T0326446

Global Risks

Dresdner Schriften zu Recht und Politik der Vereinten Nationen
Dresden Papers on Law and Policy of the United Nations

Herausgegeben von/edited by
Sabine von Schorlemer

Zentrum für Internationale Studien/
School of International Studies,
Technische Universität Dresden/
University of Dresden

Band 14

PETER LANG

Frankfurt am Main · Berlin · Bern · Bruxelles · New York · Oxford · Wien

Jana Hertwig / Sylvia Maus /
Almut Meyer zu Schwabedissen / Matthias Schuler (eds.)

Global Risks

Constructing World Order through Law,
Politics and Economics

PETER LANG
Internationaler Verlag der Wissenschaften

Bibliographic Information published by the Deutsche Nationalbibliothek
The Deutsche Nationalbibliothek lists this publication in the Deutsche Nationalbibliografie; detailed bibliographic data is available in the internet at http://dnb.d-nb.de.

ISSN 1862-443X
ISBN 978-3-631-59291-5
© Peter Lang GmbH
Internationaler Verlag der Wissenschaften
Frankfurt am Main 2010
All rights reserved.

www.peterlang.de

Acknowledgments

A book like this one is only possible with the support of many people. We were fortunate to have had the assistance of many remarkable people, only a few of whom we are able to acknowledge here.

We express our appreciation to all of the authors for their commitment to this common project, particularly for their exceptional contributions as well as for their patience and co-operation at all times.

Having been more or less novices in the field of academic editing, we are deeply grateful for generous support and advice by established scholars. In particular, we owe a great debt of gratitude to the members of the Research Council of the School of International Studies, who offered critical and constructive input during the peer review process: Professor *Monika Medick-Krakau* (Founding Director of the School of International Studies), Professor *Ulrich Fastenrath* (Academic Director of the School of International Studies), Professor *Sabine von Schorlemer*, as well as Professor *Udo Broll* and Professor *Alexander Kemnitz*. We also like to thank Professor *Cornelia Manger-Nestler*, (Leipzig University of Applied Sciences) and PD Dr. *Hans-Joachim Heintze* (Ruhr-Universität Bochum) who have supported us with their expert opinion.

We would further like to thank the commentators. Not only did they draw the academic bow in the three parts of the volume with their comments, they also greatly assisted and supported us in the process of the set up of the volume. We would like to thank *Alexander Brand*, Dr. *Regina Heller*, Dr. *Kinka Gerke-Unger*, Professor *Cornelia Manger-Nestler*, Dr. *Solveig Richter*, as well as Dr. *Tina Roeder*. In addition, we are grateful for crucial advice received at an early stage of the project by Dr. *Daniel Mügge* and Dr. *Arne Niemann* (both University of Amsterdam). All of them have enriched and valuably complemented this volume with their knowledge and experience in the field of research of the present publication.

We are indebted to our student research assistants *Carolin Erwerth, Anja Nier* and *Ronny Rammelt* who have been to a great extent responsible for editorial reviews of the manuscripts and the final formatting. Their contribution to this book cannot be summed up in words.

Our special thanks go to Professor *von Schorlemer* for including this volume into her book series "Dresden Papers on Law and Policy of the United Nations".

Last but not least we would like to thank the Vattenfall Europe AG for its generous financial support without which this publication would not have been possible.

Dresden/Berlin, March 2010
Jana Hertwig, Sylvia Maus, Almut Meyer zu Schwabedissen, Matthias Schuler

Preface

The present volume assembles the written contributions made to the interdisciplinary conference "Weltrisiken: Chancen einer Weiterentwicklung von Ordnungsstrukturen durch Recht, Wirtschaft und Politik" on the occasion of the 10th anniversary of the B.A. programme "International Relations" at the School of International Studies of the Technische Universität Dresden. The highly competitive B.A. programme, with 36 students selected out of several hundred applicants each year, is the only interdisciplinary undergraduate programme in the field of international relations in Germany.

The great majority of the authors of the present volume as well as two of the editors are alumni of the B.A. programme. The other two editors are closely involved in the programme as researchers and lecturers at chairs cooperating with the School of International Studies. Hence, this book is another contribution in the tradition of the book series "Dresdner Schriften zu Recht und Politik der Vereinten Nationen / Dresden Papers on Law and Policy of the United Nations" that has repeatedly provided a platform for the results of the latest research in cooperation with researchers at the Chair of International Law, European Union Law and International Relations.

The research topic of the present volume, global risks, also sets forth the interdisciplinary, problem-oriented teaching and research at the School of International Studies. The selected contributions show from very different academic perspectives how international actors, states as well as regional and international organisations, deal with global risks. The authors and commentators highlight that complex challenges demand multi-faceted, pluri-disciplinary, and not least multilateral solutions. It becomes clear throughout the volume that these solutions have to start with an informed and thorough assessment of the dimensions of a global risk. They have to sound out and evaluate the possibilities which international law, politics and economics offer to tackle these risks, and they have to go beyond conventional modes of governance to keep up with the pace of global change. Thus, the volume presents an inspiring point of departure for further research in this field of study.

The editor of the book series would like to thank all persons involved for their efforts and contributions to this volume and wishes the audience an insightful and inspiring reading!

Dresden, March 2010

Sabine von Schorlemer

Table of Contents

Abbreviations

ACTA	Anti-Counterfeiting Trade Agreement
APII	Protocol Additional to the Geneva Conventions of 12 August 1949, and relating to the Protection of Victims of Non-International Armed Conflicts
BIRPI	United International Bureau for the Protection of Intellectual Property
BP	British Petroleum
CAFTA	Central America Free Trade Agreement
CAT	Convention against Torture and other Cruel, Inhuman or Degrading Treatment or Punishment
CEQ	Council on Environmental Quality
CFSP	Common Foreign and Security Policy
Clwtf	costs lie where they fall
COPS	Political and Security Committee
CRTA	Committee on Regional Trade Agreements
DSB	WTO Dispute Settlement Body
EC	European Community
ECHR	European Convention for the Protection of Human Rights and Fundamental Freedoms
ECJ	European Court of Justice
ECtHR	European Court of Human Rights
EDA	European Defence Agency
EPA	Environmental Protection Agency
EPW	Senate Committee on Environment and Public Works
ESS	European Security Strategy
EU	European Union
EU-L	European Union, Treaty of Lisbon
EUFOR	European Union Force
FIH	Financial Instability Hypothesis
FTA(s)	free trade agreement(s)
GAERC	General Affairs and External Relations Council
GATS	General Agreement on Trade in Services
GATT	General Agreement on Tariffs and Trade
GBN	Global Business Network
GDP	gross national product
GE	general equilibrium
GHG	greenhouse gas
ICC	International Criminal Court
ICCPR	International Covenant on Civil and Political Rights

ICJ	International Court of Justice
ICTR	International Criminal Tribunal for Rwanda
ICTY	International Tribunal for the Former Yugoslavia
IHL	international humanitarian law
IHRL	international human rights law
IISS	International Institute for Strategic Studies
ILC	International Law Commission
ILM	International Legal Materials
IMT	International Military Tribunal at Nuremberg
IP	intellectual property
IPCC	Intergovernmental Panel on Climate Change
IR	international relations
ISPs	internet service providers
ITT	International Telephone and Telegraph
LDCs	Least-Developed Countries
MAI	Multilateral Agreement on Investment
MFN	most-favoured nation
MNCs	multinational corporations
MONUC	United Nations Organization Mission in DR Congo
MTS	multilateral trading system
NAFTA	North American Free Trade Agreement
NASA	National Aeronautics and Space Administration
NATO	North Atlantic Treaty Organization
NIC	National Intelligence Council
NIE	National Intelligence Estimate
NOOA	National Oceanic and Atmospheric Administration
OAS	Organization of American States
OAU	Organization of African Unity
OECD	Organisation for Economic Cooperation and Development
OSCE	Organization for Security and Cooperation in Europe
PLS	profit-and-loss-sharing
PTA(s)	preferential trade agreement(s)
RTA(s)	regional trade agreement(s)
RUF	Revolutionary Unity Front
SECURE	Standards Employed by Customs for Uniform Rights Enforcement
SMEs	small and medium enterprises
SPLT	Substantive Patent Law Treaty
TAR	Third Assessment Report
TPMs	technological protection measures
TRIPS	Agreement on Trade-Related Aspects of Intellectual Property Rights
UN	United Nations
UNCED	United Nations Conference on Environment and Development

UNCTAD	United Nations Conference on Trade and Development
UNFCCC	United Nations Framework Convention on Climate Change
UNHCR	United Nations High Commissioner for Refugees
UNITA	National Union for the Total Independence of Angola
UNSC	United Nations Security Council
UNTS	United Nations Treaties Series
UPOV	International Union for the Protection of New Varieties of Plants
USD	US dollar
VCLT	Vienna Convention on the Law of Treaties
WCO	World Customs Organization
WEU	Western European Union
WHO	World Health Organization
WIPO	World Intellectual Property Organization
WTO	World Trade Organization

Global Risks – An Introduction

Jana Hertwig, Sylvia Maus, Almut Meyer zu Schwabedissen, and Matthias Schuler

"Modern society has become a risk society in the sense that it is increasingly occupied with debating, preventing and managing risks that it itself has produced."[1]

Whether or not one agrees with *Ulrich Beck's* assessment of today's world, there can be little doubt that global risks, however unspecific, shape our discourse and action, not only on a national, but on a global scale. For instance, the former Secretary-General of the United Nations, *Kofi Annan*, in 2004 implemented the famous High-level Panel on Threats, Challenges and Change, in which the summoned experts dealt with contemporary perceptions of threats to peace, challenges to the current world order and potentials for change in order to pacify the international system. The experts on this panel came to state inter alia poverty, internal conflict, nuclear and biological weapons, terrorism, and transnational organised crime as threats to collective security, thus posing global risks. The Global Risk Report 2010 of the World Economic Forum, to name another example, presents a complex net of interconnected risks in the fields of economics (e.g. fiscal crises, slowing of Chinese economy), technology (e.g. data fraud, nanoparticle toxity), environment (e.g. water scarcity, extreme weather), society (e.g. migration, pandemics) and geopolitics (e.g. global governance gap, nuclear proliferation). All of these threats are inherently man-made, even though they may be entirely unintended consequences of political and economic decisions.

The contemporary structure of world order allows for a wide range of actors and agents to find ways of cooperation. From an academic point of view, there are several ways to accompany and support the global society's attempt of mitigating global risks. For one thing, academics can analyse the status quo and can ask how and why, for instance, a phenomenon is perceived as global risk. They might try to raise awareness regarding potentially risky developments or warn about potential misperception or misinterpretation of risks and the causes. Further, they can discuss possibilities for appropriate reaction to global risks and make recommendations. In doing so, academics are called to find new approaches for analysis and maybe even resolution of evolving threats and challenges on the global agenda. The academic endeavour to explain and help mitigating global risks therefore strongly depends on efforts to overcome differences between scientific disciplines and find interdisciplinary approaches in order to tackle complex global issues.

---

1   U. Beck, Living in the world risk society, in: Economy and Society, 35, 3 (2006), p. 332.

The School of International Studies at the Technische Universität (TU) Dresden, Germany, has since its foundation been devoted to multi- and interdisciplinary research and teaching. In 2008, it celebrated the 10th anniversary of its B.A. programme "International Relations". On this occasion it hosted the interdisciplinary scientific symposium "Weltrisiken – Chancen einer Weiterentwicklung von Ordnungsstrukturen durch Recht, Wirtschaft und Politik" ("Global Risks – Progress by developing structures of world order through law, economics and politics"). The event, kindly financed by Volkswagenstiftung, took place at the TU Dresden from 27–29 November 2008 and was divided into two parts. The first part of the symposium assembled distinguished experts and experienced practitioners in the fields of law, politics and economics. Bringing together one representative of each academic discipline, the three panels in this first part dealt with failed states, genocide, and multinational enterprises, respectively.

The second part of this symposium gave young academics from different disciplines the opportunity to present their PhD or other research projects. Scholars have been selected from different academic fields. Their expertise was complemented by the insights and experience of practitioners from various international institutions. With this set up, the organisers aimed at enabling the exchange and development of ideas across the divide between scientific disciplines as well as across the science-practice divide.

The present volume assembles the written contributions of all young speakers, after they had the chance to incorporate thoughts and results of the stimulating discussions in the panels. They are, as during the symposium, discussed and put in perspective by written comments by experts familiar with interdisciplinary approaches.

With their articles on global risks, the authors have bravely and earnestly contributed to a topic that suffers from severe under-specification and thus, the nine pieces of writing may look quite heterogeneous at first sight. On the one hand, this is hardly surprising, since most of the authors are alumni of the School of International Studies who have, after having gained their academic roots in International Relations, subsequently spread out to specialize in different fields. Therefore, it holds true that they treat very different fields from very different perspectives, only coming together under the broad theme of global risks. On the other hand, it is exactly the overarching theme of the book which is calling for variety. It is the firm belief of the present editors that meaningful dealing with global risks cannot be limited to one policy field but has to transcend disciplines to find sound explanations and viable solutions. It was our intent to enable multi-faceted analysis and discourse in an interdisciplinary way – not because it is one of the most fashionable academic exercises at the moment, but because we consider this as the only promising way for dealing with global risks.

In spite of the under-specification of the topic and its resulting wide array of risk-related issues to tackle, the present contributions can be subsumed under three headings: Identification and Assessment, Normative Reflections and Alternative Modes of Governance.

The first part of the volume deals with the identification of risks on three different levels: global (climate change), institutional (altering types of legal and political agreements of/with the World Trade Organization (WTO)), and regional (EU military operations in Africa). *Jörn Richert* opens up the debate by looking at the example of climate change. While over a long time only perceived as a threat to the elusive and abstract concept of "environment" or to people far away either in time or in space or both, today climate change is on everyone's lips, not only as a fact, but undoubtedly also as a global risk. This becomes also evident by the inclusion of climate change into the discourses on national and international security. *Richert* analyses how, on the one hand, this "securitization" of the topic, i.e. its treatment in a framework of security, has affected political decision-making and how, on the other hand, this very process has altered the meaning of security. By taking the climate politics in the US Senate from 2000 to 2008 as an example, he argues that the perception of climate change as risk or threat has been the main driver behind climate policy. At the same time, the perception of climate change as a threat has intensified. On the question of how the securitization is affecting climate change decision-making, empirical findings appear ambiguous. Although securitization has indeed led to traditional security legislation, as critics of securitization as strategy for agenda setting would have expected, these initiatives are outweighed by the securitization's effect on climate policy-making. Nevertheless, the debate has "allowed for a significant step forward in the climate policy of the US Senate".

In the second chapter, *Anke Dahrendorf* deals with a risk that can easily be called a global one. She examines the proliferation of bilateral agreements in the sphere of trade regulations and asks to what extent this development – both source and consequence of the standstill in multilateral trade negotiations (Doha-Round) – has to be considered a threat for the main multilateral institution in the field, the WTO. Serious weakening or even a breakdown of the WTO could indeed be qualified as a global risk. Given the global economic integration and interdependence, in short: globalisation, inability to find viable means of regulation and/or the breakdown of existing regulation can affect the whole world economy – a lesson that we have learned only recently in the different but related financial crisis. But *Dahrendorf's* chapter points to a second set of risks, namely those faced by developing countries who are usually partners to the bilateral trade agreements. For the area of intellectual property protection, *Dahrendorf* argues that the threat to the WTO is quite limited, whereas the problems of developing countries are significant, ranging from the undermining of their policy space and the exploitation of their dependence from international trade to adverse agreements largely benefitting industrialised countries. It is interesting to note, as *Dahrendorf* suggests, that public/academic awareness seems to focus much more on the risk for the WTO (e.g. end of multilateralism, spill-over effects) than on the risks for developing countries which are difficult to assess at this point.

In the third chapter of this part, *Christian Burckhardt* sets out to explain the European Union's military operations in Africa. Are they, *Burckhardt* asks, humanitarian responses to alleviate human suffering at the other end of the world? And are they intended to react to an increasing number of internal conflicts before their sheer number and scope turn into a global risk? *Burckhardt* analyses the international role of the EU as great power versus civilian power by looking at the European Security and Defence Policy (ESDP), and the EU missions in the Democratic Republic of the Congo in 2003 and 2006 in particular. He argues that the activities of the EU can best be explained in the framework of realism and by considering the EU as a great power since it intervenes to gain prestige – and not to alleviate misery and stop serious violations of human rights. Thus, *Burckhardt* concludes, the EU undertakes military intervention to serve first and foremost its own concerns and not acting out of humanitarian concerns. With regards to global risks, it seems that the EU uses situations that are commonly perceived as (global) risks, i.e. deadly internal conflicts in Africa, to put forward its own interest in strengthening its status as a great power. This behaviour, in turn, can lead to the emergence of other, new risks: less cooperation with other actors such as the UN and hence a weakening of multilateral institutions, arbitrary (non-)reaction to or disregard of situations in which reaction is really needed (e.g. Darfur), and over-emphasis of military responses to international threats to the detriment of preventive measures and international law.

In their commentary to the three chapters, *Kinka Gerke-Unger* and *Solveig Richter* note that none of the authors explicitly discusses to what extent their subject matter is a global risk. Instead, they assume the global risk character and directly enter their respective analysis from different theoretical angles. What the contributions have in common, *Gerke-Unger* and *Richter* assert, is the fact that they open the door to a subsequent set of questions, namely whether the characterisation as global risk leads to unintended and potentially ineffective consequences in the management of global risks. Especially against the background of securitization and military action, further discussion is needed on effective ways and means of prevention and reaction.

In dealing with global risks, reflections cannot stop at discussing the status quo. They have to go beyond and tackle the underlying legal and socio-political conditions with the aim of exposing possible shortcomings and room for improvement. In the second part, the authors therefore analyse existing modes of governance and point out, from a normative perspective, to what extent these must be adapted or even changed to either meet current challenges and global risks or to prevent future risks from emerging.

Vanessa Holzer's contribution is set in the context of the arguably most tangible global risk, namely armed conflict. It is obvious that armed conflict per se as well as any proliferation of armed conflict poses risks for the respective state or region and the international community as a whole. This is mirrored for instance by UN Security Council resolutions defining mass movement of refugees as threat to international peace and security. Moreover, also the consequences for individuals affected by armed conflict must be dealt with adequately. *Holzer* argues that the 1951 Convention Relating to the Status of Refugees remains the crucial international legal framework for the protection of persons fleeing from persecution. Although persecution has frequently occurred during armed conflict, as the example of "ethnic cleansing" highlights, the Refugee Convention has only to a limited extent been applied to persons escaping from armed conflict. As *Holzer's* analysis shows, the Refugee Convention's refugee definition must be interpreted in light of international human rights law and international humanitarian law with regard to claims for refugee status based on experiences during armed conflict. In doing so, certain persons fleeing from armed conflict will fall under the refugee definition. This definition requires a well-founded fear of persecution on the grounds of race, religion, nationality, membership of a particular social group, or political opinion. *Holzer* shows that the argument that such an interpretation of the refugee definition would mean to "open the floodgates" to large numbers of displaced persons is unfounded from a political and legal perspective. By extending the scope of application to certain victims of armed conflict, the legal regime for the protection of refugees mitigates the risk for the protected individual. It provides protection which is not available through the country of origin in these situations.

The second contribution in this part deals with a completely different but highly topical risk. By switching focus from state actors to private actors, *Joris Larik* searches for ways to curtail the currently largely unfettered power of multinational corporations. With yearly turnovers that sometimes exceed the gross national product of states and corresponding political influence, such corporations not only theoretically can, but in the past repeatedly have, created detrimental effects for states and individuals in their sphere of operations. On the other hand, viable international solutions to subject multinational corporations to international rules and obligations comparable to those applicable to states are missing, except for voluntary partnerships like the UN Global Compact introduced by former UN Secretary-General *Kofi Annan* or efforts to make human rights obligations applicable to multinational corporations. *Larik* therefore explores possibilities to extent the applicability of international criminal law to legal persons such as corporations. Instead of interpreting a given treaty, the author shows how often-mentioned theoretical "stumbling blocks" such as establishing a corporation's criminal intent (mens rea), corporate complicity, and means of punishment for corporations can be overcome. He demonstrates that all three issues are not irresolvable and that international criminal law bears the potential to give remedy to victims not only to crimes committed by states and individuals but also by multinational corporations. Only in extending the scope of international criminal law to multinational corporations, *Larik* argues, can the former live up to its role not only as a means to punish but also to protect.

In his contribution on the legitimacy of WTO law *Nicolas Lamp* discusses the circumstances under which the outcome of institutionalised international negotiations on legally binding rules in a specific policy field can be considered legitimate. *Lamp* analyses the current debate on the legitimacy – or to be more precise the lack of legitimacy – of WTO law, which has accompanied international trade negotiations over the last decade, and argues that this debate takes place within a legitimacy-to-power paradigm representing a discursive structure that furthers a limited view of what would be required to make WTO law legitimate. *Lamp* claims that the legitimacy-to-power paradigm directs attention towards legitimising WTO law within the framework of the prevailing power relations, instead of considering these power relations as a major obstacle to legitimate lawmaking in the first place. Thus he argues that only a reconfiguration of power relations in the WTO can lead to legitimate lawmaking processes. However, this is not a matter of redistributing coercive power to some states at the expense of others. Instead, *Lamp* suggests enhancing the role of communicative power in the lawmaking process. This contribution shows how institutional practices and discursive structures in international institutions reflect the power relations in the international system and thus reify a certain vision of global governance, which at some point might turn into a global risk itself due to its lack of democratic legitimacy.

The comment of *Alexander Brand* and *Tina Roeder* is guided by two central questions. First, they enquire about the value of normative reflections to enhance existing modes of governance in the sense of improving situations by means of legal instruments. Secondly, the specific value of normative reflections as compared to other approaches is addressed. Regarding the latter, *Brand* and *Roeder* suggest that all three contributions find a particular value of normative reflections, albeit on different levels of analysis. At the same time, they also find the limits of normative thinking in each of the chapters. In the end, they conclude, normative action cannot be considered a panacea for handling global risks. Instead it might contribute to finding a point of equilibrium between the necessary and the possible in managing risks.

The last part of the volume presents examples of alternative modes of governance in different policy fields. Naturally, the respective global risks in the three contributions appear completely distinct not only in nature but also in scope. However, this part intends to provide more than individual spot-lights on unrelated policy fields from three different academic perspectives. Instead, the focus of each of the three contributions lies on offering an alternative to traditional modes of governance in relation to the respective risks, by enlarging the perspective from which the object of study is examined and sometimes by crossing the boundaries of academic disciplines.

In the first chapter, *Susanne Lechner* introduces the triad of law, politics and economics in this part by analysing a legal provision with a tool usually found in economics to ask whether a political goal can be achieved. More precisely, *Lechner* examines whether the right to withdraw from the European Union, the exit-option, which has been established by the Treaty of Lisbon enhances the stability of the EU by furthering flexible integration. Prima facie, this seems to be a contradictory claim: how can a legal provision allowing for a withdrawal from the EU at the same time increase the stability of the very same organisation? By using a game-theoretic approach, *Lechner* critically examines the options member states now have in negotiations and bargaining situations. She concludes that on the one hand, the exit-option bears significant potential as a threatening instrument to serve the interests of member states because they gain bargaining power. On the other hand, the exit-option can also be regarded as a stabilising factor since the option for a legal withdrawal allows for flexible integration through the formation of clubs within the EU. Thus, the risk of either costly struggles for secession or a deadlock in the integration process or both is diminished by a legal provision that, prima facie, seems to have the contrary effect.

Stability is also the focus of the second chapter in which *Ewa Karwowski* scrutinises the claim that Islamic banking is more stable than conventional, i.e. Western, banking. Given the unexpected scope and consequences of the current financial crisis, the quest for better, more efficient, reliable modes of banking has to be considered an urgent global issue. *Karwowski* critically examines the three main arguments brought forward by proponents of Islamic banking, namely the advantageous behaviour of the homo islamicus as opposed to the homo oeconomicus, the developmental character of Islamic banking, and the reduction of economic fluctuations. After reviewing the theoretical foundations behind these arguments, *Karwowski* comes to the conclusion that even though Islamic banking can in some situations guarantee greater stability, this cannot be considered a general rule. Instead, as *Karwowski* concludes, Islamic banking can be as stable or instable as conventional banking since the main factor for stability is the direction and purpose of lending which is not determined by the model of banking. Using it as an alternative mode of governance thus would require more elaboration on the implementation of the concept of Islamic banking.

In the last one of the nine chapters, *Carolin Görzig* gives the issue of stability yet another turn. In contrast to the two preceding chapters, stability here is not the opposite of one or more global risks but represents itself a global risks. *Görzig* claims that various asymmetric conflicts of today, including terrorism, languish in a deadly form of stability in the sense that they are caught in the trap of self-perpetual violence without any perspective for change. The main reason for this often decade-long continuation of the "new wars" frequently lies in the fact that war is fought for its own cause, as a result of three factors: the commercialisation of warfare, terrorism as provocation and spirals of radicalisation. *Görzig* takes on a global perspective and analyses the three factors by way of three rather distinct examples from Colombia, Turkey and Egypt. She shows that traditional modes of dealing with these situations, namely deterrence and military violence, only lead to a self-perpetuation of violence on all sides. Therefore, she calls for alternative ways to effectively govern new conflicts such as terrorism, one of them being active integration of violent non-state actors through dialogue.

In their comment, *Regina Heller* and *Cornelia Manger-Nestler* compare and assess the three quite different examples for alternative modes of governance. In doing so, they ask what can be learned from such alternative approaches. And, more importantly, to what extent can the findings of each contribution be generalised to be used in other situations? On the one hand, *Heller* and *Manger-Nestler* come to the conclusion that the presented alternative modes have the advantage of being more flexible in the solution of the problems. On the other hand, the commentators also see the limits of such approaches. In particular, they point to the respective interests of the actors involved in problem-solving efforts and whether or not they want to make use of new modes of governance. Interdisciplinary research is thus useful and illuminating in discussing these kinds of questions.

The present volume does not attempt to offer final answers and ready-made solutions. Instead, the academic discussion of global risks is only at its starting point. Thus, this volume intends to serve as an inspiration for further discussion and research in the field of global risks.

We therefore hope that you will find the thoughts presented in the following chapters informative, thought provoking and inspiring.

A. Global Risks: Identification and Assessment

Climate Change and the Transformation of Security – Political Consequences of the Emerging Discourse on Capitol Hill

Jörn Richert

"[W]e need to 'desecuritize' security linguistically and epistemologically, turning it from an (objectified) concept into a (politicized) signifier."[1]

I. Introduction

Many voices have stressed the deadly consequences of a changing climate. The exact referent object, however, has been open to debate. For a long time, climate change has predominantly been perceived as threatening the environment, future generations, or geographically distant people. This has changed dramatically. Since late 2006, threats to international economy and security have begun to dominate the climate discourse. In 2007, the security implications of climate change were discused in the United Nations (UN) for the first time. Moreover, many climate policy-makers in Europe and the United States have made "climate security" their main argument.

In academic circles, the assumed security implications of climate change have been critically discussed in the light of earlier empirical and conceptual work on environmental security.[2] Respective publications aim at examining the analytical appropriateness of the "climate security" discourse. Furthermore, "climate security" has been interpreted as a case of securitization.[3] In contrast to the first approach, securitization analyses are concerned with the political force of the discourse. So far, they have mainly focused on securitising moves. The effect

---

1   A. Behnke, The Message or the Messenger?: Reflexions on the Role of Security Experts and the Securitization of Political Issues, in: Cooperation and Conflict 35 (2000), p. 96.

2   See e.g. R. Floyd, The Environmental Security Debate and its Significance for Climate Change, in: The International Spectator 43 (2008), pp. 51-65; I. Salehyan, From Climate Change to Conflict? No Consensus Yet, in: Journal for Peace Research 45 (2008), pp. 315-326; also see the special issue of Political Geography on "Climate Change and Conflict" 26 (2007).

3   J. M. Trobmetta, Environmental Security and Climate Change: Analysing the Discourse, in: Cambridge Review of International Affairs 21 (2008); O. Brown/A. Hammill/R. Mc-Ceman, Climate Change as the ‚New' Security Threat: Implications for Africa, in: International Affairs 83 (2007); M. Brzoska, The Securitization of Climate Change and the Power of Conceptions of Security, in: Sicherheit und Frieden/ Security and Peace 27 (2009).

of discourse on actual political decision-making, on the other hand, has been largely neglected. A crucial dimension of securitization analysis has thus been left out.[4] The present chapter attempts to start filling this gap. It investigates the interaction between "security" and "climate change", understood as discourses, and the effect of this interaction on policy-making.[5] The chapter analyses the ways in which the meaning of security has been altered within the climate debate and which effect the climate security frame has had on climate politics.

It concentrates on one specific case: climate politics in the Senate of the United States over the course of the two presidential terms of *George W. Bush* (2000-2008). Although the *Bush* Administration notoriously neglected climate policy, there was significant change within the United States in that period. Since the turn of the century, particularly the US Congress has made major progress towards effective climate legislation. Changes in Congress have implications far beyond Capitol Hill: A successful US climate policy needs to be approved by Congress and every substantial international agreement has to find its way through the US Senate by a 2/3 majority vote. Thus, even though a new President has raised considerable hopes by coming back to the international negotiation table, politics in the Senate remain crucial for US domestic as well as for international climate policy.

To outline the ambition of the chapter, a theoretical discussion on the meaning of security is essential. The first section will discuss security as a concept and as a discourse. It will identify several dimensions of the security concept. In doing so, it will focus on the framework of securitization. By critically examining this framework's "securityness of security", the chapter will identify additional dimensions of potential change, not included in the Copenhagen School's original framework.[6] Part three illustrates the emergence of the climate security discourse. Part four traces the influence of the discourse on politics in the US Senate between 2000 and 2008.

---

4   Trombetta provides an exception here. In her discussion about the influence of the environmental and security discourse, empirical evidence is presented rather anecdotally, however. See Trobmetta, Environmental Security and Climate Change (2008).

5   This connection has been analysed by Hough Dyer who, however, focuses on the conceptual value and integrity of "environment" and "security" rather than on the political effect of this connection. He thereby sees security as a concept, judged by its applicability and analytical value, rather than as a discourse, including political power. See H. Dyer, Environmental Security and International Relations: the Case for Enclosure, in: Review of International Studies 27 (2001).

6   B. Buzan/O. Wæver/J. de Wilde, Security: A new Framework for Analysis (1998).

II.   What is Security?

Only 20 years ago, Security Studies were widely acknowledged as being about, to speak with the well-known words of *Stephen M. Walt*, "the study of threat, use, and control of military force."[7] Security was often understood as the survival of sovereign states in an anarchic international system, ultimately to be defended by military means.[8] With the Cold War coming to an end, however, this definition was challenged by new notions of security entering the political and academic debate. One major example is that of environmental security.[9] Attempts to understand the environment in terms of security were criticized fiercely. Most criticism was based on an understanding of security as an analytical concept. From that perspective, the inclusion of environmental hazards into security definitions would merely dilute the analytical value of the concept.[10] Hence, scholars such as *Walt* attempted to prevent a broadening of the security agenda. Nevertheless, with new threats and referent objects entering the debate, conceptual uncertainties emerged. Re-defining security became "something of a cottage industry".[11]

While struggles to define security proceed, a more fundamental critique of traditional security concepts has emerged from putting security in a broader historical perspective. Such an exercise casts doubts on the very idea of security being an objectively definable concept. At the time of the Roman Empire, the phrase "securitas" did not address the security of a nation.[12] On the contrary,

---

7   S. M. Walt, The Renaissance of Security Studies, in: International Studies Quarterly 35 (1991), p. 212; also see S. Smith, The Increasing Insecurity of Security Studies: Conceptualizing Security in the Last Twenty Years, in: Contemporary Security Policy 20 (1999).

8   This is the essence of Kenneth Waltz's approach to international politics. He further qualifies the means of security policy as follows: "In politics force is said to be the ultima ratio. In international politics force serves, not only as the ultima ratio, but indeed as the first and constant one." K. Waltz, Theory of International Politics (1979), p. 112.

9   For the discussion of environmental security see, among others, J. Tuchman Mathews, Redefining Security, in: Foreign Affairs 68 (1989); R. D. Kaplan, The Coming Anarchy. How Scarcity, Crime, Overpopulation, Tribalism, and Disease are Rapidly Destroying the Social Fabric of our Planet, in: Atlantic Monthly 273 (1994); R. H. Ullman, Redefining Security, in: International Security 8 (1983); T. F. Homer-Dixon, Environment, Scarcity, and Violence (1999).

10   See e.g. D. Deudney, The Case against Linking Environmental Degradation and National Security, in: Millennium 19 (1990); M. A. Levy, Is the Environment a National Security Issue?, in: International Security 20 (1995).

11   D. A. Baldwin, The Concept of Security, in: Review of International Studies 23 (1997), p. 5.

12   For an outline of these conceptual changes in history see E. Rothschild, What is Security?, in: Daedalus 124 (1995), p. 61; also see K. Krause/M. C. Williams,

it indicated an individual and subjective state of mind. Both the objectivist quality and the focus on the nation as referent object are due to later conceptual changes: *Walt's* understanding of security only gradually emerged at the end of the *Napoleonic* Wars and the Congress of Vienna. It became particularly dominant within the context of the Cold War. *Walt's* idea of only one appropriate definition of Security Studies, has to be seen as an ahistorical reification of that specific, historically constituted understanding of security. It ignores the fluidity of the concept, overestimates its objective quality and downplays the political force inherent to such a definition.

Instead of opposing attempts to re-define security, these should be understood as part of an ongoing and open-ended process of change. To overcome the elusive quest for an objective definition and to obtain further insights into the politics surrounding "security", it is necessary to think about security not as an objective concept but as a discourse. A discourse can be defined as an "ensemble of ideas, concepts, and categories through which meaning is given to social and physical phenomena".[13] Discourses are intersubjectively shared by particular groups of individuals. Therefore, a specific definition of security is part of a particular, socially constructed "reality". The significance of the security discourse lies in its power to structure and transform social relations. It contains mind-sets prescribing imperatives of action and standards of appropriate behaviour. The Copenhagen School has provided a framework to analyse security, which comes close to this perspective. Following this group of scholars, in order to be considered a security issue, phenomena have to be securitised, i.e. they have

"to be staged as existential threats to a referent object by a securitising actor who thereby generates endorsement of emergency measures beyond rules that would otherwise bind."[14]

Furthermore, to be relevant, such a securitization move has to be accepted by a significant group of people. Hence, securitization is an "essentially intersubjective process".[15] If securitization has taken place, emergency (or extraordinary) measures can and most likely will be applied to counter the threat. From the Copenhagen School's perspective, the meaning of security has to be investigated rather than defined by scholars of security studies. The securitization framework investigates the political struggle over the response to two particular questions: "security for whom?", determining the referent object, and "security from what?", determining the threat. At the same time, however,

Broadening the Agenda of Security Studies: Politics and Methods, in: Mershon International Studies Review 40 (1996).
13   M. A. Hajer, The Politics of Environmental Discourse (1995), p. 44.
14   Buzan/Waever/de Wilde, Security (1998), p. 5.
15   Ibid., p. 30.

the Copenhagen School attempts to preserve an objective core of security: Being asked "how much security?", its proponents would reply "extraordinarily much"; being asked "security by which means?", they would respond "by means that break rules which otherwise bind". This is what *Ole Waever* calls the "securityness of security".[16] Because *Waever* sees securitization connected to a tendency of applying non-democratic ways of handling a problem, he cautions against securitization. Other scholars, such as *Levy*, have also cautioned against "brandish[ing] the environment-qua-security rhetorical sword"[17] in order to generate support for environmental protection.

Taking the notion of security as a discourse seriously, however, *Waever's* objective core does not hold. Rather than guarding any essential meaning of the concept – a form of securityness – an approach understanding security as a discourse has to acknowledge the concept's sponginess:

> "Sociopolitical concepts are like sponges: they are able to soak up and contain a variety of meanings as a result of being used in different contexts for different purposes. It is this sponginess that makes a concept increasingly ambiguous, and it is the resulting ambiguity that sometimes makes concepts constitutive of discourse."[18]

This has two implications: First, by theoretically breaking the close interconnection of "how much?" and "by which means?", "extraordinarily much" might combine with other ways of achieving security. It is important to note the consequences of this insight for the meaning of security policy. Anything can be 'real' security policy. With regard to climate change, alternative security policies have been developed by *Barnett* and *Dalby*.[19] However, the fundamental question is whether or not such academic endeavours translate into altered political behaviour. As *Deudney* notes, it might be

> "premature to characterise environmental degradation as a threat to '[common] security' until we can be more confident that people do in fact think 'common' whenever they hear 'security'."[20]

Knudsen also sees the securityness of security fixed in political interaction rather than in any kind of conceptual framwork. More optimistically than *Deudney*, he interprets the securityness of securitization as closely associated with politics

---

16   O. Waever, Securitization and De-Securitization, in: R. D. Lipschutz (ed.), On Security (1995).
17   Levy, Is the Environment a National Security Issue? (1995), p. 61.
18   J. Bartelson, Three Concepts of Globalization, in: International Sociology 15 (2000), p. 182, emphasis added.
19   See J. Barnett, The Meaning of Environmental Security. Ecological Politics and Policy in the New Security Era (2001); and S. Dalby, Environmental Security (2002).
20   Deudney, The Case Against Linking Environmental Degradation and National Security (1990).

in the Cold War and thus empirically outdated.[21] In line with this argument, *Rasmussen* and *Trombetta* have demonstrated that it has substantially changed since then.[22]

Second, opening up "how much?" to political struggle, means opening up the debate on a potential insignificance of security. It allows responding "nothing at all"[23] and thereby exposes what security actually is: a semantic device. It is not important in itself. It is important as it connects particular combinations of answers to those four questions defined above (see also fig. 1). There are no right or objective answers. Answers are valid only within a respective social context in which they are intersubjectively shared.

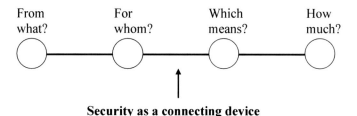

Security as a connecting device

Figure 1: Security as a connecting device

As figure one illustrates, the transformation of security is a multidimensional process. A transformation is given, when the political effect of a particular security argument deviates from the expected pattern of action associated with security in a specific context. This deviation indicates a change in the security mind-set.[24] The interplay between the four dimensions is particularly interesting: In connection to which referent object does the threat of climate change abet political action? Which policies are applied to tackle the threat and are these, in

---

21   O. Knudsen, Post-Copenhagen Security Studies: Desecuritizing Securitization, in: Security Dialogue 32 (2001), p. 359; also see J. Eriksson (ed.) Threat Politics: New Perspectives on Security, Risk and Crisis Management (2001), p. 3.

22   M. V. Rasmussen, Reflexive Security: Nato and International Risk Society, in: Millennium: Journal of International Studies 30 (2001); Trombetta, Environmental Security and Climate Change (2008) .

23   This possibility is implicitly acknowledged by Baldwin. Although Baldwin merely attempts to put security into perspective relative to other political goals, by asking "how much?" and "at what cost?" he opens up the debate to any kind of responses. Baldwin, The Concept of Security (1997), p. 18.

24   Taking the realist understanding as a starting point, the empirical investigation presented here by itself presupposes such a transformation. Climate change is seen as threat (as opposed to states as threats).

turn, connected to other dimensions, such as the specific characteristics of the threat as such? Empirical data for a respective analysis is easily accessible:

> "Securitization can be studied directly; it does not need indicators. The way to study securitization is to study discourse and political constellations: When does an argument with this particular rhetorical and semiotic structure achieve sufficient effect [...]?"[25]

Buzan and *Waever* define sufficient effect in terms of the securityness of security. In contrast, following the argument put forward above, there is no particular pre-defined threshold of effect. The effect itself is object to investigation. Methodologically, however, this does not change much. The climate discourse on Capitol Hill will be analysed. Discursive changes will be related to changes in politics. While part three reconstructs the broader debate on climate and security, the major empirical work is presented in part four where the arguments of those Senators, most active in promoting climate legislation, will be investigated. Empirically, the analysis draws on press statements and speeches accessible at the respective Senator's web sites. The focus of analysis will be on arguments related to "climate security". Alternative frames such as "economic costs of climate policy" have also been considered in the analysis, due to limited space however, they will be mentioned only briefly.

III. Climate Security blazing, Nay Sayers fading – The Construction of Climate Change as a Threat

Since the beginning of international climate politics, the Intergovernmental Panel on Climate Change (IPCC) has been the most influential body in promoting knowledge for decision-makers.

In its Second Assessment Report of Climate Science, published in 1995, it is stressed that many aspects of a changing climate "are important considerations for sustainable development".[26] While the report merely identified "a discernible human influence on global climate",[27] the Third Assessment Report (TAR) of 2001 concluded that such an influence is likely.[28]

---

25 Buzan/Waever/de Wilde, Security (1998), p. 25.
26 Intergovernmental Panel on Climate Change, Climate Change 1995: the Science of Climate Change. Summary for Policymakers and Technical Summary of the Working Group I Report (1996), p. 3.
27 Ibid., p. 5.
28 Intergovernmental Panel on Climate Change, Climate Change 2001. Synthesis Report. Summary for Policy Makers, Assessment of the Intergovernmental Panel on Climate Change (2001).

Whereas threats to human health and vulnerable ecosystems were considered, climate change was not seen as a security issue. Rather scientifically the TAR concluded:

> "Projected climate change will have beneficial and adverse effects on both environmental and socio-economic systems, but the larger the changes and rate of change in climate, the more the adverse effects predominate."[29]

1.   Climate Security blazing

The TAR also included a discussion on large-scale non-linear effects of climate change such as a shut-down of the thermohaline circulation. The report states that most climate scientists consider such an event possible only beyond the year 2100.[30] Nevertheless, the scenario was taken up by a study, conducted on behalf of the Pentagon in 2003. The authors of that study, who considered the shut-down a plausible scenario, found far reaching implications for national and international security. These included a potential disintegration of the European Union and a direct confrontation of US and Chinese military forces in the Middle East.[31] The report, however, did not have a pronounced effect on the climate debate, since the *Bush* Administration managed to get it off the Pentagon web-site before it attracted major attention. On the other side of the Atlantic, the climate security debate began heating up in 2004. The UK's Chief Scientific Advisor, Sir *David King*, criticized US policies and called climate change the far greater threat to the world than international terrorism.[32] Furthermore, in 2005, former German Minister for the Environment, *Jürgen Trittin* held a speech on the implications of climate change for international security.[33] Later that year two devastating hurricanes (Katrina and Rita) led to multi-billion dollar damages and practical anarchy in the city of New Orleans.

In the subsequent years the debate intensified substantially. In October 2006, the Stern Review on the Economics of Climate Change was published. The costs of untackled climate change were estimated to be as much as five to twenty

---

29   Intergovernmental Panel on Climate Change, Climate Change 2001 (2001).

30   Ibid., p. 15.

31   D. Randall/P. Schwartz, An Abrupt Climate Change Scenario and its Implications for United States National Security. Global Business Network (GBN) Report (2003).

32   Again, the Bush Administration reacted harshly, leading Prime Minister Tony Blair to openly criticizing his scientific advisor. See F. Müller, Einigung im Emissionshandel: Ein Beitrag zur Erosion der internationalen Klimapolitik?, in: SWP-Aktuell, Stiftung Wissenschaft und Politik (2004).

33   J. Trittin, Speech held by Jürgen Trittin on 17 February 2005: Internationale Umweltpolitik ist Sicherheitspolitik (translates roughly into "International Environmental Politics is Security Politics"), www.bmu.de/reden/ bundesumweltminister_juergen_trittindoc/35292.php (These and the following internet sources have last visited on 10 October 2009).

percent of the annual global gross domestic product "now and forever".[34] The Stern Review caught wide-spread media attention and climate change became widely accepted as posing a serious threat to the world economy – a referent object of immediate interest to practically every decision-maker. At the same time, former United Kingdom Foreign Secretary *Margaret Beckett* began to strongly emphasize the threat of climate change to national security.[35] In 2007, besides the IPCC's Fourth Assessment Report, which practically muted the political discussion on the scientific basis of climate change, several publications defined climate change as a threat to national and international security.

A group of retired US generals for example predicted that climate change would function as a threat multiplier and that the "chaos that results [from climate change] can be an incubator of civil strife, genocide and the growth of terrorism".[36] This and several other publications made social science's findings operational for policy-makers by interpreting existing uncertainties in a fundamentally different way as it had been done by the IPCC so far – in favour of a national security frame. These securitising moves brought climate change to the heart of state politics.

2.   Nay Sayers fading

While in Europe the climate science became broadly accepted at an early stage of the debate, this was not the case in the United States. Scientists who criticised scientific findings got extensive media attention and the *Bush* Administration demonstrated a remarkable ignorance towards scientific evidence.[37]

In 2002, the administration set up its own climate science program, designed to "research uncertainties".[38] In 2005, the administration finally accepted climate science internationally at the G8 summit in Gleneagles. Even then, however, it was reluctant to do so in the domestic context. Investigations of the Minority Staff Committee on Government Reform of the US House of Representatives in 2003 and 2007 proved that the *Bush* Administration had continuously distorted scientific findings of federal agencies such as the National Aeronautics and Space Administration (NASA), the Environmental Protection Agency (EPA),

---

34   N. Stern (ed.), Stern Review Report on the Economics of Climate Change (2006), p. vi.

35   M. Beckett, Berlin Speech on Climate and Security (24 October 2006), http://ukingermany.fco.gov.uk/de/newsroom/?view=Speech&id=4616005.

36   Center for Naval Analyses (ed.), National Security and the Threat of Climate Change (2007).

37   E. Benedick, U.S. Climate Policy after the Presidential Election: Continuity or Change?, in: A. Riechel/A. Venturelli (eds.), Building a Foundation for Transatlantic Climate Policy (2005).

38   White House, President Bush Discusses Global Climate Change (2001), http://georgewbush-whitehouse.archives.gov/news/releases/2001/06/20010611-2.html.

and the National Oceanic and Atmospheric Administration (NOOA). In 2007,
Philip Cooney, former Head of the White House's Council on Environmental
Quality (CEQ) (2001-2005), admitted to have manipulated more than one
hundred reports and research findings of federal agencies to cast doubt on the
scientific basis of climate change.

Congress	Nay Sayers	Science
before	-	Discernible human influence
107th	Denial	Likely human influence
108th	Denial and manipulation	Some studies and comments on significant climate threat
109th	Reluctant acceptance of science by *Bush* Administration	Further statements, Hurricanes (Rita, Katrina); End of 06: Stern Review
110th	Statement by *Cooney* over manipulating scientific findings	National and Economic Security; Very likely influence

Table 1: Development of the Climate debate.

IV.   US Climate Policy and Developments on Capitol Hill

At the United Nations Conference on Environment and Development (UNCED)
in Rio de Janeiro in 1992, the United Nations Framework Convention on
Climate Change (UNFCCC) was negotiated. While European countries were
pushing for the inclusion of quantified emission reduction targets, the *Bush
sen.* Administration blocked such attempts.[39] In Kyoto 1997, the *Clinton*
Administration (1993-2000) more productively participated and considerably
shaped the negotiations leading to the Kyoto Protocol. When the administration
signed the protocol, however, it was already clear that it would not be ratified,
since the US Senate had unanimously issued the *Byrd-Hagel* Resolution.
This resolution expressed the reluctance of the Senate to ratify any climate
agreement, which would do serious harm to the US economy and would not
include commitments from developing countries.[40] These concerns were shared

---

39   L. Krämer, The Roots of Divergence: A European Perspective, in: N. J. Vig/M. G.
      Faure (eds.), Green Giants?: Environmental Policies of the United States and the
      European Union (2004), p. 64.
40   U.S. Senate, A Resolution Expressing the Sense of the Senate Regarding the
      Conditions for the United States Becoming a Signatory to any International
      Agreement on Greenhouse Gas Emissions under the United Nations Framework
      Convention on Climate Change, S.Res.98 (1997), http://thomas.loc.gov/cgi-bin/
      bdquery/z?d105:SE00098.

by *George W. Bush* (2000-2008). In March 2001, he announced not to bring the protocol before the Senate. He followed the language of the *Byrd-t* Resolution, adding concerns about scientific uncertainties.[41] As an alternative, the US Administration merely presented a series of unhelpful initiatives.[42]

This abstract of US climate politics demonstrates two things: a general reluctance of the United States to participate in an effective international climate policy regime and the power of Congress in foreign policy. When *Bush* entered the Oval Office, the Senate had already taken up a tough stance on climate change. This stance was informend by a particularly traditional understanding of security.

It put clear emphasise on the preservation of the national well-being and capabilities as well as on the maintenance of the US position towards potential future peer competitors such as China. Instead of climate change, climate policy was seen as a threat. Since then, however, the Senate has departed considerably from its former position. Although no comprehensive climate bill was passed between 2000 and 2008, efforts to bring forward climate policy increased substantially.

1.   107th Congress (2001-2002)[43]

Although the 107th Congress of the United States saw 80 climate-related legislative attempts it did not produce any economy wide cap legislation.[44]

---

41   White House, President Bush Discusses Global Climate Change (2001).

42   The so-called "Climate Change Initiative", introduced in 2002, announced a reduction of GHG-intensity, emissions relative to output, by 18 percent in ten years. Following Blanchard and Perkaus, this would translate into an increase of 14 percent between 2002 and 2012 in absolute emissions. Christiansen calculates, that this in turn would mean an absolute increase by 30 to 40 percent between 1990 and 2008-2012. See O. Blanchard/J. F. Perkaus, Does the Bush Administration's Climate Policy mean Climate Protection?, in: Energy Policy 32 (2004), p. 1998; A. C. Christiansen, Convergence or Divergence? Status and Prospects for US Climate Strategy, Climate Policy 3 (2003), p. 346.

43   The insights presented in part IV are drawn from a discourse analysis based on press statements and speeches available on the respective senator's web sites. Furthermore Senator's statements in hearings conducted by the Senate Committee on Environment and Public Works have been included to compensate for missing data on those Senators, who have retired and thus closed down their web sites. The following citations will illustrate the findings. They will be rather anecdotal though. Insights have been drawn from the analysis of more than 250 single documents.

44   The numbers on overall climate legislation include a vast range of issues related to climate change such as proposed measures on energy efficiency, transport measures and research activity. They have been drawn from the work of the Pew Center on Global Climate Change, www.pewclimate.org.

Three bills[45], however, required CO_2 emission reductions from electric power plants, responsible for approximately 40 percent of overall emissions. After introduction into the Senate these bills were sent to the Senate Committee on Environment and Public Works (EPW). Only one bill, the Clean Power Act (promoted by Sen. *James M. Jeffords*), made it through the committee process. It was not voted on by the Senate though. *Jeffords* emphasised: "Economic development that does not factor in the environment or quality of life of those future generations [of Americans] is not sustainable."[46] He focussed on climatic impacts on the environment and public health, mostly referring to future developments. The threat of climate change did not dominate his arguments. Instead, he spent significant time defending climate science and emphasising: "[I]t is our responsibility to act and our duty to lead."[47]

The Co-sponsor of the Clean Power Act, Senator *Joseph Lieberman*, additionally named phenomena attributed to climate change:

> "Sea levels could swell up to 35 feet, potentially submerging millions of homes and coastal properties. Precipitation would become more erratic, leading to droughts that would make hunger an even more serious global problem than it is today. Diseases such as malaria and dengue fever would spread at an accelerated pace. Severe weather disturbances and storms triggered by climatic phenomena, such as El Nino, would be aggravated by global warming and become more routine."[48]

When commenting on these developments' implications for the United States, however, he also merely stressed environmental and health threats. Other senators, active in promoting climate policy, demonstrated a similar perception of the issue. Senator *Patrick J. Leahy*, Sponsor of the Clean Power Plant and Modernization Act, stated that "[w]e face an undermining of our quality of life [...] and maybe even [a threat] to the continued existence of some forms of life on our planet."[49] Besides this threat perception, he emphasised the US' "world leadership role in protecting the earth", which "the new administration wants to throw away."[50]

---

45   S. 556, Clean Power Act, James M. Jeffords; S. 1131, The Clean Power Plant and Modernization Act, Partick J. Leahy; S. 3135, The Clean Air Planning Act, Sen. Thomas Carper.
46   US Senate, Statement of Senator James Jeffords, International Environmental Commitments, July 24, 2002, http://epw.senate.gov/107th/jef_072402.htm.
47   Ibid.
48   US Senate, Colloquy Between Senators John McCain and Joe Lieberman on Cap and Trade Approach to Climate Trade, 2 August 2001, http://lieberman.senate.gov/newsroom/release.cfm?id=208276.
49   US Senate, Hearing Statement on the Bush Administrations Environmental Rollbacks at the Senate Committee on Agriculture, Nutrition, and Forestry, 29 March 2001, Patrick Leahy, http://leahy.senate.gov/press/200103/010329a.html.
50   Ibid.

Congress	Frames	Threat to...	Scope/Cap	Votes	Bills (No.)
107th	Diffused (economic, positive/ negative; leadership)	Future; ecosystems; health	Energy generation only (40%)	EPW: 10-9 Senate: no	80

Table 2: Climate Discourse in the 107th Congress.

2. 108th Congress (2003-2004)

Compared to previous years, there was a slight increase in quantity of legislation. 96 climate related bills were introduced into Congress. The Clean Air Planning Act was re-introduced. Furthermore, *Joe Lieberman* and *John McCain* introduced the first economy wide bill: the Climate Stewardship Act (S. 139).[51] The bill was designed to reduce emissions by 2010 to the 2000 level. It thus aimed at a stabilisation rather than any reduction of emissions. The Climate Stewardship Act was defeated by 43-55 votes. Nevertheless, it was the first time the Senate had ever voted on a comprehensive climate bill. Thus, Senator *Lieberman* claimed "that the political climate is changing on climate change".[52]

Regarding the impact of climate policy *Lieberman* focused, rather defensively, on limiting costs instead of highlighting opportunities. More offensively he announced: "Global warming constitutes one of the great challenges of our time, threatening our environment, our economy and our public health".[53] In contrast to *Jeffords*, *Lieberman* did not merely perceive climate change as an environmental challenge. Furthermore, in his eyes the threat was geographically closer:

"Climate change poses not only a global challenge, but a very local one, impacting the lives of Americans in critical and potentially disastrous ways. Every family has reason to fear the effects of global warming."[54]

---

51 The bill included provisions to reduce greenhouse gas (GHG) emissions from electricity, manufacturing, commercial and transportation sectors (representing approx. 85 percent of US emissions). Such bills will be called comprehensive or economy wide bills hereafter.

52 US Senate, McCain, Lieberman Look Forward to Global Warming Vote, 1 August 2003, http://lieberman.senate.gov/newsroom/release.cfm?id=207835.

53 US Senate, Senate Casts Historic Vote on McCain-Lieberman Global Warming Bill, 30 October 2003, http://lieberman.senate.gov/newsroom/release.cfm?id=214290, emphasis added.

54 US Senate, Statement of Senator Joseph I. Lieberman on the McCain-Lieberman Climate Stewardship Act Amendment (S. 139), October 29, 2003, http://lieberman. senate.gov/newsroom/release.cfm?id=214240.

The economic dimension of climate impacts, slowly entering the discussion, continuously turned more concrete. In June 2004, *Lieberman* emphasised that the "costs and consequences of inaction, [...] will ruin the economy with a certainty far more destructive than any greenhouse-gas control program ever could".[55] Senator *McCain*, on the other hand, applied a rather conservative argumentation, explaining that he did "not support the [Kyoto] Protocol's exclusion of the developing world, largely China and India".[56] Nevertheless, he believed the Protocol's "goals should be heeded".[57] He also saw the reason for this in "[t]he costs of inaction [which] are prohibitive and unacceptable".[58]

Congress	Frames	Threat to...	Scope/Cap	Votes	Bills (No.)
108th	Threat more dominant; policy impact on economy not so costly; leadership mostly constant	ecosystems; health; economy; (national security; once) less distant geographically and temporally	Economy wide 2000 = 2010	Senate: 43-55	96

Table 3: Climate Discourse in the 108th Congress.

3.   109th Congress (2005-2006)

The quantity of climate legislation continued to increase. 106 climate related proposals were introduced into the 109th Congress. Climate politics were dominated by attempts of *Lieberman* and *McCain* to re-introduce their earlier bills. The Climate Stewardship Act was re-introduced in February 2005. In May, they furthermore introduced the Climate Stewardship and Innovation Act,

55   US Senate, Preserving our Planet Remarks by Senator Joe Lieberman, 24 June 2004, http://lieberman.senate.gov/newsroom/release.cfm?id=223150&&. In early 2004, referring to the Pentagon study mentioned above, Lieberman even said: "Finally, there has been increasing concern about global warming among the nation's national security experts." At that stage, national security entered the debate. However, framing climate change this way stayed a singular incident (cf. Bush's reaction to the study). US Senate, (2004b) Lieberman Pledges Action this Spring on Global Warming Bill, Tells Commerce Committee Support for Bill is Broadening, 3 March 2004, http://lieberman.senate.gov/newsroom/release.cfm?id=218618.

56   US Senate, Lieberman, McCain Welcome Russia's Action on Global Warming, Senators Encouraged by Russian Cabinet's Approval of Kyoto Protocol, 30 September 2004, http://lieberman.senate.gov/newsroom/release.cfm?id=226968.

57   Ibid.

58   US Senate, Statement of Senator Joseph I. Lieberman on the McCain-Lieberman Climate Stewardship Act Amendment (p. 139), 29 October 2003, http://lieberman.senate.gov/newsroom/release.cfm?id=214240.

which included additional incentives for the development of climate-friendly technologies. Both bills were sent to the EPW. They were not reported back to the Senate. The Climate Stewardship and Innovation Act was also offered as an amendment to the Energy Policy Act of 2005. The attempt was defeated by a 38-60 vote against the amendment. As a reaction, however, *Jeff Bingaman* issued a non-binding resolution, expressing the sense of the Senate

"that, before the end of the first session of the 109th Congress, Congress should enact a comprehensive and effective national program of mandatory, market-based limits on emissions of greenhouse gases that slow, stop, and reverse the growth of such emissions at a rate and in a manner that-- (1) will not significantly harm the United States economy; and (2) will encourage comparable action by other nations that are major trading partners and key contributors to global emissions." (S. Amdt. 866)

The resolution also acknowledged the growing consensus among climate scientists. For the first time, a majority had acknowledged the immediate need of comprehensive climate legislation.[59] Furthermore, besides *McCain* and *Lieberman*, other senators introduced economy wide climate legislation into the 109th Congress. In July 2006, *James Jeffords* and *Barbara Boxer* introduced the Global Warming Pollution Reduction Act and, in September, *John Kerry* and *Olympia Snowe* proposed the Global Warming Reduction Act.[60] Both bills were referred to the EPW and not reported back to the Senate. In contrast to the *McCain/Lieberman* bills, these two proposals included medium and long term reduction targets. The sponsors thereby proposed a significantly more vigorous answer to "how much?".

a)   *McCain* and *Lieberman*

Only minor changes occurred in the arguments put forward by *McCain* and *Lieberman*. There was practically no change in the perception of economic effects of climate policy. Leadership as a motive for policy-making was mentioned somewhat more frequently in the wake of the Kyoto Protocol coming into force in February 2005. While perceived threats further included an environmental and an economic dimension, they became more concrete. *John McCain* for example asserts "that earlier climate models are being validated today by actual conditions. The only surprise is that the rate of change is even faster than predicted."[61]

---

59   More concretely, it was accepted by voice vote after a motion to table, which would have defeated the resolution and ended the debate, was rejected by a 44-53 vote.

60   While the former bill was aiming at a reduction of GHG emissions to 1990 levels by 2020 and to 80 percent below 1990 levels by 2050, the latter proposed GHG emission reductions of 15 percent by 2020 and 65 percent by 2050 using a 2010 base line.

61   US Senate, Statement of Senator John McCain on the Climate Stewardship Act of 2005, 10 February 2005, http://mccain.senate.gov/public/index.

b)   Kerry and Snowe

With the presentation of the Global Warming Reduction Act, *Kerry* and *Snowe* had outpaced the prior climate champions in ambition (see table 4). They also intensified the discussion on climate impacts. Senator *John Kerry* demonstrated similar concerns about leadership. Furthermore, however, he called climate change "a matter of [...] our own security"[62] and presented it as "the other mortal threat to America after terrorism".[63] With the latter, he drew a clear connection to policies much more salient to the US Administration. Similarly, Senator *Snowe* emphasised that climate change poses a "threat not only to our economy, but to our environment, [and] our national security".[64] She continuously discussed the potential of non-linear, abrupt climate change.

c)   Jeffords and Boxer

Similar to his fellow climate policy-makers, *Jeffords* mentioned health, environmental and economic effects. He framed these in a more positive way by emphasising the potential of climate policy to avoid these impacts. Nevertheless, *Jeffords* also warned that "[w]e may go beyond the tipping point and be forced to confront the reality of irreversible climate change".[65] He also emphasised the need for leadership and business opportunities. As in earlier statements of *Jeffords* (108th Congress), there is no particular issue dominating his argumentation. His Co-Sponsor, Senator *Boxer*, had not paid much attention to the climate issue before 2006.[66] Then, however, she forcefully entered the debate by stating: "Nowhere is there a greater threat to future generations than the disastrous effects of global warming."[67] She mainly focused on the threat

---

cfm?FuseAction=PressOffice.FloorStatements&ContentRecord_id=178d377c-a1bb-419e-8b21-7ce6c9e27e8a&Region_id=&Issue_id.

62   US Senate, John Kerry on Climate Change: Its Time for America to Re-engage with the Rest of the World on this Very Real Problem, 16 February 2005, http://kerry.senate.gov/cfm/record.cfm?id=232209.

63   US Senate, John Kerry: Three New Bold Ideas for Energy Independence and Global Climate Change, 26 June 2006, http://kerry.senate.gov/cfm/record.cfm?id=261502.

64   US Senate, Snowe Hails Release of International Climate Change Report, Urges Formation of New G8+ Group to Address Climate Change, 25 January 2005, http://snowe.senate.gov/public/index.cfm?FuseAction=PressRoomPressReleases&ContentRecord_id=59e954e2-fa30-4a05-8fcf-21b83a98d441&Region_id=&Issue_id.

65   US Senate, U.S. Senate Committee on Environment & Public Works, Hearing Statements, Statement of Senator James M. Jeffords, Examining Approaches Embodied in the Asia Pacific Partnership, 20 September 2006, http://epw.senate.gov/hearing_statements.cfm?id=263553.

66   No single climate related press release or speech in 2005.

67   US Senate, California Senator Vows to Focus on Global Warming and Children's Health; Names Longtime Aide Bettina Poirier as First Female Staff Director and Chief

of climate change, which she perceived as endangering "our nation's public health, economic growth and environment".[68] More than others, she emphasised potential irreversible changes and tipping points.

Climate policy in the 109th Congress is particularly insightful since three different approaches can be compared. First, *Lieberman* and *McCain* continued their efforts, accompanied by a largely constant threat perception. Second, with the *Bingaman* Resolution, a majority was found for the first time. This majority vote is interesting since it can be related to particular policy measures. *Bingaman* himself introduced the Climate and Economy Insurance Act, presumably in the spirit of his own resolution. The respective bill, potentially representing a middle-ground on climate policy at that time, was significantly less ambitious than those bills discussed so far. It merely demanded GHG intensity targets and included a safety valve, restricting the potential price of emission allowances. Hence, although a majority of senators seemed to acknowledge the threat frame offered by *McCain* and *Lieberman*, traditional security concerns (economic harm; position vis-à-vis peer competitors) stayed particularly important and impeded comprehensive climate legislation. Third, arguments put forward to legitimate new proposals were heavily focussed on the threat frame, going as far as explicitly calling climate change a threat to security. New security concerns coincided with more ambitious policy proposals. Furthermore, securitization of climate change in terms of national security (as opposed to e.g. environmental or health security) was accompanied by enforced mitigation measures rather than a shifting focus towards traditional security policy. These observations challenge the fixed nature of the connection between the security dimensions of "how much?" and "by which means?".

Counsel of EPW, 14 November 2006, http://boxer.senate.gov/news/releases/record.cfm?id=265868.

68   US Senate, Boxer, Feinstein Tell President to Let California Fight Global Warming National Highway Traffic and Safety Administration's Rule Wrongly Tries To Undermine State Climate Change Laws, 31 March 2006, http://boxer.senate.gov/news/releases/record.cfm?id=253405.

Congress	Frames	Threat to...	Scope/Cap	Votes	Bills (No.)
109th	Mostly constant, threat frames emerging as dominant part of discourse	ecosystems; health; economy; in America/now	All economy wide 2000 = 2010	Senate: 38 – 60	106
		.. plus tipping points	1990 = 2020 2050= -80%	no	
		.. plus national security	2010 = 2010 2020 = -15% 2050 = -65%	no	
		.. including caveats	"meaningful"	53-44	

Table 4: Climate Discourse in the 109th Congress.

4.   110th Congress (2007-2008)

Already before the 110th Congress of the United States was officially inaugurated, *Barbara Boxer*, *Jeff Bingaman* and *Joseph Lieberman* urged President *Bush* to join the new Congress, now under a new democratic majority, to produce meaningful climate legislation. They emphasised:

> "Scientists are now warning that we may be reaching a 'tipping point' beyond which it will be extremely difficult, or perhaps impossible, to avoid the worst consequences of climate change. If the world continues on its current path of emissions increases, we could risk global climatic disasters on an unprecedented scale, ranging from dangerous sea level rise, to increasingly damaging hurricanes (such as Hurricanes Katrina and Rita), increased deaths from air pollution and disease, to widespread geo-political instability. A recent report by Sir Nicholas Stern finds that leaving climate change unchecked could cost between 5%-20% of global GDP."[69]

Although additional voices entered the climate debate, *Joe Lieberman* resumed his role as the most active climate legislator. Together with *John McCain* he introduced an enhanced version of the Climate Stewardship and Innovation Act. Together with *John Warner*, a distinguished security expert and voice of authority within Senate, he furthermore introduced the Climate Security Act. Altogether five comprehensive climate bills were introduced into the Senate.

---

69   US Senate, Boxer, Bingaman and Lieberman Ask President to Commit to Workingwith Congress to Fight Global Warming, 15 November 2006, http://www.boxer.senate.gov/news/releases/record.cfm?id=265906.

All of them included emission targets for 2050 (see table 5). The proposals of *Lieberman-Warner*, *McCain-Lieberman* and *Kerry-Snowe* were roughly comparable regarding their ambitions. Two bills revealed differences though: On the one hand, the most ambitious bill, proposed by *Boxer* and *Sanders* (who had succeeded Jeffords in Senate), called for an emission reduction of 80 percent by 2050 and applying a 1990 base line. On the other hand, the *Bingaman-Specter* proposal was less ambitious than other bills. It merely demanded an emission reduction of 60 percent until 2050, applying a 2006 base line.[70] Additionally, this bill included a so-called safety valve; potentially further diluting the bill's effect by limiting the market price of carbon.

Although all bills were referred to the EPW, only the Climate Security Act was reported back to Senate. It was reported to the EPW by the EPW's Subcommittee on Private Sector and Consumer Solutions to Global Warming by a 4-3 vote in January 2007 and by the EPW to the Senate by an 11-8 vote in May 2008. It thereby was the first comprehensive climate bill to be reported to the Senate. However, there was no final vote on the bill.

a) *Lieberman-Warner/Lieberman-McCain*

While considerations about the cost of climate policy remained defensive, *Lieberman* stressed:

> "Indeed, if we fail to start substantially reducing greenhouse gas emissions in the next couple of years, we risk catastrophic damage. Insect-borne diseases such as malaria will spike as tropical ecosystems expand; hotter air will exacerbate the pollution that sends children to the hospital with asthma attacks; food insecurity from shifting agricultural zones will spark border wars; and storms and coastal flooding from sea-level rise will cause mortality and dislocation."[71]

Although *Lieberman* did not refer to national security in particular, this statement implies a clear notion of respective challenges by mentioning migration (dislocation) and interstate (border) wars. *Lieberman's* companion *McCain* expressed a more obvious change in threat perception. The costs of climate change, "the consequences of which so directly affects our national interests", were said to be "enormous, and the national security concerns related to our inaction cannot be ignored."[72]

---

70 The baseline used for calculation is important since emissions have risen by approximately 14 percent between 1990 and 2006.

71 US Senate, The Turning Point on Global Warming, The Boston Globe, by John McCain and Joe Lieberman, 13 February 2007, http://lieberman.senate.gov/ newsroom/release.cfm?id=269205.

72 US Senate, Lieberman, McCain Reintroduce Climate Stewardship and Innovation Act, 12 January 2007, http://lieberman.senate.gov/newsroom/release.cfm?id=267559.

Sponsors	Lieberman-Warner	McCain-Lieberman	Sanders-Boxer	Kerry-Snowe	Bingaman-Specter
Name of Bill	Climate Security Act	Climate Stewardship and Innovation Act	Global Warming Pollution Reduction Act	Global Warming Reduction Act	Low Carbon Economy Act
Aspired reduction	2012: 4% 2020: 19% 2050: 71% (Base year 2005)	2020: 0% 2030: 20% 2050: 60% (Base year 1990)	2010: Stabilisation 2020: 0% 2030: 27% 2040: 53% 2050: 80% (Base year 1990)	2010: Stabilisation 2020: 0% 2050: 62% (Base year 1990)	2012: Stabilisation 2020 = 2006 2030 = 1990 2050: ≥ 60% safety valve (Base year 2006)

Table 5: Major Climate Bills in 110th Congress.

The influence of climate security turns even more obvious in the case of Senator *John Warner*. Not demonstrating any distinguished stance on the climate issue before, in June 2007 he announced his collaboration with *Lieberman* and stressed the fact that "[i]n my 28 years in the Senate, I have focused above all on issues of national security, and I see the problem of global climate change as fitting squarely within that focus."[73] He issued this statement only two months after the CNA report, featuring several high-ranking retired military officers, had been published.

b)   *Kerry-Snowe*

Both sponsors basically continued their previous lines of argumentation. *Kerry* called climate change a threat "which could have a greater long-term impact on our security than any other."[74] Additionally, he once emphasised the role of China as a major force in the development of innovative energy technologies, thereby beginning to reverse the peer competitor argument in favour of climate policy. *Snowe* compared the relevance of the 2005 Hurricanes Rita and Katrina for US policy to that of the terrorist attacks on 9/11.

---

73   US Senate, Senators Lieberman, Warner Drafting New Bipartisan Bill on ClimateChange, 27 June 2007, http://lieberman.senate.gov/newsroom/release.cfm?id=277907.
74   US Senate, Kerry Offers Post-Kyoto Global Climate Change Approach, 30 October 2007, http://kerry.senate.gov/cfm/record.cfm?id=286291.

c) *Sanders-Boxer*

Barbara Boxer emphasised the "horrific impact"[75] of climate change. *Bernie Sanders*, although a newcomer in the Senate, was the most ambitious of all senators actively involved in climate politics. He directly criticised *Lieberman* and *Warner* for not going far enough. He urged to "wage a war on global warming".[76] This stance on the issue was based on a double motivation: Beside acknowledging "that global warming poses a significant threat to the national security and economy of the United States, to public health and welfare, and to the global environment,"[77] he predicted that an ambitious climate policy will "create millions of good-paying jobs."[78]

d) *Bingaman-Specter*

Congress	Frames	Threat to...	Scope/Cap	Votes	Bills (No.)
110th	threat frames dominating the debate (energy security and "green jobs" slowly emerging)	Economy and national security	e.g. 2050 = -71% (base 2005)	EPW Sub-Committee: 4-3 EPW: 11-8	>235

Table 6: Climate Discourse in the 110th Congress

The sponsors of the least ambitious economy wide draft presented in the 110th Congress did not demonstrate a similar level of concern. Although *Jeff Bingaman* mentioned potential climate impacts, he focused on the economic impacts of climate policy. He discussed positive and negative consequences, emphasising the need to "strike the right balance".[79] He also paid more attention to energy security. Similarly, *Arlen Specter* accepted climate change as a "major problem" that the Senate "ought to deal with".[80] He, however, cautioned against the *Lieberman-Warner* bill since it might imply too much economic costs.

---

75 US Senate, Boxer Discusses Global Warming with UN Secretary-General, Tuesday, 17 July 2007, http://boxer.senate.gov/news/releases/record.cfm?id=279125.

76 US Senate, Summary of the Global Warming Pollution Reduction Act (p. 309), as introduced January 2007, 15 January 2007, Bernie Sanders, http://sanders.senate.gov/newsroom/news/?id=f99cc6a4-1b10-4a0e-8d91-75bd0b3ab1bd.

77 Ibid.

78 US Senate, International Solutions, 13 November 2008, Bernie Sanders, http://www.sanders.senate.gov/news/record.cfm?id=304950.

79 US Senate, Jeff Bingaman, A Step Toward Clean Energy, 4 September 2007, http://bingaman.enews.senate.gov//common/mailings/?id=109.

80 US Senate, Senator Arlen Specter Proposes Amendments on Emission Caps, 3 June

e)   Security Policy

Most policy initiatives to tackle climate change were aimed at reducing GHG
emissions. With the emergence of the national security discourse, these efforts
were enforced significantly. Moreover, however, initiatives considering
traditional security instruments to tackle the impact of climate change emerged
within this context. The Global Climate Change Security Oversight Act, a bill
sponsored by Senator *Richard Durbin*, demanded the National Intelligence
Council (NIC) to prepare a National Intelligence Estimate (NIE) on the
geopolitical effects of climate change. It also required the Secretary of State
and the Secretary of Defence to consider the implications of the NIE's findings
for military operations and US national security interests. Although the bill was
not voted on, similar measures were approved as an amendment to the National
Defence Authorization Act for Fiscal Year 2008.

It is worthwhile taking a look at the co-sponsors of the Global Climate
Change Security Oversight Act. The legislation was supported by only one of
those senators involved in drafting economy wide bills: *John Kerry*.[81] Most
active climate legislators supported different strategies to counter the threat.
This becomes clear in a resolution, sponsored by *Joe Biden* (S. Res. 30). The
resolution promoted international cooperation and emission reductions as
the right way to counter the national security implications of climate change.
Furthermore, the resolution demanded to establish a bipartisan Senate observer
group to monitor international negotiations. It was co-sponsored by, among
others, *Barbara Boxer, Joe Lieberman, Jeff Bingaman, Bernie Sanders, Olympia
Snowe, Arlen Specter, John Warner* and *John Kerry*.[82] Senator *Richard Durbin*,
and several other Sponsors of the Global Climate Change Security Oversight
Act, also supported the *Biden* Resolution, demonstrating that security policies
are perceived as an additional and not as the first and foremost strategy to tackle
the national security impacts of climate change.

2008,   http://specter.senate.gov/public/index.cfm?FuseAction=NewsRoom.ArlenSpe
cterSpeaks&ContentRecord_id=50780340-eec5-5b38-c8c3-1aca7f3ec13f&Region_
id=&Issue_id=bd504b78-7e9c-9af9-7434-429fb23e40e3.

81   Further Co-Sponsors: Sen. Richard Lugar [R-IN], Sen. Maria Cantwell [D-WA], Sen.
      Joseph Biden [D-DE], Sen. Sheldon Whitehouse [D-RI], Sen. Robert Casey [D-PA],
      Sen. Charles Hagel [R-NE], Sen. Evan Bayh [D-IN], Sen. Dianne Feinstein [D-CA].

82   Sen. Amy Klobuchar [D-MN], Sen. Robert Menéndez [D-NJ], Sen. Susan Collins
      [R-ME], Sen. Richard Lugar [R-IN], Sen. Benjamin Cardin [D-MD], Sen. Maria
      Cantwell [D-WA], Sen. Debbie Ann Stabenow [D-MI], Sen. Russell Feingold [D-WI],
      Sen. Richard Durbin [D-IL], Sen. Carl Levin [D-MI], Sen. Christopher Dodd [D-CT],
      Sen. Jim Webb [D-VA], Sen. Thad Cochran [R-MS], Sen. Sherrod Brown [D-OH],
      Sen. Robert Casey [D-PA], Sen. Evan Bayh [D-IN], Sen. Barack Obama [D-IL], Sen.
      Dianne Feinstein [D-CA], Sen. Jon Tester [D-MT], Sen. Frank Lautenberg [D-NJ].

V. Conclusions

This chapter set out to investigate the policy effect of securitization of climate change, and to evaluate these processes' power to transform the meaning of security. In other words: it attempted to investigate the co-constitution of agent based political action and socially constructed structure. The analysis has shown that both, an amplified threat perception and enforced efforts in climate policy occurred. Several arguments support the claim that threat perception has been the major driver of climate policy: First, while the debate was diffused in the beginning, more concrete efforts in climate policy coincided with a growing domination of threat frames. Second, increased efforts were accompanied not only by a more dominant position of the threat frame compared to other frames but also by a perception of threat, continuously coming closer geographically and temporally. Third, while there was significant change in threat perception, conceptions of e.g. the cost of climate policy and ambitions to exercise a leadership role in international politics stayed relatively constant. A detailed observation of these processes allows inferences about the nature of security itself: Although security is still understood as national security in the Senate, the ways of handling threats has transformed. The *Byrd-Hagel* Resolution of 1997 emphasised threats from climate policy to the nation's international power position and economy, resulting in a 95-0 vote. In other words, Congress started off at a decisively traditional position on security. Although Senate started to acknowledge climate change as a threat ("from what?") early within the considered time frame, major shifts in efforts ("how much?") were dependent upon the notions of national security ("for whom?"). Although the threat to other referent objects also provoked action, ambitions most visibly accelerated when the referent object continuously approached the entity most capable to act: the state.

The relation of "how much?" and "by which means?" was also presented as crucial in part II. *Ole Waever* in particular opted for desecuritising environmental problems as these dimensions are necessarily connected. Regarding this argument, the empirical analysis presents an ambiguous picture. On the one hand, calling climate change a national security issue has resulted in traditional security policy legislation in the 110th Congress. On the other hand, this legislation was not the major part of the answer to climate change as a national security threat. Most initiatives still are situated within the realm of climate policy (mitigation action). *Joe Biden* makes this clear with his resolution. Nevertheless, one has to bare in mind the intersubjective quality of security. Even in the US Senate, there is no security concept shared by all senators. Not only threat perceptions vary, security mind-sets vary too. This becomes clear since distinct groups of senators have been identified with regard to different policy strategies. Altogether, however, mitigation measures dominated the debate and were also accepted by those senators considering traditional security policy measures. Although *Waever's* securityness of security and his call for caution can serve as a helpful reminder that traditional security concepts are still taken seriously, it fails in providing a valid definition of security as occurring in concrete social relations. The discursive power of security has allowed for a significant step forward in the climate policy of the US Senate. This implies a clear transformation of security as defined in part II.

The analysis of security as a discourse has provided insights into the dynamics of politics and security beyond the scope of more orthodox approaches to Security Analysis. Although it is absolutely necessary to generate precise predictions of climate impacts, approaches which understand security as analytical concepts of an objective quality are blind to transformations of "security" within concrete political contexts. Instead, "most of the literature on security studies is not so much a study of the practice as the very practice itself."[83]

Bibliography

Baldwin, D. A., The Concept of Security, in: Review of International Studies 23 (1997), pp. 5–26.

Barnett, J., The Meaning of Environmental Security. Ecological Politics and Policy in the New Security Era (2001).

Bartelson, J., Three Concepts of Globalization, in: International Sociology, 15 (2000), pp. 180-192.

Beck, U., Weltrisikogesellschaft: auf der Suche nach der verlorenen Sicherheit (2007).
—   World Risk Society (1999).

Behnke, A., The Message or the Messenger?: Reflexions on the Role of Security Experts and the Securitization of Political Issues, in: Cooperation and Conflict 35 (2000), pp. 89-105.

Beckett, M., Berlin Speech on Climate and Security, 24 October 2006, http://ukingermany.fco. gov.uk/de/newsroom/?view=Speech&id=4616005.

Benedick, R. E., U.S. Climate Policy after the Presidential Election: Continuity or Change?, in: A. Riechel/A. Venturelli (eds.), Building a Foundation for Transatlantic Climate Policy (2005), pp. 15-25.

Blanchard, O./J. F. Perkaus, Does the Bush Administration's Climate Policy mean Climate Protection?, in: Energy Policy 32 (2004), pp. 1993-1998.

Brown, O./A. Hammill/R. McCeman, Climate Change as the 'New' Security Threat: Implications for Africa, in: International Affairs 83 (2007), pp. 1141-1154.

Brzoska, M., The Securitization of Climate Change and the Power of Conceptions of Security, in: Sicherheit und Frieden/Security and Peace 27 (2009), pp. 137-145.

Buzan, B./O. Wæver/J. de Wilde, Security: A new Framework for Analysis (1998).

Center for Naval Analyses (eds.), National Security and the Threat of Climate Change (2007).

---

83   Smith, The Increasing Insecurity of Security Studies (1999), p. 96.

Christiansen, A. C., Convergence or Divergence? Status and Prospects for US Climate Strategy, Climate Policy 3 (2003), pp. 343-358.

Dalby, S., Environmental Security (2002).

Deudney, D., The Case Against Linking Environmental Degradation and National Security, in: Millenium 19 (1990), pp. 461-476.

Dyer, H., Environmental Security and International Relations: The Case for Enclosure, in: Review of International Studies 27 (2001), pp. 441-450.

Eriksson, J. (ed.), Threat Politics: New Perspectives on Security, Risk and Crisis Management (2001).

Floyd, R., The Environmental Security Debate and its Significance for Climate Change, in: The International Spectator 43 (2008), pp. 51-65.

Hajer, M. A., The Politics of Environmental Discourse (1995).

Homer-Dixon, T. F., Environment, Scarcity, and Violence (1999).

Intergovernmental Panel on Climate Change, Climate Change 1995: The Science of Climate Change. Summary for Policymakers and Technical Summary of the Working Group I Report (1996), http://www.ipcc.ch/pdf/climate-changes-1995/ipcc-2nd-assessment/2nd-assessment-en.pdf.

Intergovernmental Panel on Climate Change, Climate Change 2001. Synthesis Report. Summary for Policy Makers, Assessment of the Intergovernmental Panel on Climate Change (2001), http://www.ipcc.ch/pdf/climate-changes-2001/synthesis-spm/synthesis-spm-en.pdf.

Kaplan, R. D., The Coming Anarchy. How Scarcity, Crime, Overpopulation, Tribalism, and Disease are Rapidly Destroying the Social Fabric of our Planet, in: Atlantic Monthly 273 (1994), pp. 44-76.

Knudsen, O., Post-Copenhagen Security Studies: Desecuritizing Securitization, in: Security Dialogue 32 (2001), pp. 355-368.

Krämer, L., The Roots of Divergence: A European Perspective, in: N. J. Vig/M. G. Faure (eds.), Green Giants?:Environmental Policies of the United States and the European Union (2004), pp. 53-72.

Krause, K./M. C. Williams, Broadening the Agenda of Security Studies: Politics and Methods, in: Mershon International Studies Review 40 (1996), pp. 229-254.

Lacy, M., Security and Climate Change: International Relations and the Limits of Realism (2005).

Levy, M. A., Is the Environment a National Security Issue?, in: International Security 20 (1995), pp. 35-62.

Müller, F., Einigung im Emissionshandel: Ein Beitrag zur Erosion der internationalen Klimapolitik?, in: SWP-Aktuell, Stiftung Wissenschaft und Politik. (2004).

Randall, D./P. Schwartz, An Abrupt Climate Change Scenario and Its Implications for United States National Security. Global Business Network (GBN) report (2003).

Rasmussen, M. V., Reflexive Security: Nato and International Risk Society, in: Millennium: Journal of International Studies 30 (2001), pp. 285-309.

Rothschild, E., What is Security?, in: Daedalus, 124 (1995), pp. 53-98.

Salehyan, I., From Climate Change to Conflict? No Consensus Yet, in: Journal for Peace Research 45 (2008), pp. 315-326.

Stern, N. (ed.), Stern Review Report on the Economics of Climate Change (2006), http://www.hm-treasury.gov.uk/d/CLOSED_SHORT_executive_summary.pdf.

Smith, S., The Increasing Insecurity of Security Studies: Conceptualizing Security in the Last Twenty Years, in: Contemporary Security Policy 20 (1999), pp. 72-101.

Tuchman Mathews, T., Redefining Security, in: Foreign Affairs 68 (1989), pp. 162-177.

Trittin, J., Speech held by Jürgen Trittin on 17 February 2005: Internationale Umweltpolitik ist Sicherheitspolitik, www.bmu.de/reden/bundesumweltminister_juergen_trittin/doc/35292.php.

Trobmetta, J. M., Environmental Security and Climate Change: Analysing the Discourse, in: Cambridge Review of International Affairs 21 (2008), pp. 585-602.

Ullman, R. H., Redefining Security, in: International Security 8 (1983), pp. 129-153.

US House, Hearing of the Committee on Oversight and Government Reform United States House of Representatives: Statement of Philip A. Cooney (2007), http://oversight.house.gov/documents/20070319103626-14718.PDF.

US House, Politics and Science in the Bush Administration (2003), http://oversight.house.gov/features/politics_and_science/pdfs/pdf_politics_and_science_rep.pdf.

US Senate, A Resolution Expressing the Sense of the Senate Regarding the Conditions for the United States Becoming a Signatory to any International Agreement on Greenhouse Gas Emissions under the United Nations Framework Convention on Climate Change, S.Res.98, (1997), http://thomas.loc.gov/cgi-bin/bdquery/z?d105:SE00098:.

US Senate, Colloquy Between Senators John McCain and Joe Lieberman on Cap and Trade Approach to Climate Trade, August 2, 2001, http://lieberman.senate.gov/newsroom/release.cfm?id=208276.

US Senate, Hearing Statement on the Bush Administrations Environmental Rollbacks at the Senate Committee on Agriculture, Nutrition, and Forestry, 29 March 2001, Patrick Leahy, http://leahy.senate.gov/press/200103/010329a.html.

US Senate, Statement of Senator James Jeffords, International Environmental Commitments, 24 July 2002, http://epw.senate.gov/107th/jef_072402.htm.

US Senate, McCain, Lieberman Look Forward to Global Warming Vote, 1 August 2003, http://lieberman.senate.gov/newsroom/release.cfm?id=207835.

US Senate, Senate Casts Historic Vote on McCain-Lieberman Global Warming Bill, 30 October 2003, http://lieberman.senate.gov/newsroom/release.cfm?id=214290.

US Senate, Statement of Senator Joseph I. Lieberman on the McCain-Lieberman Climate Stewardship Act Amendment (p. 139), 29 October 2003, http://lieberman.senate.gov/newsroom/release.cfm?id=214240.

US Senate, Preserving Our Planet Remarks By Senator Joe Lieberman, 24 June 2004, http://lieberman.senate.gov/newsroom/release.cfm?id=223150&&.

US Senate, Lieberman Pledges Action This Spring on Global Warming Bill, Tells Commerce Committee support for bill is broadening, 3 March 2004, http://lieberman.senate.gov/newsroom/release.cfm?id=218618.

US Senate, Lieberman, McCain Welcome Russia's Action on Global Warming, Senators encouraged by Russian cabinet's approval of Kyoto Protocol, 30 September 2004, http://lieberman.senate.gov/newsroom/release.cfm?id=226968.

US Senate, Text of Senator Liebermans Floor Statement on Climate Change, 10 February 2005, http://lieberman.senate.gov/newsroom/release.cfm?id=231966.

US Senate, Statement of Senator John McCain on the Climate Stewardship Act of 2005, 10 February 2005, http://mccain.senate.gov/public/index.cfm?FuseAction=PressOffice.FloorStatements&ContentRecord_id=178d377c-a1bb-419e-8b21-7ce6c9e27e8a&Region_id=&Issue_id.

US Senate, John Kerry on Climate Change: Its Time for America to Re-engage with the Rest of the World on this Very Real Problem, 16 February 2005, http://kerry.senate.gov/cfm/record.cfm?id=232209.

US Senate, Snowe Hails Release of International Climate Change Report, Urges Formation of New G8+ Group to Address Climate Change, 25 January 2005, http://snowe.senate. gov/public/index.cfm?FuseAction=PressRoom.PressReleases&ContentRecord_ id=59e954e2-fa30-4a05-8fcf-21b83a98d441&Region_id=&Issue_id.

US Senate, John Kerry: Three New Bold Ideas for Energy Independence and Global Climate Change, 26 June 2006, http://kerry.senate.gov/cfm/record.cfm?id=261502.

US Senate, U.S. Senate Committee on Environment & Public Works, Hearing Statements, Statement of Senator James M. Jeffords, Examining Approaches Embodied in the Asia Pacific Partnership, 20 September 2006, http://epw.senate.gov/hearing_statements. cfm?id=263553.

US Senate, California Senator Vows to Focus on Global Warming and Children's Health; Names Longtime Aide Bettina Poirier as First Female Staff Director and Chief Counsel of EPW, 14 November 2006, http://boxer.senate.gov/news/releases/record.cfm?id=265868.

US Senate, Boxer, Feinstein Tell President to Let California Fight Global Warming National Highway Traffic and Safety Administration's Rule Wrongly Tries To Undermine State Climate Change Laws, 31 March 2006, http://boxer.senate.gov/news/releases/record. cfm?id=253405.

US Senate, Boxer, Bingaman and Lieberman Ask President to Commit to Working with Congress to Fight Global Warming, 15 November 2006, http://www.boxer.senate.gov/ news/releases/record.cfm?id=265906.

US Senate, Kerry Offers Post-Kyoto Global Climate Change Approach, 30 October 2007, http://kerry.senate.gov/cfm/record.cfm?id=286291.

US Senate, Boxer Discusses Global Warming with UN Secretary-General, 17 July 2007, http:// boxer.senate.gov/news/releases/record.cfm?id=279125.

US Senate, Summary of the Global Warming Pollution Reduction Act (p. 309), as introduced January 2007, 15 January 2007, Bernie Sanders, http://sanders.senate.gov/newsroom/ news/?id=f99cc6a4-1b10-4a0e-8d91-75bd0b3ab1bd.

US Senate, Jeff Bingaman, A Step Toward Clean Energy, 4 September 2007, http://bingaman. enews.senate.gov//common/mailings/?id=109.

US Senate, International Solutions, 13 November 2008, Bernie Sanders, http://www.sanders. senate.gov/news/record.cfm?id=304950.

US Senate, Senator Arlen Specter Proposes Amendments on Emission Caps, 3 June 2008, http:// specter.senate.gov/public/index.cfm?FuseAction=NewsRoom.ArlenSpecterSpeaks& ContentRecord_id=50780340-eec5-5b38-c8c3-1aca7f3ec13f&Region_id=&Issue_ id=bd504b78-7e9c-9af9-7434-429fb23e40e3.

US Senate, The Turning Point on Global Warming, The Boston Globe, by John McCain and Joe Lieberman, 13 February 2007, http://lieberman.senate.gov/newsroom/release. cfm?id=269205.

US Senate, Lieberman, McCain Reintroduce Climate Stewardship and Innovation Act, 12 January 2007, http://lieberman.senate.gov/newsroom/release.cfm?id=267559.

US Senate, Senators Lieberman, Warner Drafting New, Bipartisan Bill on Climate Change, 27 June 2007, http://lieberman.senate.gov/newsroom/release.cfm?id=277907.

Waever, O., Securitization and De-Securitization, in: R. D. Lipschutz (ed.), On Security (1995), pp. 62-65.

Walt, S. M., The Renaissance of Security Studies, in: International Studies Quarterly 35 (1991), pp. 211-239.

Waltz, K., Theory of International Politics (1979).

White House, President Bush Discusses Global Climate Change (2001), http://georgewbush-whitehouse.archives.gov/news/releases/2001/06/20010611-2.html.

Williams, M. J., (In)Security Studies, Reflexive Modernization and the Risk Society, in: Cooperation and Conflict 43 (2008), pp. 57-79.

Global Proliferation of Bilateral and Regional Trade Agreements: A Threat for the World Trade Organization and/or for Developing Countries?

Anke Dahrendorf

I. Introduction

Aim of this contribution is to answer the two questions raised in the title, in particular for the area of intellectual property (IP) protection. In light of the recent proliferation of bilateral trade agreements on a large territorial scale that regulate manifold trade-related and trade-unrelated issues, the question arises whether the relevance of the World Trade Organization (WTO) as the multilateral forum of trade relations is undermined through this development. By looking at the legal basis for such bilateral agreements in the relevant WTO agreements, in particular the Agreement on Trade-Related Aspects of Intellectual Property Rights[1] (hereinafter TRIPS Agreement), and the development of international regulation of intellectual property protection, an answer to this question is sought. While it is not only important to look at a possible deadlock in the WTO resulting from this development, equally pressing is the question as to whether or not developing countries have encountered problems through the proliferation of bilateral trade agreements. Four problems for developing countries will be discussed in the remainder of this contribution, being:

1) TRIPS-plus provisions (with a focus on IP provisions in free trade agreements concluded by the United States);
2) the absence of a regional integration exception in the TRIPS Agreement;
3) secret and non-transparent negotiations (with a focus on IP provisions in free trade agreements concluded by the United States); and
4) a broader strategy by industrialised countries to increase the global protection of IP, in particular enforcement issues.

II. Recent Proliferation of Bilateral and Regional Trade Agreements

Over the last ten years, there has been a considerable rise in bilateral and regional trade agreements (RTAs).[2] This proliferation of bilateral and regional

---

1   Agreement on Trade-Related Aspects of Intellectual Property Rights, 33 I.L.M. 1197 (1994). This chapter inlcudes information up until June 2009.
2   See M. Wilson, Friend or Foe? Regional Trade Agreements and the WTO, in: ICTSD-BRIDGES Monthly Review 12 (2008), p. 19; S. Lester/B. Mercurio (eds.), Bilateral and Regional Trade Agreements: Case Studies (2009); J. Bhagwati, Termites in the

trade agreements has not only taken place in areas concerning trade issues, such as trade in goods and services, but also in fields such as investment, trade facilitation, government procurement, environmental and labour standards, competition policy, and, in particular, protecting intellectual property.[3] In the 2006 update on the regional trade agreements notified to the WTO, the Trade Policies Review Division of the WTO secretariat describes the increasing number of RTAs as a prominent feature of the multilateral trading system and as an important trade policy tool for virtually all WTO members.[4] The number of regional trade agreements notified before the establishment of the WTO and after its establishment confirms the claimed proliferation of regional trade agreements: during the years under the General Agreement on Tariffs and Trade 1947[5] (hereinafter GATT 1947), 124 RTAs were notified, while during the WTO years 243 RTAs were registered.[6] This amounts to an annual average of 20 notifications for the WTO years (from 1995 until December 2006) and less than three regional trade agreements notifications per year during the 47 years of the GATT 1947 regime (from 1947 until 1994). Furthermore, the results suggest that the regional trade agreements, at a proposal stage, reflect a significant increase in bilateral RTAs (compared with plurilateral) as well as in cross-regional RTAs (compared with intra-regional). In other words, we can observe a "shift from using regional trade agreements as an instrument for regional integration to vehicles for strategic market access"[7] in regions other

Trading System: How Preferential Agreements Undermine Free Trade (2008); F. M. Abbott, A New Dominant Trade Species Emerges: Is Bilateralism a Threat?, in: Journal of International Economic Law 10 (2007), p. 571; M. Schaefer, Ensuring That Regional Trade Agreements Complement The WTO System: US Unilateralism a Supplement to WTO Initiatives?, in: Journal of International Economic Law 10 (2007), p. 585; H. Gao/C. L. Lim, Saving the WTO From the Risk of Irrelevance: The WTO Dipsute Settlement Mechanism as a 'Common Good' for RTA Disputes, in: Journal of International Economic Law 11 (2008), p. 899.

3   See Wilson, Friend or Foe? (2008), p. 19.

4   RTAs notified to the WTO include free trade agreements (FTAs), customs unions or partial scope agreements in the areas of goods and services. They include the notifications made under GATT Article XXIV, GATS Article V, the Enabling Clause, as well as accessions to existing RTAs. However, these agreements are not limited to the areas of goods and services, but contain, in the majority of cases, also rules for the protection of IPRs. 84 percent of the notified RTAs in force as of December 2006 are FTAs. According to the authors of the report, this reflects the fact that FTAs do respond best to the needs of trading partners nowadays, being the clearly preferred option. See R. V. Fiorentino/L. Verdeja/C. Toqueboeuf, The Changing Landscape of Regional Trade Agreements: 2006 Update, Discussion Paper (2007), pp. 1 ff.

5   General Agreement on Tariffs and Trade, UNTS Vol. 55 (1950), No. I-814, p. 187.

6   See Fiorentino/Verdeja/Toqueboeuf, The Changing Landscape of Regional Trade Agreements, (2007), p. 4.

7   Ibid., p. 8.

than the traditional geographically contiguous countries. When looking at the type of partners involved in such regional trade agreements, it is evident that the majority of the regional trade agreements in force are between developed and developing countries, i.e. so-called North-South agreements.[8] Almost all of these regional trade agreements include references to WTO-plus issues, including the protection of intellectual property.[9]

Many of the issues covered in the preferential trade agreements (PTAs)[10] are WTO-plus provisions.[11] The term WTO-plus is used to describe provisions that differ from the nature and level of WTO rules in one of the following two ways: 1) WTO members have not agreed to negotiate or not concluded multilateral rules in a particular issue area in the framework of the WTO, and hence the rules contained in a bilateral or regional trade agreement deal with a new issue; or 2) the PTA imposes obligations that go beyond existing WTO rules in a certain issue area. The first category of provisions mainly concerns areas of economic relations for which the WTO framework does not yet provide general multilateral rules,[12] such as on investment, public procurement, environmental and labour standards, competition, finance, insurances, etc. These types of rules so far have not been regulated in the WTO framework. When looking at the latter category of WTO-plus rules, one type of such rules are the rights and obligations in the area of protecting intellectual property rights. The WTO already deals with IP rules in the TRIPS Agreement, which is a multilateral agreement annexed to the Agreement Establishing the World Trade Organization[13] (hereinafter WTO Agreement). To the extent that the provisions included in PTAs go beyond the standard set in the TRIPS Agreement, they are called TRIPS-plus provisions.

There are several ways to define the TRIPS-plus nature of a provision. The most encompassing definition includes three elements while other authors[14] refer

---

8   Note that the number of RTAs among developing countries and among transition countries only are considerable as well. See Fiorentino/Verdeja/Toqueboeuf, The Changing Landscape of Regional Trade Agreements (2007), p. 10.

9   Ibid., p. 13.

10   Bilateral, regional or plurilateral agreements are often referred to as preferential trade agreements. Preferential trade agreements can take the form of free trade agreements, trade promotion agreements, customs unions, partnership agreements, etc.

11   See Wilson, Friend or Foe? (2008), p. 19.

12   The WTO framework contains two plurilateral agreements, one on trade in civil aircraft and another one on public procurement. These agreements are only binding on those WTO members that are party to these agreements. As they are not part of the body of WTO law that is multilaterally accepted, they are also not recognized as WTO rules for the matter of WTO-plus rules.

13   Agreement Establishing the World Trade Organization, 33 I.L.M. 1144 (1004).

14   Among these authors are Peter Drahos in P. Drahos, BITs and BIPs: Bilateralism in Intellectual Property, in: Journal of World Intellectual Property 4 (2001), p. 792/3; and El-Said, M., The European TRIPS-plus Model and the Arab World: From Cooperation

only to the last two elements. TRIPS-plus provisions take the following forms: 1) the inclusion of a new area of intellectual property rights not yet dealt with in the TRIPS Agreement (e.g. the protection of the content of databases); 2) the implementation of more extensive standards of intellectual property protection and enforcement than contained in the TRIPS Agreement (e.g. extended period of copyright protection); and 3) the elimination of an option or flexibility available under the TRIPS Agreement (e.g. requiring that patents are available to protect plants).[15] In section 5.1 of this contribution, examples of TRIPS-plus provisions in the area of public health, which are included in free trade agreements concluded by the United States, are analyzed.

III.   The Legal Basis for PTAs in the WTO Agreements

Preferential trade agreements among WTO members usually contain rules that grant more preferential treatment to certain countries being part of the preferential trading area. Such preferential treatment is inconsistent with the most-favoured nation (MFN) treatment obligation that is contained in the General Agreement on Tariffs and Trade 1994[16] (hereinafter GATT 1994), the General Agreement on Trade in Services[17] (hereinafter GATS) and the TRIPS Agreement. This important non-discrimination principle requires WTO members to grant no less favourable treatment than they grant to products, services/ service providers or IP right holders from any country, to any like product, like service/service provider or national from another member of the WTO. WTO members are also required to do so immediately and unconditionally.[18]

---

      to Association – A New Era in the Global IPRs Regime, in: Liverpool Law Review 27 (2007), p. 158.

15   See B. Mercurio, TRIPS-Plus Provisions in FTAs: Recent Trends, in: L. Bartels/F. Ortino (eds.), Regional Trade Agreements and the WTO Legal System (2006), p. 219; R. Kampf, TRIPS and FTAs: A World of Preferential or Detrimental Relations, in: C. Heath/A. Kamperman Sanders (eds.), Intellectual Property in Free Trade Agreements (2007), p. 102; D. Vivas-Eugui, Regional and Bilateral Agreements and a TRIPS-plus World: the Free Trade Area of the Americas (2003), p. 4.

16   General Agreement on Tariffs and Trade 1947, 33 I.L.M. 1154 (1994).

17   General Agreement on Trade in Services, 33. I.L.M. 1164 (1994).

18   The MFN treatment obligations provided for in the three agreements differ slightly from each other. See Article I:1 of the GATT 1994, Article II:1 of the GATS, and Article 4 of the TRIPS Agreement. For example, the MFN treatment obligation in the GATT 1994 prohibits discrimination on the basis of the national origin or destination of a product between other countries. The MFN treatment obligation in the GATS prohibits dis-crimination on the basis of the national origin of the service or the nationality of a service supplier. The MFN treatment obligation in the TRIPS Agreement prohibits discrimination on the basis of the nationality of intellectual property right holders with regard to the protection as defined in footnote 3 to the

If PTAs stipulate preferential treatment to goods, services or IP right holders from particular countries, all three MFN treatment obligations are breached if the same treatment is not extended to other WTO members. However, some of the WTO agreements provide for exceptions from the MFN treatment obligations, through which an inconsistency with an obligation of WTO law can be justified. Such exceptions are the regional integration exceptions and are regulated in Article XXIV of the GATT 1994 and Article V of the GATS. The regional integration exception for trade in goods is elaborated further in the Understanding on the Interpretation of Article XXIV of the GATT 1994. These exceptions only apply to preferential treatment in the context of trade in goods and services, not to preferential treatment of intellectual property right holders. The purpose of the two exceptions in the GATT 1994 and the GATS is to allow inconsistencies with the MFN treatment obligation, as long as they are necessary for the pursuit of regional economic integration, either in the form of a customs union or a free trade area. Article XXIV:4 of the GATT 1994 summarizes the rationale for such an exception.

The contracting parties recognize the desirability of increasing freedom of trade by the development, through voluntary agreements, of closer integration between the economies of the countries parties to such agreements. They also recognize that the purpose of a customs union or of a free-trade area should be to facilitate trade between the constituent territories and not to raise barriers to the trade of other contracting parties with such territories. Similarly, Article V:4 of the GATS recognizes the purpose of facilitating trade between the parties to such agreements.

For a WTO member to invoke these exceptions, a number of substantive and procedural requirements need to be fulfilled.[19] An important procedural condition is the notification requirement stipulated in Article XXIV:7(a) of the GATT 1994 and in Article V:7(a) of the GATS. WTO members therefore must promptly notify the Committee on Regional Trade Agreements (CRTA) of the decision to enter into a customs union or free trade area, or an agreement that liberalizes trade in services. The CRTA would have to determine the consistency of the notified agreement with GATT 1994 and/or GATS rules. However, in practice this exercise turned out to be very difficult as consensus among the committee's members to adopt a report on the GATT/GATS-consistency of a

---

TRIPS Agreement. Another important difference of the MFN treatment obligation incorporated in the GATT 1994 on the one hand and in the TRIPS Agreement on the other is the subject matter of discrimination. In the GATT 1994, the treatment of like products originating from WTO members must not be discriminatory, whereas in the TRIPS Agreement, the treatment given to nation-als of WTO members with regard to the protection of intellectual property must not be less favourable.

19 For a detailed analysis of these requirements, see P. van den Bossche, The Law and Policy of the World Trade Organization: Text, Cases and Materials (2008), pp. 699-713.

RTA could hardly ever be reached.[20] The TRIPS Agreement does not provide for an exception to justify preferential treatment of intellectual property rights holders in the pursuit of economic integration. Although there are a number of exceptions to the MFN treatment obligation stipulated in Article 4:a) – d) of the TRIPS Agreement, these exceptions do not apply to preferential trade agreements concluded after the entry into force of the WTO Agreement.[21] As a result, the TRIPS Agreement does not allow for preferential treatment of IP right holders in preferential trade agreements concluded after the entry into force of the WTO Agreement. The more extensive protection of intellectual property rights required in recent bilateral and regional trade agreements will therefore have to be granted to any other national from a WTO member state. The absence of a regional integration exception, such as that provided for in the GATT 1994 and the GATS, does not mean that the TRIPS Agreement discourages the adoption of higher standards of intellectual property protection. To the contrary, it incorporates the principle of minimum protection which allows for the pursuit of higher standards of protection outside the WTO framework. The TRIPS Agreement requires WTO members to conform to a certain level of protection of intellectual property (so-called minimum standards), whereas it does not set a ceiling how far protection may go (so-called maximum standards). The principle of minimum standards is reflected in Article 1.1 of the TRIPS Agreement which expressly allows WTO members to adopt "more extensive protection", provided that such protection does not contravene the disciplines of the agreement. With regard to enforcement provisions, some barriers to enhanced protection can be identified in the preamble of the TRIPS Agreement. It is stated there that "measures and procedures to enforce intellectual property rights (...) [should] not themselves become barriers to legitimate trade." Such explicit limitation to more extensive protection, however, is not provided for with regard to substantive standards of intellectual property protected by the TRIPS Agreement.

---

20   Consensus on the GATT-consistency was reached so far in only one case, being the Czech-Republic-Slovak Customs Union. See P. Sutherland, The Future of the WTO: Addressing Institutional Challenges in the New Millennium, Report by the Consultative Board to the Director-General Supachai Panitchpakdi (2004), p. 22.

21   Article 4 (d) of the TRIPS Agreement provides for an exception that applies to international agreements related to the protection of intellectual property which entered into force prior to the entry into force of the WTO Agreement, not after 1 January 1995.

IV.   Does the Proliferation of PTAs Lead to a Deadlock in the WTO?

A vigorous debate is reflected in the literature about the question as to whether PTAs are a "stumbling block" or a "building block" of the multilateral system.[22] Arguments in support of PTAs, and therefore reflecting the original intention of including a regional integration exception in the GATT 1947, emphasize the role of PTAs in facilitating more liberalisation between its partners. Such liberalisation at bilateral or regional level would create spin-offs for the multilateral system in the long run through the principle of "competitive liberalisation". However, during the last years, arguments against this belief have become dominant. When observing the increasing number of PTAs that are concluded while the Doha Development Round is deadlocked, it seems that the failing trade talks at the multilateral level spur talks at the bilateral level, and not vice versa.[23]

This contribution will not focus on the question of benefits and disadvantages of bilateral and regional trade agreements for multilateral negotiations.[24] Instead, by looking at two developments in the international protection of intellectual property, the point is made that the recent proliferation of bilateral trade agreements fits very well in the dialectic development of intellectual property protection. There is reason to believe that the multilateral organisation will become the preferred option again.

1.   The Dialectic Development of International Intellectual Property Protection

The proliferation of PTAs in recent years has been significant, as demonstrated by the Trade Policies Review Division Report of 2006 mentioned above.[25] At the same time, efforts to conclude multilateral trade agreements have become increasingly difficult at various forums, most prominently at the WTO.[26] This

---

22   See Sutherland, The Future of the WTO (2004), p. 19; R. Bhala, Competitive Liberalization, Competitive Imperialism, and Intellectual Property, in: Liverpool Law Review 28 (2007); Bhagwati, Termites in the Trading System (2008), Sutherland, The Future of the WTO (2004), pp. 81ff.; Abbott, A New Dominant Trade Species Emerges (2007); M. Khor, Bilateral and Regional Free Trade Agreements (2008), pp. 3 ff.; N. Limão, Are Preferential Trade Agreements with Non-trade Objectives a Stumbling Block for Multilateral Liberalization?, in: Review of Economic Studies 74 (2007).

23   See Bhala, Competitive Liberalization (2007), p. 82.

24   See L. Crump, Global Trade Policy Development in a Two-Track System, in: Journal of International Economic Law 9 (2006).

25   See Fiorentino/Verdeja/Toqueboeuf, The Changing Landscape of Regional Trade Agreements (2007).

26   Negotiations on the Doha Development Agenda which began in 2001 have been suspended. For the latest developments, see www.wto.org/english/tratop_e/dda_e/

suggests that WTO members currently prefer to regulate their trade relations at the bilateral/regional level, as opposed to the multilateral level. However, such periods of preference for one level, in the present case the bilateral or regional, instead of another level, the multilateral, are not new. The recent proliferation of bilateral/regional agreements should be seen as merely one element in a larger cycle of IP protection that alternates between bilateralism/regionalism and multilateralism, and is evident since the beginning of the international system of intellectual property protection.[27] An increasing interest in international cooperation in the field of intellectual property protection was first expressed through bilateral agreements among major European countries. In the area of copyright, typical features of such agreements were the reciprocity provisions.[28] These provisions assured that each party to the agreement protected the creative efforts and works of the nationals of both parties. By the late 19th century, a comprehensive network of bilateral copyright conventions had developed among European and Latin American states.[29] Also in the field of industrial property, European states started cooperating internationally through bilateral treaties. By 1883, there were at least 69 bilateral agreements, the majority of which dealt with trademarks and designs or models.[30] The international protection of patents, however, remained inadequate. Overall, the network of bilateral treaties in the field of copyright and industrial property and its lack of uniformity led to the common understanding of states to create multilateral pillars for regulating the protection of intellectual property.

The development of a multilateral system to protect intellectual property was initiated by the establishment of the Paris Convention for the Protection of Industrial Property[31] and the Berne Convention for the Protection of Literary

---

dda_e.htm (12 June 2009). Futhermore, efforts to conclude a Substantive Patent Law Treaty at the WIPO have not been successful for various years. See T. Balasubramaniam, WIPO Patent Committee Embarks on Positive Agenda (2008), www.keion-line.org/index.php?option=com_jd-wp&Itemid=39&p=124 (12 June 2009).

27   See also Mercurio, TRIPS-Plus Provisions in FTAs (2006), p. 216.
28   The early agreements between the Kingdom of Prussia and other German states in the years 1827 to 1829 were based on simple reciprocity. They accorded national treatment to the works of the other state without embodying common rules. Subsequent agreements, such as the one between Austria and the Kingdom of Sardinia in May 1840, added to the principle of national treatment the so-called material or substantive reciprocity. This reciprocity assured an approximate parity between the level of protec-tion in each state. See S. Ricketson, The Birth of the Berne Union, in: Columbia-VLA Journal of Law and the Arts 11 (1986), pp. 14 f.
29   See Ricketson, The Birth of the Berne Union (1986), p. 15.
30   See P. S. Ladas, Patents, Trademarks, and Related Rights: National and International Protection (1975), pp. 43 ff.
31   Paris Convention for the Protection of Industrial Property of 20 March 1883, Including Revisions, UNTS Vol. 828 (1972), No. I-11851, p. 306 (hereinafter Paris Convention).

and Artistic Works[32], which were adopted in 1883 and 1886 respectively. These two multilateral pillars were further formalized by the creation of the United International Bureau for the Protection of Intellectual Property (BIRPI), the predecessor of the World Intellectual Property Organization (hereinafter WIPO). It was primarily under the framework of the BIRPI that the 20th century saw the proliferation of multilateral treaties in the field of intellectual property.[33] The intellectual property regime developed in the areas of trademarks, designs, patents, micro-organisms, indication of origins, performance, audiovisual works, internet, etc. Outside the WIPO framework, the intellectual property regime expanded to areas such as the protection of plant varieties.[34]

These two multilateral conventions marked the first multilateral phase. Despite these multilateral efforts, countries did not seem to be satisfied with the developments at the WIPO and started using bilateral treaties again.[35] First, the bilateral commercial treaties between European countries developed into an important tool in extending protection of intellectual property to the colonized territories in Africa, Asia, and the Pacific.[36] The purpose of this extension was to secure national economic interests against other European countries in their colonies. Second, bilateral investment treaties became the new instrument for addressing a variety of private economic issues, including the protection of intellectual property.[37] They have first been used in the late 1950s by European countries,[38] but only became very popular with European countries during the

---

32   Berne Convention for the Protection of Literary and Artistic Works of 9 September 1886, Completed at Paris on 4 May 1896, Including Revisions, UNTS Vol. 828 (1972), No. I-11850, p. 222 (hereinafter Berne Convention).

33   For detailed information on all treaties that are administered by WIPO to date, see WIPO website, www.wipo.int/treaties/en/.

34   The International Convention for the Protection of New Varieties of Plants (UPOV Convention) was adopted in November 1961 and entered into force in 1968. The convention is administered by the International Union for the Protection of New Varieties of Plants (UPOV), an intergovernmental organisation with its headquarters in Geneva. See International Convention for the Protection of New Varieties of Plants of 2 December 1961, Including Revisions, UNTS Vol. 1867 (1995), No. I-31696, p. 281.

35   Note that Article 19 of the Paris Convention and Article 20 of the Berne Convention grant member states the right to enter into special agreements for the protection of industrial property and authors rights, insofar as they do not contravene the provisions of the conventions.

36   See R. Okediji, The International Relations of Intellectual Property: Narratives of Developing Country Participations in the Global Intellectual Property System, in: Singapore Journal of International & Comparative Law 7 (2003), p. 324.

37   See R. Okediji, Back to Bilateralism? Pendulum Swings in International Intellectual Property Protection, in: University of Ottawa Law & Technology Journal 1 (2003), p. 138.

38   The first BIT was signed between Germany and Pakistan in 1959 and entered into force in 1962. See UNCTAD, Bilateral Investment Treaties: 1959-1999 (2000), p. 57.

1970s. Those agreements addressed, among other things, the protection of intellectual property by including intellectual property rights in the definition of investment, although not in detail.[39] The United States, by contrast, did not start using bilateral investment treaties until the early 1980s.[40] In January 1982, the United States Trade Representative announced the formulation of the first prototype Bilateral Investment Treaty.[41] Since then, the use of bilateral investment treaties by the United States has increased drastically, in particular with the negotiations of the Uruguay Round. While the provisions on intellectual property protection in the first bilateral investment treaties were still limited, the level of detail with which the intellectual property provisions were drafted increased rapidly over the years.[42] In 1995, the TRIPS Agreement came as an intermission to that bilateral phase. Being part of the WTO framework, the TRIPS Agreement incorporated the protection of intellectual property into the multilateral trading regime.[43]

This multilateral agreement reached an unprecedented scope of substantive intellectual property protection, membership, and level of enforcement. However, immediately after the conclusion of this significant agreement, another bilateral phase started with the recent proliferation of bilateral/regional trade agreements that often include so-called TRIPS-plus provisions.

2.   The Strategy of Forum-shifting

As a whole, the development of the international protection of intellectual property can be described as a dialectic one where bilateral/regional phases

---

39   For two examples, see Article 1(a)(iv) of Agreement for the Promotion and Protection of Investments, United Kingdom of Great Britain and Northern Ireland and Singapore, signed at Singapore on 22 July 1975, United Nations Treaty Series, Vol. 1018, No. 14935, p. 175; see Article 1(1)(d) of Treaty concerning the promotion and reciprocal protection of investments, Federal Republic of Germany and Singapore, signed at Singapore on 3 October 1973, United Nations Treaty Series, Vol. 1008, No. 14792, p.229.

40   See M. S. Bergman, Bilateral Investment Protection Treaties: An Examination of the Evolution and Significance of the U.S. Prototype Treaty, in: New York University Journal of International Law & Policy 16 (1983), p. 3.

41   See Office of the United States Trade Representative, Reagan Administration Initiates Bilateral Treaty Negotiations, Press Release 13 January 1982.

42   See Okediji, Back to Bilateralism? (2003), p. 138.

43   The membership to WIPO and to the WTO is not identical. To date, there are 179 members to the Convention Establishing the World Intellectual Property Organization, while 153 countries/customs territories have become members to the WTO. The relationship between the two organisations is governed, according to Article V of the WTO Agreement and Article 68 of the TRIPS Agreement, by the Agreement Between the World Intellectual Property Organization and the World Trade Organization, 35 I.L.M. 754 (1996).

have been followed by multilateral phases and vice versa. In other words, the development of the international regime of protecting intellectual property is a history of forum-shifting. The recent proliferation of bilateral trade agreements seems to fit into this history of forum-shifting.

Forum-shifting is an important strategy which *Helfer* defines as an

"attempt to alter the status quo ante by moving treaty negotiations, lawmaking initiatives, or standard setting activities from one international venue to another."[44]

States make use of this forum-shifting strategy when they seek to enhance their negotiating power.[45] *Braithwaite* and *Drahos* analyze three kinds of strategies that forum-shifting encompasses:

- moving an agenda from one organisation to another;
- abandoning an organisation; and
- pursuing the same agenda in more than one organisation.

They argue that:

"[The] thinking behind abandonment is that the abandoned international organization will be shocked into a more compliant mode of behaviour, endeavouring to woo back the world's most powerful state (and its financial contribution) with more favourable policies and attitudes."[46]

According to these authors, forum-shifting is a strategy that only the powerful and well-resourced countries can use; indeed, it was during US hegemony after World War II that this strategy was used for the first time with a certain frequency;[47] no other country has made use of forum-shifting on such a regular basis that one can speak about a strategy. The forum-shifting strategy has prominently been used by the United States in the area of intellectual property protection.

Drahos has described this development as the "global intellectual property ratchet". The ratchet builds upon bilateral and regional agreements which

---

44   L. R. Helfer, Regime Shifting: The TRIPs Agreement and New Dynamics of International Intellectual Property Lawmaking, in: The Yale Journal of International Law 29 (2004), p. 14. Note that Helfer talks about regime shifting instead of forum-shifting. For the purpose of defining the phenomenon, the difference between regime and forum does not play a role. For further discussion of forum-shifting in the area of IP, see also J. Braithwaite/P. Drahos, Global Business Regulation (2000), pp. 564-571; Mer-curio, TRIPS-Plus Provisions in FTAs (2006), pp. 216-224.

45   See P. Yu, Currents and Crosscurrents in the International Intellectual Property Regime, in: Loyola of Los Angeles Law Review 38 (2004), p. 412.

46   Ibid., p. 564.

47   See ibid., pp. 564 f.

increase standards of intellectual property protection and are eventually taken to the higher, multilateral level to become international standards.[48] He not only observes the recurring shifts of forums, but he also recognizes that each wave of bilateral/regional agreements or multilateral agreements never derogates from existing standards and that they even go beyond those standards by creating new standards. The standards adopted in the TRIPS Agreement built upon the intellectual property standards established by the North American Free Trade Agreement (NAFTA) of 1993. Similarly, recent bilateral agreements that contain TRIPS-plus provisions will most probably be the basis for future multilateral agreements addressing intellectual property protection.

Drahos found the following three factors to be essential for the ratchet to function: 1) A process of forum-shifting which allows countries to choose the forum where they will encounter least resistance to their intellectual property agenda; 2) Co-ordinated bilateral, regional, and multilateral intellectual property strategies that are adapted to the situations faced at the respective forum; and 3) The principle of minimum standards that is included in every agreement and preserves the option to establish higher standards in future agreements.[49] Therefore, each wave of bilateralism and multilateralism consistently expands intellectual property protection at a global level and makes the global intellectual property ratchet work. *Okediji* has identified this ratchet as being an ongoing explicit strategy by the United States and the European Union (EU) in which they aim to use bilateral trade agreements in order to expand global intellectual property rights.[50] In conclusion, the recent proliferation of bilateral/regional agreements is not something extraneous to the international development of intellectual property protection. It rather forms part of a larger cycle of shifting forums between the multilateral, regional and bilateral level.

The rationales for forum-shifting indicate that countries will continue to use the available forums to shift rule-making from venues that are unfavorable for them to forums that are more advantageous to their needs. This, however, does not mean that the multilateral forum will not be the favored option in the future. In the past, it was often the case that bilateral, and regional trade agreements have functioned as a sort laboratory for future multilateral agreements. PTAs can lead to new agreements at the WTO.

Furthermore, the WTO offers features that have often been praised as being more effective compared to other forums. If it is possible to make these features even more attractive in the future, a deadlock in the WTO seems unlikely.[51]

---

48   See P. Drahos, Expanding Intellectual Property's Empire: the Role of FTAs, Paper
      (2003), p. 8.
49   See ibid., p. 7.
50   See Okediji, Back to Bilateralism? (2003), pp. 128 f.
51   Some suggestions for reform have been made. Changing the voting structure to enable
      "less than consensus" agreements is certainly an idea that should be followed up. See

V.   Important Problems for Developing Countries

Even if the WTO does not experience a crisis resulting from the recent proliferation of bilateral trade agreements, developing countries are facing severe problems resulting from this development. Four major problems will be discussed in the following, with a focus on the free trade agreements that the United States has been concluding with developing countries, and, in particular, with regard to the IP provisions related to public health.

1.   TRIPS-plus Provisions Reduce Public Policy Space

It exceeds the scope of this paper to give a comprehensive overview of TRIPS-plus provisions that are included in recent bilateral trade agreements and how they reduce the policy space available to developing countries policy makers. The areas which contain TRIPS-plus provisions range over the entire spectrum of intellectual property issues and vary according to the actors that pursue the conclusion of PTAs. For example, the free trade agreements concluded by the United States contain strong TRIPS-plus provisions in the areas of public health, access to information in the digital environment, trademarks, protection of life forms and enforcement. The bilateral trade agreements concluded by the European Union, in contrast, focus on the increased protection of geographical indications and enforcement provisions.[52] This contribution will present some of the most important TRIPS-plus provisions related to public health that are contained in the free trade agreements concluded by the United States and developing countries.

It is fair to say that the provisions related to public health in United States FTAs have been criticized most. The issues that these provisions deal with are significant and have been analyzed in detail by different scholars.[53] The five

---

Abbott, A New Dominant Trade Species Emerges (2007), p. 582.

52   Since the launch of the strategy "Global Europe", the European Union has started to negotiate and conclude trade agreements which contain more and more TRIPS-plus provisions also in other areas, such as industrial design protection, utility model protect, the protection of copyright material in the digital environment, etc. See European Commission, Global Europe: competing in the world (2006).

53   See F. M. Abbott, The Doha Declaration on the TRIPS Agreement and Public Health and the Contradictory Trend in Bilateral and Regional Free Trade Agreements, Occasional Paper (2004); S. K. Sell, TRIPS-plus Free Trade Agreements and Access to Medicines, in: Liverpool Law Review 28 (2007); J.-F. Morin, Tripping up TRIPs Debates: IP and Health in Bilateral Agreements, in: International Journal of Intellectual Property Management 1-2 (2006); F. Rossi, Free Trade Agreements and TRIPS-plus Measures, in: International Journal of Intellectual Property Management 1 (2006); C. Fink/P. Reichenmiller, Tightening TRIPS: The Intellectual Property Provisions of Recent US Free Trade Agreements, in: Trade Note of The World Bank

most important issues will be illustrated below: the protection of undisclosed information/data exclusivity, the linkage between the drug registration and patent protection, the extension of the patent term for pharmaceutical and chemical patents, restrictions on parallel imports, and restrictions on compulsory licenses.

a)   The Protection of Undisclosed Information/Data Exclusivity

Probably the most contentious requirement among the public health provisions is the protection of undisclosed information. United States FTAs drastically increase the protection of undisclosed information that is submitted by a patent applicant to a regulatory agency for marketing approval of his pharmaceutical product. The data exclusivity requirements have been described as "another form of monopoly (…) [that is granted in United States FTAs] in ways TRIPS Agreement does not require".[54] Consequently, "brand name pharmaceutical companies, in effect, have acquired a new form of intellectual property right in their test data".[55]

    Data exclusivity provisions intend to protect the information submitted by a pharmaceutical company which proves the safety and efficacy of a new chemical entity (=drug). This data is submitted to regulatory authorities and is kept undisclosed. The question arises in how far third parties, in particular generic pharmaceutical producers, can rely on that same data in order to apply for marketing approval for their generic version of the original pharmaceutical. Relying on the data submitted by the originator is essential for generic producers as it is very expensive to produce test data.

    In order to protect the data of originators, the TRIPS Agreement requires in Article 39.3 that WTO members must protect undisclosed test data on pharmaceutical products against unfair competition. The rationale of this provision is the protection against unfair commercial use, not against any use by third parties. That is, however, how United States FTAs have interpreted this provision of the TRIPS Agreement.[56] The core prohibition required by United

---

      Group 20 (2005); Mercurio, TRIPS-Plus Provisions in FTAs (2006), pp. 224-235; M. P. Pugatch, The International Regulation of IPRs in a TRIPs and TRIPs-plus Worlds, in: Journal of World Investment and Trade 6 (2005), pp. 13-20; J. Kuanpoth, TRIPS-Plus Rules under Free Trade Agreements: An Asian Perspective, in: C. Heath/A. Kamperman Sanders (eds.), Intellectual Property in Free Trade Agreements (2007), pp. 32-41; S. Reid Smith, Intellectual Property in Free Trade Agreements (2008), pp. 7-16.

54   Abbott, The Doha Declaration on the TRIPS Agreement and Public Health (2004), p. 7.

55   Sell, TRIPS-plus Free Trade Agreements and Access to Medicines (2008), p. 60.

56   It is interesting to know that the domestic law of the United States also provides for data exclusivity. However, US law also foresees exceptions to the exclusivity rights.

States FTAs is that generic producers of new pharmaceutical products cannot rely on the undisclosed data submitted by the originator for a period of five years from the date of marketing approval in that country, unless the consent of the originator is given.[57] In this prohibition, no reference is made to protecting the data against unfair commercial use; it rather introduces exclusivity for the originator for at least five years. This means, a member that wishes to register a generic drug for public non-commercial use in clinics will not be able to rely on the data submitted by the originator, without his consent, for marketing approval during the five-year period of market exclusivity.

These provisions clearly prolong the period in which generic producers of essential drugs cannot receive marketing approval. Without competition from generic producers, patented originator drugs can be sold at high(er) prices due to their monopoly position. This extended period of market exclusivity leads to high(er), unaffordable drug prices for patients in developing countries for an even longer period of time.

b)   Linkage Between the Drug Registration and Patent Protection

Related to the protection of undisclosed information is the issue concerning the linkage between drug registration and patent protection. A link is created by making the marketing approval for a generic drug dependant on the expiry of the patent for the original drug. The TRIPS Agreement does not provide any rules on this linkage. United States FTAs require that state parties prevent the marketing of a generic drug that relies on the information on safety and efficacy submitted by the originator of the patented drug, unless by consent of that patent owner.[58] This provision effectively extends the term of data protection to the full term of a patent, rather than the five years referred to above.[59] However, the difference with the data exclusivity provision is that one can only get data

---

For example, the information submitted by originators can be used for the purpose of research, as the research exemption establishes. Such exemptions cannot be found in the FTAs and therefore establish even higher protection compared to the US law standard.

57   See Article 15.10(1)(a) of the US-CAFTA-DR; Article 15.10.1 of the US-Morocco FTA; Article 14.9.1(a) of the US-Bahrain FTA. Note that the US-CAFTA-DR encompasses the Central American countries Costa Rica, El Salvador, Guatemala, Honduras and Nicaragua, as well as the Dominican Republic.

58   See Article 15.10.2(a) of the US-CAFTA-DR; Article 15.10.4(a) of the US-Morocco FTA; Article 16.8.4(c) of the US-Singapore FTA; Article 17.10.2(c) of the US-Chile FTA; Article 15.10.4 of the US-Panama TPA. Note that the agreements with Peru, Colombia, and Panama are called "Trade Promotion Agreement" rather than "Free Trade Agreement". They have the same effect though.

59   See Abbott, The Doha Declaration on the TRIPS Agreement and Public Health (2004), p. 8.

protection for the full patent term if a patent is granted; the five years of data exclusivity are granted also to drugs that finally do not receive patent protection. In addition, the patent owner must be notified of the identity of the third party that requests marketing approval during the term of his patent.[60]

These provisions do not only restrict the marketing of a generic drug during the term of a patent, they also restrict the use of compulsory licenses or government use as a drug can only receive marketing approval if the patent owner consents. In essence, although a compulsory license has been granted to the generic producer, he will not be able to market the product on regulatory grounds unless he gathers his own test data. This is very expensive and difficult for generic producers.

c) Extension of the Patent Term

A third issue dealt with in the public health provisions of United States FTAs is the extension of the patent term. The patent term recognized by the TRIPS Agreement lasts 20 years.[61] This is the nominal term of protection that foresees 20 years of protection regardless of delays in the patent examination procedure or the marketing approval procedure.[62] United States FTAs, in contrast, require an effective term of protection that takes into account delays in these procedures. In fact, there are two possibilities for patent holders to receive a prolongation of the nominal patent term: 1) by receiving compensation for unreasonable delays in granting the patent; and 2) by receiving compensation for unreasonable curtailment as a result of the marketing approval procedure.

Concerning delays in the granting procedure, unreasonable delay is defined by some FTAs as a delay of four years from the date of filing of the application or two years after a request for examination has been made, whichever is later.[63] Other FTAs have stipulated that unreasonable delays in the granting procedure are delays of more than five years from the filing date and three years after the request for examination was made.[64] These rules specify under which conditions

---

60   See Article 17.10.4(b) of the US-Australia FTA; Article 14.9.4(b) of the US-Bahrain FTA; Article 4(23)(b) of the US-Jordan FTA.

61   See Article 33 of the TRIPS Agreement.

62   Note that Article 62(2) of the TRIPS Agreement requires members to ensure that these procedures permit the grant or approval within a reasonable period of time so as to avoid the unwarranted curtailment of the period of protection. The article does not specify further what a reasonable period of time is and what compensation a patent holder should get in case of un-warranted curtailment.

63   See Article 14.7.6(a) of the US-Bahrain FTA; Article 16.7.7 of the US-Singapore FTA; Article 15.9.7 of the US-Morocco FTA; Article 17.9.8(a) of the US-Australia FTA.

64   See Article 15.9.6(a) of the US-CAFTA-DR; Article 17.9.6 of the US-Chile FTA. The most recently concluded FTAs between the United States and Panama, Peru and Colombia do not apply this compensation rule for pharmaceutical patents, see Article

unreasonable delay exists, which needs to be compensated; however, they do not define how much compensation needs to be granted to the patent applicant.

The second possibility of prolonging the term of a patent is through receiving compensation for unwarranted curtailment of the effective patent term as a result of the marketing approval procedure.[65] It has not been further specified what an unwarranted curtailment is, how long the effective patent term is and how much of the curtailment will be compensated.[66]

By prolonging the patent term, the monopoly that the original makers of a patented drug hold is also extended. Competitors and generic producers are therefore prohibited from producing, making, using, offering for sale, selling or importing that drug for an even longer period of time. The beneficial effects of competition on drug prices are therefore also postponed and leave citizens of developing countries even longer without affordable drugs.

d)   Prohibition of Parallel Importation

A fourth issue dealt with in United States FTAs concerns the prohibition of parallel importation. The TRIPS Agreement refers indirectly to parallel importation of intellectual property goods by stating that nothing in the Agreement addresses the issue of the exhaustion of intellectual property rights.[67] In other words, members are free to adopt the exhaustion principle they prefer, be it the national exhaustion principle, and therefore preventing parallel imports, or the principle of international exhaustion which allows parallel imports to the country where, for example, a patent has been granted. Some United States FTAs do not leave this choice to members but require that patent owners shall have the exclusive right to prevent the importation of the patented product; this right also shall not be limited by the sale or distribution of that product outside its territory.[68] In other words, parallel importation of the patent product can be prevented by the patent owner and therefore amounts to the imposition of the national exhaustion regime.

15.9.6(b) of the US-Panama TPA; Article 16.9.6(b) of the US-Peru TPA and the US-Colombia TPA.

65   See Article 15.10.3 of the US-Morocco FTA; Article 16.8.4(a) of the US-Singapore FTA; Article 4(23)(a) of the US-Jordan FTA; Article 16.9.6(c) of the US-Peru TPA and the US-Colombia TPA.

66   Note that the latest FTAs specify that the compensation should be the restoration of the patent erm or patent rights; see Article 16.9.6(c) of the US-Peru TPA and the US-Colombia TPA.

67   See Article 6 of the TRIPS Agreement.

68   See Article 15.9.4 of the US-Morocco FTA; Article 17.9.4 of the US-Australia FTA. The US-Singapore FTA provides in a slightly different form for the same obligation, see Article 16.7.2.

By prohibiting parallel imports, it will not be possible for country "A" to allow imports of the same drug that have also been marketed in country "B". Therefore, this prohibition prevents competitive prices and the affordability of essential medicines for citizens of developing countries.

e)   Restrictions on Compulsory Licensing

The last issue discussed in the context of public health provisions in United States FTAs regards the restrictions on compulsory licensing. A compulsory license is an authorisation that the government gives to a third party in order to use the patented invention without the consent of the patent holder. The TRIPS Agreement allows granting compulsory licenses under certain conditions specified in Article 31. United States FTAs restrict the use of compulsory licenses beyond the numerous conditions laid down in Article 31 of the TRIPS Agreement. They do so in two manners: first, the use of compulsory licenses is restricted by the linkage between drug registration and patent protection, as explained above. A second and more direct restriction is the limitation of the grounds on which compulsory licenses can be issued. In contrast to the TRIPS Agreement, United States FTAs restrict the use of compulsory licenses to specified cases. The grounds to which some FTAs restrict the use of compulsory licenses are anti-competitive practice, public non-commercial use, national emergency, other circumstances of extreme urgency and the failure to meet working requirements.[69] Article 31 of the TRIPS Agreement, however, does not contain an exhaustive list of grounds and therefore offers some discretion for WTO members to add other grounds. Note that other FTAs concluded by the United States with Chile, Central America and the Dominican Republic, Bahrain, Morocco, Peru, Colombia, and Panama do not contain these restrictions. This seems to reflect the United States' deference to the Doha Declaration on the TRIPS Agreement and Public Health which grants all WTO members the right to determine for themselves the grounds upon which compulsory licenses can be granted.[70] Compulsory licenses are an important exception with which the rights of a patent holder, as stipulated in Article 28 of the TRIPS Agreement, can be set aside for the promotion of a public interest. This exception is one of the most important tools for developing countries to fight their public health crisis. Generic producers are granted a license to produce and market a certain patented drug at lower prices. By restricting the grounds for granting compulsory licenses to an exhaustive list, a crucial

---

69   See Article 17.9.7 of the US-Australia FTA; Article 4(20) of the US-Jordan
      Agreement; Article 16.7.6 of the US-Singapore Agreement.
70   See WTO Ministerial Conference Doha, Declaration on the TRIPS Agreement and
      Public Health, Doc. WT/MIN(01)/DEC/2 of 20 November 2001, paragraph 5(b).

flexibility, emphasised by the Doha Declaration on the TRIPS Agreement and Public Health, for developing countries is curtailed.

2. Absence of a Regional Integration Exception from the MFN Treatment Obligation

Because of the lack of a regional integration exception similar to that included in Article XXIV of the GATT 1994 and in Article V of the GATS, the most-favoured nation treatment obligation in Article 4 of the TRIPS Agreement applies in full to bilateral trade agreements. In other words, WTO members which accept TRIPS-plus standards in bilateral trade agreements must accord the same treatment "immediately and unconditionally to the nationals of all other members"[71] of the WTO. With currently 153 member states, the WTO is made up by the vast majority of countries involved in international trade. The reach of TRIPS-plus provisions further increases with the territorial expansion of bilateral or regional agreements concluded in virtually all parts of the world. If ever more countries in the world have to adhere to TRIPS-plus provisions, the bilateral or regional standard will become the *de facto* global standard.

The problem for developing countries manifests itself if one considers that *de facto* global standards are set at the bilateral and/or regional level. They are not adopted at a global/multilateral forum, such as the WTO or the World Intellectual Property Organization (WIPO). Circumventing the multilateral venue for setting new international standards of intellectual property protection deprives developing countries of the option of multilateral coalition-building. At the multilateral level, developing countries could increase their bargaining leverage through allying with like-minded countries in order to oppose efforts proposed by countries such as the United States, European states or Japan. At the bilateral or regional level, power asymmetries between negotiating partners are substantial and leave the weaker party with little chances to successfully oppose higher demands of intellectual property protection if access to agricultural or textiles markets is offered in exchange.

3. Secret and Non-transparent Negotiations

One of the much criticized characteristics of the FTA negotiations led by the United States, but also by many other countries, is the lack of transparency that surrounds the negotiations. Official information is either not made public at all or merely in summary version just before or after the agreement has been signed. In the case of the US-CAFTA-DR, when demanded by civil society organisations, the draft texts of the proposed agreement were not made public.[72]

---

71   Article 4, TRIPS Agreement.
72   See Oxfam America, Make Trade Fair for Central America: Agriculture, Investment

Costa Rican negotiators signed a confidentiality agreement that prevented the disclosure of meeting agendas or substantive information about the agreement to the public.[73] In the case of the US-Chile FTA, the Chilean government made available brief summaries just before the agreement was signed.[74] Although it is true that most developing countries that face the United States in bilateral negotiations can learn from earlier experiences of other countries, the lack of official information opens up much room for speculation which often does not increase the support for the FTA.

Another aspect of transparency is whether negotiations are open to the public. This is not to say that most international negotiations are usually open to the public. However, when free trade agreements encompass a big variety of areas which are sought to be liberalized, and hence their content undoubtedly has an enormous impact on the lives of the people living in these countries, there is a need for a certain degree of openness and involvement of interest groups in the negotiations. While private sector interest groups are often informed about issues in the FTA that are relevant for them, and also invited to discuss their views thereon with the government, this is generally not the case for civil society organisations. In the FTA negotiations between the United States and Thailand, the Thai government was heavily criticized for deepening inequalities between different interest groups. "Business people" were given privileged access and therefore could decide the main issues together with "bureaucrats".[75] The negotiations between the United States and CAFTA states took

> "place in closed quarters, with a side room available for selected interested parties. (...) The business sector has privileged access to the negotiating process but civil society organizations have limited or no access".[76]

Also in the US-Chile FTA negotiations, limited participation by interest groups has been noticed.[77]

4.   The Broader Context: Strategy to Strengthen IP Protection at a Global Level

Developing countries do not only face higher demands of intellectual property protection at the bilateral and regional level, but also at various other forums.

---

and Intellectual Property: Three Reasons to Say No to CAFTA (2003), p. 7.

73   See R. Rajkumar, The Central American Free Trade Agreement: an End Run Around the DOHA Declaration on TRIPS and Public Health, in: Albany Law Journal of Science & Technology 15 (2004), p. 465.

74   See Vivas-Eugui, The Free Trade Area of the Americas (2003), p. 15.

75   See Kuanpoth, TRIPS-Plus Rules under Free Trade Agreements (2007), p. 29.

76   Oxfam America, Make Trade Fair for Central America (2003), p. 6.

77   See Vivas-Eugui, The Free Trade Area of the Americas (2003), p. 15.

The problems described above, with which developing countries are confronted at the bilateral or regional level, repeat themselves in the context of other negotiations, such as the negotiations on a Substantive Patent Law Treaty (SPLT) at the WIPO and negotiations on higher IP enforcement standards at the World Customs Organization (WCO) and in the framework of G8 countries. Consequently, developing countries find themselves trapped in a global IP ratchet, as *Drahos* has described the explicit strategy by some industrialised countries to achieve higher levels of IP protection and enforcement standards.

The negotiations on a SPLT are part of the WIPO Patent Agenda which represents a new initiative to develop an international patent system. The SPLT aims at harmonizing substantive patent standards such as priority art, novelty, utility, inventiveness, requirements relating to sufficient disclosure, the drafting of patent claims, etc.[78] Harmonizing substantive concepts of patent law are likely to result in TRIPS-plus provisions. The TRIPS Agreement grants WTO members the flexibility to interpret and implement substantive patent concepts in accordance with their local conditions. If the SPLT gives a clear definition of the concepts concerned, this flexibility is eliminated. In 2005, negotiations on the SPLT had been suspended for three years due to polarised views among WIPO members. In June 2008, the WIPO Standing Committee on the Law of Patents met for the first time again after the collapse and was able to produce a positive agenda on a work program for future negotiations on the SPLT.[79] Since then, the SCP has met in March 2009 and will meet again in January 2010.

Negotiations on higher IP enforcement standards are conducted at various multilateral and plurilateral forums by developed countries, in particular G8 countries.[80] One multilateral forum that has seen the development of increased enforcement standards is the WCO. Since 2005, the WCO has dedicated much attention to the development of model legislation and best practices in the area of enforcement of intellectual property. This model legislation relates to border measures and customs legislation and has been developed by the WCO Working Group on the Provisional Standards Employed by Customs for Uniform Rights Enforcement (SECURE). The SECURE Model Provisions presented in June 2008 contain significant TRIPS-plus provisions.[81] These provisions mainly

---

78   See S. F. Musungu/G. Dutfield, Multilateral agreements and a TRIPS-plus world: The World Intellectual Property Organization (WIPO) (2003), p. 12.

79   See Balasubramaniam, WIPO Patent Committee Embarks on Positive Agenda (2009).

80   For a detailed analysis of these efforts, see E. T. Biadgleng/V. Muñoz Tellez, The Changing Structure and Governance of Intellectual Property Enforcement (2008); D. Matthews, The Fight Against Counterfeiting and Piracy in the Bilateral Trade Agreements of the EU, Briefing Paper (2008); S. K. Sell, The Global IP Upward Ratchet, Anti-Counterfeiting and Piracy Enforcement Efforts: The State of Play (2008). See also the analysis of the developments of the ACTA below.

81   The Secure working draft is contained in the WCO, Report of SECURE Working Group, Doc. SP0269E1a of 9 June 2008.

grant increased powers to customs authorities to suspend the clearance of goods which are suspected of infringing intellectual property rights.[82] A number of concerns have been expressed with regard to the activity of the SECURE working group establishing such standards. These concerns relate to problems of transparency, involvement of developing countries and the WCO's mandate which arguably does not include the setting of voluntary standards in the area of IP enforcement.[83]

One of the most recent activities of developed countries to increase intellectual property enforcement are the negotiations of an Anti-Counterfeiting Trade Agreement (ACTA). On the basis of efforts within the G8 framework,[84] the United States, the European Commission, Japan and Switzerland initiated negotiations on a plurilateral agreement that would apply new, stricter legal and enforcement standards to the trade in goods that are protected by some form of IP right.[85] Representatives of Canada, Mexico, Australia, New Zealand, South Korea, Singapore, Morocco, the United Arab Emirates, and Jordan have been invited to participate.[86] The first informal negotiations were held in October 2007. The United States announced on 23 October 2007 that

> "the goal is to set a new, higher benchmark for enforcement that countries can join on a voluntary basis. The negotiations represent a cooperative effort by the governments involved, and will not be conducted as part of any international organization".[87]

Since then, participating countries have held further meetings in January, June, July, October, and December 2008, discussing details of the ACTA. According to the European Commission, negotiations are continuing in 2009.[88] The elements in the ACTA that could be of a TRIPS-plus nature regard the extension

---

82   See X. Li, SECURE: A Critical Analysis and Call for Action, in: South Bulletin 15 (2008), p. 5.

83   See D. Cronin, World Customs Organization Recommends Far-Reaching New Rules on IP (2008), www.ip-watch.org/weblog/index.php?p=939 (12 June 2009); A. Shaw, The Problem with the Anti-Counterfeiting Trade Agreement (and What to Do About It), in: Knowledge Ecology Studies 2 (2008), p. 2; Matthews, The Fight Against Counterfeiting and Piracy in the Bilateral Trade Agreements of the EU (2008), p. 23.

84   See G8, Reducing IPR Piracy and Counterfeiting Through More Effective Enforcement (2005), www.g7.utoronto.ca/summit/2005gleneagles/ipr_piracy.pdf (12 June 2009).

85   See Shaw, The Problem with the Anti-Counterfeiting Trade Agreement, p. 1.

86   See K. Weatherall, The Anti-Counterfeiting Trade Agreement: What's It All About? (2008), http://works.bepress.com/kimweatherall/18 (12 June 2009), p. 1.

87   See USTR Press Release, Ambassador Schwab Announces US Will Seek New Trade Agreement to Fight Fakes (2007), www.ustr.gov/ambassador-schwab-announces-us-will-seek-newtrade-agreement-fight-fakes (12 June 2009).

88   See European Commission, The Anti-Counterfeiting Trade Agreement (ACTA): Fact Sheet (2008), http://trade.ec.europa.eu/doclib/docs/2008/october/tradoc_140836.11.08.pdf (12 June (2009), p. 4.

of criminal liability, the reinforced use of technological protection measures (TPMs) and the cutting of legal safeguards that protect internet service providers (ISPs). This initiative has also received much criticism.[89]

VI. Is there Scope for Action in Political or Legal Bodies in the WTO?

In view of the described problems that developing countries are confronted with, the question arises as to whether or not there are possibilities for developing countries to address these issues within the World Trade Organization. In general, there will not be many developing countries that want to criticize the proliferation of TRIPS-plus provisions outside the WTO within that same forum as they mostly form part of this development: they agree to these provisions in bilateral/regional agreements. In fact, it is WTO members that consciously have chosen for the bilateral/regional avenue to regulate higher IP protection. It seems unlikely that these same members would discuss the desirability of this development within the forum that they are circumventing. Rather than the members of the WTO, it has been the Director General *Pascal Lamy* who has addressed the recent proliferation of RTAs at several occasions.

> "I think that it would be fair to say that proliferation is breeding concern —
> concern about incoherence, confusion, exponential increase of costs for business,
> unpredictability and even unfairness in trade relations."[90]

Lamy emphasizes the "downside of an exponential expansion" of RTAs in general, rather than the TRIPS-plus nature of their provisions in particular. However, the Director General of the WTO does not represent the opinion of WTO members. If a WTO member would also like to raise its concerns with regard to this development, it could do so either in political bodies of the WTO, such as the Committee on Regional Trade Agreements or the TRIPS Council, or before a judicial body of the WTO, a WTO panel.

The CRTA[91] is one venue in which WTO members could try to discuss the desirability of the recent proliferation of TRIPS-plus provisions. The newly established transparency procedure[92] presents an opportunity for members

---

89   See R. Gross, IP Justice White Paper on the Proposed Anti-Counterfeiting Trade Agreement (ACTA) (2008), http://ipjustice.org/wp/2008/03/25/ipj-white-paper-acta-2008/ (12 June 2009); Shaw, The Problem with the Anti-Counterfeiting Trade Agreement (2008), pp. 2 f.

90   P. Lamy, Proliferation of Regional Trade Agreements "Breeding Concern", in: WTOSpeeches (10 September 2007).

91   See part 3 of this contribution.

92   In the context of the Doha mandate, the Negotiation Group on Rules has developed a new mechanism to enhance the transparency of bilateral/regional agreements

to criticize certain provisions of the agreement, possibly also TRIPS-plus provisions.[93] To the author's knowledge, no member has so far made use of this possibility. The TRIPS Council presents another forum in which members could discuss the TRIPS-plus nature of bilateral, regional or plurilateral agreements concluded outside the WTO framework. Recently, Brazil and India have used two TRIPS Council meetings to criticize the seizure of generic pharmaceuticals by Dutch and German customs authorities on their way from India to Brazil and the Republic of Vanuatu.[94] In this context, in the 9 March 2009 meeting of the TRIPS Council, the Indian delegation drew members' attention to the proliferation of TRIPS-plus provisions:

> "This is the effort to implement the protection and enforcement of IPRs in a maximalist manner and thereby upset the delicate balance between rights of IPR holders and the public policy objectives under the TRIPS Agreement. (…) There is an attempt to enlarge the definition of counterfeits beyond its definition in the TRIPS Agreement, to set maximalist enforcement norms, and to include TRIPS plus provisions in RTAs. These are subtle and concerted ways of circumscribing the flexibilities of the TRIPS Agreement."[95]

This suggests that India and Brazil are willing to discuss this trend with other WTO members and that the TRIPS Council is used for this purpose.

While the recent development of TRIPS-plus provisions has been brought up in a political body of the WTO, it is rather unlikely that a member would start a judicial procedure before a WTO panel involving a dispute about an alleged conflict of a TRIPS provision and a RTA provision. Regardless of the political

---

concluded by WTO members. Paragraph 29 of the Doha Ministerial Declaration gives the mandate for "negotiations aimed at clarifying and improving disciplines and procedures under the existing WTO provisions applying to regional trade agreements, (…) tak[ing] into account development aspects." See WTO Ministerial Conference, Doha Ministerial Declaration, Doc. WT/MIN(01)/DEC/1 of 20 November 2001, paragraph 29.

93   See WTO General Council, Transparency Mechanism for Regional Trade Agreements, Doc. WT/L/671 of 18 December 2006, paragraph 7b.

94   See T. Balasubramaniam, India: Intervention at WTO TRIPS Council on Public Health Dimension of the TRIPS Agreement (2009), www.keionline.org/blogs/2009/03/09/indiatrips-council/ (12 June 2009); T. Balasubramaniam, Statement by Brazil at TRIPS Council: Public Health dimension of TRIPS Agreement (2009), www.keion-line.org/blogs/2009/03/04/brazilian-intervention-at-trips-council/ (12 June 2009); K. Mara, Generic Drug Delay Called „Systemic" Problem At TRIPS Council (2009), www.ip-watch.org/weblog/2009/06/09/generic-drug-delay-called-%E2%80%9Csystemic%E2%80%9D-problem-at-trips-council/ (12 June 2009).

95   Balasubramaniam, India: Intervention at WTO TRIPS Council on public health dimension of the TRIPS Agreement (2009). As the minutes of these meetings have not published yet, it is not clear whether or not a discussion has taken place following these statements.

reluctance of members to start a dispute settlement procedure, this is also due to several judicial factors that will inhibit a WTO member from bringing a dispute to the WTO Dispute Settlement Body (DSB).[96]

VII. Conclusions

The recent proliferation of bilateral and regional agreements can be described by two significant features: 1) being mainly North-South agreements; and 2) covering trade-related and non-trade-related issues, that go beyond the liberalisation or protection recognized by the WTO. These so-called WTO-plus issues also extend to the area of intellectual property protection.

This contribution aimed at analyzing whether the described recent development poses a threat to the WTO or to developing countries. While focusing particularly on the field of intellectual property protection, the author pointed out that the threat of a deadlock in the WTO is unlikely. The strategy of forum-shifting during the international development of intellectual property protection suggests that the bilateral/regional level on the one hand and the multilateral level on the other alternate and will continue to do so. This does not mean that the efficiency of WTO law will not suffer from the proliferation of PTAs that impose WTO-plus rules. Therefore, it is necessary to investigate further what the possibilities are to mitigate the negative effects of PTAs for the multilateral system and how to improve the attractive features of the WTO.[97]

For developing countries, the proliferation of PTAs that contain TRIPS-plus issues poses significant problems which need to be addressed. The pace with which bilateral and regional agreements proliferate threatens to undermine a large part of the policy space of developing countries. However, it seems doubtful whether the proliferation of such agreements can be stopped as their benefits in areas of trade in agricultural and textile products seem to outweigh the reduction of policy space in areas such as intellectual property. It is therefore important to raise awareness among the public, and developing countries in particular, of the costs of TRIPS-plus standards concluded in bilateral and regional trade agreements. This is also the aim of this contribution.

---

96 For a discussion of the judicial difficulties, see A. Dahrendorf, Free Trade Meets Cultural Diversity: The Legal Relationship Between WTO Rules and the UNESCO Convention on the Protection of the Diversity of Cultural Expressions, in: H. Schneider/P. van den Bossche (eds.), Protection of Cultural Diversity From a European and International Perspective (2008).

97 One possibility is to use the WTO dispute settlement mechanism as a venue for resolving RTA disputes and to develop a body of common law on RTAs. See Gao/Lim, Saving the WTO from the Risk of Irrelevance (2008), p. 911.

Bibliography

Abbott, F. M., The Doha Declaration on the TRIPS Agreement and Public Health and the Contradictory Trend in Bilateral and Regional Free Trade Agreements, Occasional Paper (2004).
—   A New Dominant Trade Species Emerges: Is Bilateralism a Threat?, in: Journal of International Economic Law 10 (2007), pp. 571-583.
Balasubramaniam, T., WIPO Patent Committee Embarks on Positive Agenda (2008), www. keionline.org/index.php?option=com_jd-wp&Itemid=39&p=124 (12 June 2009).
—   Statement by Brazil at TRIPS Council: Public Health Dimension of TRIPS Agreement (2009), www.keionline.org/blogs/2009/03/04/brazilian-intervention-t-trips-council/ (12 June 2009).
—   India: Intervention at WTO TRIPS Council on Public Health Dimension of the TRIPS Agreement (2009), www.keionline.org/blogs/2009/03/09/india-trips-council/ (12 June 2009).
Bergman, M. S., Bilateral Investment Protection Treaties: An Examination of the Evolution and Significance of the U.S. Prototype Treaty, in: New York University Journal of International Law & Policy 16 (1983), pp. 1-43.
Bhagwati, J., Termites in the Trading System: How Preferential Agreements Undermine Free Trade (2008).
Bhala, R., Competitive Liberalization, Competitive Imperialism, and Intellectual Property, in: Liverpool Law Review 28 (2007), pp. 77-105.
Biadgleng, E. T./V. Muñoz Tellez, The Changing Structure and Governance of Intellectual Property Enforcement (2008).
Braithwaite, J./P. Drahos, Global Business Regulation (2000).
Cronin, D., World Customs Organization Recommends Far-Reaching New Rules on IP (2008), www.ip-watch.org/weblog/index.php?p=939 (12 June 2009).
Crump, L., Global Trade Policy Development in a Two-Track System, in: Journal of International Economic Law 9 (2006), pp. 487-510.
Dahrendorf, A., Free Trade Meets Cultural Diversity: The Legal Relationship between WTO Rules and the UNESCO Convention on the Protection of the Diversity of Cultural Expressions, in: H. Schneider/P. van den Bossche (eds.), Protection of Cultural Diversity From a European andInternational Perspective (2008), pp. 31-83.
Drahos, P., BITs and BIPs: Bilateralism in Intellectual Property, in: Journal of World Intellectual Property 4 (2001), pp. 791-808.
—   Expanding Intellectual Property's Empire: the Role of FTAs, Paper (2003).
El-Said, M., The European TRIPS-plus Model and the Arab World: From Co-operation to Association - A New Era in the Global IPRs Regime, in: Liverpool Law Review 27 (2007), pp. 143-174.
European Commission, Global Europe: competing in the world (2006), http://trade.ec.europa. eu/doclib/docs/2006/october/tradoc_130376.pdf (12 June 2009).
European Commission, The Anti-Counterfeiting Trade Agreement (ACTA): Fact sheet (2008), http://trade.ec.europa.eu/doclib/docs/2008/october/tradoc_140836.11.08.pdf (12 June 2009).
Fink, C./P. Reichenmiller, Tightening TRIPS: The Intellectual Property Provisions of Recent US Free Trade Agreements, in: Trade Note of The World Bank Group 20 (2005).
Fiorentino, R. V./L. Verdeja/C. Toqueboeuf, The Changing Landscape of Regional Trade Agreements: 2006 Update, Discussion Paper (2007).

Gao, H./C. L. Lim, Saving the WTO From the Risk of Irrelevance: The WTO Dispute Settlement Mechanism as a 'Common Good' for RTA Disputes, in: Journal of International Economic Law 11 (2008), pp. 899-925.

Gross, R., IP Justice White Paper on the Proposed Anti-Counterfeiting Trade Agreement (ACTA) (2008), http://ipjustice.org/wp/2008/03/25/ipj-white-paper-acta-2008/ (12 June 2009).

G8, Reducing IPR Piracy and Counterfeiting Through More Effective Enforcement (2005), www.g7.utoronto.ca/summit/2005gleneagles/ipr_piracy.pdf (12 June 2009).

Helfer, L. R., Regime Shifting: The TRIPs Agreement and New Dynamics of International Intellectual Property Lawmaking, in: The Yale Journal of International Law 29 (2004), pp. 1-83.

Kampf, R., TRIPS and FTAs: A World of Preferential or Detrimental Relations, in: C. Heath/A Kamperman Sanders (eds.), Intellectual Property in Free Trade Agreements (2007), pp. 87-125.

Khor, M., Bilateral and Regional Free Trade Agreements (2008).

Kuanpoth, J., TRIPS-Plus Rules under Free Trade Agreements: An Asian Perspective, in: C. Heath/A. Kamperman Sanders (eds.), Intellectual Property in Free Trade Agreements (2007), pp. 28-45.

Ladas, P. S., Patents, Trademarks, and Related Rights: National and International Protection (1975).

Lamy, P., Proliferation of Regional Trade Agreements "Breeding Concern", in: WTO Speeches (10 September 2007).

Lester, S./B. Mercurio (eds.), Bilateral and Regional Trade Agreements: Case Studies (2009).

Li, X., SECURE: A Critical Analysis and Call for Action, in: South Bulletin 15 (2008), pp. 4-5.

Limão, N., Are Preferential Trade Agreements with Non-trade Objectives a Stumbling Block for Multilateral Liberalization?, in: Review of Economic Studies 74 (2007), pp. 821-855.

Mara, K., Generic Drug Delay Called "Systemic" Problem At TRIPS Council (2009),www.ip-watch.org/weblog/2009/06/09/generic-drug-delay-called-%E2%80%9Csystemic%E2%80%9D-problem-at-trips-council/ (12 June 2009).

Matthews, D., The Fight Against Counterfeiting and Piracy in the Bilateral Trade Agreements of the EU, Briefing Paper (2008).

Mercurio, B., TRIPS-Plus Provisions in FTAs: Recent Trends, in: L. Bartels/F. Ortino (eds.) Regional Trade Agreements and the WTO Legal System (2006), pp. 215-227.

Morin, J.-F., Tripping up TRIPs debates: IP and Health in Bilateral Agreements, in: International Journal of Intellectual Property Management 1-2 (2006), pp. 37-53.

Musungu, S. F./G. Dutfield, Multilateral agreements and a TRIPS-plus world: The World Intellectual Property Organization (WIPO) (2003).

Okediji, R., The International Relations of Intellectual Property: Narratives of Developing Country Participations in the Global Intellectual Property System, in: Singapore Journal of International & Comparative Law 7 (2003), pp. 15-385.

—   Back to Bilateralism? Pendulum Swings in International Intellectual Property Protection, in: University of Ottawa Law & Technology Journal 1 (2003), pp. 125-147.

Oxfam America, Make Trade Fair for Central America: Agriculture, Investment and Intellectual Property: Three Reasons to Say No to CAFTA (2003).

Pugatch, M. P., The International Regulation of IPRs in a TRIPs and TRIPs-plus Worlds, in: Journal of World Investment and Trade 6 (2005), pp. 231-265.

Rajkumar, R.,The Central American Free Trade Agreement: an End Run Around the DOHA Declaration on TRIPS and Public Health, in: Albany Law Journal of Science & Technology 15 (2004), pp. 433-475.

Reid Smith, S., Intellectual Property in Free Trade Agreements (2008).

Ricketson, S., The Birth of the Berne Union, in: Columbia-VLA Journal of Law and the Arts 11 (1986), pp. 9-32.

Rossi, F., Free trade agreements and TRIPS-plus measures, in: International Journal of Intellectual Property Management 1 (2006), pp. 150-172.

Schaefer, M., Ensuring That Regional Trade Agreements Complement The WTO System: US Unilateralism a Supplement to WTO Initiatives?, in: Journal of International Economic Law 10 (2007), pp. 585-603.

Sell, S. K., TRIPS-plus Free Trade Agreements and Access to Medicines, in: Liverpool Law Review 28 (2007), pp. 41-75.

—   The Global IP Upward Ratchet, Anti-Counterfeiting and Piracy Enforcement Efforts: The State of Play (2008).

Shaw, A., The Problem with the Anti-Counterfeiting Trade Agreement (and What to Do About It), in: Knowledge Ecology Studies 2 (2008), pp. 1-9.

Sutherland, P., The Future of the WTO: Addressing Institutional Challenges in the New Millennium, Report by the Consultative Board to the Director-General Supachai Panitchpakdi (2004).

UNCTAD, Bilateral Investment Treaties: 1959-1999 (2000).

USTR Press Release, Ambassador Schwab Announces US Will Seek New Trade Agreement to Fight Fakes (2007), www.ustr.gov/ambassador-schwab-announces-us-will-seek-new-trade-agreement-fight-fakes (12 June 2009).

Van den Bossche, P., The Law and Policy of the World Trade Organization: Text, Cases and Materials (2008).

Vivas-Eugui, D., Regional and Bilateral Agreements and a TRIPS-plus World: the Free Trade Area of the Americas (FTAA) (2003).

WCO, Report of SECURE Working Group, Doc. SP0269E1a of 9 June 2008.

Weatherall, K., The Anti-Counterfeiting Trade Agreement: What's It All About? (2008), http://works.bepress.com/kimweatherall/18 (12 June 2009).

Wilson, M., Friend or Foe? Regional Trade Agreements and the WTO, in: ICTSD BRIDGE Monthly Review 12 (2008), pp. 19-20.

WTO General Council, Transparency Mechanism for Regional Trade Agreements, WT/L/671 of 18 December 2006.

WTO Ministerial Conference, Doha Ministerial Declaration, WT/MIN(01)/DEC/1 of 20 November 2001.

WTO Ministerial Conference Doha, Declaration on the TRIPS Agreement and Public Health, WT/MIN(01)/DEC/2 of 20 November 2001.

Yu, P., Currents and Crosscurrents in the International Intellectual Property Regime, in: Loyola of Los Angeles Law Review 38 (2004), pp. 323-443.

Building a Better World? Assessing the European Union's Military Operations in Africa

Christian Burckhardt[1]

I. Introduction

A patrol of the European Union's (EU) military force (EUFOR) in Chad was shot upon near the city Guereda on 18 August 2008. The soldiers returned fire, the ambushers withdrew. A follow-up search, aided by two helicopters, was not successful. The armed group had disappeared into the night.[2]

This episode is just one of many encountered by EU soldiers in Africa in recent years. Since 2003, the EU has conducted 22 operations so far; nine of them have taken place in sub-Saharan Africa, four have been military missions. The article aims to explain the EU's recent surge of military activity "out of area": Why does the EU intervene in Africa? Is it really only for humanitarian aims as Brussels claims? The answer to this question matters. From a policy-perspective, it allows us to speculate upon the future of EU military missions and the potential for cooperation with the United Nations (UN). Theoretically, the issue area of defence is crucial for a general assessment of the nature of the EU as an international actor. Furthermore, it potentially offers a fertile ground for applying realism – a theory which focuses on military power – to the area of EU foreign policy.[3]

The chapter proceeds as follows. First, it presents two divergent concepts of the EU's international role: great power and civilian power. It defines them according to their foreign policy aims, instruments and decision-making procedures. The second section analyses the European Security and Defence Policy (ESDP) according to these three criteria. Third, the chapter turns to the EU's military interventions in Africa, in particular the 2003 and 2006 missions in Congo. It argues that the EU actions in this issue area are best explained by realism – the EU intervenes in Africa to gain international prestige. Finally, the conclusion highlights key risks of this finding for Europe, Africa, and the international system.

1   Any opinions expressed in the chapter are the sole responsibility of the author and do not represent the official position of the United Nations.
2   European Union, EUFOR Troops Challenge and Disperse Ambushers, Press Release, 19 August 2008.
3   Obviously, there exist many possible objections to the application of realism to a supra-national organisation like the EU. This is not the place to comprehensively address these objections. It suffices to note that the ESDP military missions are an additional proof that the EU is a relatively cohesive actor in international relations.

II.   Two Concepts to Analyse the EU's International role

Today, the EU is most commonly depicted as a civilian power. *François Duchêne*, then-director of the International Institute for Strategic Studies (IISS) in London, introduced the civilian power concept in 1972. Two brief chapters in two edited volumes contained one brief paragraph each about the new concept – taken together, these were less than two pages. Clearly, *Duchêne* "never developed his vision into a detailed and comprehensive scheme"[4]. Nonetheless, civilian power quickly became "one of the main conceptual anchors for debate over the sources of EU influence in the world"[5]. Civilian powers' ultimate aim is to

"bring to international problems the sense of common responsibility and structures of contractual politics which have in the past been associated almost exclusively with 'home' and not foreign, that is, alien affairs"[6]

More than 20 years later, he did not doubt as to whether the EU had achieved that aim:

"with all its imperfections, the Community domesticates the balance of power into something which, if not as democratic as domestic norms,has made the international system in Europe take a huge step in their direction. Relations between states reflect domestic standards instead of threatening them."[7]

The traditional antonym of civilian power is great power or superpower.[8] The term "great power" (Großmacht in German, l'Europe puissance in French) has a long history. Lord *Caslereagh*, former British Foreign Secretary, used it with reference to the Congress of Vienna in 1814. Great power has remained in the diplomatic vocabulary ever since. One of the first academics to apply the term to the European Integration process was *Johann Galtung*. In 1973, he called the European Community (EC) a "superpower in the making"[9]. More recently, *Helene Sjursen* argues that the ESDP could signify a shift away from civilian

---

4   J. Zielonka, Explaining Euro-paralysis: Why Europe is Unable to Act in International Politics (1998), p. 226.
5   K. Nicolaïdis/R. Howse, 'This is my EU-topia': Narrative as Power, in: Journal of Common Market Studies 40 (2002), p. 770.
6   F. Duchêne, The European Community and the Uncertainties of Interdependence, in: M. Kohnstamm/W. Hager (eds.), A Nation Writ Large? Foreign-Policy Problems before the European Community (1973), p. 19.
7   F. Duchêne/J. Monnet, The First Statesman of Interdependence (1994), p. 405.
8   I will not elaborate on the differences between great power and superpower. It suffices to note that it is much harder to qualify as a superpower in the international system. In the following, I employ the term great power.
9   J. Galtung, The European Community: A Superpower in the Making (1973).

power and make "EU policy more akin to that of traditional 'great powers'"[10]. The term is currently high on the agenda because of an alleged return of traditional balance of power politics. Europe needs to hold ground against other great powers, such as America and China. Former Prime Minister *Tony Blair*, for instance, stated that "we are building a *new world superpower*. The EU is about the projection of collective power, wealth and influence."[11]

Both concepts are notoriously difficult to define. However, it is possible to identify three distinct aspects (see table 1).[12] First, a civilian power pursues particular foreign policy objectives: the deepening and widening of multilateral forums, in particular the UN and the Organization for Security and Cooperation in Europe (OSCE); the promotion of democracy and the respect for human rights; the fight against corruption, international crime, and the development of a participatory market economy (good governance); and finally, responsibility for the global environment ("sustainable development"). These are what *Arnold Wolfers* calls "milieu goals"[13]. A great power, on the other hand, pursues "possession goals" to further the national interest: weakening of multilateral institutions and a strong preference for unilateral initiatives; enlargement of its territory and the acquisition of natural resources; disregard for human rights and the environment. Second, a civilian power uses particular foreign policy instruments – apart from traditional peacekeeping activities under the auspices of the United Nations, a civilian power uses exclusively political, economic, and cultural instruments. A great power instead employs the full range of foreign policy instruments, including military force. A civilian power uses its means in a particular way. The foreign policy style of a civilian power relies on "soft power" (latent influence) and on persuasion; a great power does not sway another actor's decisions, it compels through force or deterrence. Finally, the foreign policy processes of a civilian power and that of a superpower differ substantially: civilian powers favour open decision-making processes which are subject to civilian, democratic control, whereas the decision-making processes of a superpower are secretive and made within a small, confined circle.

What about our particular area of interest: military missions under UN auspices in African countries without any immediate security or economic significance for the EU? *Andrew Moravcsik* and *Kalypso Nicolaïdis* explicitly mention peacekeeping as being part of "civilian power"[14]. The Center for

---

10   H. Sjursen, What Kind of Power?, in: Journal of European Public Policy 13 (2006), p. 171.
11   T. R. Reid, The United States of Europe: the Superpower Nobody Talks About - From the Euro to Eurovision (2005), p. 4, emphasis added.
12   See C. Burckhardt, Civilian Power Europe? The Nature of European Union Foreign Policy (2010).
13   A. Wolfers, Discord and Collaboration: Essays on International Politics (1965), p. 73.
14   A. Moravcsik/K. Nicolaïdis, How to Fix Europe's Image Problem, in: Foreign Policy 148 (2005), p. 67.

Global Development in Washington and Foreign Policy magazine rank the rich countries by their commitment to development. They use six variables, contributions to peacekeeping being one of them.[15] The positive view on peacekeeping can be explained by its definition:

> "A United Nations' presence in the field (normally involving civilian and military personnel) that, with the consent of the conflicting parties, implements or monitors arrangements relating to the control of conflicts and their resolution, or ensures the safe delivery of humanitarian relief."[16]

	Civilian Power	**Great Power**
Foreign policy philosophy	Domestication of international relations	Self-help in anarchical system
1. Aims	1.1 Monopolise use of force by supporting cooperative and collective security arrangements 1.2 Widening and deepening of international organisation 1.3 Advance international law 1.4 Promotion of human rights 1.5 Promotion of democracy 1.6 Preservation of environment 1.7 Helping the poor (development and humanitarian aid) 1.8 Enhancement of fair international trading system 1.9 Leadership/model without claiming exclusive leadership status	1.1 Autonomy 1.2 National security 1.3 Control of natural resources/energy security 1.4 Enhancement of economic position
2. Instruments	2.1 Emphasis on diplomacy, economic and cultural means 2.2 Persuasion, offering and granting rewards	2.1 Emphasis on military means 2.2 Threats and coercion
3. Process	Pluralistic	Centralised

Table 1: Overview of the Two Concepts

Even "robust" peacekeeping on the basis of Chapter VII of the UN-Charter merely allows peacekeepers "to use all necessary means" to protect civilians in

---

15   T. Garton Ash, Free World: Why a Crisis of the West Reveals the Opportunity of Our Time (2005), pp. 169 ff.

16   United Nations, What is Peacekeeping?, http://www.un.org/Depts/dpko/dpko/field/body_pkeep.htm (accessed: 1 November 2009).

their immediate vicinity and prevent violence against UN staff and personnel. The UN Secretary-General has stressed that the use of force should always be seen as a measure of last resort.[17] The participation of civilian powers in peacekeeping operations strengthens the UN, advances international peace, the respect of human rights, and it takes place only with the consent of all parties involved. Humanitarian intervention is notoriously difficult to define.[18] The main difference between peacekeeping and humanitarian intervention is that, concerning the latter, no permission is given by the state within whose territory force is applied. Unauthorized humanitarian intervention refers to humanitarian intervention that has not been authorized by the UN Security Council under Chapter VII of the Charter.[19] In contrast to *Hanns W. Maull*[20], I argue that unauthorized interventions are not compatible with a civilian power posture. They clearly violate international law, create the risk of undermining international inhibitions against the use of force, seriously damage the credibility of a civilian power as a proponent of world-wide legitimate governance and lead to an "interventionism à la carte"[21]. Authorized humanitarian interventions are in conformity with civilian power norms. It is widely accepted among international lawyers that the UN Security Council can authorize humanitarian interventions through an expansive interpretation of Article 39 of the UN Charter, Article I of the Genocide Convention, and numerous other international conventions.[22] In the cases where the UN has authorized humanitarian interventions, the humanitarian case has been strong.[23] Faced with particularly grave human rights violations, a civilian power tries to prevent widespread human suffering.[24] Great powers, on the other hand, do not care much about "widespread human suffering", but focus upon extending or at least maintaining their (relative) power position.[25] They "behave like large states do, with regard for their own concerns before any other values come

17   United Nations, Peacekeeping: Frequently Asked Questions, www.un.org/Depts/dpko/dpko/faq/q9.htm (accessed: 1 November 2009).

18   J. M. Welsh, Humanitarian Intervention and International Relations (2004), p. 3.

19   J. L. Holzgrefe, The Humanitarian Intervention Debate, in R. O. Keohane/J. L. Holzgrefe (eds.), Humanitarian Intervention: Ethical, Legal, and Political Dilemmas (2003), p. 1.

20   H. W. Maull, Germany and the Use of Force: Still a „Civilian Power"?, in: Survival 42 (2000).

21   S. v. Schorlemer, Menschenrechte und „humanitäre Interventionen", in: Internationale Politik 55 (2000), p. 47.

22   Holzgrefe, The Humanitarian Intervention Debate (2003), pp. 40-44.

23   T. J. Farer, Humanitarian Intervention Before and After 9/11: Legality and Legitimacy, in: J. L. Holzgrefe/R. O. Keohane (eds.), Humanitarian Intervention: Ethical, Legal, and Political Dilemmas (2003), p. 76.

24   A. Linklater, A European Civilising Process?, in: C. Hill/M. Smith (eds.), International Relations and the European Union (2005), p. 378.

25   K. N. Waltz, Theory of International Politics (1979), p. 111.

into play"[26]. International engagement is ruled out if their own interests are not directly affected.[27] This obviously would rule out military engagement in most African countries. Nevertheless, maximal realism provides an alternative interpretation. Great powers may intervene in third countries if it offers opportunities to demonstrate and assert their power and leadership.[28] This, in turn, increases the prestige of the actor in question. Prestige, defined as the "probability that a command with a given specific content will be obeyed by a given group of persons"[29], is one of the main components in the governance of the international system. It is the reputation for power, and military power in particular.[30] Like power, prestige ensures that the weaker states in the system will obey the commands of the dominant ones.[31] The EU is more likely than others to yearn for prestige. Its role as a security actor in the international sphere is recent and still in flux. Actors who are "unsure" of themselves accord a much higher importance to third-party views. Prestige counts more if your own identity is fragile.[32] However, maximal realism does not depart entirely from realist assumptions: the intervention takes place only if the number of expected casualties is low and the probability of success is high.[33]

To summarize, civilian powers intervene in far-away, economically and strategically unimportant countries to alleviate misery and defend basic human rights of the local population. Great powers, by contrast, intervene to gain international prestige.

III. EU Defence Policy at Ten

ESDP was not the first attempt of the Europeans to forge a common defence policy. The European security community (1950-1954) and the *Fouchet* Plan (1958-1963) were ambitious but ultimately unsuccessful plans. Subsequently,

---

26   C. Hill, European Foreign Policy: Power Bloc, Civilian Power, or Flop?, in: R. Rummel (ed.), The Evolution of an International Actor: Western Europe's New Assertiveness (1990), p. 41.

27   K. Kirste, Rollentheorie und Außenpolitikanalyse. Die USA und Deutschland als Zivilmächte (1998), pp. 50-55.

28   B. R. Posen/A. L. Ross, Competing Visions for US Grand Strategy, in: International Security 21 (1997), p. 32.

29   R. Dahrendorf, Class and Class Conflict in Industrial Society (1959), p. 30.

30   R. Gilpin, War and Change in World Politics (1981), p. 31.

31   See E. H. Carr, The Twenty Years' Crisis, 1919-1939: An Introduction to the Study of International Relations (1964).

32   See R. Wolf, Respekt: Ein unterschätzter Faktor in den Internationalen Beziehungen, in: Zeitschrift für Internationale Beziehungen 15 (2008), p. 22; Y. Huo/L. E. Molina, Is Pluralism a Viable Model of Diversity? The Benefits and Limits of Subgroup Respect, in: Group Processes and Intergroup Relations 9 (2006), p. 372.

33   See R. J. Art, A Defensible Defense, in: International Security 15 (1991), pp. 5-53.

it took more than four decades for the EU to re-enter the security and defence realm. From the mid-90s onwards, European states – for a variety of reasons – were no longer content with having only the North Atlantic Treaty Organization (NATO) and the Western European Union (WEU) as defence institutions.[34] Thus, following the British-French St. Malo Declaration of 4 December 1998, ESDP was born in 1999: the Cologne European Council meeting in June 1999 fixed the institutional basis while the Helsinki European Council meeting in December defined the military capacity objectives.

Ten years on, how to evaluate the objectives, instruments and decision-making process of EU defence policy? The objectives of the EU's foreign policy as stipulated in the Lisbon Treaty point towards a strong civilian power orientation. The EU seeks to advance

"democracy, the rule of law, the universality and indivisibility of human rights and fundamental freedoms, respect for human dignity, the principles of equality and solidarity, and respect for the principles of the United Nations Charter and international law".[35]

The common security and defence policy shall provide the EU with an operational capacity to achieve these aims. It may employ forces

"on missions outside the Union for joint disarmament operations, humanitarian and rescue tasks, military advice and assistance tasks, conflict prevention and peacekeeping tasks, tasks of combat forces in crisis management, including peace-making and post-conflict stabilisation".[36]

A qualitative content analysis of speeches and documents by leading EU politicians and officials seems to confirm the "benign" foreign policy objectives of the Union.[37] The former EU Commissioner for External Affairs and European Neighbourhood Policy, *Benita Ferrero-Waldner*, assured hat the EU does not wish to "start a geo-political zero-sum game" and is not interested in "extending its zones of influence"[38]. In 2000, only one year after the European Council decided to "progressively frame a European defence policy"[39], former EU High Representative for the Common Foreign and Security Policy (CFSP), *Javier*

---

34   See J. Howorth, From Security to Defence: the Evolution of the CFSP, in: C. Hill/M. Smith (eds.), International Relations and the European Union (2005), p. 183.
35   European Union, Treaty of Lisbon, 2007/C 306/01, 15 April 2007, p. 121.
36   Ibid., pp. 42 f.
37   See Burckhardt, Civilian Power Europe? (2010).
38   B. Ferrero-Waldner, Europa als globaler Akteur – Aktuelle Schwerpunkte Europäischer Außen- und Nachbarschaftspolitik, SPEECH/05/30 (accessed: 24 January 2005).
39   European Council, Declaration on Strengthening the Common European Policy on Security and Defence, 4 June 1999.

Solana, made it clear that the purpose of the CFSP "is not to exercise power for its own sake"[40]. A study of the Council's discourse of the same year confirms the EU's civilian power orientation.[41] From then on, however, attitudes in the *Justus Lipsius* building seem to change. *Solana* felt that the EU has not received the respect on the world stage it deserves due to a lack of unity and military capability.[42] ESDP is a means for the EU to be "larger", "more influential"[43] and "a leading strategic actor"[44]. It will aid the EU in defending its material and security interests in a dangerous world.[45] This might entail "early, rapid and (...) robust intervention"[46]. It is even more surprising to hear similar statements from *Solana's* Commission colleagues. They embody the "civilian" aspect of European foreign policy. With the advent of ESDP, the Council gained while the Commission lost influence. Nevertheless, *Romano Prodi* believed that "the EU cannot be strong without ESDP"[47]. It will turn the EU into "a more self-confident player (...) in global leadership"[48], "a new power pole" and, perhaps most intriguingly, "a serious counterpart to the United States".[49] The instruments of EU defence policy are difficult to assess. The first factor to consider is the volume of defence expenditure. In 2004, the EU-25 spent almost 230 billion US dollar (USD) on defence; more than half the US defence budget for that year: 456 billion USD. EU expenditure is equal to the combined total of China, Russia, Japan, Saudi Arabia, India, and South Korea. Usually China and Russia get accused of great power posturing. When it comes to defence spending, however, the EU is the second-largest power on the planet. This finding does not apply to all member states. Italy, France, the United Kingdom, and Germany

---

40   J. Solana, Europe Has the Will to Build a Common Foreign and Security Policy, in: European Affairs (2000), http://www.europeanaffairs.org/Spring-2000/europe-has-the-will-to-build-a-common-foreign-and-security-policy.html (accessed: 14 February 2010).

41   H. Larsen, The Discourse on the EU's Role in the World, in: B. Hansen/B. Heurlin (eds.), The New World Order: Contrasting Theories (2000), p. 338.

42   See J. Solana, European Defence: The Task Ahead, European Voice, 24 October 2001.

43   J. Solana, Towards a Stronger Alliance, in: European Affairs 12 April 2000.

44   J. Solana, Annual Speech at the European Union Institute for Security Studies, 2003.

45   Solana adds that "other countries defend theirs as well, so there is no need to be apologetic about this.", J. Solana, Annual Speech at the European Union Institute for Security Studies, S279/06, 6 October 2006.

46   Council of Ministers, European Security Strategy: A Secure Europe in a Better World, 12 December 2003, EU Doc. 15895/03, 8 December 2003.

47   R. Prodi, A Stronger Foreign and Security Policy for Europe, SPEECH/02/465, 9 October 2002.

48   R. Prodi, The New Europe in the Transatlantic Partnership, SPEECH/01/204, 9 May 2001.

49   C. Patten, The Role of the European Union on the World Stage, Speech/01/23, 25 January 2001.

account for nearly 75 percent of EU defence expenditure.[50] Furthermore, not all spending is relevant for missions outside the EU. European forces still own 10,000 main battle tanks and 2,500 combat aircraft. Only 30 percent of two million active service personnel can actually be employed outside European territory either because of legal restrictions or inadequate training.[51] The EU devised the "battle-groups" concept precisely because of the un-readiness of the majority of European troops for interventions abroad. Battle-groups are elite units between 1,500 and 2,200 troops which are operational within five to ten days and sustainable in the field for at least one month. A battle-group consists of a combined-arms battalion-size force, reinforced with combat support and combat service support elements. It has a force headquarter and designated operational and strategic enablers such as logistics and strategic airlift.[52] The EU battle-groups reached full operational capacity in January 2007; two are on standby at all times. They have not been used yet: whenever the opportunity arose, the nation in charge was reluctant to intervene. The two main reasons for this disinclination are costs and chronic shortages of airlift capacity. The EU deployment to Chad had to be delayed by six months because of a failure to locate 16 helicopters and ten transport aircraft, for instance. The long-term solution, the Airbus A400M, has been the victim of prolonged delays. The first batch of aircraft is not expected before 2012.[53] The European Defence Agency (EDA) was created in 2004 to avoid similar incidents in the future. The objectives of the EDA are to improve military capabilities, consolidate defence research, and to promote armaments cooperation.[54] These issues have never before been discussed within the EU framework. The EDA is guided by a Steering Board comprised of the National Defence Ministers; the Board is headed by the High Representative for the CFSP.[55]

The following diagram illustrates the Union's complex decision-making procedures in the realm of defence (see figure 1). The figure presents the situation under the Treaty of Nice.[56] The policy process usually works like this: A policy initiative may be proposed by a variety of actors (governments, Political and Security Committee (COPS), Council Secretariat, Commission), is scrutinized by all member states, modified through recommendations proposed

---

50   J. Howorth, From Security to Defence: the Evolution of the CFSP, in: C. Hill/M. Smith (eds.), International Relations and the European Union (2005), p. 188.
51   International Institute for Strategic Studies, European Military Capabilities: Building Armed Forces for Modern Operations (2008).
52   J. Howorth, Security and Defence Policy in the European Union (2007), pp. 107 f.
53   C. Bretherton/J. Vogler, The European Union as a Global Actor (2006), p. 234.
54   Council of Ministers, Council Joint Action on the Establishment of the European Defence Agency, 2004/551/CFSP, 12 July 2004.
55   Howorth, Security and Defence Policy in the European Union (2007), p. 109.
56   At the time of writing (end of 2009), the exact division of competencies in the area of ESDP under the Lisbon Treaty is not clear.

by specialist working groups, sent to COPS for general discussion, forwarded to the General Affairs and External Relations Council (GAERC), and finally approved by the EC.[57] This is not the place to elaborate on each single institution depicted. It suffices to note the striking dispersion of power between them. That is why the EU is structurally better suited to smaller-scale crisis management than to larger military interventions.[58] Even among the member states, a directoire of Germany, the United Kingdom and France does not exist. While the "Big Three" undoubtedly dominate the proceedings, other member states, notably Italy, Sweden, and the Netherlands have stubbornly resisted attempts to institutionalize any kind of leadership group when it comes to politico-strategic decisions.

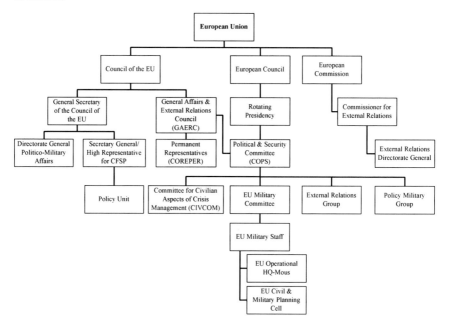

Figure 1: ESDP institutional structures[59]

Nevertheless, the Lisbon Treaty presents a major step towards stronger centralisation. The High Representative of the Union for Foreign Affairs and Security Policy as a Vice-President of the European Commission and the

---

57   Howorth, Security and Defence Policy in the European Union (2007), p. 91.
58   A. Menon, Empowering Paradise? The ESDP at Ten, in: International Affairs 85 (2009), p. 237.
59   Based on Howorth, Security and Defence Policy in the European Union (2007), p. 69.

Chairperson of the GAERC will be the first person in the history of European Integration to combine the inter-governmental and supranational sides of policy-making. She will be assisted by an External Action Service, an embryonic EU diplomatic corps.[60]

IV. Military Interventions in Africa

Since the inception of the ESDP, the EU has launched a total of 22 operations, 12 of which are still on-going. Concerning the nature of the missions, six were military operations (see table 2), seven police missions, four border missions, one a planning mission, three rule of law missions, three monitoring missions, two assistance missions and two were security sector reform missions.[61] They have ranged in size from tiny (15 personnel assigned to security sector reform mission in Guinea-Bissau) to Operation Althea in Bosnia and Herzegovina, which at its peak was 7,000 man strong. Nine out of the 22 missions and four out of the six military operations have taken place in sub-Saharan Africa. Why has the EU chosen Africa as the main location for its first steps as a military actor? Because it offers the opportunity of deploying troops "without trespassing on the interest spheres of more powerful actors"[62]. One Commission official, in making the case for the intervention in Darfur in 2004, pointed out that "here we have a low-technology, low-intensity conflict taking place in a region where we would not trespass on the interest spheres of Russia or the US".[63]It is not a coincidence that for all the missions the EU has carried out, it has been a mere bystander when major conflicts erupted in the Middle East, the Gulf, and the Caucasus.[64]

It is difficult to evaluate the EU's operations in Chad and in Somalia. The former concluded very recently, while the latter is still on-going.[65] Thus, I focus on the two operations in Congo. Due to space limitations, the role of the EU's trade, development and humanitarian aid, police and security sector reform policies vis-à-vis Congo are not considered – the focus is squarely on the military side.

---

60   European Union, Treaty of Lisbon, 2007/C 306/01, 15 April 2007, art. 27.
61   Council of Ministers, European Security and Defence Policy, http://consilium.europa. eu/showPage.aspx?id=268&lang=EN (accessed: 20 April 2009).
62   A. Toje, The European as a Small Power, or Conceptualizing Europe's strategic actorness, in: European Integration 30 (2008), p. 208.
63   A. Toje, The Consensus Expectation Gap: Explaining Europe's Ineffective Foreign Policy, in: Security Dialogue 39 (2008), p. 136, emphasis added.
64   See Menon, Empowering paradise? (2009), p. 244.
65   As of April 2009.

Name of mission	Concordia	Artemis	EUFOR-Althea	EUFOR-RD Congo	EUFOR-Chad/RCA	EU NAVFOR Atalanta
Country	Macedonia	DR Congo	BiH	DR Congo	Chad/Central African Rep.	Somalia, Gulf of Aden
Dates	31/03/03-15/12/03	05/06/03-01/09/03	12/04 - date	06/06-12/06	28/01/08-15/03/09	08/12/08-date
No. of personnel	400	1,800	7,000	2,000	3,700	1,500
No. of countries	26	17	33	18	26	>8
Budget	6.2 + clwtf	7	clwtf	149	119,6	8,3
UN mandate	No	Yes	Yes	Yes	Yes	Yes
Head	Adm. Rainer Feist	Gen. Bruno Neveux	Adm. Hans-Jochen Wittauer	Gen. Karl-Heinz Viereck	Gen. Patrick Nash	Adm. Philip Jones
Aegis	ESDP	ESDP	ESDP	ESDP	ESDP	ESDP
Command chain	Berlin Plus	EU-only	Berlin Plus	EU-only	EU-only	EU-only

Table 2: ESDP Military Missions

The French-led operation Artemis, in accordance with UN Resolution 1484[66], had the following aims:

---

66   UN Doc. S/RES/1484, 30 May 2003.

"to contribute to the stabilization of the security conditions and the improvement of the humanitarian situation in Bunia, to ensure the protection of the airport, the internally displaced persons in the camps in Bunia and, if the situation requires it, to contribute to the safety of the civilian population, United Nations personnel and the humanitarian presence in the town".[67]

In the town of Bunia, the Lendu and Hema communities violently clashed. Several hundred people were killed. There was a great anxiety that the unrests would spread: on 6 May 2003, 7,000 Ugandans fled from Bunia. The UN force was not capable of providing a secure environment in and around the city. The EU operation was planned and conducted by France's Centre Planification et Conduite des Opérations instead of NATO. In contrast to Operation Concordia, Artemis was therefore the first time when EU troops were deployed outside of Europe and independently from NATO. Artillery and fixed-wing Mirage 2000 ground attack jets supported the force. It got into skirmishes with Lendu militia in June 2003. A month later, the soldiers encountered more serious resistance from Union of Congolese Patriots forces. They killed at least twenty militia members. European forces re-established security in Bunia, weakened the rival Lendu and Hema militias, and then handed responsibility back to UN forces.[68]

The EU itself and most observers claim that the operation was a great success. *Jolyon Howorth* noted that it demonstrated the EU's capacity for

"rapid deployment, logistics, a single command structure, well and appropriately trained forces, clear rules of engagement allowing for tactical evolution in the theatre, good incorporation of multinational elements, excellent inter-service cooperation, and adequate communications".[69]

Indeed, it was – but the mission's terms of reference were extremely limited in time and space. European forces managed to guarantee civilian safety only in a small area for three months.[70] The militia were driven out of Bunia, but continued their massacres throughout the rest of the Ituri province. That is why the International Crisis Group argued that the mission was "totally insufficient"[71].

The decision to send troops to Bunia does not seem to have been based on considerations related to African security but motivated by the desire to prove the ESDP as being operational. According to interviews with French officials,

---

67   Ibid., para. 1.
68   United Nations Peacekeeping Best Practices Section, Operation Artemis: The Lessons of the Interim Emergency Multinational Force, New York, October 2004.
69   Howorth, Security and Defence Policy in the European Union (2007), p. 232.
70   Médecins sans Frontières, Ituri: Unkept Promises? A Pretence of Protection and Inadequate Assistance, Report, 25 July 2003.
71   International Crisis Group, Congo Crisis: Military Intervention in Ituri Africa, Report No 64, 13 June 2003, p. i (in executive summary).

"France badly wanted a mission to show the EU was capable of acting alone, where NATO would not be involved"[72]. A reluctant Britain and Germany followed the French lead, but only after ensuring that their military contributions would be minuscule.

Another ESDP military operation in the Democratic Republic of Congo was launched in June 2006[73]. It was intended to support the UN mission in Congo (MONUC) during the run-up to the presidential election from July to October. Like Artemis, EUFOR RD Congo was an autonomous EU mission under Chapter VII of the UN Charter. Germany and France supplied over 60 percent of all troops. The force headquarter was based in Kinshasa, but the majority of the force was stationed in neighbouring Gabon, only to be called upon in the event of an emergency. The narrow aims of the missions were defined by the UN as the following:

"EUFOR was authorized to take all necessary measures to support MONUC in case the Mission faced serious difficulties in fulfilling its mandate; contribute to the protection of civilians under imminent threat of physical violence, without prejudice to the responsibility of the Congolese Government; contribute to airport protection in Kinshasa; ensure the security and free movement of EUFOR R.D Congo personnel and the protection of its installations; and execute limited operations to extract individuals in danger".[74]

The EU mission fulfilled its very limited terms of reference, but not without committing two faux pas. French military jets flew low over the house of *Jean-Pierre Bemba*, one of the candidates, provoking a riot which cost the life of six civilians. The next day, a Belgian air-force drone smashed into a house, injuring five. Nevertheless, the elections did take place peacefully throughout the country. The extent to which EUFOR was responsible for this success is debatable. The mission was "more about European form than African substance"[75], for at least four reasons. First, the number of troops deployed in Congo – a maximum of 1,000 – was clearly not sufficient for a huge country with over 50,000 polling stations. Second, the troops were based in Kinshasa – a city which was already largely pacified – and not in the more unstable eastern part of the country. Third, the stationing of the majority of the force in Gabon further heightened the impression that the operation was "largely cosmetic"[76]. Presidential candidate *Christophe Mboso* was not the only one in Congo who

72   Cited in: C. Gegout, Causes and Consequences of the EU's Military Intervention in the Democratic Republic of Congo: A Realist Explanation, in: European Foreign Affairs Review 10 (2005), p. 437.
73   UN Doc. S/RES/1671, 25 April 2006.
74   Ibid., para. 8.
75   J.-Y. Haine/B. Giegerich, Congo, a Cosmetic EU Operation, in: International Herald Tribune, June 12 (2006).
76   Ibid.

was bewildered by the EU's strategy. He rhetorically asked whether "the elections are taking place in Gabon?"[77]. Finally, the EU withdrew at exactly the moment when the situation was the most delicate: after the announcement of the election results. If the EU had been as interested in enhancing security as it was in enhancing its international prestige, its troops would have remained on the ground into 2007. Even a sympathetic observer like *Howorth* concluded that "accusations that EUFOR RD Congo was primarily intended to get some good coverage for the EU are hard to avoid"[78].

V. Conclusions

The chapter inquired about the motivation of the European Union to intervene militarily in Africa. It presented two contrasting possible explanations, one centred upon the willingness to improve the humanitarian conditions on the ground, the other one upon the desire to demonstrate to European citizens and to third countries that ESDP works beyond the EU's immediate neighbourhood. The former is associated with the civilian power concept, the later with great power and realism. The analysis of ESDP revealed that the aims and the instruments of the policy are more akin to a great power, while the decision-making process is closer to the civilian power ideal type, although the Lisbon Treaty increases the degree of centralisation. An analysis of the 2003 and the 2006 interventions of the EU in the Democratic Republic of Congo revealed that they were largely symbolic: limited terms of reference, small number of troops, short deployment period, and no real impact on the ground.

The findings of this chapter could be strengthened by an evaluation of the ESDP civilian and police missions in Africa. The chapter does not attempt to make a mono-causal claim: international prestige is one of the main drivers in this policy area, but certainly not the only one. A neo-colonial quest for regional influence by France and the hunt for natural resources in (some) African countries might constitute important independent variables. Nevertheless, these two other possible explanatory factors also fall squarely into the "realist camp". They do not change the conclusion of this chapter: future military interventions in Africa will continue to serve first and foremost the EU's "own concerns before any other values come into play"[79].

The yearning for recognition as a serious military actor poses risks for the UN, the EU itself, people in Africa and potentially for the stability of the international system. Unnecessary posturing can damage effective collaboration

---

77   Howorth, Security and Defence Policy in the European Union (2007), p. 239.
78   Ibid.
79   Hill, European Foreign Policy: Power Bloc, Civilian Power, or Flop? (1990), p. 41.

with existing multilateral missions run by other institutions.[80] *Claudia Major*, in a detailed case study, showed how poorly the EU cooperated with the UN in Congo.[81] In some instances, the most effective way for Europeans to deploy outside Europe would be to provide forces directly to UN missions rather than acting through the ESDP.[82] *Giovanna Bono* took this as a proof that the EU "uses the UN as a way of legitimizing their own military operations and actions to develop ESDP"[83]. Second, the desire to "build Europe" hinders European politicians and officials to honestly assess the effectiveness of the ESDP. *Solana*, for instance, claimed that "where we have acted, we have succeeded".[84] *Anand Menon* rightly argued that "such a self-congratulatory approach to assessment hampers the ability of the Union to draw accurate conclusions from its operations and learn from its mistakes (...)".[85] Only recently has the EU moved to establish a proper "lessons learned" mechanism after a mission has ended. More importantly, by selecting operations that require relatively little force and risk, the EU neglects operations which might have helped to protect populations from massive human rights violations or even from genocide, as in Darfur.[86] Scarce resources are diverted away from less visible civilian activities to highly visible military ones. For example, a Commission official worried that in the case of the NAVFOR Atalanta mission "we spent too much on warships and not enough on improving the situation in Somalia."[87] That is difficult to accept, particularly concerning an actor who incessantly presents itself as a "force for peace in the world"[88]. The least tangible, but the most serious risk in the long-term is the finding that the ESDP might turn the EU into a great power. One of the potentially most powerful actors in the international system is no longer contributing

---

80   J. Dobbins/S. G. Jones/K. Crane *et al.*, Europe's Role in Nation-Building: From the Balkans to the Congo (2008), p. 107.

81   C. Major, EU-UN Cooperation in Military Crisis Management: the Experience of EUFOR RD Congo in 2006, in: EUISS Occasional Paper 72 (2008).

82   Dobbins *et al.*, Europe's Role in Nation-building (2008), p. 109.

83   G. Bono, The Perils of Conceiving EU Foreign Policy as a "Civilizing Force", in: Internationale Politik und Gesellschaft 1 (2006), p. 160.

84   J. Solana, Address to the Conference of Defence Committee Chairpersons of the 27 National Parliaments, S139/07, 23 April 2007.

85   Menon, Empowering Paradise? (2009), pp. 242 f.

86   A. J. K. Bailes, The EU and a 'Better World': What Role for the European Security and Defence Policy?, in: International Affairs 84 (2008), p. 120.

87   Interviews in Brussels, April 2009, done by the author in April 2009.

88   B. Ahern, The European Union : A Force for Peace in the World, Speech at University of Ulster, 4 March 2004. Recently, the EU declared that it "holds a shared responsibility to protect populations from genocide, war crimes, ethnic cleansing and crimes against humanity", J. Solana, Report on the Implementation of the European Security Strategy: Providing Security in a Changing World, Eu Doc. S407/08, 11 December 2008.

"to a different kind of international relations, in which civilian instruments are wielded on behalf of a collectivity which had renounced the use of force among its members and encouraged others to do the same".[89]

Instead of being a distinctive model, the EU acts more like a big state. The consequences of this development are debatable, of course. Nevertheless, a prediction informed by realist thinking would point towards a stronger emphasis on relative gains, military means, the "securitization" of various policy areas,[90] and a less favourable attitude towards the UN and international law. On a systemic level, the addition of another power pole to what still remains a unipolar system dominated by the United States, might increase frictions and balancing tendencies.[91] That is why proponents of a further strengthening of the EU's military dimension should heed *Martin Wright's* 1966 warning:

"Practical problems of international politics are often described in terms of building a bigger and better state – a European Union, without seeing that such an achievement would leave the problems of interstate politics precisely where they were."[92]

Bibliography

Ahern, B., The European Union: A Force for Peace in the World, Speech at University of Ulster, 4 March 2004.

Art, R. J., A Defensible Defense, in: International Security 15 (1991), pp. 5-53.

Bailes, A. J. K., The EU and a 'Better World': What Role for the European Security and Defence Policy?, in: International Affairs 84 (2008), pp. 115-130.

Bono, G., The Perils of Conceiving EU Foreign Policy as a "Civilizing Force" in: Internationale Politik und Gesellschaft 1 (2006), pp. 150-163.

Bretherton, C./J. Vogler, The European Union as a Global Actor (2006).

Burckhardt, C., Civilian Power Europe? The Nature of European Union Foreign Policy (2010).

Carr, E. H., The Twenty Years' Crisis, 1919-1939: An Introduction to the Study of International Relations (1964).

Dahrendorf, R., Class and Class Conflict in Industrial Society (1959).

Dobbins J./S. G. Jones/K. Crane/C. S. Chivvis/F. A. Radin/S. Larrabee/N.Bensahel/B. K. Stearns/B. W. Goldsmith, Europe's Role in Nation-building: From the Balkans to the Congo (2008).

Duchêne, F., The European Community and the Uncertainties of Interdependence, in: M. Kohnstamm/W. Hager (eds.), A Nation Writ Large? Foreign-Policy Problems before the European Community (1973), pp.1-21.

---

89   K. E. Smith, The Instruments of European Union Foreign Policy, in: EUI RSC Working Paper 97/68 (1997), p. 18.

90   Immigration policy and space policy are prime examples.

91   B. Posen, ESDP and the Structure of World Power, in: International Spectator 39 (2004).

92   M. Wight, Why is there no international relations theory?, in: H. Butterfield/M. Wight (eds.), Diplomatic Investigations (1966), p. 21.

Duchêne, F./J. Monnet, The First Statesman of Interdependence (1994), p. 405.

Farer, T. J., Humanitarian Intervention before and After 9/11: Legality and Legitimacy, in: J. L. Holzgrefe/R. O. Keohane (eds.), Humanitarian Intervention: Ethical, Legal, and Political Dilemmas (2003).

Ferrero-Waldner, B., Europa als globaler Akteur – Aktuelle Schwerpunkte Europäischer Außen- und Nachbarschaftspolitik, SPEECH/05/30 (accessed: 24 January 2005).

Galtung, J., The European Community: A Superpower in the Making (1973).

Garton Ash, T., Free World: Why a Crisis of the West Reveals the Opportunity of Our Time (2005).

Gegout, C., Causes and Consequences of the EU's Military Intervention in the Democratic Republic of Congo: A Realist Explanation, in: European Foreign Affairs Review 10 (2005),pp. 427-443.

Gilpin, R., War and Change in World Politics (1981).

Haine, J.-Y./B. Giegerich, Congo, a Cosmetic EU Operation, in: International Herald Tribune June 12 (2006).

Hill, C., European Foreign Policy: Power Bloc, Civilian Power, or Flop?, in: R. Rummel (ed.), The Evolution of an International Actor: Western Europe's New Assertiveness (1990), pp. 31-55.

Holzgrefe, J. L., The Humanitarian Intervention Debate, in R. O. Keohane/J. L. Holzgrefe (eds.), Humanitarian Intervention: Ethical, Legal, and Political Dilemmas (2003), pp.275-298.

Howorth, J., From Security to Defence: the Evolution of the CFSP, in: C. Hill/M. Smith (eds.), International Relations and the European Union (2005), pp. 179-204.

—   Security and Defence Policy in the European Union (2007).

Huo Y./L. E. Molina, Is Pluralism a Viable Model of Diversity? The Benefits and Limits of Subgroup Respect, in: Group Processes and Intergroup Relations 9 (2006), pp. 359-376.

International Crisis Group, Congo Crisis: Military Intervention in Ituri Africa, Report No 64, 13 June 2003.

International Institute for Strategic Studies, European Military Capabilities: Building Armed Forces for Modern Operations (2008).

Kirste, K., Rollentheorie und Außenpolitikanalyse. Die USA und Deutschland als Zivilmächte (1998).

Larsen, H., The Discourse on the EU's Role in the World, in: B. Hansen/B. Heurlin (eds.), The New World Order: Contrasting Theories (2000).

Linklater, A., A European Civilising Process?, in: C. Hill/M. Smith (eds.), International Relations and the European Union (2005), pp. 367-387.

Major, C., EU-UN cooperation in military crisis management: the experience of EUFOR RD Congo in 2006, in: EUISS Occasional Paper 72 (2008).

Maull, H. W., Germany and The Use of Force: Still a "Civilian Power"?, in: Survival 42 (2000), pp. 56-80.

Médecins sans Frontières, Ituri: Unkept Promises? A Pretence of Protection and Inadequate Assistance, Report, 25 July 2003.

Menon, A., Empowering Paradise? The ESDP at Ten, in: International Affairs 85 (2009), pp. 227-246.

Moravcsik, A./K. Nicolaïdis, How to Fix Europe's Image Problem, in: Foreign Policy 148 (2005).

Nicolaïdis K./R. Howse, 'This is my EU-topia': Narrative as Power, in: Journal of Common Market Studies 40 (2002), pp. 767-792.

Patten C., The Role of the European Union on the World Stage, Speech/01/23, 25 January 2001.

Posen, B. R./A. L. Ross, Competing Visions for US Grand Strategy, in: International Security 21 (1997), pp. 49-88.

Posen, B. R., ESDP and the Structure of World Power, in: International Spectator 39 (2004), pp. 5-17.

Prodi, R., A Stronger Foreign and Security Policy for Europe, SPEECH/02/465, 9 October 2002.

— The New Europe in the Transatlantic Partnership, SPEECH/01/204, 9 May 2001.

Reid, T. R., The United States of Europe: The Superpower Nobody Talks About - From the Euro to Eurovision (2005).

Schorlemer, S. von, Menschenrechte und „humanitäre Interventionen", in: Internationale Politik 55 (2000), pp. 41-47.

Sjursen, H., What kind of power?, in: Journal of European Public Policy 13 (2006), pp. 169-181.

Smith, K. E., The Instruments of European Union Foreign Policy, in: EUI RSC Working Paper 97/68 (1997).

Solana, J., European defence: the task ahead, European Voice, 24 October 2001.

— Europe Has the Will to Build a Common Foreign and Security Policy, in: European Affairs (2000), http://www.europeanaffairs.org/Spring-2000/europe-has-the-will-to-build-a-common-foreign-and-security-policy.html (accessed: 14 February 2010).

— Annual Speech at the European Union Institute for Security Studies, 2003.

— Annual Speech at the European Union Institute for Security Studies, S279/06, 6 October 2006.

— Address to the Conference of Defence Committee chairpersons of the 27 national parliaments, S139/07, 23 April 2007.

— Report on the Implementation of the European Security Strategy: Providing Security in a Changing World, S407/08, 11 December 2008.

Toje, A., The European as a Small Power, or Conceptualizing Europe's Strategic Actorness, in: European Integration 30 (2008).

— The Consensus Expectation Gap: Explaining Europe's Ineffective Foreign Policy, in: Security Dialogue 39 (2008), pp. 121-141.

Waltz, K. N., Theory of international politics (1979).

Welsh, J. M., Humanitarian intervention and International Relations (2004).

Wight, M., Why is there no International Relations Theory?, in: H. Butterfield/M. Wight (eds.), Diplomatic Investigations (1966), pp. 17-34.

Wolf, R., Respekt: Ein unterschätzter Faktor in den Internationalen Beziehungen, in: Zeitschrift für Internationale Beziehungen 15 (2008).

Wolfers, A., Discord and Collaboration: Essays on International Politics (1965).

Zielonka, J., Explaining Euro-paralysis: Why Europe is Unable to Act in International Politics (1998).

Global Risks: Identification, Assessment and Management

Kinka Gerke-Unger and Solveig Richter

Globalisation, the flow of information, goods, capital, and people across political and geographical borders has led to an unprecedented level of economic integration and interdependence. While this process had many beneficial effects such as increased global wealth, it also produced numerous undesired effects such as environmental degradation, resource scarcity, the uneven distribution of wealth or internal conflicts in failing states. Globalisation in short created global risks, i.e. effects that arise with a certain probability from an event and that harm or endanger the attainment of specific goals or the preservation of past achievements and that are felt without spatial or geographical limit. It is the ubiquity, the supra- or transnational character of these effects, the "border sublating dynamic of the danger" that turn a risk into a global risk as *Ulrich Beck* pointed out.[1] The fact that the effects of a certain event are felt worldwide and practically nobody can escape from them does not imply that the degree to which these effects are felt is evenly distributed, that people of different regions, different states, and different social classes are evenly affected by them. Global risks can threaten peace and security directly, as the food riots in Haiti 2008 or the violent demonstrations of farmers in Madagascar against the land grabbing by an international corporation 2009 clearly show. But they can also increase the probability of violent conflict or growing global injustice since the capacity of international actors to manage these risks diminishes.

This supra- or transnational character of global risks poses a challenge for traditional actors. The post-modern world is characterised by the loss of full control of a nation state and its people over its own affairs within its national territory. In order to address the problems created by the globalisation process, to steer it or at least mitigate its adverse effects, international regimes were established that facilitate the convergence of expectations, cooperation and joint decision-making in a given issue area. Subsequently, not only the global risks which these formal and informal institutions were supposed to address featured prominently in the academic debate but also the risks to the effectiveness and the maintenance of these organisations began to be considered as aggravating global risk. Apparently, the most effective actors in world politics – nation states and intergovernmental organisations – came under pressure to adapt their strategies and instruments. The UN's High-Level Panel on Threats, Challenges and Change concluded in 2004 that there is a real danger that the accomplishments of the United Nations to meet the international challenges will be reversed

---

1   U. Beck, Risikogesellschaft. Auf dem Weg in eine andere Moderne (1986), p. 7.

unless the world strengthens the UN to respond effectively to the full range of threats. In sum, this creates a complex situation with global risks increasing and the capacity of traditional actors to respond decreasing.

The three articles in this section analyse different types of risks associated with developments in three different policy fields (environment, economics, security). And all three authors approach their subject from a different theoretical angle. Neither of them explicitly designates its subject matter as global risk, begging the question, if their analytical object is indeed a global risk – as defined above – or what it is that makes it at least potentially one. They all touch different aspects of the analysis of global risks. *Jörn Richert* contributes to the debate with a focus on how processes of securitisation can transform a global ecological phenomenon into a risk and thus making it a security issue for policy makers. *Anke Dahrendorf* looks at global risks from a different angle. She focuses on the unintended side effects of globalised trade which may augment wealth but also harm the public health policy of developing countries. *Christian Burckhart* does not put an emphasis on the analysis of a global risk but asks what role international organisations, i.e. the EU, play. His assessment that the EU's foreign policy resembles more that of great power, is insofar surprising as one would expect the EU to increase its civilian capacity instead of military capacity to manage global risks.

Jörn Richert: Climate Change as a Global Risk Due to Securitisation?

Richert's contribution focuses on the issue of climate change and the effects that the "securitization" of the climate change discourse had on political decision-making in the US Senate on climate policy during President *George W. Bush's* term in office (2000-2008). By analysing the interaction between "security" understood not as an objective concept but a discourse, i.e. a context dependent, socially constructed, changing concept, and the notion of "climate change", he attempts to show how discursive changes result in changes in actual political decision-making. From a constructivist perspective, he starts out by critically discussing the neo-realistic notion of "security" and moves on to describe the process of "securitization". The latter entails attributing specific notions of threat to a referent object that imply the imperative for action. This imperative provides the sense of urgency necessary to justify taking measures in violation of rules that otherwise would bind. In that sense, security then becomes a semantic device that enables to connect means with ends. Before describing in more detail the effects of securitization of the climate policy debate in the US Senate, *Richert* reconstructs briefly how climate change was gradually constructed as a threat in the global debate on climate change. At the beginning, the immediate impact on the environment, on future generations, and distant people were at the centre of this debate. To the extent that the economic dimension of climate change (loss of gross national product (GDP), property values, spread of diseases, quality of life) and known sources of military conflict (resource wars, dislocation) came into view, climate change was increasingly perceived as a threat to the nation state, the national welfare and standard of living, and US supremacy. In the US Senate, this discursive change made it possible to garner increasing political support for political measures to stop climate change despite the stubborn denial of the *Bush* administration that climate change is taking place and its persistent opposition to a climate saving policy.

Richert concludes that the perception of climate change was the key driver of a change in US climate policy in the Senate. The article leaves the question unanswered if the securitization of climate change was prompted by the deliberate attempt of environmental groups to expand their political basis, or was necessitated by the political circumstances of an administration that was largely opposed to environment protection policy so that the continuation of that policy was only possible by re-labelling climate protection as "energy security" or "energy independence" and semantically linking it to its core political objectives and values. It also leaves open, what impact the discursive change at the global level had on the US domestic decision making process. An interaction that is of particular relevance it seems for global risks that require a global response. Finally, it would be worthwhile to analyse the consequences that the discursive change had or might have on the choice of policy instruments. The price for averting the risk of leaving an issue unaddressed until the damage caused is irreversible, might come at the risk of applying unsuitable, military means to the problem at hand.

Anke Dahrendorf: **Trade Agreements as a Global Risk for Public Health Policy?**

The second article by *Dahrendorf* has already executed the discursive change by asking if the global proliferation of bilateral and regional trade agreements that has taken place over the last ten years[2], is a threat to the World Trade Organization (WTO) and/or for developing countries. Contrary to what the title suggests, her focus is not on the general impact of bilateral and regional trade agreements on the effectiveness and reputation of the WTO and the multilateral trading system (MTS) and developing countries, but on the specific effects that bilateral and regional agreements on intellectual property rights have on public health policy. She concludes that they do not pose so much a risk to the WTO as an institution, as to the ability a specific group of WTO members

---

2   The concern over regional trade agreements (RTAs) dates much further back, however, to the creation of the European Economic Communities that prompted the quantitative increase of RTAs in the 1980s.

– developing countries – to independently decide on their public health policy. The "forum-shifting" strategy that particularly the USA and the European Union (EU) have cyclically used as a means to enhance their negotiating power vis-à-vis developing countries, has resulted in a significantly higher level of protection for intellectual property. The price that developing countries paid for this development is a reduction of their public policy space. In particular their ability to pursue a public health policy that serves the needs of the poorest of their population was significantly curtailed. Apart from making it very difficult or impossible to loosen patent protection through, for example, compulsory licenses, the secretiveness with which these negotiations were conducted and the fact that only selected, privileged business groups are allowed to participate in the negotiations calls into question their democratic legitimisation. To overcome the latter problem, *Dahrendorf* advocates raising public awareness in developing countries. While her analysis of the effects of enhanced patent protection through restrictions on compulsory licensing, extension of patent registration and protection of undisclosed information, is very detailed, she pays little or no attention to the institutional short-comings of the WTO that make "forum-shifting" an attractive strategy. When and why it is ever in the interest of the US and the EU to shift back to a multilateral organisation or forum, that mitigates power imbalances by enabling developing countries to form powerful coalitions regrettably is also not stated. Just as the treatment of developing countries as a homogenous group does not adequately describe the reality of the world trading system. Likewise, a discussion of why and when it is in the interest of particular actors in developing countries to agree to such agreements would have benefitted the analysis. Lastly, the threat described by her is a threat to the attainment of certain policy objectives by a certain group of countries that affect in particular certain sections of their population. What makes this deplorable fact a global threat requires further elaboration.

Christian Burckhart: Can the EU as Great Power Manage Global Risks?

After *Richert's* constructivist approach to the analysis of climate change politics, the actor-centred approach of *Dahrendorf* to international trade policy, *Burckhardt* tries to explain the recent surge of EU military operations "out of area" in Sub-Sahara Africa within the analytical framework of realism. More specifically, he tries to shed light on the motives behind the policy of the EU that claims to be a global player.

Indeed, since the European Security and Defence Policy (ESDP) emerged into the light of the day in 1999, the EU's role in preventing international conflicts and dealing with transnational risks and threats has grown steadily. The European Security Strategy (ESS) of 2003 emphasises the EU's "responsibility for global security and in building a better world." Along with terrorism and the proliferation of weapons of mass destruction the ESS lists regional conflicts, state failure and organised crime as key threats and calls for a more active EU engagement in addressing these threats by applying "the full spectrum of instruments", including military activities. For analysts and policy makers it is the prima facie evidence of the EU's changing identity. Traditionally, the focus of research was mainly on the EU's capacity for a common foreign and security and asked, if and how the EU can act coherently. Thus, keeping in mind the militarising process of the ESDP, it is more than necessary to critically reflect the EU's role as foreign policy actor.

In the academic debate the EU was for a long time mainly portrayed as a civilian power. The two global risks *Burckhardt* discusses are that of a civilian power turning into a great power that tries to defend and enhance its international position militarily and promote its objectives at the expense of others as well as the risk of damaging effective international cooperation through posturing.

As such a civilian power, *Burckhardt* posits, the EU should only pursue certain foreign policy objectives, such as enhancing of multilateral fora, promoting democracy, human rights, sustainable development, and good governance. It should furthermore be restrained to the use of political, economic, and cultural instruments of foreign policy. If it applies force, it should only do so in the form of UN-mandated peacekeeping missions. Otherwise it should rely on "soft power" and persuasion. Finally, its foreign policy process should be characterised as open and subject to civilian, democratic control. According to *Burckhardt*, few if any of these criteria apply to the ESDP and the military interventions in Africa, even though Brussels justifies them with purported humanitarian aims. Rather than resembling the foreign policy of a true civilian power, the EU meets the criteria of a "great power", *Burckhardt* argues. The key objective for its military interventions was not to prevent or mitigate widespread human suffering, as claimed, but its longing to gain international prestige and respect as a strategic international actor. The byzantine, highly complex, and secretive decision-making process of the ESDP also does not fit the ideal of an open democracy, just as the fact that it did not ask the UN to authorise its military missions. As additional prove that the EU is not a civilian but a "great power", he cites the EU's defence spending that is the second largest worldwide. And last not least, the choice of Africa as a location to take its first steps as military actor, was motivated by geopolitical and "spheres of interest" considerations, i.e. it chose to intervene in a region where it would not violate the spheres of interest of Russia and the US. His analysis, *Burckhardt* claims, revealed that the aims and instruments of the EU's policy are more akin to a greater power, while the decision-making process resembles more that of the civilian power type. The EU's yearning for international recognition as a serious military actor, make it potentially a risk for the UN as well as for itself, the people in Africa, and potentially the stability of the international system, since it would imply the return to an unstable multi-polar world. The ESDP, however, poses the most serious, albeit least tangible risk, since it might turn the EU fully into a great power, thus, proving that its decisions and motives are best explained by realism.

Burckhardt is, in his assessment of the EU as great power, not alone. His analysis fits well with a recent tendency in the scientific community to conceptualise the EU as more traditional, military actor in world politics. But it is apparent that such a paradigmatic change which ignores the normative power of the EU's foreign policy lacks explanatory power. The EU presents itself as a normative force and emphasises international law, democracy, human rights and multilateralism. The success of the EU's military mission in its near abroad cannot be understood without the linkage to its norm based enlargement and neighbourhood policy. Also in out-of-area missions, it might not always be in line with humanitarian civilian ideals, but sometimes military intervention might just be required in order to pacify a region enough to enable aid workers to do their job.

And to come full circle to our starting point, a more fundamental question arises: If *Burckhardt* is right in his analysis and the EU is becoming a great power based on military capacities, and if we keep in mind that these traditional concepts and instruments are not sufficient to address global risks, how can the EU keep the expectations of playing a global role in the medium- to long term? Is the EU following the wrong strategy to address the challenges of an interdependent world? Neither of the authors nor this comment has yet answers to these questions, so the floor is open for more academic and policy oriented research.

B. Normative Reflections to Enhance Existing Modes of Governance

The Relevance of the 1951 Refugee Convention for the Protection of Individuals Forced to Flee Armed Conflicts

Vanessa Holzer

I. Introduction

There are about ten million refugees worldwide.[1] The 1951 Convention relating to the Status of Refugees[2] – the Refugee Convention – is the only universal treaty for the protection of refugees. Article 1A(2) of the Refugee Convention defines a refugee as a person

> "who owing to a well-founded fear of being persecuted for reasons of race, religion, nationality, membership of a particular social group or political opinion is outside the country of his nationality and is unable or, owing to such fear, is unwilling to avail himself of the protection of that country (…)".

Armed conflicts are the primary reason why people feel compelled to leave their state of origin. The prevailing understanding has long been that the Refugee Convention does not protect "mere" victims of armed conflict since they were subjected to general, indiscriminate violence and were not targeted for one of the Convention grounds.[3] This stands in stark contrast to the experiences of many displaced people during recent armed conflicts. These experiences often resemble the requirements in the refugee definition. Numerous current internal armed conflicts are at least in part motivated by ethnic or religious concerns. Frequently, forced displacement has become an objective rather than a mere consequence of hostilities, as the practice of "ethnic cleansing" in the former Yugoslavia illustrates.[4] Sexual violence against women has been employed as a calculated method of warfare in various armed conflicts such as those in Bosnia

---

1   See United Nations High Commissioner for Refugees (UNHCR), Statistical Yearbook 2007, http://www.unhcr.org/cgi-bin/texis/vtx/home/opendoc.pdf?id=4981c4812&tbl=S TATISTICS (This internet source and the following ones: 22 June 2009). The author thanks Dr. Freya Baetens and PD Dr. Hans-Joachim Heintze for helpful comments on an earlier draft of this chapter.

2   189 UNTS 137, as adopted on 25 July 1951 and as amended by the 1967 Protocol Relating to the Status of Refugees, 606 UNTS 267.

3   See W. Kälin, Flight in Times of War, in: International Review of the Red Cross 843 (2001), p. 629 and p. 642.

4   See R. Lubbers, Foreword by the High Commissioner for Refugees, in: International Review of the Red Cross 843 (2001), p. 578.

and Herzegovina, Liberia, and Sierra Leone.[5] Often, these atrocities are not
arbitrary acts of violence but constitute a calculated endeavour to dehumanize
and destroy entire communities.[6] Thus, while the mere fact of having fled
from an armed conflict in itself is not enough to qualify as a refugee under
the Refugee Convention, a person's well-founded fear of persecution may
nonetheless arise out of experiences during armed conflict. Nevertheless, these
persons often face serious obstacles in obtaining protection under the Refugee
Convention.[7] This article analyses how international law protects persons
compelled to leave their state of origin because of armed conflicts. The aim is
to critically assess the relevance of the Refugee Convention for their protection.
Hence, the focus is on individuals who are outside their state of origin rather
than on internally displaced persons. It is suggested that despite the existence
of several international legal instruments for the protection of persons who had
to flee their home countries due to armed conflict, the Refugee Convention
remains of pivotal importance for their protection. In the context of armed
conflict, the refugee definition must be interpreted in the light of human rights
law and international humanitarian law so as to adequately account for the
international legal framework in which such claims are embedded. The second
part of this chapter analyses the extent to which protection under international
legal instruments other than the Refugee Convention is available in situations of
armed conflict. The refugee definition is scrutinized in the third part in order to
determine its meaning and scope in armed conflicts. The fourth part addresses
concerns about "opening the floodgates" to large groups of people in situations
of armed conflict before a final conclusion is drawn in the fifth part.

II. Protection Based on International Legal Instruments Other Than the Refugee Convention

Apart from the Refugee Convention, there are different international legal
instruments at the global and regional level for the protection of individuals
compelled to leave their state of origin because of armed conflicts. This part
analyses whether these instruments render the Refugee Convention redundant as
a basis for the protection of these persons under international law. The focus is
therefore on the scope *ratione personae* of these instruments. Where necessary,
their scope *ratione materiae* is also compared to the Refugee Convention.

---

5   See Report of the Secretary General on the Protection of Civilians in Armed Conflict
     of 28 October 2007, UN Doc. S/2007/643 of 28 October 2007, pp. 46 f.
6   See ibid, p. 45.
7   See J. Fitzpatrick, Human Rights and Forced Displacement: Converging Standards, in:
     A. F. Bayefski/J. Fitzpatrick (eds.), Human Rights and Forced Displacement (2000),
     p. 5.

1. Expanded Refugee Definitions

At the regional level, expanded refugee definitions have been adopted. Article I(2) of the 1969 Organization of African Unity Convention on the Specific Aspects of Refugee Problems in Africa[8] (OAU Convention) broadens the Refugee Convention's refugee definition by stating that

> "[t]he term 'refugee' shall also apply to every person who, owing to external aggression, occupation, foreign domination or events seriously disturbing public order in either part or the whole of his country of origin or nationality, is compelled to leave his place of habitual residence in order to seek refuge in another place outside his country of origin or nationality".

This provision recognises that persons who fled their state of origin due to events of a more general nature may be in need of international protection. The expanded refugee definition has gained particular relevance in the context of armed conflicts throughout the African continent. In the Latin American region, the 1984 Cartagena Declaration on Refugees[9] includes a similarly broad refugee definition and refers more overtly to flight prompted by armed conflicts.[10] This legally non-binding declaration "represents endorsement by the States concerned of appropriate and applicable standards of protection and assistance"[11]. The legally non-binding 1966 Bangkok Principles on Status and Treatment of Refugees as adopted in 2001 by the Asian-African Legal Consultative Organization should also be mentioned here. They include an expanded refugee definition which is very similar to the OAU definition.[12] In contrast to the OAU Convention and the Cartagena Declaration, the Bangkok Principles have hardly had an apparent impact on state practice with regard to refugees.[13]

Thus, expanded refugee definitions are only relevant at the African and Latin American level. The Cartagena Declaration as such is not legally binding and the OAU Convention expressly acknowledges that it is a complement to the universal Refugee Convention.[14] Therefore, these instruments do not render the

---

8   1001 UNTS 45.
9   Organization of American States (OAS), OAS/Ser.L/V/II.66, Doc. 10, Rev. 1, pp. 109-193.
10   See para. 3 of the Cartagena Declaration.
11   G. S. Goodwin-Gill/J. McAdam, The Refugee in International Law (2007), p. 38; see also I. C. Jackson, The Refugee Concept in Group Situations (1999), pp. 405-414.
12   Article I(2) of the Bangkok Principles. The Bangkok Principles were adopted at the 40th session of the AALCO in New Delhi (Res. 40/3 of 24 June 2001, www.aalco.int).
13   See S. E. Davies, The Asian Rejection? International Refugee Law in Asia, in: Australian Journal of Politics and History 52 (2006), p. 564.
14   See preamble of the OAU Convention (ninth and tenth recital) and Article VIII(2) of the OAU Convention which stress the OAU Convention's complementarity regarding the Refugee Convention.

Refugee Convention irrelevant for the protection of persons who had to leave their state of origin because of armed conflicts.

2.   Protection from *Refoulement*

Rejected asylum seekers whom the receiving state wants to send back to a state where an armed conflict is taking place may be protected from *refoulement* under international human rights law. *Non-refoulement* is the central element of complementary protection in international law, i.e. protection granted to individuals on the basis of a legal obligation other than the Refugee Convention.[15] The prohibition of *refoulement* is expressly entailed in Article 3 of the 1984 Convention against Torture and other Cruel, Inhuman or Degrading Treatment or Punishment[16] (CAT). It is also implied in the prohibitions of torture, inhuman or degrading treatment or punishment in Article 7 of the 1966 International Covenant on Civil and Political Rights[17] (ICCPR) and Article 3 of the European Convention for the Protection of Human Rights and Fundamental Freedoms[18] (ECHR). While all three articles are potentially relevant to the protection of aliens who face expulsion to a state with an ongoing armed conflict, the following section analyses Article 3 ECHR because particularly elaborate jurisprudence exists regarding this provision.

Although the European Court of Human Rights (ECtHR) has repeatedly stated that the ECHR does not include a right to asylum, several rejected asylum-seekers have been granted protection from *refoulement* under Article 3 ECHR.[19] In its jurisprudence, the ECtHR has developed the prohibition of *refoulement* under Article 3 ECHR. According to the Court, where there are substantial grounds to believe that an alien would be at real risk of being subjected to treatment proscribed by Article 3 ECHR, a state party to the ECHR must not send the person back to the state in question. The existence of an armed conflict alone will hardly be enough for the applicability of Article 3

---

15   See J. McAdam, Complementary Protection in International Refugee Law (2007), pp. 2 f. and p.23. *Refoulement* is also prohibited under customary international law. This prohibition is a rule of *jus cogens*. See E. Lauterpacht/D. Bethlehem, The Scope and Content of the Principle of *Non-Refoulement*: Opinion, in: E. Feller/V. Türk/F. Nicholson (eds.), Refugee Protection in International Law. UNHCR's Global Consultations on International Protection (2003), p. 140 and pp. 150-155.

16   1465 UNTS 85.

17   999 UNTS 171.

18   213 UNTS 222.

19   See for example *Vilvarajah and Others v. the United Kingdom*, Application Nos. 13163/87, 13164/87, 13165/87, Judgement of 30 October 1991, para. 102; *Ahmed v. Austria*, Application No. 33449/96, Judgement of 27 November 1996, para. 38.

ECHR in such cases. The risk of ill-treatment must be personal.[20] The ECtHR stipulated in *Vilvarajah and others v. the Netherlands* that a "mere possibility of ill-treatment" is not in itself sufficient to give rise to a breach of Article 3 ECHR.[21] In this case, the applicants were Sri Lankan Tamils from an area of Sri Lanka where despite the general improvement of the situation in Sri Lanka, "there was a persistent threat of violence and a risk that civilians might become caught up in the fighting"[22]. The ECtHR suggested that the applicants would have to be more at risk than other members of the minority to which they belonged, e.g. because they exhibit special distinguishing features.[23] There is considerable tension between this reasoning and the absolute nature of the prohibition in Article 3. After all, it does not make the applicants' plight upon return more tolerable if other persons in Sri Lanka are subjected to comparable ill-treatment.[24] In its judgement in *Salah Sheek v. the Netherlands*, the ECtHR signalled a departure from *Vilvarajah*, although it based its reasoning on the facts of the case. In *Salah Sheek*, the Court reiterated that the mere possibility of ill-treatment does not suffice to give rise to a violation of Article 3. Yet the ECtHR also stated that

"[i]t might render the protection offered by that provision illusory if, in addition to the fact of his belonging to the [minority group] (...), the applicant were required to show the existence of further special distinguishing features".[25]

The ECtHR emphasised in its subsequent judgement in *N.A. v. the United Kingdom* that it

"has never excluded the possibility that a general situation of violence in a country of destination will be of a sufficient level of intensity as to entail that any removal to it would necessarily breach Article 3 of the Convention".[26]

The Court stressed, however, that this would only be the case in the most extreme cases of general violence in which there is a real risk of ill-treatment simply by virtue of the individual's presence in the area in question.[27] This finding indicates that in situations in which the intensity of general violence

20   See N. Mole, Asylum and the European Convention on Human Rights (2007), pp. 30-33.
21   See *Vilvarajah and Others v. the United Kingdom*, para. 111.
22   *Vilvarajah and Others v. the United Kingdom*, para. 109.
23   See ibid., para. 112. The same approach was adopted in the judgement in *Muslim v. Turkey* of 26 April 2005 (Application No. 53566/99) with regard to returns to Iraq.
24   See Mole, Asylum (2007), p. 33.
25   *Salah Sheekh v. The Netherlands*, Application No. 1984/04, Judgement of 11 January 2007, para. 149.
26   *N.A. v. the United Kingdom*, Application No. 25904/07, Judgement of 17 July 2008, para. 115.
27   See *N.A. v. the United Kingdom*, para. 115.

prevailing in the state of destination reaches very high levels, there is no need to examine the personal circumstances of the applicant. Simply by being in the state in question, there would be a real risk that the applicant experiences the ill-treatment subscribed by Article 3 ECHR. Such situations are, however, exceptional. General violence in the state of destination is normally not enough for a violation of Article 3 in case of expulsion. In situations with low levels of general violence, the personal circumstances of the applicants, for instance their membership of a group systematically subjected to ill-treatment or other distinguishing features, must be considered. It remains unclear how the intensity of the general violence in the state of destination must be assessed.

The ECHR thus potentially protects certain persons against *refoulement* to a state with an ongoing armed conflict, provided the criteria stipulated in the ECtHR's case law are met. But the ECHR, as well as the ICCPR and the CAT, remain silent regarding the domestic legal status of the beneficiaries and the corresponding rights. Consequently, their legal statuses vary significantly in the different domestic legal systems.[28] The vast majority of the states with codified complementary protection systems provide beneficiaries with fewer entitlements than granted to refugees.[29] Thus, protection from *refoulement* under the ECHR does not make the Refugee Convention irrelevant for persons who escaped from armed conflicts. The same is true for protection from *refoulement* under the ICCPR and the CAT. Regarding these treaties, it must be noted in addition that their respective treaty bodies cannot issue binding views on the communications which they receive.

3. Subsidiary Protection

Within the European Union (EU), a specific system for complementary protection, here referred to as subsidiary protection, was introduced by the 2004 Council Directive 2004/83/EC on 28 April 2004, the so-called Qualification Directive.[30] For the first time at the European level, a legally binding supranational instrument was adopted that establishes criteria which individuals must fulfil in order to qualify as refugees or as persons otherwise in need of

---

28 See McAdam, Complementary Protection (2007), pp. 2 f. and pp. 54 f.
29 See Goodwin-Gill/McAdam, The Refugee in International Law (2007), p. 332. When comparing to rights that attach to refugee status under the Refugee Convention and the rights that beneficiaries of other forms of protection enjoy, the structure of the entitlements under the Refugee Convention must be taken into account: While all refugees are granted certain basic rights, other rights depend on the nature and duration of the attachment to the host country. See J. C. Hathaway, The Rights of Refugees Under International Law (2005), p. 154.
30 For the legal basis and background of the Qualification Directive, see P. Piotrowicz/C. van Eck, Subsidiary Protection and Primary Rights, in: International and Comparative Law Quarterly 53 (2004), p. 109.

international protection and which sets out the rights attached to their respective status.[31] A person eligible for subsidiary protection is defined in Article 2(e) of the Qualification Directive as

> "a third country national (...) who does not qualify as a refugee but in respect of whom substantial grounds have been shown for believing that the person concerned, if returned to his or her country of origin (...), would have a real risk of suffering serious harm as defined in Article 15 (...) and is unable, or, owing to such risk, unwilling to avail himself or herself of the protection of that country".

Article 15 of the Qualification Directive defines serious harm as:

> "(a) death penalty or execution; or (b) torture or inhuman or degrading treatment or punishment of an applicant in the country of origin; or (c) serious and individual threat to a civilian's life or person by reason of indiscriminate violence in situations of international or internal armed conflict".

Articles 15(a) and (b) have their roots in ECHR provisions.[32] Article 15(c) reflects the consistent, but varied European state practice of granting some form of complementary protection to persons fleeing indiscriminate effects of armed conflicts or generalized violence without a specific link to Convention grounds.[33] The definition of "serious harm" in Article 15(c) is ambiguous because the requirement that the threat be "individual" is difficult to reconcile with the fact that it must arise by reason of "indiscriminate" violence in situations of armed conflict. After all, indiscriminate violence is generally understood to mean "the exercise of force not targeted at a specific object or individual"[34]. Therefore, the requirement that the threat be individual cannot reasonably signify that a person must be singled out in the context of indiscriminate violence.[35] If Article 15(c) is to have an independent value next to Articles (a) and (b), it must provide protection from serious risks that are not individually targeted

---

31   See M.-T. Gil-Bazo, Refugee Status, Subsidiary Protection, and the Right to be Granted Asylum under EC Law, New Issues in Refugee Research. Research Paper No. 136 (2006), http://www.unhcr.org/research/RESEARCH/455993882.pdf, pp. 1 f.

32   The legal basis for Article 15(a) Qualification Directive is Protocol No. 6 to the ECHR which prohibits the imposition of the death penalty in peacetime. Article 15(b) is based on the prohibition of *refoulement* implied in Article 3 ECHR and the corresponding jurisprudence of the ECtHR. See Piotrowicz/van Eck, Subsidiary Protection (2004), p. 109.

33   See Goodwin-Gill/McAdam, The Refugee in International Law (2007), pp. 326 f.

34   UNHCR, Statement on Subsidiary Protection Under the EC Qualification Directive for People Threatened by Indiscriminate Violence (2008), www.unhcr.org/cgi-bin/texis/vtx/refworld/rwmain?docid=479df7472&page=search, p. 3.

35   See Recital 26 of the Directive's Preamble; see also McAdam, Complementary Protection (2007), p. 72.

but situational.[36] In its judgement of 17 February 2009, the European Court of Justice (ECJ) tried to resolve these ambiguities. The ECJ clarified that for the existence of a serious and individual threat to the applicant's life or person, they must not necessarily show that they are specifically targeted because of their personal circumstances. According to the ECJ, a threat may also be individual in exceptional situations in which the degree of indiscriminate violence is so high that there are substantial grounds to believe that the person, upon return to the respective state, would face a substantial risk of being subjected to this risk by virtue of their mere presence in this state.[37] The Court continued that the more the applicant is specifically affected because of their personal circumstances, the lower the level of indiscriminate violence necessary for them to qualify for subsidiary protection.[38] Article 15(c) of the Qualification Directive hence seems to cover threats arising from armed conflicts characterised by a very high level of generalized violence in which virtually anyone is at risk of serious harm. Conversely, a relatively minor degree of violence may also suffice if the applicant proves that they are personally targeted. It remains to be seen how these factors are to be balanced and in which way this understanding of Article 15(c) of the Qualification Directive differs from protection *non-refoulement* under Article 3 ECHR on which Article 15(b) of the Qualification Directive is based.

Article 17 of the Qualification Directive in essence incorporates the Refugee Convention's exclusion clause in Article 1F. Moreover, Article 17(1)(c) of the Qualification Directive stipulates that persons who constitute a danger to the community or the security of the Member State in question are not eligible for subsidiary protection. This provision apparently draws from Article 33(2) of the Refugee Convention. The absolute prohibition of *refoulement* in Article 3 ECHR, on which Article 15(b) of the Qualification Directive is based, does not include any exception. By allowing such exceptions, the Qualification Directive may create protection gaps.

Under the Qualification Directive, the status of beneficiaries of subsidiary protection is formalized and certain rights are granted to them. In many fields such as the family circle, residence permits, access to employment, health care and integration facilities, the entitlements are less extensive than under the Refugee Convention.[39] The Refugee Convention therefore remains pertinent as a legal basis for the protection of persons who had to leave their home country because of armed conflicts.

---

36   See UNHCR, Statement on Subsidiary Protection Under the EC Qualification Directive for People Threatened by Indiscriminate Violence (2008), p. 6.
37   ECJ, 17 February 2009, C-465/07, *Elgafaji v. Staatssecretaris van Justitie*, para. 43.
38   Ibid., para. 39.
39   See H. Battjes, European Asylum Law and International Law (2006), pp. 490-493.

4. Temporary Protection

Persons forced to flee from armed conflict in their state of origin may also benefit from temporary protection. Temporary protection is, as the term implies, limited in time and constitutes a pragmatic, exceptional mechanism. It is designed for situations of mass influxes of displaced persons which threaten to overwhelm the asylum system of the receiving state. With its origins in the *ad hoc* responses to mass population flows in Southeast Asia in the 1970-80s,

> "[t]he contemporary international law understanding of 'temporary protection' is based predominantly on European practice, and describes the exceptional, time-bound response of granting protection to a mass influx of asylum seekers fleeing armed conflict, endemic violence, or a serious risk of systematic or generalized violations of human rights".[40]

At the European level, temporary protection was formally established by the so-called Temporary Protection Directive in 2001.[41] In Article 2(c)(i) of this Directive, "persons who have fled areas of armed conflict or endemic violence" are expressly mentioned as a group of displaced persons that may benefit from temporary protection.

This form of protection is important because even if the refugee definition is interpreted broadly, many people escaping armed conflicts will not fulfil its criteria.[42] The Temporary Protection Directive envisages temporary protection as an interim measure prior to the beneficiaries either being recognized as refugees, receiving subsidiary protection, or returning home. While the content of temporary protection is in many respects close to the Refugee Convention, the Temporary Protection Directive does not confirm that its beneficiaries are entitled to all benefits which the Refugee Convention grants to unrecognised refugees.[43] Moreover, temporary protection is generally only available in

---

40 Goodwin-Gill/McAdam, The Refugee in International Law (2007), p. 340. For a detailed account of the evolution of temporary protection at the international and European level, see U. Davy, Temporary Protection: Neue Konzepte der EU-Flüchtlingspolitik und ihr Verhältnis zur Gewährung von Asyl, in: H. Tretter (ed.), Temporary Protection für Flüchtlinge in Europa. Analysen und Schlussfolgerungen (2005), pp. 17-89.

41 Council Directive 2001/55/EC of 20 July 2001 on Minimum Standards for Giving Temporary Protection in the Event of a Mass Influx of Displaced Persons and on Measures Promoting a Balance of Efforts between Member States in Receiving such Persons and Bearing the Consequences thereof. Temporary Protection Pursuant to this Directive has not been activated yet.

42 See W. Kälin, Temporary Protection in the EC: Refugee Law, Human Rights and the Temptations of Pragmatism, in: German Yearbook of International Law 44 (2001), p. 215.

43 See Battjes, European Asylum Law (2006), p. 512.

situations of large-scale influx. It complements the Refugee Convention, but cannot replace the latter as a protection instrument for persons who escaped from armed conflicts.

III.   The Refugee Definition in Article 1A(2) of the Refugee Convention

It has been shown that the existence of other international legal instruments does not render the Refugee Convention obsolete for the protection of persons who had to leave their state of origin due to armed conflict. But "[t]oo often, the existence of civil conflict is perceived by decision-makers as giving rise to situations of general insecurity that somehow exclude the possibility of persecution".[44] Even the Handbook on Refugee Status Determination of the United Nations High Commissioner for Refugees (UNHCR) mistakably reiterates that persons who had to leave their state of origin because of an armed conflict are normally not considered to fall within the refugee definition.[45] Indeed, claims for refugee status arising out of experiences during armed conflict raise particular difficulties with regard to the interpretation of the refugee definition in Article 1A(2) of the Refugee Convention. The most essential of these difficulties are analysed in the following sections which, notwithstanding the need for further inquiry into these difficulties, suggest entry points for potential solutions.

1.   The Interpretation of Persecution in Times of Armed Conflict

Persecution is the key element of the refugee definition. Assessing its meaning and scope is particularly difficult when it comes to claims for refugee status based on experiences during armed conflicts since typically, many people try to escape from serious harm in such situations. How, then, should persecution be assessed in the context of armed conflicts?

In pursuing this question, it is important to differentiate between international and non-international armed conflicts. States have the to right resort to self-defence in accordance with Article 51 of the United Nations Charter[46]. In respect of international armed conflicts, it has been argued that a victim of a

---

44   Goodwin-Gill/McAdam, The Refugee in International Law (2007), p. 126.

45   See UNHCR, Handbook on Procedures and Criteria for Determining Refugee Status under the 1951 Convention and the 1967 Protocol relating to the Status of Refugees (1992), www.unhcr.org/publ/PUBL/3d58e13b4.pdf, para. 164.

46   1 UNTS XVI. In its Advisory Opinion on the Legality or Use of Nuclear Weapons, the International Court of Justice (ICJ) stressed "the fundamental right of every State to survival, and thus its right to resort to self-defence". See ICJ, Advisory Opinion on the Legality or Use of Nuclear Weapons, [1996] ICJ Reports 226, at p. 263, para. 96. See also Y. Dinstein, War, Aggression and Self Defence (2005), p. 175.

government's military operations is not persecuted even if he or she has been personally targeted because the state is merely exercising its legitimate right of self-defence.[47] While this understanding can be seen as a consequence of state sovereignty, it is nonetheless problematic because it is tantamount to a blank cheque for states involved in an armed conflict. The rights of states parties to an international armed conflict to engage in military activities are not unfettered. They must be exercised in accordance with the applicable bodies of international law such as international human rights law (IHRL) and international humanitarian law (IHL). It must be kept in mind that IHL and IHRL deal with the methods adopted for exercising these rights, not with the right to use force as such. Once an international armed conflict begins, the applicability of IHL is independent from the question of the legality of the use of force, which is a matter of the *jus ad bellum*.[48] IHL constitutes the principal, but not exclusive international legal framework for assessing the legality of the actions of a party to an armed conflict *vis-à-vis* civilians and other protected persons.

In non-international armed conflicts, the exercise of states' right to maintain public order and to fend off non-state actors' violence is also limited by IHL and IHRL. Mere reference to the exercise of this right does not suffice to repel allegations of persecution. The rules of IHL applicable in non-international armed conflicts, which can mainly be found in Common Article 3 to the Geneva Conventions[49] and the 1977 Protocol II Additional to the Geneva Conventions of 12 August 1949[50] (APII), are less elaborate than those applicable in international armed conflicts. International humanitarian treaty law contains different thresholds of applicability.[51] Even in situations not covered by the existing norms, however, elementary considerations of humanity must be respected in all circumstances.[52]

47	See Kälin, Flight in Times of War (2001), p. 643, who refers to this criticism but does not share it.

48	See C. Greenwood, Historical Development and Legal Analysis, in: D. Fleck (ed.), The Handbook of International Humanitarian Law (2008), p. 1.

49	Geneva Convention I for the Amelioration of the Condition of the Wounded and Sick in Armed Forced in the Field (75 UNTS 31), Geneva Convention II for the Amelioration of the Condition of the Wounded, Sick and Shipwrecked Members of Armed Forces at Sea (75 UNTS 85), Geneva Convention III Relative to the Treatment of Prisoners of War (75 UNTS 135), Geneva Convention IV Relative to the Protection of Civilian Persons in Time of War (75 UNTS 287), all adopted on 12 August 1949.

50	1977 Protocol II Additional to the Geneva Conventions of 12 August 1949, and Relating to the Protection of Victims of Non-International Armed Conflicts (APII), 1125 UNTS 609.

51	Common Article 3 of the Geneva Conventions has a lower threshold of applicability than the APII.

52	The origin of this rule lies in the so-called Martens Clause. See D. Fleck, The Law of Non-International Armed Conflicts, in D. Fleck (ed.), The Handbook of International Humanitarian Law (2008), pp. 608 and 619 f.

The drafters of the Refugee Convention consciously left persecution undefined because they deemed it impossible to list in advance all potential future ill-treatments that would amount to persecution.[53] According to a widely accepted understanding of persecution in international law, the latter means

> "the sustained or systemic failure of state protection in relation to one of the core entitlements which has been recognized by the international community"[54].

To determine these core entitlements, IHRL is normally used because of the close affinity between this body of law and the Refugee Convention. In times of armed conflict, be it of an international or non-international character, these core entitlements should also be conceived in terms of the applicable IHL norms.[55] The relationship between IHL and IHRL is very complex and cannot be explored here comprehensively. Suffice it to make the following remarks: A case in point for the use of both IHL and IHRL in refugee status determination is the right to life. A state's failure to ensure that an individual is not unlawfully deprived of his or her right to life is under any circumstances tantamount to persecution. In situations of armed conflict in which killing is lawful under certain conditions, it is IHL which determines whether an unlawful deprivation of life has occurred.[56] Moreover, IHRL generally aims at societies during peacetime whereas IHL addresses the abnormal situations created by armed conflicts and more specifically tackles the latter's realities. In contrast to IHRL, most IHL provisions are non-derogable.[57] Thus, regarding claims for refugee status arising out of armed conflicts, the sole recourse to IHRL in interpreting the notion of persecution does not adequately reflect the international legal framework in which the feared harm is situated. IHL norms must be additionally taken into account.

---

53   See Hathaway, Law of Refugee Status (1991), p. 108.
54   Ibid., p. 112.
55   In its Advisory Opinion on the Legal Consequences of the Construction of a Wall in the Occupied Palestinian Territories stressed that some rights are exclusively matters of IHRL, other rights are exclusively matters of IHL, and a third category of rights are matters of both bodies of international law. See ICJ, Advisory Opinion on the Legal Consequences of the Construction of a Wall in the Occupied Palestinian Territories, [2004] ICJ Reports 136, at p. 178, para. 106.
56   See ICJ, Advisory Opinion on the Legality or Use of Nuclear Weapons (1996), p. 240, para. 25.
57   See H. Storey/R. Wallace, War and Peace in Refugee Law Jurisprudence, in: American Journal of International Law 95 (2001), pp. 356-359.

While an interpretation of the refugee definition which draws upon IHRL and IHL has frequently been proposed,[58] its accordance with the rules on treaty interpretation, notably Articles 31 and 32 of the 1969 Vienna Convention on the Law of Treaties[59] (VCLT), has been scarcely scrutinized. Nothing in the wording of the refugee definition precludes its application to a person whose wellfounded fear of persecution is related to an armed conflict. The interpretation of the refugee definition in light of IHRL corresponds to the Convention's human rights-inspired object and purpose.[60] Notwithstanding the differences between IHL and IHRL, as well as the Refugee Convention, all aim at safeguarding individuals from serious threats to their physical and psychological integrity.[61] There is some overlap between IHRL and IHL, e.g. the prohibition of torture, inhuman or degrading treatment or punishment. Although IHRL and IHL share some objectives and exhibit similar provisions, they can also come into conflict. For the purpose of interpreting the refugee definition, the two bodies of law should not be brought into accordance through the use of the *lex specialis* maxim. This would lead to derogation by priority. Instead, the goal should be mutual reinforcement on a case-by-case basis.[62] Acknowledging the relevance of IHL for refugee status determination is not tantamount to saying that IHL must necessarily be applied to every single refugee applicant from a country where an armed conflict is occurring. Some applicants may well succeed in showing a well-founded fear of persecution in the context of an armed conflict based on human rights violations.[63]

Furthermore, the terms of the refugee definition must be interpreted in their context which can consist of "any subsequent agreement between the parties

---

58   See for example Immigration and Refugee Board of Canada, Civilian Non-Combatants Fearing Persecution in Civil War Situations. Guidelines Issued by the Chairperson Pursuant to Section 65(3) of the Immigration Act (1996), pp. 2 f.; M. v. Sternberg, The Grounds of Refugee Protection in the Context of International Human Rights and Humanitarian Law. Canadian and United States Case Law Compared (2002), p. 116; Kälin, Flight in Times of War (2001), pp. 629-650; Fitzpatrick, Human Rights and Forced Displacement (2002), pp. 3-25; S. Jaquemet, The Cross-Fertilization of International Humanitarian Law and International Refugee Law, in: International Review of the Red Cross 83 (2001), pp. 651-674.

59   1155 UNTS 331. The VCLT was adopted after the Refugee Convention, but its provisions are widely accepted as customary international law and hence are pertinent to the Refugee Convention. For an assessment of the most adequate approach to the interpretation of the Refugee Convention, see Hathaway, The Rights of Refugees (2005), pp. 48-74.

60   See Foster, International Refugee Law (2007), pp. 41-49.

61   See Sternberg, The Grounds of Refugee Protection (2002), p. 318.

62   See R. Kolb, Human Rights and Humanitarian Law, in R. Wolfrum (ed.), Max Planck Encyclopedia of Public International Law (2009), para. 44.

63   See Storey/Wallace, War and Peace (2001), p. 359.

regarding the interpretation of the treaty or the application of its provisions"[64]. The Conclusions on International Protection issued by the UNHCR Executive Committee can arguably be considered as evidencing subsequent agreement between the parties to the Refugee Convention on the meaning of the refugee definition.[65] In 2003, the Executive Committee stressed that

> "[i]f someone is forced to flee armed conflict in their country because of human rights violations and breaches of humanitarian law, these factors will be part of what determines that person's refugee status".[66]

Pursuant to Article 31(3)(b) VCLT, subsequent state practice should also be taken into account in interpreting the refugee definition. While there are some states which grant refugee protection to certain victims of armed conflict, there are also many others which exclude experiences during armed conflict from the purview of Article 1A(2) of the Refugee Convention.[67] Reliance on inconsistent state practice to interpret the duties of all parties to a treaty is problematic. Moreover, it must be recalled that the Refugee Convention serves human rights purposes. International human rights treaties constitute special international treaties insofar as they are specifically designed to limit state conduct for the benefit of human beings. This purpose would essentially be obstructed if the obligations which states parties undertook in ratifying the treaty would be determined by precisely those state practices which were sought to be restricted in the first place.[68]

The Convention's *travaux préparatoires*, which are supplementary means of interpretation pursuant to Article 32 VCLT, illustrate that although the Refugee Convention was originally envisaged as a response to victims of war, the drafters' intention was not to grant refugee status to all those displaced by

---

64   Article 31(3)(a) of the VCLT.
65   It must be acknowledged that not all states parties to the Refugee Convention are members of the Executive Committee at one point of time, nor are all members of the Executive Committee parties to the Convention or its Protocol. The Notes on International Protection by the Executive Committee are hence imperfect portraits of subsequent agreements between parties. Nevertheless, Hathaway correctly concludes that "it is difficult to imagine in practical terms how subsequent agreement among 145 states parties to the Refugee Convention could more fairly be generated". Hathaway, The Rights of Refugees (2005), pp. 54 f.
66   UNHCR Executive Committee, Note on International Protection, UN Doc. A/AC.96/975 of 2 July 2004, p. 53.
67   See Fitzpatrick, Human Rights and Forced Displacement (2000), p. 5. For a detailed assessment of the impact of the Directive's subsidiary protection regime, consult European Council on Refugees and Exiles, The Impact of the EU Qualification Directive on International Protection (2008), www.ecre.org/files/ECRE_QD_study_full.pdf.
68   See Hathaway, The Rights of Refugees (2005), pp. 68-73.

armed conflicts.[69] This desire resulted in the limitation of the Convention's scope *ratione personae* in Article 1. An interpretation of the refugee definition in light of IHRL and IHL is in accordance with this tenet of the *travaux* since not all violations of IHL will amount to persecution just as not all infringements of IHRL are tantamount to persecution.

In sum, an interpretation of the refugee definition that draws upon IHRL and IHL is in accordance with the rules on treaty interpretation.

2.   Acts Which Constitute Persecution

As argued above, persecution can be understood as the sustained or systemic violation of core norms of human rights, demonstrative of a failure of protection by the state of origin. In situations of armed conflict, certain violations of IHL may amount to persecution. It is generally accepted that refugee law should deal with actions that infringe a person's dignity. If read in conjunction with Article 33(1) of the Refugee Convention, the refugee definition comprises, as a minimum, persons who face threats against their physical and psychological integrity, life, and freedom.[70] Violations of non-derogable human rights amount to persecution under any circumstances. Examples include the right not to be arbitrarily deprived of one's life and the prohibition of torture, cruel, inhuman or degrading treatment or punishment. Most of these rights are also guaranteed by Common Article 3 of the Geneva Conventions, which contains the minimum standards of treatment in international and non-international armed conflicts. Common Article 3 stipulates, for instance, that persons taking no active part in hostilities and persons *hors de combat* shall in all circumstances be treated humanely. It expressly prohibits, *inter alia*, outrages upon personal dignity, in particular humiliating and degrading treatment.

Other harmful actions can also be tantamount to persecution, depending on the severity of the infringement, the circumstances of the case, and the "psychological make-up of individuals"[71]. Various measures which individually would not amount to persecution can, if taken as a sum, constitute persecution.[72] In assessing such measures, IHL should play a significant role because it contains norms expressly designed for the context of armed conflicts and

---

69   See Hathaway, Law of Refugee Status (1991), p. 185; K. Hailbronner, Rechtsfragen der Aufnahme von „Gewaltflüchtlingen" in Westeuropa – am Beispiel Jugoslawien, in: Schweizerische Zeitschrift für internationales und europäisches Recht 4 (1993), pp. 524 f.

70   See U. Brandl, Die Anwendbarkeit des Flüchtlingsbegriffs der Genfer Flüchtlingskonvention auf Bürgerkriegsflüchtlinge, in: H. Tretter (ed.), Temporary Protection für Flüchtlinge in Europa. Analysen und Schlussfolgerungen (2005), pp. 186 f.

71   See UNHCR, Handbook Determining Refugee Status, para. 52.

72   See ibid. para. 53.

thereby provides more adequate benchmarks. *Stéphane Jaquemet* understands the application of IHL and refugee law as a continuum and conceives protection under the Refugee Convention as a response to certain forms of defiance of IHL.[73] He focuses on those infringements of IHL which entail individual criminal responsibility under international law and argues that war crimes blatantly violate human dignity and therefore always constitute persecution.[74] According to this view, the victims of war crimes fall within the meaning of the refugee definition, provided they fulfil the other criteria of the refugee definition.[75] This continuous application of IHL and refugee law does have certain merits, for instance enhancing the coherence of the two bodies of international law. The prohibition of the forced displacement of civilians in IHL illustrates another advantage of this approach. Forceful displacement has been a recurrent phenomenon in many armed conflicts.[76] It was often part and parcel of "ethnic cleansing" and hence was undertaken at least partly for one of the reasons stipulated in Article 1A(2) of the Refugee Convention. While both IHL and IHRL prohibit such practices, the IHL provisions are more detailed in this respect.[77] The Statutes of the International Tribunal for the Former Yugoslavia (ICTY) and the International Criminal Court (ICC) list forced displacement as an international crime.[78] There is a significant body of jurisprudence which fleshes out the elements of this crime that can be used in refugee status determination.

But this approach also entails certain difficulties regarding, for example, the different standards of proof in refugee status determination and in the assessment of individual criminal responsibility. A refugee applicant must not be required to demonstrate that he or she has become the victim of an international crime since this would entail a higher standard of proof than normally used during refugee status determination. It is hardly possible to say that all violations of IHL which contain individual criminal responsibility automatically constitute persecution. Hence, while the rich jurisprudence in the field of international criminal law may be of assistance during refugee status determination,

---

73   See Jaquemet, Cross-Fertilization (2001), p. 664.; Storey/Wallace, War and Peace (2001), pp. 627 f.
74   Jaquemet, Cross-Fertilization (2001), p. 667.
75   See ibid., pp. 665-669.
76   See Lubbers, Foreword (2001), p. 578.
77   See Articles 45 and 49 of the Fourth Geneva Convention as well as Article 76 of Additional Protocol I. See also Jaquemet, Cross-Fertilization (2001), p. 669.
78   Statute of the International Tribunal for the Prosecution of Persons Responsible for Serious Violations of International Humanitarian Law Committed in the Territory of theFormer Yugoslavia since 1991 (1993), Security Council Resolution 827 (1993), Articles 2(g) and 5(d); Rome Statute of the International Criminal Court, Adopted on 17 July 1998, UN Doc. A/CONF.183/9, Articles 7(1)(d), 8(2)(a)(vii), and 8(2)(b)(vii), 8(2) (e)(vii).

persecution remains a function of the severity of the infringement and the individual circumstances.

3.   The Personal Risk of Being Persecuted

It is necessary to differentiate between the refugee applicant's risk of incidentally becoming the victim of generalized violence on the one hand and the existence of a well-founded fear of persecution on the other. This analysis is closely related to the assessment of whether a person fears persecution *for reasons of* race, religion, nationality, membership of a particular social group, or political opinion. The extent to which a refugee applicant must demonstrate a risk of being singled out for ill-treatment during armed conflict remains controversial. This requirement has frequently been used to deny refugee protection to claimants from armed conflict situations.[79] It is therefore the subject of scrutiny in this section.

Two principal approaches can be distinguished in refugee law scholarship and jurisprudence. The so-called differential risk analysis examines whether the claimant, as an individual or member of a group, faces a differential risk arising from the armed conflict if compared to other civilians. Where such risk merely arises out of the conflict itself or where it affects all alike, there can be no differential risk.[80] This view essentially introduces an additional threshold for meeting the criteria of the refugee definition in times of armed conflict, namely that the applicant must be at greater risk than other civilians or even other members of their group. It implies that certain harm is not persecution when it affects a large number of people. This understanding is rather artificial and difficult to reconcile with the wording, object and purpose of the Refugee Convention. In contrast, the so-called non-comparative approach stipulates that persecution under the Convention exists as long as persecutory intent can be identified, regardless of whether a differential impact on the side of the applicant can be established. Accordingly, it is irrelevant whether the persecutory intent arises out of the conflict or whether persecution affects all alike; what matters is the nexus between the serious harm feared and a Convention ground.[81] This approach can be critizised as ignoring the particularities of armed conflicts.

A possible way to reconcile these approaches is to classify victims of armed conflicts as refugees if they are subjected to differential victimisation based on their civil or political status, their ethnicity, etc. Differential victimisation means that those victims of armed conflicts who qualify as refugees are different

---

79   See Brandl, Anwendbarkeit des Flüchtlingsbegriffs (2005), p. 203.
80   See Storey/Wallace, War and Peace (2001), p. 352. A related approach is called the differential impact analysis and scrutinizes whether the person is more at risk than other members of their group.
81   Ibid., p. 354.

from other victims of armed conflict in that their victimisation is premised on persecution for Convention reasons. This approach acknowledges that armed conflicts can be used as instruments of persecution and that the Refugee Convention merely protects a subset of those at risk during armed conflicts. The Convention may thus cover situations in which violence is not generalized but aimed at a particular group defined by its race, religion, nationality, or political opinion or at a particular social group. It may also be applicable in situations in which violence is generalized but in which the applicant's fear nonetheless stems from specific forms of disfranchisement within their home country.[82]

Hugo Storey and *Rebecca Wallace* proposed that IHL can assist in discerning claims for refugee status in which the personal nature of the risk must be demonstrated and cases in which it must not, because the scale of abuses directed against individuals on account of their religion or ethnicity amounts to severe and systemic infringements of IHL.[83] This proposal acknowledges that there are situations in which a certain group experiences blatant IHL violations and in which it may suffice that a refugee applicant shows their membership of this group, without additionally having to proof the personal nature of the risk. During refugee status determination, the general situation of human rights violations in the state of origin is often taken into account, but is usually not enough on its own as a basis for refugee status. Similar limitations may be pertinent in assessing the degree of compliance with IHL in the home country. Nevertheless, the ascertainment of the fact that certain persons experience severe and systemic violations of IHL for one of the Convention reasons should create a strong presumption for refugee status.

4.   Availability of Protection by the State of Origin

International refugee protection is surrogate protection for persons who are no longer protected by their state of origin. Persecution is understood here as the violation of core IHRL or IHL norms which demonstrate the failure of the state of origin's obligation to protect its nationals. Moreover, Article 1A(2) of the Refugee Convention stipulates that a refugee is unable or, due to their well-founded fear of persecution, unwilling to avail him- or herself of the protection of their home country. In the following, it is examined how the lack of protection by the state of origin which is a party to an armed conflict should be determined.

Historically, protection by the state of origin as referred to in the refugee definition has meant "external protection", i.e. diplomatic protection accorded

---

82   For the approach regarding differential victimisation, see Hathaway, Law of Refugee Status (1991), pp. 185 f. and p. 188.

83   See Storey/Wallace, War and Peace (2001), p. 359.

by states to their nationals abroad.[84] Yet this form of protection has lost most of its original function, namely to secure the basic rights of citizens abroad at a time when the major human rights treaties were inexistent. In light of the Refugee Convention's human rights purpose and by logically extending the original rationale of diplomatic protection, protection can also be understood as internal protection, i.e. protection from violations of core human rights which the state must accord within its territory.[85] In situations of peace, such protection has rightly been described as

> "measures and mechanisms designed to establish the rights of the person and at setting up mechanisms to ensure that these can effectively be claimed and exercised, prevent the violation of the person's rights, and provide remedies where such violations occur".[86]

In times of armed conflict, the determination of what constitutes protection is less straightforward. It surely comprises promotional, preventive, and remedial measures regarding non-derogable human rights. States parties to the Geneva Conventions pledge themselves to respect and to ensure respect for these Conventions in all circumstances.[87] This obligation can serve to determine the protection which a state party to an armed conflict owes to its citizens. More precisely, the minimum standards of treatment in Article 3 common to the Geneva Conventions may be used as a yardstick for determining the core of such protection. It has been argued in refugee law literature and jurisprudence that in situations of armed conflict in which the state has no effective control over the territory and state power has virtually dissolved, the Refugee Convention does not apply. According to this so-called accountability view,[88] the Convention as an international treaty is premised on the existence of a sovereign state or of an entity that exercises state-like functions. The Refugee Convention connects refugee status with the disregard of international legal obligations to respect certain core human rights. Where there is no subject of international law to which human rights violations can be attributed, the Refugee Convention does

---

84   See A. Fortin, The Meaning of 'Protection' in the Refugee Definition, in: International Journal of Refugee Law 12 (2001). For a strong criticism of this view, see J. C. Hathaway/M. Foster, Internal Protection/Relocation/Flight Alternative as an Aspect of Refugee Status Determination, in E. Feller/V. Türk/F. Nicholson (eds.), Refugee Protection in International Law. UNHCR's Global Consultations on International Protection (2003), pp. 373-381.

85   See W. Kälin, Non-State Agents of Persecution and the Inability of the State to Protect, in: Georgetown Immigration Law Journal 15 (2000-2001), pp. 427-482. For a criticism of this view, see Fortin, The Meaning of Protection (2001).

86   Fortin, The Meaning of Protection (2001), p. 552.

87   Article 1 Common to the Geneva Conventions.

88   See Brandl, Anwendbarkeit des Flüchtlingsbegriffs (2005), p. 209.

not provide protection.[89] However, this understanding is difficult to reconcile with the object and purpose of the Refugee Convention, namely to protect those whom their state of origin no longer protects. The reason why the home country fails to provide protection, for instance the lack of a state apparatus, is not relevant from a legal point of view. What counts is the resulting lack of protection. To refuse protection in these situations would lead effective refugee protection *ad absurdum*.[90]

Closely intertwined with the availability of protection by the state of origin is the issue of the agent of persecution. The lack of protection by the state of origin is apparent when the feared persecution originates directly from state agents or when persecution is carried out by non-state actors with the instigation, condoning, or tolerance of the state. It remains controversial whether persecution by non-state actors who are in such control over a territory that they can be seen as *de facto* authorities or persecution by private entities in situations where the state has collapsed fall within the refugee definition.[91] A closer look at the wording of the refugee definition reveals that there is no express requirement that persecution be carried out by state agents. The inability or unwillingness of the home country to provide protection is a separate element in the definition. Non-state actors such as rebel groups or guerrilla movements play a significant role in many armed conflicts. The law of non-international armed conflict binds all parties to the conflict, i.e. states and non-state actors.[92] It would therefore be illogical to exclude *per se* persecution by non-state actors from the purview of the refugee definition.

Where an armed conflict takes place in part, but not all, of a state's territory and where the feared persecution originates from non-state actors, the question arises of whether an internal protection alternative exists, that would render international refugee protection unnecessary.[93] In armed conflicts, the threats from which people flee can be geographically confined.[94] The internal protection alternative has been criticized as a device to limit states' duties to provide refugee protection. It was originally drafted in a vague and ambiguous way

---

89   For the whole paragraph, see Hailbronner, Gewaltflüchtlinge (1993), pp. 528 f., who
       refers to German jurisprudence, and Brandl, Anwendbarkeit des Flüchtlingsbegriffs
       (2005), pp. 209-212.
90   See J. C. Hathaway, Is Refugee Status Really Elitist? An Answer to the Ethical
       Challenge, in: J.-Y. Carlier/D. Vanheule, Europe and Refugees: A Challenge?
       L'Europe et les Refugiés: Un Défi? (1997), pp. 82 f.
91   See Kälin, Non-State Agents of Persecution (2000-2001), p. 416.
92   See D. Fleck, The Law of Non-International Armed Conflicts (2008), p. 620.
93   The internal protection alternative has also been called internal flight or relocation
       alternative, see Hathaway/Foster, Internal Protection Alternative (2003), pp. 357-359.
94   UNHCR, Handbook on Procedures and Criteria for Determining Refugee Status under
       the 1951 Convention and the 1967 Protocol relating to the Status of Refugees, para.
       91.

by the UNHCR and has since been developed by various domestic courts, the UNHCR, and refugee law scholars. Its roots in the refugee definition remain unclear. While the UNHCR suggests that the internal flight alternative is part of the well-founded fear of persecution test, *James C. Hathaway* and *Michelle Foster* have shown that it should more appropriately be treated as part of the test whether national protection is available to the applicant.[95] Four criteria must be satisfied if a person is not to be granted refugee status because of the existence of an internal protection alternative: Firstly, access to protection available elsewhere in the home country must be practical, safe and legal; secondly, it must be a veritable "antidote" to the original well-founded fear of persecution; thirdly, no new risks of persecution must arise in the alternative location, nor must there be a risk of *refoulement*; and fourthly, the state must provide a minimum standard of protection in the alternative location.[96] In situations of armed conflict, it will be difficult to fulfil these conditions. Even if the state party to an armed conflict is not itself persecuting, it may prove too weak to provide efficient protection throughout its territory, especially if no central state authority exists and different parties to the conflict control different parts of the territory.[97]

IV. "Opening the Floodgates?"

Concerns may be raised that granting protection under the Refugee Convention to individuals who fled the perils of armed conflict could "open the floodgates". Purportedly, huge numbers of refugee applicants from countries experiencing armed conflicts would overwhelm the reception capacities of host states. The floodgates concern is a political, not a legal argument, but it may influence the interpretation of the refugee definition by decision-makers in the domestic realm and therefore merits closer scrutiny.

The floodgates argument seems to assume that a clear-cut understanding of persecution exists from which decision-makers should not deviate in order to avoid providing protection to an "unhealthy" number of people. But there is no such commonly agreed meaning of persecution in international law. Interpreting the refugee definition in light of IHRL and IHL is not tantamount to saying that every victim of armed conflict is a refugee. Nor does every violation of an IHL norm suffice to qualify for refugee status. Applicants still must fulfil the other criteria of the refugee definition, notably the requirement that their fear

---

95   See Hathaway/Foster, Internal Protection Alternative (2003), p. 372.
96   See ibid., p. 389.
97   See Brandl, Anwendbarkeit des Flüchtlingsbegriffs (2005), p. 214.

of persecution be for reasons of a Convention ground.[98] Furthermore, the vast majority of refugees worldwide remain within their regions of origin. In this respect, developing states already carry a far larger burden than industrialised states. There is no adequate system of burden sharing in place between states parties to the Refugee Convention. Thus, there are valid reasons to question the validity of the floodgates concern.

There are indeed states who expressly accept certain asylum seekers from situations of armed conflicts as refugees. Canada for instance, a major state of destination for migrants and refugees, officially recognizes that persons having fled civil war situations can qualify for refugee status. While it is true that Canada is quite far away from the regions where most current armed conflicts take place, Canada did face numerous refugee claims in the past from persons who fled the armed conflicts and generalized violence in Honduras and Haiti.[99] Furthermore, the floodgates argument is premised on a mass influx scenario. For such situations, temporary protection is available as an interim means of protection that acknowledges the limited capabilities of the domestic asylum systems. But the question of whether persons who fled armed conflicts qualify for refugee status does not only arise in situations of mass influx. There are also individual refugee applicants who base their claims on experiences during armed conflicts. If they do not arrive in the context of a mass influx, some domestic refugee status determination procedures do not provide for their individual protection under the Refugee Convention because they are deemed war-displaced, rather than individually persecuted.[100] Thus, the floodgates concern is largely unfounded.

V.   Conclusions

Although the Refugee Convention is not a panacea against all forms of conflict-induced flight, it is of considerable relevance for the protection of persons who had to leave their state of origin due to armed conflicts. Protection under the Refugee Convention is not rendered obsolete by the existence of other international legal bases for protection. The refugee definition in Article 1A(2) must be interpreted in light of IHRL and IHL when it comes to assessing claims for refugee status arising out of experiences during armed conflicts. This interpretative approach is in line with the rules on treaty interpretation. IHRL

---

98   For the above reasoning in general, see Foster, International Refugee Law (2007), pp. 74-79.

99   For a selection of Canadian and U.S. cases, see Sternberg, The Grounds of Refugee Protection (2002), pp. 82-123.

100   See UNHCR, Note on International Protection of 30 June 1999, UN Doc. A/AC.96/914, para. 42.

and IHL together provide an adequate yardstick for assessing such claims. IHL norms, particularly those whose violation entails individual criminal responsibility under international law, can be used to highlight which forms of serious harm amount to persecution in armed conflicts. They can also inform the assessment of whether there is a personal risk of being persecuted. Protection by the state of origin during armed conflict comprises promotional, preventive, and remedial activities for the fulfilment of fundamental IHRL and IHL obligations. The Refugee Convention provides surrogate protection where the state apparatus has ceased to exist due to armed conflicts. Protection by the home country is deemed unavailable if no adequate international protection alternative exists, a situation which frequently occurs in armed conflicts. Concerns that this understanding of the refugee definition would "open the floodgates" to large groups of displaced people are hardly convincing. Although uncertainties remain concerning the personal scope of the Refugee Convention in times of armed conflict, it has nonetheless become apparent that this Convention remains crucial for tackling today's refugee problems.

Bibliography

Battjes, H., European Asylum Law and International Law (2006).

Brandl, U., Die Anwendbarkeit des Flüchtlingsbegriffs der Genfer Flüchtlingskonvention auf Bürgerkriegsflüchtlinge, in: H. Tretter (ed.), Temporary Protection für Flüchtlinge in Europa. Analysen und Schlussfolgerungen (2005), pp. 179-219.

Davies, S. E., The Asian Rejection? International Refugee Law in Asia, in: Australian Journal of Politics and History 52 (2006), pp. 562-575.

Davy, U., Temporary Protection: Neue Konzepte der EU-Flüchtlingspolitik und ihr Verhältnis zur Gewährung von Asyl, in: H. Tretter (ed.), Temporary Protection für Flüchtlinge in Europa. Analysen und Schlussfolgerungen (2005), pp.17-89.

Dinstein, Y., War, Agression and Self Defence (2005).

European Council on Refugees and Exiles, The Impact of the EU Qualification Directive on International Protection (2008), www.ecre.org/files/ECRE_QD_study_full.pdf (accessed 22 June 2009).

Fitzpatrick, J., Human Rights and Forced Displacement: Converging Standards, in: A. F. Bayefski/J. Fitzpatrick (eds.), Human Rights and Forced Displacement (2000), pp. 3-25.

Fleck, D., The Law of Non-International Armed Conflicts, in: D. Fleck (ed.), The Handbook of International Humanitarian Law (2008), pp. 605-634.

Fortin, A., The Meaning of 'Protection' in the Refugee Definition, in: International Journal of Refugee Law 12 (2001), pp. 548-576.

Foster, M., International Refugee Law and Socio-Economic Rights. Refuge from Deprivation (2007).

Gil-Bazo, M.-T., Refugee Status, Subsidiary Protection, and the Right to be Granted Asylum under EC Law, New Issues in Refugee Research. Research Paper No. 136 (2006), www.unhcr.org/research/RESEARCH/455993882.pdf (accessed 22 June 2009).

Goodwin-Gill, G. S./J. McAdam, The Refugee in International Law (2007).

Greenwood, C., Historical Development and Legal Analysis, in: D. Fleck (ed.), The Handbook of International Humanitarian Law (2008), pp. 1-44.

Hailbronner, K., Rechtsfragen der Aufnahme von „Gewaltflüchtlingen" in Westeuropa - am Beispiel Jugoslawien, in: Schweizerische Zeitschrift für internationales und europäisches Recht 4 (1993), pp. 517-538.

Hathaway, J. C., The Law of Refugee Status (1991).

—   Is Refugee Status Really Elitist? An Answer to the Ethical Challenge, in: J.-Y. Carlier/D. Vanheule (eds.), Europe and Refugees: A Challenge? L'Europe et les Refugiés: Un Défi? (1997), pp. 79-88.

—   The Rights of Refugees under International Law (2005).

Hathaway, J. C./M. Foster, Internal Protection/Relocation/Flight Alternative as an Aspect of Refugee Status Determination, in: E. Feller/V. Türk/F. Nicholson (eds.), Refugee Protection in International Law. UNHCR's Global Consultations on International Protection (2003), pp. 357-417.

Jackson, I. C., The Refugee Concept in Group Situations (1999).

Jaquemet, S., The Cross-Fertilization of International Humanitarian Law and International Refugee Law, in: International Review of the Red Cross 843 (2001), pp. 651-674.

Kälin, W., Flight in Times of War, in: International Review of the Red Cross 843 (2001), pp. 629-650.

—   Non-State Agents of Persecution and the Inability of the State to Protect, in: Georgetown Immigration Law Journal 15 (2000-2001), pp. 415-430.

—   Temporary Protection in the EC: Refugee Law, Human Rights and the Temptations of Pragmatism, in: German Yearbook of International Law 44 (2001), pp. 202-236.

Kolb, R., Human Rights and Humanitarian Law, in: R. Wolfrum (ed.), Max Planck Encyclopedia of Public International Law (2009).

Lauterpacht, E./D. Bethlehem, The Scope and Content of the Principle of *Non-Refoulement*: Opinion, in: E. Feller/V. Türk/F. Nicholson (eds.), Refugee Protection in International Law. UNHCR's Global Consultations on International Protection (2003), pp. 89-177.

Lubbers, R., Foreword by the High Commissioner for Refugees, in: International Review of the Red Cross 843 (2001), pp. 577-579.

McAdam, J., Complementary Protection in International Refugee Law (2007).

Mole, N., Asylum and the European Convention on Human Rights (2007).

Piotrowicz, R./C. van Eck, Subsidiary Protection and Primary Rights, in: International and Comparative Law Quarterly 53 (2004), pp. 107-138.

Rogers, A.P.V., Law on the Battlefield (2004).

Sternberg, M. v., The Grounds of Refugee Protection in the Context of International Human Rights and Humanitarian Law. Canadian and United States Case Law Compared (2002).

Storey, H./R. Wallace, War and Peace in Refugee Law Jurisprudence, in: American Journal of International Law 95 (2001), pp. 349-366.

United Nations High Commissioner for Refugees, UNHCR Statement on Subsidiary Protection Under the EC Qualification Directive for People Threatened by Indiscriminate Violence (2007), www.unhcr.org/cgi-bin/texis/vtx/refworld/rwmain?doc id=479df7472&page=search (accessed 22 June 2009).

United Nations High Commissioner for Refugees, Handbook on Procedures and Criteria for Determining Refugee Status under the 1951 Convention and the 1967 Protocol relating to the Status of Refugees (1992), http://www.unhcr.org/refworld/docid/3ae6b3314.html (accessed 22 June 2009).

Corporate International Criminal Responsibility: Oxymoron or an Effective Tool for 21st Century Governance?

Joris Larik

I. Introduction: Multinational Corporations and the Rise of International Criminal Law

In this contribution, two great phenomena of our times will be brought together: on the one hand globalisation and the emergence of multinational corporations and on the other hand the rapid development of international criminal law.[1] The former describes a trend through which corporate actors have gained significantly in power on the international stage and by virtue of their

> "ubiquitous presence, and consequently intrusion into many aspects of people's lives (...) can and [do] occasionally impact detrimentally on the enjoyment of internationally recognised human rights".[2]

The latter, it will be argued, can provide means to punish and prevent such a detrimental impact, at least in its most appalling forms.

It is widely recognized that corporations, and particularly the multinational corporations, have assumed an increasingly significant role on the international stage.[3] Today, the most powerful corporations by far outweigh most countries both in terms of economic leverage and political influence.[4] As the UN Special Rapporteur on the Working Methods and Activities of Transnational Corporations *El Hadji Guissé* concluded in 1998:

---

1   The latter development has been called, maybe somewhat confusingly, the "criminalization of international law" by T. Meron, Is International Law Moving Towards Criminalization?, in: European Journal of International Law 9 (1998), pp. 18 ff.

2   S. Joseph, Taming the Leviathans: Multinational Enterprises and Human Rights, in: Netherlands International Law Review 46 (1999), p. 172.

3   A historical account of their rise to power is provided in P. Muchlinki, Multinational Enterprises and the Law (1995), pp. 19 ff.

4   See e.g. B. Hocking/M. Smith, World Politics: An Introduction to International Relations (1996), p. 100; D. Carreau/P. Juillard, Droit International Économique (1998), pp. 31 ff.; P. Willetts, Transnational Actors and International Organizations in Global Politics, in: J. Baylis/S. Smith (eds.), The Globalization of World Politics: An Introduction to International Relations (2005), pp. 429 ff.; and C. Wells/J. Elias, Catching the Conscience of the King: Corporate Players on the International Stage, in: P. Alston (ed.), Non-State Actors and Human Rights (2005), pp. 146 ff.

"Transnational corporations play an important part in international economic life. Of the 100 biggest concentrations of wealth in the world, 51 per cent are owned by transnational corporations and 49 per cent by States. Mitsubishi's turnover exceeds Indonesia's gross national product (GNP); Ford's turnover exceeds South Africa's GNP; and Royal Dutch Shell earns more than Norway."[5]

However, views diverge on the assessment of the consequences of the increased power of corporations: While some present a sunny image of corporations being on the whole beneficial to development, employment, and human rights[6], others paint a much gloomier picture[7]. In any case, it seems uncontroversial to state that this augmented power at least constitutes a global risk, as it inevitably entails an increased ability to create detrimental effects.[8] At various occasions, this risk materialized, often in the form of large-scale incidents.[9] All of this should therefore merit these powerful actors in international relations to be "distrusted"[10] to a heightened degree, and to have them checked more

---

5   United Nations Economic and Social Council, Commission on Human Rights, Sub-
     Commission on Prevention of Discrimination and Protection of Minorities, The
     Realization of Economic, Social and Cultural Rights: The Question of Transnational
     Corporations, Working Document on the Impact of the Activities of Transnational
     Corporations on the Realization of Economic, Social and Cultural Rights, Prepared by
     Mr. El Hadji Guissé, UN Doc. E/CN.4/Sub.2/1998/6 of 10 June 1998, p. 7.
6   See e.g. the seminal study of W. Meyer, Human Rights and MNCs: Theory Versus
     Quantitative Analysis, in: Human Rights Quarterly 18 (1996), pp. 368 ff.
7   See e.g. S. Hymer/G. Modelski, The Multinational Corporation and the Law of
     Uneven Development, in: G. Modelski (ed.), Transnational Corporations and World
     Order (1979), pp. 386-403; or J. Smith/M. Bolyard/A. Ippolito, Human Rights and
     the Global Economy: A Response to Meyer, in: Human Rights Quarterly 21 (1999),
     pp. 207 ff. For a concise general discussion see D. Shelton, Protecting Human Rights
     in a Globalizing World, in: C. Ku/P. Diehl (eds.), International Law: Classic and
     Contemporary Readings (2003), pp. 336 ff.
8   C. Vázquez, Direct vs. Indirect Obligations of Corporations Under International Law,
     in: Columbia Journal of Transnational Law 43 (2004/2005), p. 949.
9   Some cases including nothing less than the overthrow of government 1954 in
     Guatemala and 1973 in Chile with the active involvement of United Fruit and
     International Telephone and Telegraph (ITT) respectively, or the 1984 Bhopal disaster
     where 2.000   people were killed and over 200.000 injured due to the lax safety
     regulations at Union Carbide. For these and other examples see Wells/Elias, Catching
     the Conscience of the King (2005), pp. 143-146; Joseph, Taming the Leviathans
     (2000), p. 76; S. Agbakwa, A Line in the Sand: International Dis(Order) and the
     Impunity of Non-State Corporate Actors in the Developing World, in: A. Anghie *et
     al.* (eds.), The Third World and International Order: Law, Politics, and Globalization
     (2003), p. 8; see also the more recent examples of corporate involvement in human
     rights abuses of e.g. Shell in Nigeria, British Petroleum (BP) in Colombia, and
     Nike in Indonesia, N. Jägers, Corporate Human Rights Obligations: in Search of
     Accountability (2002), p. 9, and the literature indicated in footnotes 36, 37, and 38.
10   Thus extending the famous dictum of James Madison at the Philadelphia Convention

effectively. How has the international legal framework thus far responded to this? The first observation to be made is that corporations have been granted an increased amount of legal remedies in order to protect their interests. Even though the legal personality of (multinational) corporations is disputed or even still plainly denied,[11] by virtue of legal developments in the area of trade and investment protection, corporations have in several instances been given standing before courts and arbitration tribunals on equal footing with states.[12] Hence, one could say that the international community has acknowledged the greater *de facto* weight that corporations wield by granting them possibilities to defend their rights. However, the same can by no means be said about the obligations side. In fact, it is undeniable that there is a grave imbalance, or in other words a "fundamental institutional misalignment"[13] or "regime deficit"[14], between the international rights and obligations of corporations, and *a fortiori* regarding the avenues to enforce them respectively.

Discussions of this imbalance and ways to rectify it have become a veritable trend in international legal scholarship as well as in civil society. Policy-makers have not remained unaffected by this, as is evidenced, for instance, by the proposition of a Global Compact between the business world and the international community by the UN Secretary-General in 1999 or the

---

on 11 July 1787 "that all men having power ought to be distrusted" to corporations, cited in M. Farrand, The Records of the Federal Convention of 1787 (1966), Vol. 1, p. 584.

11   M. Herdegen, Internationales Wirtschaftsrecht (2005), p. 58; see also S. Hobe/O. Kimmenich, Einführung in das Völkerrecht (2004), p. 158. At least, one might see them as "participants" in international law, to use the term coined by R. Higgins, Problems and Process: International Law and How We Use It (1994), p. 46.

12   A prominent example being the Convention on the Settlement of Investment Disputes between States and Nationals of Other States, Art. 1, para. 2 and Art. 25. As the envisaged coronation of this corporate-friendly trend, one should also note the Negotiating Group on the Multilateral Agreement on Investment (MAI), OECD Multilateral Agreement on Investment, Draft Consolidated Text, DAFFE/MAI(98)7/ REV1 of 22 April 1998, which would grant corporations wide non-reciprocal rights vis-à-vis host states (see pp. 69 ff. on "Investor-State Procedures"). However, negotiations on it were discontinued in 1998.

13   Human Rights Council, Implementation of General Assembly Resolution 60/251 of 15 March 2006 entitled "Human Rights Council", Report of the Special Representative of the Secretary-General on the Issue of Human Rights and Transnational Corporations and Other Business Enterprises, John Ruggie, Business and Human Rights: Mapping International Standards of Responsibility and Accountability for Corporate Acts, UN Doc. A/HRC/4/35 of 19 February 2007, p. 3; see also M. Kamminga/S. Zia-Zarifi, Liability of Multinational Corporations Under International Law: An Introduction, in: M. Kamminga/S. Zia-Zarifi (eds.), Liability of Multinational Corporations Under International Law (2000), pp. 5 ff.

14   Agbakwa, A Line in the Sand (2003), p. 5, who also proposes the harsher, and exaggerated term "false edifice of privileged impunity", p. 18.

appointment of *John Ruggie* as Special Representative of the Secretary-General on the issue of human rights and transnational corporations and other business enterprises in 2005. However, this trend has largely focussed on the general human rights framework.[15] What has so far only been addressed marginally, as a sort of by-road of the human rights regime, is the issue of international criminal responsibility of corporations.[16] This is quite astonishing, with international criminal law being one of the most remarkable developments in modern international law. It has evolved out of the understanding that holding states alone responsible for violating the "elementary considerations of mankind"[17] is insufficient.

Therefore, it seems worthwhile to explore the extent to which international criminal law has the potential to set right the imbalance outlined above. It is beyond the scope of this contribution to devise a comprehensive framework of what might be called "corporate international criminal law". Instead, what needs to be done in the first place is to overcome a number of conceptual stumbling blocks that make the attempt to sketch out such a framework appear like an improbable exercise. To this end, arguably the three most prominent of such stumbling blocks will be discussed, and shown to be surmountable. First, the intricate issue of establishing a corporation's criminal intent (*mens rea*); secondly, the increasingly important issue of corporate complicity; and thirdly, the different ways to punish a corporation.

II.   Determining Corporate *Mens Rea*

The first question that needs to be answered when dealing with the legal fiction of a corporation is: How would something that has "no soul"[18] develop intent, i.e. a will of its own? This is of essential importance in view of the emphasis

---

15   Note e.g. Jägers, Corporate Human Rights Obligations (2002); S. Ratner, Corporations and Human Rights: A Theory of Legal Responsibility, in: Yale Law Journal 111 (2001/2002), pp. 443 ff.; or A. Clapham, Human Rights Obligations of Non-State Actors (2006). Note also that John Ruggie's precise term of mandate is "human rights and transnational corporations and other business enterprises".

16   The only prominent exception of an article fully devoting itself to this topic is that of A. Clapham, The Question of Jurisdiction Under International Criminal Law Over Legal Persons: Lessons from the Rome Conference on an International Criminal Court, in: M. Kamminga/S. Zia-Ziarifi (eds.), Liability of Multinational Corporations Under International Law (2000), pp. 139 ff.

17   To use the expression used by the International Court of Justice, *Corfu Channel Case*, ICJ Reports (1949), p. 22.

18   Excerpt borrowed from the famous statement by Lord Chancellor Edward, First Baron Thurlow, cited in L. Dunford/A. Ridley, 'No Soul to be Damned, No Body to be Kicked'[1]: Responsibility, Blame and Corporate Punishment, in: International Journal of the Sociology of Law 21 (1996), p. 1.

international criminal law places on *mens rea*. Considering the crimes enumerated in the Rome Statute of the International Criminal Court (ICC), genocide[19] requires *dolus specialis*, i.e. "the specific intention, required as a constitutive element of the crime, which demands that the perpetrator clearly seeks to produce the act charged"[20], namely the eradication in whole or in part of a group of people. For crimes against humanity,[21] it is necessary that, next to criminal intent for the actual crime, the perpetrator commit it "as part of a widespread or systematic attack directed against any civilian population, with knowledge of the attack".[22] As for the yet to be defined crime of aggression,[23] it can also be assumed that

> "it must be shown that [the perpetrators] were parties to the plan or conspiracy [to wage a war of aggression], or, knowing of the plan, furthered its purpose and objective by participating in the preparation for aggressive war".[24]

Eventually, for the category of war crimes,[25] the Rome Statute stresses the importance of a specific plan or policy[26] and requires intent for the overwhelming majority of war crimes.[27] Furthermore, regarding the complex relationship the corporation shares with its organs, an additional question that could be asked is: To which extent can, and should corporate responsibility replace individual responsibility?

Concerning these questions, different relevant approaches from both international and national law will be discussed: Historically, there is the so-called "Nuremberg construction"[28], i.e. the possibility "to prosecute membership in groups declared as criminal"[29]. An inversion of this construction can be found in the final French proposal at the Rome Conference on the ICC to include the responsibility of legal persons,[30] by virtue of which "the company

---

19   Rome Statute of the International Criminal Court, Art. 6.
20   International Criminal Tribunal for Rwanda, *Prosecutor vs. Akayesu*, Case No. ICTR-96-4-T, Judgement of 2 September 1998, para. 498.
21   Rome Statute of the International Criminal Court, Art. 7.
22   Ibid., Art. 7, para. 1.
23   Ibid., Art. 5, para. 1 (d), and para. 2.
24   United States Military Tribunal, *Trial of Carl Krauch and Twenty-Two Others (The I.G. Farben Trial)*, Case No. 57, in: Law Reports of Trials of War Criminals, Selected and Prepared by the United Nations War Crimes Commission (1949), Vol. 10, p. 35; cp. also A. Cassese, International Criminal Law (2003), pp. 115 f.
25   Rome Statute of the International Criminal Court, Art. 8.
26   Ibid., para. 1.
27   Ibid., Art. 8, para. 2; see also Art. 30, para. 1 as the general rule.
28   Jägers, Corporate Human Rights Obligations (2002), p. 226.
29   M. Frulli, Jurisdiction *Ratione Materiae*, in: A. Cassese *et al.* (eds.), The Rome Statute of the International Criminal Court: A Commentary (2002), Vol. 1, p. 531, footnote 16.
30   United Nations Diplomatic Conference of Plenipotentiaries on the Establishment of

would have been tried as a sort of 'accessory' to the individual's crime"[31], thus "implicat[ing] the legal person, once the natural had been convicted of a crime"[32]. From a domestic-comparative viewpoint, there is "no single, broadly accepted theory of corporate blameworthiness"[33] yet. However, there are four main approaches discernible, namely the "agency", the "identification", the "aggregation", and the "holistic" theory.

Under the Charter of the International Military Tribunal at Nuremberg[34] (IMT) it was possible to implicate individual responsibility from membership in an organisation that was declared criminal. The obvious doctrinal shortcomings of this approach were that it both excluded the liability of the corporation as such and allowed for the indiscriminate punishment of large numbers of members, without taking note of their specific intentions to join and their acts within the organisation. As was demonstrated by the marginal use of this principle by the IMT itself,[35] this model appears on the whole not purposeful.

During the negotiations leading up to the Rome Statute, however, the "Nuremberg construction" was turned upside down in a French proposal, according to which legal persons could be held criminally liable for crimes of which a natural person had already been convicted and if that natural person had acted on behalf of and with the explicit consent of the corporation in question – as well as in the course of its activities – and, on top of that, if that person had been in a position of control within the corporation (as defined in the domestic law of the state of registration).[36] It already becomes clear from this range of cumulative requirements that this would constitute a rather restrictive approach. Criminal responsibility of corporations is inseparably linked to that of a natural

---

an International Criminal Court, Committee of the Whole, Working Group on General Principles of Criminal Law, UN Doc. A/CONF.183/C.1/WGGP/L.5/Rev.2 of 3 July 1998, Draft Art. 23, paras. 5 and 6.

31   Clapham, The Question of Jurisdiction Under International Criminal Law Over Legal Persons (2000), p. 153.

32   Jägers, Corporate Human Rights Obligations (2002), p. 229.

33   Anonymous, Corporate Crime: Regulating Corporate Behaviour Through Criminal Sanctions, in: Harvard Law Review 92 (1978/1979), p. 1241; also C. Wells, Corporations and Criminal Responsibility (2001), p. 84.

34   Charter of the International Military Tribunal, Art. 9.

35   The Nuremberg Judgement excludes such members of criminal organisations "who had no knowledge of the criminal purposes or acts of the organization [...], unless they were personally implicated in the commission of acts declared criminal by Article 6 of the [IMT] Charter as members of the organization". International Military Tribunal (Nuremberg), Judgement and Sentences, October 1, 1946, in: American Journal of International Law 41 (1947), p. 251.

36   United Nations Diplomatic Conference of Plenipotentiaries on the Establishment of an International Criminal Court, Committee of the Whole, Working Group on General Principles of Criminal Law, UN Doc. A/CONF.183/C.1/WGGP/L.5/Rev.2 of 3 July 1998, Draft Art. 23, paras. 5 and 6.

person, rendering the former a by-product of individual responsibility. Although it is not explicitly mentioned, it is to be assumed that the *mens rea* of that natural person can thus be transferred onto the legal one. This is supported by the requirement that the natural person had to be in a directing position.

The last mentioned point distinguishes this approach from the "agency" theory (also known as *respondeat superior* in the United States), which "is based on the principle whereby a corporation is taken to be the agent of all its employees".[37] Thus, by "imputing to the corporation (…) the mental state of any employee"[38] a corporation is rendered "blameworthy even when a single agent commits a crime for the benefit of the corporation."[39] In fact, it is as unjust as the Nuremberg construction: Instead of punishing individuals just for joining an organisation, it punishes companies just for employing somebody. Furthermore, since this approach is predominantly used for regulatory offences,[40] and not for graver offences requiring *mens rea*, it seems utterly inappropriate to be applied to international crimes.

Actually, the reversed Nuremberg construction is much closer to the theory of "identification" (sometimes also called "directing mind" or "*alter ego*" theory),[41] which appears to be the most common approach in modern national legislation that provides for criminal responsibility of legal persons.[42] This theory "identifies a limited layer of senior officers within the company as its 'brains' and renders the company liable for their culpable transgressions, not for those of other workers".[43] It is important to note that "the person who acts is not speaking or acting for the company. He is speaking as the company and his mind which directs his acts is the mind of the company."[44] For our purposes, the "identification" theory is of particular interest, since its introduction "marked the first recognition of corporations as capable of committing serious non-regulatory offences"[45], i.e. offences requiring *mens rea*. At least in theory, this would render it possible for a corporation to commit even international crimes with an extremely high threshold such as genocide, since individuals can be, and indeed have been, convicted for this crime.

---

37   Wells, Corporations and Criminal Responsibility (2001), p. 85.
38   Anonymous, Corporate Crime (1978/1979), p. 1242.
39   Ibid.
40   Wells, Corporations and Criminal Responsibility (2001), p. 85, concerning England.
41   D. Stuart, Canadian Criminal Law: A Treatise (1995), pp. 576 f.
42   The fact that French criminal law also employs the identification theory shows that it is not only suitable for common law countries. See the French Code Pénal, Art. 121-2, para. 1; and J. Pradel, Manuel de droit pénal général (2004), p. 478.
43   Wells, Corporations and Criminal Responsibility (2001), p. 85.
44   As expressed by Lord Reid in the leading English case on the matter, House of Lords, *Tesco Supermarkets Ltd. vs. Nattrass*, AC 153, 1972, p. 170 (emphasis added).
45   Ibid., p. 101.

However, it poses certain difficulties. First of all, since corporate responsibility remains a derivative of certain cases of individual responsibility, it is imperative to establish the radius of this inner circle of directing minds within a corporation. In other words: Where to draw the borderline between what constitutes the "brain" and the "hands" of a company.[46] Presumably, the "mind" includes "directors, the managing director, the company secretary and other superior officers responsible for managing the affairs of the corporation".[47] Moreover, employees that have been delegated the power from these to act independently are also to be included.[48] The final French proposal at the Rome Conference avoided this problem by leaving this question to be determined by "the national law of the State where the juridical person was registered at the time the crime was committed".[49] In any case, this circle of persons with such extensive powers is bound to be rather limited, which has a very unfortunate consequence: The "identification" theory makes it "particularly difficult to convict larger companies".[50] The larger the corporation, the more complex and wide-spread, the more difficult it becomes to determine one of the limited few "directing minds" at the top who intended the commission of a specific crime. Therefore, while the narrow "identification" theory facilitates the conviction of smaller businesses, it shields larger, i.e. more powerful (multinational) corporations, which eventually contradicts the very rationale of this undertaking, namely to bring actual power and legal restraints into a fair balance.

Some relief could be provided by a broader definition of "identification". According to Canadian jurisprudence, for instance, it suffices that the acts in question be "performed by the manager within the sector of corporation operation assigned to him by the corporation".[51] The assigned sector can be either geographical or functional.[52] Interestingly, this was specifically done in view of the fact that in Canada "corporate operations are frequently geographically widespread".[53] As clarified in a later Canadian judgement,

---

46   To use the image provided by Lord Justice Denning in House of Lords, *H.L. Bolton (Engineering) Co. Ltd. vs. T.J. Graham & Sons Ltd.*, 1 QB 159, 1957, p. 172.
47   M. Allen, Textbook on Criminal Law (2005), p. 231.
48   Ibid.; similarly Pradel, Manuel de droit pénal général (2004), pp. 484 f.
49   United Nations Diplomatic Conference of Plenipotentiaries on the Establishment of an International Criminal Court, Committee of the Whole, Working Group on General Principles of Criminal Law, UN Doc. A/CONF.183/C.1/WGGP/L.5/Rev.2 of 3 July 1998, Draft Art. 23, para. 5 (c).
50   Stuart, Canadian Criminal Law (1995), p. 580.
51   Taken from the leading decision by the Supreme Court of Canada, *Canadian Dredge & Dock Co. vs. The Queen*, 1 SCR 662 (1985), p. 21.
52   Ibid.
53   Ibid, p. 32.

"[t]he key factor which distinguishes directing minds from normal employees is the capacity to exercise decision-making authority on matters of corporate policy, rather than merely to give effect to such policy on an operational basis, whether at head office or across the sea".[54]

This is inspirational, *a fortiori*, when dealing with multinational corporations that operate in a multitude of countries.

Another approach for broadening the possibilities for corporate criminal responsibility is the so-called "aggregation" theory. According to this approach "corporate culpability does not have to be contingent on one individual employee's satisfying the relevant culpability criterion".[55] Here, the "fragmented knowledge of a number of individuals is fitted together to make one culpable one".[56] It underlines the fact that corporations indeed have a separate personality and that aggregation would clarify that "it is the whole which is judged, not the parts".[57]

Both theoretically and practically, however, it appears quite problematic to "add an innocent state of mind to an innocent state of mind and get as a result a dishonest state of mind".[58] In view of the special emphasis on *mens rea* and knowledge required for most international crimes, it is hardly conceivable how a systematic plan for genocide or persecution could be patched together from different individual wills not being aware themselves of this. This is not to be confused with the approach taken by the International Criminal Tribunal for Rwanda (ICTR) in the *Akayesu* case, namely that "intent can be inferred from a certain number of presumptions of fact".[59] Whereas the Tribunal put together a number of pertinent facts to construe a *mens rea*, the "aggregation" theory aims at putting together different mindsets to add up to one, which separately do not constitute a *mens rea*. All the same, this problem disappears when the threshold is merely (gross) negligence.[60] For "at least some limited categories

---

54   Supreme Court of Canada, *The "Rhône" vs. The "Peter A.B. Widener"*, 1 SCR 497 (1993), p. 526.
55   Wells, Corporations and Criminal Responsibility (2001), p. 156.
56   Ibid.
57   Ibid.
58   As it has been brought to the point in House of Lords, *Armstrong vs. Strain*, 1 KB 232, 1952, p. 246; also sceptical J. Smith/B. Hogan, Criminal Law (2005), p. 239; in other jurisdictions, this is severely criticised, too, see e.g. G. Stratenwerth, Schweizerisches Strafrecht (2005), p. 413.
59   International Criminal Tribunal for Rwanda, *Prosecutor vs. Akayesu* (1998), p. 523.
60   Smith/Hogan, Criminal Law (2005), pp. 239 f.; also Allen, Textbook on Criminal Law (2005), pp. 232 f., with more case law on the matter. Note also Dutch practice, see S. Field/N. Jorg, Corporate Liability and Manslaughter: Should we be Going Dutch?, Criminal Law Review 156 (1991), pp. 156 ff.

of war crimes"[61] where "gross or culpable negligence (*culpa gravis*) may be sufficient"[62] it remains an appealing option.

Finally, the most progressive approach is the so-called "holistic" theory, which "locates corporate blame in the procedures, operating systems, or culture of a company".[63] The most prominent example of this in national law is Section 12.3 of the Australian criminal code,[64] featuring "a broader conception of corporate responsibility than any other common law models".[65] It was introduced especially in order to remedy the fact that only few acts of large, multinational corporations would be covered under the "identification" theory.[66] Taking it further than the "aggregation" theory, it appreciates the fact that "[c]orporate behaviour is not just the sum of individual employee behaviour but must be considered in the context of the organization's structure and culture".[67] In stark contrast to the "agency" and "identification" theories, it endeavours to separate also in criminal law the legal person from the natural one, arguing that "responsibility can flow both from the individual to the corporations and can be found in the corporation's structures themselves".[68]

However intriguing or modern one might find this approach, one eventually remains stuck with the same problem as with "aggregation". True, it is not beyond imagination to construe some form of collective negligence. However, it appears inapt for *mens rea* offences. For it is virtually impossible to find in such vague terms as corporate "ethos", "culture" or "structure" the specific intent to commit a war crime, let alone plans for, say, systematic extermination. Furthermore, such terms are prone to subjectivism and finding an internationally accepted definition for them will doubtlessly prove to be very difficult. This is of course without prejudice to the to-be-welcomed possibility to expose structures which are favourable to the commission of such crimes. This, however, will not suffice to prove the existence of intent.[69]

In conclusion, this discussion shows that there are indeed workable conceptual approaches available to determine the criminal intent of a corporation. These different theories show great potential, especially when

---

61   Cassese, International Criminal Law (2003), p. 58.
62   Ibid. Cassese names certain cases of superior responsibility and wanton destruction of private property as possible examples, pp. 58 f. (emphasis in the original).
63   Wells, Corporations and Criminal Responsibility (2001), p. 85.
64   Australian Criminal Code Act 1995, Sec. 12.3.
65   Wells, Corporations and Criminal Responsibility (2001), p. 138.
66   Ibid., p. 137; see also A. Rose, 1995 Australian Criminal Code Act: Corporate Criminal Provisions, in: Criminal Law Forum 6 (1995), pp. 129 ff.
67   Stuart, Canadian Criminal Law (1995), p. 588.
68   Wells, Corporations and Criminal Responsibility (2001), p. 157 (emphasis added).
69   Except, of course, one were to accept such unconventional concepts as "reactive corporate fault", see B. Fisse/J. Braithwaite, Corporations, Crime and Accountability (1993), pp. 44 ff.

it comes to offences with a negligence requirement. However, in the realm of international criminal law, where crimes tend to have a high threshold, the overwhelming majority requiring specific intent, only a resort to the "identification" theory seems viable. It remains the most workable basis for three main reasons: Firstly, in comparison to the more daring approaches, it would definitely constitute a more acceptable compromise to the international community and in particular the parties of the Rome Statute. Secondly, it would not require a far-reaching remodelling and therefore questioning of the Rome Statute, or the drafting of some special corporate crimes statute, the success of which is highly doubtful. Thirdly, it would more easily connect with the previous jurisprudence of the war crimes tribunals of the Second World War, since the people convicted in the German industrialist cases were mostly in a position that would plainly qualify as "directing mind".[70] Its main disadvantage, the difficult applicability to multinational corporations, could be mitigated through a more flexible approach modelled after Canadian criminal law. This would allow expanding the circle of "directing minds" in order to include regional or functional bearers of responsibility. Finally, having reached this conclusion, the question whether there should be concurrent or alternative convictions of the legal and natural person is also answered, since individual guilt is a precondition for corporate guilt under "identification".

III. Addressing Corporate Complicity

When moving on to the second conceptual stumbling block, it is important to recall a corporation's true *raison d'être*, which is to conduct business in a profitable way. Therefore, even though it is by no means excluded that a company might engage directly in criminal conduct, it is much more likely to assist indirectly in the commission of a crime while pursuing its commercial purposes. This raises the important issue of "corporate complicity", the roots of which go back as far as Nuremberg.[71] In recent years, it has received heightened

---

70   See e.g. United States Military Tribunal, *Trial of Carl Krauch and Twenty-Two Others* (1949), pp. 1 ff.; also United States Military Tribunal, *Trial of Alfried Felix Alwyn Krupp von Bohlen und Halbach and Eleven Others*, Case No. 58, in: Law Reports of Trials of War Criminals, selected and prepared by the United Nations War Crimes Commission (1949), Vol. 10, pp. 1 ff.; also United States Military Tribunal, *Trial of Alfried Felix Alwyn Krupp von Bohlen und Halbach and Eleven Others* (1949), Vol. 10, pp. 69 ff.; and British Military Court, *Trial of Bruno Tesch and Two Others (The Zyklon B Case)*, Case No. 9, in: Law Reports of Trials of War Criminals, selected and prepared by the United Nations War Crimes Commission (1949), Vol. 1, pp. 93 ff.

71   See for a detailed assessment of the industrialist cases with regard to complicity W. Schabas, Enforcing International Humanitarian Law: Catching the Accomplices, in: International Review of the Red Cross 83 (2001), pp. 441 ff.

attention,[72] which is motivated by the massive investment of multinational corporations in countries with repressive regimes, or at least countries more readily willing to sacrifice the protection of their citizens in the increasingly fierce competition for foreign investment (a phenomenon that has come to be known as "race to the bottom").[73] This constitutes a certain historical turn: After the generally opposite positions of developing countries and multinational corporations during the 1970s and 1980s,[74] we are now facing the prospect of their acting increasingly hand in hand, also to the detriment of their citizens. The bleak bottom line is that

> "[m]any if not most of the humanitarian law violations committed in Kosovo, Sierra Leone, East Timor, Chechnya and the numerous other theatres of conflict in today's world could not take place without the assistance of arms dealers, diamond traders, bankers and financiers"[75],

in short, the corporate world. Therefore, it is imperative that acts of "corporate complicity" should also find their legal counterpart in order to repress and punish them. In international criminal law, the concept of "complicity" is firmly established when used to describe individual conduct. Both the statutes of the Nuremberg and Tokyo Tribunals included provisions on complicity,[76] as did the ensuing Nuremberg Principles[77] and the later Draft Code of Crimes against the Peace and Security of Mankind[78]. Also, all the modern statutes of international tribunals include provisions on complicity.[79] According to the International

---

72   A. Ramasastry, Corporate Complicity: From Nuremberg to Rangoon. An Examination of Forced Labour Cases and Their Impact on the Liability of Multinational Corporations, in: Berkeley Journal of International Law 20 (2002), p. 91.
73   Jägers, Corporate Human Rights Obligations (2002), pp. 8 f.
74   This opposition manifested itself in the call for a "New International Economic Order" on part of the developing countries, see United Nations General Assembly, Declaration on the Establishment of a New International Economic Order, UN Doc. A/RES/S-6/3201 of 1 May 1974; see also Muchlinki, Multinational Enterprises and the Law (1995), pp. 3 ff.
75   Schabas, Enforcing International Humanitarian Law (2001), p. 441.
76   Charter of the International Military Tribunal, Art. 6; and Charter of the International Military Tribunal for the Far East, Art. 5.
77   International Law Commission, Principles of International Law Recognized in the Charter of the Nürnberg Tribunal and in the Judgment of the Tribunal, in: Yearbook of the International Law Commission (1950), Vol. 2, principle VII.
78   International Law Commission, Draft Code of Crimes against the Peace and Security of Mankind, in: Yearbook of the International Law Commission (1996), Vol. 2 (Part 2), pp. 17 ff., Art. 2, para. 3 (d).
79   Rome Statute of the International Criminal Court, Art. 25, para. 3 (b) on soliciting and inducing the (attempted) commission of a crime, para. 3 (c) on aiding, abetting, or otherwise assisting in the (attempted) commission of a crime, and para. 3 (d) on contribution the (attempted) commission of a rime by a group with a common

Criminal Tribunal for the Former Yugoslavia (ICTY), individual complicity also has "a basis in customary international law".[80]

We will now turn to the contents of individual complicity. As for the objective element, terms such as "to solicit" or "to induce" are "applicable to cases in which a person is influenced by another to commit a crime".[81] This influence is "normally of a psychological nature but may also take the form of physical pressure within the meaning of vis compulsiva"[82]. If this cannot be proved, the threshold for at least aiding, abetting or otherwise assisting might still be reached. A distinction has occasionally been brought forward between "aiding" and "abetting".[83] However, a general definition for both is "practical assistance, encouragement, or moral support which has a substantial effect on the perpetration of the crime".[84] Under the Rome Statute, however, there is no reference to the contribution having to be "substantial", which might be seen as indicating a lower objective threshold.[85] Under certain exceptional circumstances, the mere "presence" of a person can amount to complicity as well, "if the presence can be shown or inferred, by circumstantial or other evidence, to be knowing and to have a direct and substantial effect"[86] or "a significant legitimising or encouraging effect on the principal offender"[87]. Concerning the subjective element, unlike stronger forms such as soliciting and inducing, which require a *mens rea* to commit the crime in question, in regard of aiding, abetting and otherwise assisting, the ICTY ruled that it is only necessary that the person

---

purpose; see also Statute of the International Criminal Tribunal for the Former Yugoslavia, Art. 7, para. 1; Statute of the International Criminal Tribunal for Rwanda, Art. 6, para.1.

80   International Criminal Tribunal for the Former Yugoslavia, *Prosecutor vs. Tadić*, Case No. IT-94-1, Trial Chamber Opinion and Judgement of 7 May 1997, para. 666.

81   K. Ambos, Article 25: Individual Criminal Responsibility, in: O. Triffterer (ed.), Commentary on the Rome Statute of the International Criminal Court (1999), p. 481.

82   Ibid.

83   International Criminal Tribunal for Rwanda, *Prosecutor vs. Akayesu* (1998), para. 484: "Aiding and abetting, which may appear to be synonymous, are indeed different. Aiding means giving assistance to someone. Abetting, on the other hand, would involve facilitating the commission of an act by being sympathetic thereto".

84   International Criminal Tribunal for the Former Yugoslavia, *Prosecutor vs. Furunzija*, Case No. IT-95-17/1, Judgement of 10 December 1998, p. 249. This is also in line with the residual clause of the Rome Statute of the International Criminal Court, Art. 25, para. 3 (c) of "otherwise assists".

85   A. Clapham, On Complicity, in: M. Henzelin/R. Roth (eds.), Le droit pénal à l'épreuve de l'internationalisation (2002), pp. 254 f.

86   International Criminal Tribunal for the Former Yugoslavia, *Prosecutor vs. Tadić* (1997), para. 689.

87   International Criminal Tribunal for the Former Yugoslavia, *Prosecutor vs. Krnojelac*, Case No. IT-97-25, Trial Chamber Judgement of 25 March 2002, para. 89.

"knew (in the sense that he was aware) that his own acts assisted in the commission of the specific crime in question by the principal offender. The aider and abettor must be aware of the essential elements of the crime committed by the principal offender, including the principal offender's mens rea"[88].

However, concerning the wording of the Rome Statute (viz. "For the purpose of facilitating"[89]), it has been argued that this "implies a specific subjective requirement stricter than mere knowledge".[90] In any case, "it is not necessary for the accomplice to share the mens rea of the perpetrator, in the sense of positive intention to commit the crime."[91] Interestingly, it has been suggested that this knowledge may not only be derived from official or specialized documents, but also through mass media coverage.[92] On top of this, "a person may very well be tried as an accomplice, even where the principal perpetrator of the crime has not been identified, or where, for any other reasons, the latter's guilt can not be proven".[93]

When we now attempt to extend international criminal jurisdiction to corporations, the concept of complicity harbours some interesting potential due to its special features. Firstly, the different degree of intent, which can be detached from the *mens rea* of the perpetrator, and which could also be inferred from a factual situation,[94] would make it remarkably easier to convict a corporation. Whereas it is rather unlikely, for instance, to find a leading

---

88   Ibid., para. 90.
89   Rome Statute of the International Criminal Court, Art. 25, para. 3 (c).
90   Ambos, Article 25 (1999), p. 483.
91   International Criminal Tribunal for the Former Yugoslavia, *Prosecutor vs. Furunzija* (1998), para. 245; see also International Criminal Tribunal for Rwanda, *Prosecutor vs. Akayesu*, Case No. ICTR-96-4-T, Judgement of 2 September 1998, para. 531.
92   Referring to the Sierra Leone conflict and its coverage by the media, William Schabas noted that "a court ought to have little difficulty in concluding that diamond traders, airline pilots and executives, small arms suppliers and so on have knowledge of their contribution to the conflict and to the offences being committed". Schabas, *Enforcing International Humanitarian Law* (2001), p. 451.
93   International Criminal Tribunal for Rwanda, *Prosecutor vs. Musema*, Case No. ICTR-96-4-T, Judgement and Sentence of 27 January 2007, para. 174.
94   Note British Military Court, *Trial of Bruno Tesch and Two Others* (1949), pp. 100 ff., where two of the accused individuals were convicted because they must have known from the mere quantity of poison gas that was supplied, that it did not serve a legitimate purpose; note also the dictum by the International Criminal Tribunal for Rwanda that "in the absence of a confession from the accused, his intent can be inferred from a certain number of presumptions of fact", International Criminal Tribunal for Rwanda, *Prosecutor vs. Akayesu*, Case No. ICTR-96-4-T, Judgement of 2 September 1998, para. 523, even for the crime of genocide (as was the case here); for complicity to genocide see International Criminal Tribunal for Rwanda, *Prosecutor vs. Musema*, Case No. ICTR-96-4-T, Judgement and Sentence of 27 January 2007, paras. 884-936.

individual within a corporation with the intent to commit genocide or crimes against humanity on behalf of that corporation, it seems much more easily conceivable to find one who could reasonably have been expected to be aware that his or her company is contributing to the commission of such crimes (in accordance with the theory of "identification", as outlined in the preceding section).

Secondly, there are different forms of typical corporate behaviour discernible that might be covered by the legal notion of complicity. For instance, a company might provide active assistance to a crime while rendering its services to the actual perpetrators. Such cases might involve construction companies covering up mass graves, warehouses providing storage room for arms later used for massacres, or radio stations broadcasting hate speech in order to incite genocide or other grave crimes, as well as the financing, for instance, of security forces that are likely to abuse protestors.[95] It is to be stressed once more that the activity in question need not be a crime *per se*. It is through knowingly assisting in the crime of the other that it becomes criminal conduct.[96] Moreover, joint ventures, undertaken by a corporation and a government that are likely to lead to abuses in pursuing its part of the deal, might be seen as active assistance or at least as substantial encouragement.[97]

Finally, the fact that mere presence can amount to complicity if it can reasonably be assumed to lend significant legitimacy or moral support to abuses has also great potential. If a large multinational corporation, which obviously has the choice of location, decided to continue its presence, production, and tax paying in a certain host country, despite the fact that massive atrocities are taking place there, this might in extreme circumstances make this corporation an accomplice to the country's regime. This would constitute a remarkable advancement, namely rendering the (laudable) voluntary decision of a company to disinvest in the face of massive human rights violations[98] into an obligation sustained by criminal sanctions. Especially in view of the above-mentioned ever-fiercer competition for foreign investment, this seems an intriguing remedy.

---

95 International Council on Human Rights Policy, Beyond Voluntarism: Human Rights and the Developing International Legal Obligations of Companies (2002), p. 126.
96 According to the concept of "borrowed criminality" ("criminalité d'emprunt"), see International Criminal Tribunal for Rwanda, *The Prosecutor v. Akayesu* (1998), para. 528.
97 International Council on Human Rights Policy, Beyond Voluntarism (2002), pp. 128 f.
98 A rare example being Levi Strauss' withdrawal from Burma (Myanmar) in 1992 due to the military government's bad human rights record, see C. Avery, Business and Human Rights in a Time of Change, in: M. Kamminga/S. Zia-Ziarifi (eds.), Liability of Multinational Corporations under International Law (2000), p. 54.

IV.   Forms of Punishment for Corporations

As the third big conceptual stumbling block to be moved out of the way, the question of the forms of punishment applicable to a corporation should be addressed. Evidently, contrary to natural persons, a corporation is a discarnate fiction with "[n]o body to be kicked"[99], or alternatively, to be put in prison. This is regrettable, for it is true that "incarceration is one cost of business that you [cannot] pass to the consumer"[100], but remains an unalterable fact.

However, this is no insurmountable obstacle for prosecuting corporations, since there is a variety of other sanctions conceivable. It is interesting to note that the Draft Statute of the ICC used to include a special provision for penalties applicable to legal persons, reading:

> "A legal person shall incur one or more of the following penalties:
> (i) fines;
> [(ii) dissolution;]
> [(iii) prohibition, for such period as determined by the Court, of the exercise of activities of any kind;]
> [(iv) closure, for such a period as determined by the Court, of the premises used in the commission of the crime;]
> [(v) forfeiture of [instrumentalities of crime and] proceeds, property and assets obtained by criminal conduct;] [and] [(vi) appropriate forms of reparation.]"[101]

An even wider range was spelled out in a Council of Europe recommendation on corporate liability dating from 1988, which included:

> "-   warning, reprimand, recognisance;
> -   a decision declaratory of responsibility, but no sanction;
> -   fine or other pecuniary sanction;
> -   confiscation of property which was used in the commission of the offence or represents the gains derived from the illegal activity;
> -   prohibition of certain activities, in particular exclusion from doing business with public authorities;

---

99   Lord Chancellor Edward, First Baron Thurlow, cited in Dunford/Ridley, "No Soul to be Damned, No Body to be Kicked" (1996), p. 1.

100   Quoting the Chief Executive of the Environmental Crimes Division of the United States Department of Justice, cited in N. Smith, No Longer Just a Cost of Doing Business: Criminal Liability of Corporate Officials for Violations of the Clean Water Act and the Resource Conservation and Recovery Act, in: Louisiana Law Review 53 (1992/1993), p. 126.

101   United Nations Diplomatic Conference of Plenipotentiaries on the Establishment of an International Criminal Court, Report of the Preparatory Committee on the Establishment of an International Criminal Court: Draft Statute for the International Criminal Court, UN Doc. A/CONF.183/2/Add.1 of 14 April 1998, Draft Art. 76 (footnotes omitted, the square brackets indicate that these were propositions and not consolidated draft provisions).

- exclusion from fiscal advantages and subsidies;
- prohibition upon advertising goods or services;
- annulment of licences;
- removal of managers;
- appointment of a provisional caretaker management by the judicial authority;
- closure of the enterprise;
- winding-up of the enterprise;
- compensation and/or restitution to the victim;
- restoration of the former state;
- publication of the decision imposing a sanction or measure.

These sanctions and measures may be taken alone or in combination, with or without suspensive effect, as main or as subsidiary orders."[102]

The most common sanction in domestic law seems to be the fine. In some national systems, this is the only penalty applicable to corporations.[103] Its obvious advantages are that it is easy to administer and that it directly addresses the basic corporate rationale, namely profitability. If thus certain conduct incurs sensitive additional costs in the form of a fine, the rational company will adjust its behaviour according to basic economic theory.[104] However, the effects can be rather limited, since the costs can be passed on to the shareholders, employees or consumers. Apart from that, especially with regard to large multinational corporations, fines tend to be so small in relation to their overall turnovers and profits that they will not have any effect at all.[105] Close to a fine, but more appealing, seems the possibility to order punitive reparations to the victims, which combines mere punishment with relief for those affected by corporate criminal conduct. It should be stressed that this was one of the major arguments in favour of the French proposal at the Rome Conference, since corporations are much more likely to actually have sufficient funds at their disposal than

---

102   Council of Europe Committee of Ministers, Recommendation No. R (88) 18 of the Committee of Minister of Member States Concerning Liability of Enterprises Having Legal Personality for Offences Committed in the Exercise of Their Activities of 20 October 1988, Appendix to Recommendation No. R (88) 18, p. 7.

103   E.g. in Switzerland (Swiss Strafgesetzbuch, Art. 102); in Germany for regulatory offences, since there is no criminal corporate responsibility (Gesetz über Ordnungswidrigkeiten, § 30); or in England and Wales for most violations (see M. Jefferson, Corporate Criminal Liability: The Problem of Sanctions, in: Journal of Criminal Law 65 (2001), p. 236).

104   Jefferson, Corporate Criminal Liability (2001), pp. 238 ff.

105   See Wells, Corporations and Criminal Responsibility (2001), pp. 32 f. E.g., a comparatively large fine of £750.00 was imposed on British Petroleum (BP) in 1987, but which represented only 0.05 percent of the corporation's after tax profits alone (i.e. not turnover!); ibid., p. 33. See also extensively B. Fisse, Sentencing Options against Corporations, in: Criminal Law Forum 1 (1990), pp. 214 ff.

individuals in order to provide for an appropriate amount of reparations.[106] One downside of this measure, however, is that "the dividing line between civil and criminal action may be becoming blurred".[107]

The general problem with monetary penalties can also be seen from a moral view-point, since they do not necessarily "convey the message that serious corporate offences are socially intolerable"[108]. Instead, "they create the impression that corporate crime is permissible provided the offender merely pays the going price".[109] Therefore, it is imperative to move beyond a purely monetary approach to sanctions and provide for forms of punishment that might have both greater punitive and deterrent effects on companies, such as dissolution, suspension of certain activities etc., as they have been elaborated in the above-mentioned documents.[110] Arguably the most effective, and also relatively easy to administer penalty is adverse publicity. Whereas the Council of Europe recommendation included its modest version, namely "publication of the decision imposing a sanction or measure", its more sophisticated version might "take the form of advertising in the media or sending newsletters to shareholders and consumers"[111] at the expense of the convicted corporation. This approach is interesting for several reasons. First, it is a well-known fact that prestige and image are of remarkable importance in the modern business world.[112] This is not least true for globally acting multinational corporations.[113] For instance, the opening words of Shell's corporate code of conduct are telling

---

106   See also Schabas, Enforcing International Humanitarian Law (2001), p. 453.
107   Meron, Is International Law Moving towards Criminalization? (1998), p. 20. Note in this context also the U.S. Alien Tort Claims Act and the jurisprudence connected with it, which has received much attention in literature (see e.g. Clapham, Human Rights Obligations of Non-State Actors (2006), pp. 252 ff.; and B. Stephens, Corporate Accountability: International Human Rights Litigation Against Corporations in US Courts, in: M. Kamminga/S. Zia-Ziarifi (eds.), Liability of Multinational Corporations under International Law (2000), pp. 209 ff.).
108   Fisse, Sentencing Options against Corporations (1990), p. 220.
109   Ibid.
110   See on alternative punishments in a domestic context Wells, Corporations and Criminal Responsibility (2001), pp. 37 ff.; Jefferson, Corporate Criminal Liability (2001), pp. 244 ff., as well as Fisse, Sentencing Options against Corporations (1990), pp. 229 ff.
111   Jefferson, Corporate Criminal Liability (2001), p. 256. See generally the extensive study of B. Fisse/J. Braithwaite, The Impact of Publicity on Corporate Offenders (1983).
112   See generally C. Fombrun, Reputation: Realizing Value from the Corporate Image (1996); also Avery, Business and Human Rights in a Time of Change (2000), pp. 25 f.
113   See e.g. the massive publicity campaign launched by PanAm after the Lockerbie incident, by P&O after the Herald of Free Enterprise disaster (see Wells, Corporations and Criminal Responsibility (2001), p. 38), or by Union Carbide after the Bhopal tragedy (see Jefferson, Corporate Criminal Liability (2001), p. 259).

in this regard: "Reputations are hard won and easily lost. We can all play a part in protecting and building Shell's reputation. Be sure."[114] Doubtlessly, one can be even surer when using the stigma generally attached to a criminal conviction to this end, and which would be significantly amplified when pronounced by an international tribunal, due to its authoritativeness and global exposure. It has been argued that this may well have a significant deterrent effect on corporations,[115] thus fulfilling one of the fundamental functions of criminal justice.

Furthermore, while multinational corporations might try to avoid enforcement of sanctions through their complex structure of a network of subsidiaries in different countries, adverse publicity targets the entity as whole, leaving little possibility for avoidance.[116]

Moreover, consideration might be given to the contents of the adverse publicity. It does not necessarily need to be limited to a statement that the corporation was convicted of certain crimes. For example, victims of corporate criminal conduct "may be alerted to the possibility of bringing civil claims [domestically], and shareholders may be encouraged to assert control over the wrongdoers".[117] Finally, it could also raise awareness of the general problem complex. Illuminating is in this respect the example of an American corporation convicted of unlawful disposal of toxic waste that was sentenced to put an advert in a large newspaper, addressing pollution and environmental protection.[118] This would have great potential when applied to gross human rights violations. Here again, it is the multinational corporations that could actually afford launching regional or even global media campaigns.

Moreover, this point might also have further implications with regard to complicity: Since such publicity actions would greatly contribute in raising general "knowledge" and "awareness" among the public, fewer persons, both natural and legal, could hide behind a veil of ignorance while further contributing to the perpetuation of certain grievances. Adverse publicity might thus create a sort of "snowball effect" to the benefit of fundamental human rights.

In sum, it can plainly be stated that there is a wide variety of sanctions available for corporations. Which sanction, or which combination of sanctions, will be most appropriate will depend on the case at hand.

---

114 Shell Code of Conduct: How to Live by the Shell General Business Principles, www. static.shell.com/static/aboutshell/downloads/who_we_are/code_of_conduct/english. pdf (last accessed: 8 June 2009), p. 3.
115 Jefferson, Corporate Criminal Liability (2001), p. 258.
116 Fisse, Sentencing Options against Corporations (1990), p. 243.
117 Jefferson, Corporate Criminal Liability (2001), p. 258.
118 Fisse, Sentencing Options against Corporations (1990), p. 242.

V.   Concluding Observations

Following the discussion of these major questions, which would need to be answered in order to enable the application of international criminal law to corporate actors, the following main conclusion can be drawn: None of these conceptual stumbling blocks proved to be insuperable. First, it could be shown that today there exists a number of interesting, and workable theories to determine corporate *mens rea*. For international criminal law, however, a broad, functional version of the "identification" theory seems most advisable for both doctrinal and practical reasons. Second, the rising problem of corporate complicity in international crimes can also be addressed by drawing on the existing international criminal framework for individual complicity. Third, both on the international and national levels, a great number of different forms of punishment for the convicted corporation are available, ranging from mere fines to dissolution, from which judges could select a combination most suitable to prevent further misconduct, as well as to guarantee redress for the victims. Of particular potential would be the penalty of "adverse advertising".

   Hence, there seem to be no cogent reasons to prevent the use of the fast-expanding framework of international criminal law to rectify the regime deficit in terms of corporate accountability commensurate with corporate power on the international stage. To the contrary, it can be argued that international criminal law has a vast potential to fill, at least partially, the gap that traditional approaches such as classic state responsibility, the international human rights regime and so-called corporate self-regulation have failed to close.

   Of course, it ultimately will become, as it is often the case in international affairs, a question of political will to bring about this extension of international criminal jurisdiction to corporate actors. In this regard, this final consideration might serve as a source of motivation. We should ask ourselves: What is the principal reason for having international criminal law? Is it solely there to punish, or not rather to protect? I prefer to choose the latter option, for although a corporation "[h]as no soul to be damned, no body to be kicked"[119], the actual and potential human victims of its power certainly do.

---

119   Once again quoting Lord Chancellor Edward, First Baron Thurlow, cited in Dunford/ Ridley, 'No Soul to be Damned, No Body to be Kicked' (1996), p. 1.

Bibliography

Agbakwa, S., A Line in the Sand: International Dis(Order) and the Impunity of Non-State Corporate Actors in the Developing World, in: A. Anghie *et al.* (eds.), The Third World and International Order: Law, Politics, and Globalization (2003), pp. 1-18.

Allen, M., Textbook on Criminal Law (2005).

Ambos, K., Article 25: Individual Criminal Responsibility, in: O. Triffterer (ed.), Commentary on the Rome Statute of the International Criminal Court (1999), pp. 475-492.

Anonymous, Corporate Crime: Regulating Corporate Behaviour Through Criminal Sanctions, in: Harvard Law Review 92 (1978/1979), pp. 1227-1375.

Avery, C., Business and Human Rights in a Time of Change, in: M. Kamminga/S. Zia-Ziarifi (eds.), Liability of Multinational Corporations under International Law (2000), pp. 17-73.

British Military Court, Trial of Bruno Tesch and Two Others (The Zyklon B case), Case No. 9, in: Law Reports of Trials of War Criminals, Selected and Prepared by the United Nations War Crimes Commission (1949).

Carreau, D./P. Juillard, Droit International Économique (1998).

Cassese, A., International Criminal Law (2003).

Clapham, A., The Question of Jurisdiction Under International Criminal Law Over Legal Persons: Lessons from the Rome Conference on an International Criminal Court, in: M. Kamminga/S. Zia-Ziarifi (eds.), Liability of Multinational Corporations under International Law (2000), pp. 139-195.

— On Complicity, in: M. Henzelin/R. Roth (eds.), Le droit pénal à l'épreuve de l'internationalisation (2002), pp. 241-275.

— Human Rights Obligations of Non-State Actors (2006).

Council of Europe Committee of Ministers, Recommendation No. R (88) 18 of the Committee of Minister of Member States Concerning Liability of Enterprises Having Legal Personality for Offences Committed in the Exercise of Their Activities of 20 October 1988, Appendix to Recommendation No. R (88) 18.

Dunford L./A. Ridley, "No Soul to be Damned, No Body to be Kicked"[1]: Responsibility, Blame and Corporate Punishment, International Journal of the Sociology of Law 21 (1996), pp. 1-19.

Farrand, M., The Records of the Federal Convention of 1787 (1966).

Field, S./N. Jorg, Corporate Liability and Manslaughter: Should we be going Dutch?, Criminal Law Review 156 (1991), pp. 156-171.

Fisse, B./J. Braithwaite, The Impact of Publicity on Corporate Offenders (1983).

— Corporations, Crime and Accountability (1993).

Fisse, B., Sentencing Options against Corporations, Criminal Law Forum 1 (1990), pp. 211-258.

Fombrun, C., Reputation: Realizing Value from the Corporate Image (1996).

Frulli, M., Jurisdiction Ratione Materiae, in: A. Cassese *et al.* (eds.), The Rome Statute of the International Criminal Court: A Commentary (2002), Vol. 1, pp. 527-541.

Herdegen, M., Internationales Wirtschaftsrecht (2005).

Higgins, R., Problems and Process: International Law and How We Use It (1994).

Hobe, S./O. Kimmenich, Einführung in das Völkerrecht (2004).

Hocking, B./M. Smith, M., World Politics: An Introduction to International Relations (1996).

House of Lords, Armstrong vs. Strain, 1 KB 232, 1952.

House of Lords, H.L. Bolton, (Engineering) Co. Ltd. vs. T.J. Graham & Sons Ltd., 1 QB 159, 1957.

House of Lords, Tesco Supermarkets Ltd. vs. Nattrass, AC 153, 1972.

Human Rights Council, Implementation of General Assembly Resolution 60/251 of 15 March 2006 entitled "Human Rights Council", Report of the Special Representative of the Secretary-General on the Issue of Human Rights and Transnational Corporations and Other Business Enterprises, John Ruggie, Business and Human Rights: Mapping International Standards of Responsibility and Accountability for Corporate Acts, UN Doc. A/HRC/4/35 of 19 February 2007.

Hymer, S./G. Modelski, The Multinational Corporation and the Law of Uneven Development, in: G. Modelski (ed.), Transnational Corporations and World Order (1979), pp. 386-403.

International Council on Human Rights Policy, Beyond Voluntarism: Human Rights and the Developing International Legal Obligations of Companies (2002).

International Court of Justice, Corfu Channel case, ICJ Reports (1949).

International Criminal Tribunal for Rwanda, Prosecutor vs. Akayesu, Case No. ICTR-96-4-T, Judgement of 2 September 1998.

International Criminal Tribunal for Rwanda, Prosecutor vs. Musema, Case No. ICTR-96-4-T, Judgement and Sentence of 27 January 2007.

International Criminal Tribunal for the Former Yugoslavia, Prosecutor vs. Furunzija, Case No. IT-95-17/1, Judgement of 10 December 1998.

International Criminal Tribunal for the Former Yugoslavia, Prosecutor vs. Krnojelac, Case No. IT-97-25, Trial Chamber Judgement of 25 March 2002.

International Criminal Tribunal for the Former Yugoslavia, Prosecutor vs. Tadić, Case No. IT-94-1, Trial Chamber Opinion and Judgement of 7 May 1997.

International Law Commission, Draft Code of Crimes against the Peace and Security of Mankind, in: Yearbook of the International Law Commission (1996), Vol. 2 (Part 2), pp. 17-56.

International Law Commission, Principles of International Law Recognized in the Charter of the Nürnberg Tribunal and in the Judgment of the Tribunal, in: Yearbook of the International Law Commission (1950), Vol. 2, pp. 181-195.

International Military Tribunal (Nuremberg), Judgement and Sentences, 1 October 1946, in: American Journal of International Law 41 (1947), pp. 172-233.

Jägers, N., Corporate Human Rights Obligations: in Search of Accountability (2002).

Jefferson, M., Corporate Criminal Liability: The Problem of Sanctions, in: Journal of Criminal Law 65 (2001), pp. 235-261.

Joseph, S., Taming the Leviathans: Multinational Enterprises and Human Rights, in: Netherlands International Law Review 46 (1999), pp. 171-203.

Kamminga M./S. Zia-Zarifi, Liability of Multinational Corporations under International Law: An Introduction, in: M. Kamminga/S. Zia-Zarifi (eds.), Liability of Multinational Corporations under International Law (2000), pp. 1-15.

Meron, T., Is International Law Moving towards Criminalization?, in: European Journal of International Law 9 (1998), pp. 18-31.

Meyer, W., Human Rights and MNCs: Theory Versus Quantitative Analysis, in: Human Rights Quarterly 18 (1996), pp. 368-397.

Muchlinki, P., Multinational Enterprises and the Law (1995).

Negotiating Group on the Multilateral Agreement on Investment (MAI), OECD Multilateral Agreement on Investment, Draft Consolidated Text, DAFFE/MAI(98)7/REV1 of 22 April 1998.

Pradel, J., Manuel de droit pénal général (2004).

Ramasastry, A., Corporate Complicity: From Nuremberg to Rangoon. An Examination of Forced Labour Cases and Their Impact on the Liability of Multinational Corporations, in: Berkeley Journal of International Law 20 (2002), pp. 91-159.

Ratner, S., Corporations and Human Rights: A Theory of Legal Responsibility, in: Yale Law Journal 111 (2001/2002), pp. 44-545.

Rose, A., 1995 Australian Criminal Code Act: Corporate Criminal Provisions, in: Criminal Law Forum 6 (1995), pp. 129-142.

Schabas, W., Enforcing International Humanitarian Law: Catching the Accomplices, in: International Review of the Red Cross 83 (2001), pp. 439-459.

Shell Code of Conduct: How to Live by the Shell General Business Principles, www.static. shell.com/static/aboutshell/downloads/who_we_are/code_of_conduct/english.pdf (last accessed: 8 June 2009).

Shelton, D., Protecting Human Rights in a Globalizing World, in: C. Ku/P. Diehl (eds.), International Law: Classic and Contemporary Readings (2003), pp. 333-365.

Smith, J./B. Hogan, Criminal Law (2005).

Smith, J./M. Bolyard/A. Ippolito, Human Rights and the Global Economy: A Response to Meyer, in: Human Rights Quarterly 21 (1999), pp. 207-219.

Smith, N., No Longer Just a Cost of Doing Business: Criminal Liability of Corporate Officials for Violations of the Clean Water Act and the Resource Conservation and Recovery Act, Louisiana Law Review 53 (1992/1993), pp. 119-161.

Stephens, B., Corporate Accountability: International Human Rights Litigation Against Corporations in US Courts, in: M. Kamminga/S. Zia-Ziarifi (eds.), Liability of Multinational Corporations under International Law (2000), pp. 209-229.

Stratenwerth, G., Schweizerisches Strafrecht (2005).

Stuart, D., Canadian Criminal Law: A Treatise (1995).

Supreme Court of Canada, Canadian Dredge & Dock Co. vs. The Queen, 1 SCR 662 (1985).

Supreme Court of Canada, The "Rhône" vs. The "Peter A.B. Widener", 1 SCR 497 (1993).

United Nations Diplomatic Conference of Plenipotentiaries on the Establishment of an International Criminal Court, Committee of the Whole, Working Group on General Principles of Criminal Law, UN Doc. A/CONF.183/C.1/WGGP/L.5/Rev.2 of 3 July 1998.

United Nations Diplomatic Conference of Plenipotentiaries on the Establishment of an International Criminal Court, Report of the Preparatory Committee on the Establishment of an International Criminal Court: Draft Statute for the International Criminal Court, UN Doc. A/CONF.183/2/Add.1 of 14 April 1998.

United Nations Economic and Social Council, Commission on Human Rights, Sub-Commission on Prevention of Discrimination and Protection of Minorities, The Realization of Economic, Social and Cultural Rights: The Question of Transnational Corporations, Working Document on the Impact of the Activities of Transnational Corporations on the Realization of Economic, Social and Cultural Rights, Prepared by Mr. El Hadji Guissé, UN Doc. E/CN.4/Sub.2/1998/6 of 10 June 1998.

United Nations General Assembly, Declaration on the Establishment of a New International Economic Order, UN Doc. A/RES/S-6/3201 of 1 May 1974.

United States Military Tribunal, Trial of Alfried Felix Alwyn Krupp von Bohlen und Halbach and Eleven Others, Case No. 58, in: Law Reports of Trials of War Criminals, Selected and Prepared by the United Nations War Crimes Commission (1949).

United States Military Tribunal, Trial of Carl Krauch and Twenty-Two Others (The I.G. Farben Trial), Case No. 57, in: Law Reports of Trials of War Criminals, Selected and Prepared by the United Nations War Crimes Commission (1949).

Vázquez, C., Direct vs. Indirect Obligations of Corporations Under International Law, in: Columbia Journal of Transnational Law 43 (2004/2005), pp. 927-959.

Wells, C., Corporations and Criminal Responsibility (2001).

Wells, C./J. Elias, Catching the Conscience of the King: Corporate Players on the International Stage, in: P. Alston (ed.), Non-State Actors and Human Rights (2005), pp. 141-157.

Willetts, P., Transnational Actors and International Organizations in Global Politics, in: J. Baylis/S. Smith (eds.), The Globalization of World Politics: An Introduction to International Relations (2005), pp. 425-447.

Democracy in the WTO –
The Limits of the Legitimacy Debate

Nicolas Lamp[1]

I. Introduction

Ever since the widely publicised protests at the Seattle Ministerial in 1999 brought the World Trade Organization's (WTO) legitimacy crisis into sharp relief, trade lawyers and international relations scholars have been debating ways to enhance the legitimacy of WTO law. While there are sharp disagreements on the merits of the question, the debate has largely taken place within a legitimacy-to-power paradigm, i.e. the argument is about what power the WTO exercises and how that power could be legitimised. As I will argue, this discursive structure furthers a limited view of what would be required to make WTO law legitimate: First, it largely restricts the discussion to the passive dimension of self-determination, i.e. the need to secure states' freedom from imposed constraint by ensuring the accountability of whoever exercises power. Second, the focus on the need to legitimise the law that emanates from the existing power constellations promotes the assumption that steps to enhance the legitimacy of WTO law would, would have to, and indeed could leave these power constellations essentially unaffected. In short, the current debate attempts to legitimise lawmaking in the WTO in a way that accommodates current power relations, instead of interrogating and de-legitimising the practices that sustain these power relations with a view to opening up space for legitimate lawmaking in the first place.

In the present paper, I seek to counter this legitimacy-to-power paradigm with two arguments. First, I argue that for an international organisation such as the WTO to be considered legitimate, it is not sufficient for it not to constrain states in unjustifiable ways. The organisation must also enable its members to regulate globalisation effectively and thus to recover and preserve their political autonomy under circumstances of increasing interconnectedness and (inter) dependence. This active dimension of self-determination, however, has been largely ignored in the current legitimacy debate. Second, I argue that attempts to enhance the legitimacy of WTO law will remain superficial to the extent that they do not contribute to a reconfiguration of power relations in the WTO. By this I do not mean the redistribution of coercive power to some states at

---

1   The author would like to thank Nico Krisch, Andrew Lang, Colin Scott, and Monika Medick-Krakau for their helpful comments on earlier drafts of this chapter. All remaining errors and misconceptions are entirely the author's responsibility.

the expense of others but rather the need to enhance the role of what *Jürgen Habermas* calls communicative power, i.e. the transformative capacity that flows from the persuasive force of arguments, in the lawmaking process. This approach directs our attention to institutional practices and discursive structures that currently inhibit the formation of communicative power in the WTO.

I present my argument in the following steps. In the second section, I sketch the current legitimacy debate and show how the legitimacy-to-power paradigm, and in particular a bias towards passive self-determination and an agnostic attitude towards existing power relations, cuts across and hence unites what are often presented as alternative ways of conceptualising the legitimacy of WTO law. I then present the theoretical case for a stronger focus on active self-determination and communicative power, and discuss what can be described as a paradigmatic case for this perspective, namely the amendment of the TRIPS provisions on compulsory licensing in response to concerns about their detrimental effect on least-developed countries' capacity to address public health crises. Thirdly, I offer a preliminary analysis of the main obstacles to active self-determination and the formation of communicative power in the WTO's lawmaking culture, focusing on the role of reciprocity. I conclude with a short summary of the argument.

II.   Democracy in the WTO – Anatomy of a Debate[2]

The protests at the Seattle Ministerial of the WTO form the starting point of many discussions of the organisation's legitimacy not only in a literal[3] but also in a theoretical sense. These protests epitomise what is often seen as the essence of the legitimacy crisis of the WTO: the perception that the WTO is an increasingly powerful international institution which is disconnected from and unaccountable to the public. From this starting point, commentators tend to take either one of two positions: they either argue that the WTO as such does not exercise any power and hence is not in need of legitimisation, or they concede

---

2   Drawing the boundaries of a debate is necessarily beset by a degree of arbitrariness. In my analysis of the WTO "legitimacy debate", I will largely focus on contributions which explicitly address questions of legitimacy and democracy in the WTO. My observations are based on this sample, and it is entirely possible that one would arrive at different conclusions if one adopted a broader definition of what kind of scholarship represents a contribution to the "legitimacy debate". I thank Andrew Lang for drawing my attention to this point.

3   See e.g. D. Esty, The World Trade Organization's Legitimacy Crisis, in: World Trade Review 1 (2002); M. Elsig, The World Trade Organization's Legitimacy Crisis: What Does the Beast Look Like?, in: Journal of World Trade 41 (2007).

that the WTO indeed exercises power and then discuss how that power could be legitimised. *Robert Howse* makes this line of reasoning most explicit. As he puts it,

> "to understand the nature of the legitimacy question with respect to the WTO, it is first of all necessary to consider the kind of power that the WTO exercises".[4]

He then identifies several ways in which the WTO exercises power and considers potential sources of legitimacy. Other authors establish a similar connection between the WTO's increased authority as compared to the General Agreement on Tariffs and Trade (GATT) and the need for "new foundations for its legitimacy".[5]

The same premise – that the WTO only needs legitimacy to the extent that it exercises power – underlies the argument that concerns about a "democratic deficit" in the WTO are misplaced. Thus, *James Bacchus*, a former member of the Appellate Body, argues that the WTO's critics fail to appreciate "the essential 'legitimacy' of the WTO, and (...) the extent of the 'democratic governance' that already prevails in the WTO", because they do not understand that the WTO is "only a label" and hence not something that could "impose its arbitrary will on the sovereign nations of the world".[6] Similarly, *Mike Moore*, the former Director-General of the WTO, claims that it is "difficult to conceive of a system that could be more democratic" than the WTO on the grounds that the WTO is not more than a common enterprise of its member states and hence wields no power of its own.[7] And it is the fundamental powerlessness of international institutions that forms the basis of *Andrew Moravcsik's* seminal argument that we should stop worrying about the democratic deficit of international institutions such as the European Union (EU).[8]

While these commentators thus come to radically different conclusions regarding the legitimacy of the WTO and its law, they share what could be called a legitimacy-to-power paradigm, i.e. their analysis focuses on the

---

4   R. Howse, The Legitimacy of the World Trade Organization, in: J.-M. Coicaud/V. Heiskanen (eds.), The Legitimacy of International Organizations (2001), p. 357.

5   Esty, The World Trade Organization's Legitimacy Crisis (2002), p. 10.

6   J. Bacchus, A Few Thoughts on Legitimacy, Democracy, and the WTO, in: E.-U. Petersmann (ed.), Reforming the World Trading System. Legitimacy, Efficiency, and Democratic Governance (2005), pp. 429 f.

7   M. Moore, The Democratic Roots of the World Trade Organization, in: P. Macrory/A. Appleton/M. Plummer (eds.), The World Trade Organization. Legal, Economic and Political Analysis, Vol. 1 (2005), p. 40 and passim; this is also the WTO's own position, see World Trade Organization, Ten Common Misunderstandings About the WTO (2007).

8   See A. Moravcsik, In Defence of the 'Democratic Deficit': Reassessing Legitimacy in the European Union, in: Journal of Common Market Studies 40 (2002).

question whether the WTO exercises power and, in case they conclude that it does, how that power could be legitimised. As I argue, these terms of debate do two things: they focus attention on the law that has been made instead of the law that could (and perhaps should) have been made and hence limit the view to the passive dimension of self-determination (1). Moreover, they tailor the debate towards the need to legitimise the law that emanates from the existing power constellations rather than the need to reconfigure these power relations in a way that would make legitimate lawmaking possible in the first place (2).

(1) While some commentators advocate minor changes in the substance of WTO law, in particular a greater sensitivity to policy objectives other than "free trade" narrowly conceived,[9] the focus of the legitimacy debate is clearly on legitimising the law as it stands. This is most evident in the contributions by those who consider the WTO's legitimacy a non-issue due to the centrality of the consensus procedure in WTO lawmaking and hence the theoretical capacity of any member to veto a decision.[10] These commentators conceive of legitimacy in purely negative terms: as the absence of imposed constraint. From this perspective, no more is needed to establish the legitimacy of WTO law than an analysis of whether it has been imposed on a country. Given that no country is legally obliged to join the WTO and almost all decisions are taken by consensus, these commentators quickly come to the conclusion that the legitimacy of WTO law is unproblematic.

Howse goes beyond this purely formal and negative conception of legitimacy by supplementing it with a notion of "social" legitimacy, i.e. the "broad, empirically determined, societal acceptance" of a system of government.[11] He then marshals an impressive array of potential sources for the social legitimacy of WTO law. It is only in his conclusion that he concedes that the "doubts about the wisdom and justice of the kind of economic liberalization that provides an important dimension to the substantive legitimacy of the WTO"[12] may be such that even judicial interpretations of WTO law that are sensitive to other values may not be sufficient to legitimise the WTO. Even though *Howse* advocates "caution or even a standstill on issues like investment and intellectual property", he does not propose any major revisions of WTO law even in those areas in

---

9   See Esty, The World Trade Organization's Legitimacy Crisis (2002); Howse, Legitimacy of the World Trade Organization (2001), pp. 391 ff.; on the need to question what "free trade" should mean in the first place, see A. Lang, Reflecting on 'Linkage': Cognitive and Institutional Change in the International Trading System, in: Modern Law Review 70 (2007).

10   See Bacchus, A Few Thoughts on Legitimacy (2005); Moore, Democratic Roots (2005).

11   Howse, Legitimacy of the World Trade Organization (2001), p. 361.

12   Ibid. p. 395.

which his own analysis clearly shows that the law systematically disadvantages developing countries.[13]

Overall, the fixation on legitimising the law as it stands is symptomatic of the whole legitimacy debate. The possibility that to make WTO law legitimate one might actually have to change it, is rarely even considered.[14] One reason for this may be that even when legitimacy is not conceptualised in purely formal terms, the legitimacy crisis of the WTO is often portrayed as a problem of a lack of acceptance of the (pre-existing) law which has to be remedied by building "new connections to the publics around the world in whose name trade policy is advanced" or by reason-giving.[15] Moreover, many trade lawyers perceive the project of trade liberalisation as essentially sound and therefore see the problem of its legitimacy as one of enlightening the public and developing countries as to its value.[16]

I argue that a conception of legitimacy as freedom from imposed constraint is inherently limited, and a debate focused on showing that WTO law is not imposed or should not be perceived as such misses an important point. For an international institution such as the WTO to be legitimate, it is arguably not sufficient that is does not constrain states in unjustifiable ways. The organisation must also enable its members to govern themselves effectively and thus to recover and preserve their political autonomy under circumstances of increasing interconnectedness and (inter)dependence. In other words, the idea of a legitimate system of governance does not only necessitate that its members are not subjected to rules and decisions which cannot meet with general assent, but also that they must be capable of actually making and implementing those rules and decisions which can meet with general assent. As *Claus Offe* and *Ulrich Preuss* have put it:

---

13   This is particularly true for the TRIPS agreement; see ibid. and M. Trebilcock/R. Howse, The Regulation of International Trade (2005), chapter 13.

14   At the same time, this proposition appears to be widely accepted as soon as one looks beyond the confines of the legitimacy debate; see e.g. J. Stiglitz/A. Carlton, Fair Trade for All. How Trade Can Promote Development (2005).

15   Esty, The World Trade Organization's Legitimacy Crisis (2002), p. 9: "Public acceptance of the authority and decisions that emerge from the World Trade Organization can no longer be taken for granted in many countries"; cf. Steffek's and Nanz's defintion of legitimacy, adopted in Elsig, The World Trade Organization's Legitimacy Crisis (2007), p. 80, fn. 17: "Legitimacy can be understood as a general compliance of the people with decisions of a political order that goes beyond coercion or the contingent representation of interests", P. Nanz/J. Steffek, Global Governance, Participation and the Public Sphere, in: Government and Opposition 39 (2004), p. 315.

16   See in particular S. Cho, A Quest for WTO's Legitimacy, in: World Trade Review 4 (2005), p. 398, who argues for the use of "social marketing" so that "everyday people" are "informed and educated about WTO norms" in an "osmotic process of enlightenment"; cf. Moore, Democratic Roots (2005).

"A system of rule in which rulers are held perfectly accountable by the ruled yet cannot accomplish anything is as much a caricature, or an impoverished version, of democracy as a system of rule that is highly effective in shaping conditions and developments without being accountable to the ruled."[17]

This active dimension of self-determination is sometimes conceptualised as "output legitimacy", i.e. the effectiveness of a system of rule in achieving certain socially desired ends.[18] This terminology might give rise to the impression that "input" and "output" legitimacy are alternatives. However, I would argue that the two are inseparable: Without "input", it is impossible to know which "output" is desired. For example, it would be implausible to claim that the trade system has "output" legitimacy because it enhances global wealth if what states really care about is food security and the preservation of traditional livelihoods. I therefore propose to conceptualise active and passive self-determination as two dimensions of a practice that an international institution has to facilitate in order to produce legitimate outcomes. From this perspective, we have to consider not only the decisions but also the non-decisions made in the WTO; not only the constraints it imposes, but also the privileges it confers; and not only the WTO's power but also its powerlessness.

(2) A related and arguably more important and pervasive blind spot of the current debate is its agnostic attitude towards power relations. In the legitimacy-to-power paradigm, power is the fixed variable: either power is exercised or not – what matters is whether it is legitimised and held accountable. Some authors – especially *Howse* – provide sophisticated discussions of the different forms of power which the WTO exercises; their approach to the legitimacy question, however, consistently leads them to ask how one could bring legitimacy to this power, rather than how one might have to reconfigure these power relations in order to make legitimate lawmaking possible in the first place. In *Howse's* analysis, there is a clear recognition that it might ultimately be impossible to legitimise WTO law in its current form because of the "gap between formal and social legitimacy that exists even in the rules themselves".[19] But rather than embracing the obvious conclusion – that the rules, and by implication the power relations that stand behind those rules, need to be changed –, the only potential remedy that *Howse* considers, and ultimately discards, is the "sensitive exercise of judicial power" by the Appellate Body.[20]

Howse's analysis has the merit of clearly showing the limits of any attempt to legitimise WTO law in its current form. In many other contributions, the current rules represent the unproblematic parameters within which conceptual

---

17   C. Offe/U. Preuss, The Problem of Legitimacy in the European Polity. Is Democratization the Answer?, in: Constitutionalism Webpapers 6 (2006), p. 5.
18   See e.g. F. Scharpf, Governing in Europe: Effective and Democratic? (1999).
19   Howse, Legitimacy of the World Trade Organization (2001), p. 395.
20   See ibid.

and practical problems of transferring democracy to the international sphere are discussed. This set-up of the legitimacy debate not only ties in neatly with narratives about the international trading system which retrospectively make the expansion of international trade law into areas such as intellectual property rights and trade in services appear as an entirely natural and irreversible development; it also reifies the power of the WTO, or more precisely the power relations between states as they play out in the WTO. As a result, these power relations do not appear as something that would have to change to make legitimate lawmaking possible.

However, when one follows the WTO lawmaking process, for example the protracted agricultural negotiations, one is left with the impression that it is hardly conceivable that the current power relations will lead to legitimate outcomes. As I argue, these can only be envisioned if we can devise strategies to change the way in which power is exercised within the WTO, and it is these strategies that the legitimacy debate should focus on. Of course, changing the way power is exercised in the WTO is not an easy proposition. Indeed, one of the reasons many contributors to the legitimacy debate have adopted an agnostic attitude to power relations may be that they see no way how these relations can be changed in the short term. As I will argue below, however, this view is rooted in an overly narrow conception of power as coercive power – the capacity to impose one's will despite resistance. By adopting a broader conception of power, I hope to show two things: first, the dominant position of some nations in WTO lawmaking is not solely a result of their economic clout but is to a significant extent sustained by a particular culture of WTO lawmaking; second, forms of power other than coercive power are not only more readily available to developing countries, but they also make it more likely that the resulting law will be considered legitimate by all member states. From this perspective, the question of the legitimacy of WTO law becomes one of reconfiguring power relations in a way that brings those forms of power most conducive to legitimate lawmaking to the fore.

III. Broadening the Debate – Active Self-Determination and Communicative Power

Before I can analyse in more detail how the lawmaking culture in the WTO inhibits active self-determination and the formation of those forms of power most conducive to legitimate lawmaking, I need to elaborate on the theoretical foundations of these concepts. To this end, I first set out the conception of legitimacy with which I operate. I then analyse how the requirement of consent can under certain circumstances constitute an obstacle to active self-determination and hence be detrimental to the legitimacy of outcomes. Thirdly,

I examine the theoretical foundations of the concept of communicative power which, I will argue, not only represents a form of power that is more easily accessible to states which are weak in terms of coercive power, but also has an internal connection to legitimate lawmaking. Finally, I discuss a paradigmatic case for an approach to the legitimacy of WTO law that focuses on active self-determination and the use of communicative power: the amendment of the Agreement on Trade-Related Aspects of Intellectual Property Rights (TRIPS) provisions on compulsory licensing.

1.   A Discourse Theoretical Conception of Legitimacy

As to any other concept, a whole range of different meanings can be ascribed to the concept of legitimacy.[21] In the context of politics, the nowadays most widely accepted conception of legitimacy holds that the laws which govern a political community are legitimate when they are based on the consent of the members of the community. It is for a good reason that this "democratic" understanding of legitimacy has gained so widespread currency:[22] after the process of rationalisation which is characteristic of the modern age and which in many societies has seen the unquestioning acceptance of traditional belief systems undermined,[23] any appeal to a normative authority other than the will of the people to justify a particular form of social order has become difficult to sustain. Even output legitimacy – the idea that a form of government can draw legitimacy from its effectiveness in achieving particular outcomes – is ultimately dependent on some kind of popular will-formation in order to determine which outcomes are desired and at what costs in the first place. And while particular traditional or religious visions of the good life still maintain a strong hold on many societies, proponents of these visions increasingly rely on popular support, if not in order to directly legitimise the law's content (which is deemed legitimate due to its divine or historical providence), then at least to receive a mandate to institute and administer it in a particular manner.[24]

In pluralist modern societies, the procedural idea of self-government, i.e. the notion that people should only be subject to laws to which they have themselves assented, has replaced metaphysical or historical authorities as the primary

---

21   See S. Mulligan, The Uses of Legitimacy in International Relations, in: Millennium 34 (2005).
22   As Susan Marks puts it, democracy is now recognised as a "byword for legitimate authority", S. Marks, Democracy and International Governance, in: J.-M. Coicaud/V. Heiskanen (eds.), The Legitimacy of International Organizations (2001), p. 47.
23   See W. Collony, Introduction: Legitimacy and Modernity, in: W. Collony (ed.), Legitimacy and the State (1984); cf. J. Habermas, Theorie des kommunikativen Handelns. Vol. 1: Handlungsrationalität und gesellschaftliche Rationalisierung (1981).
24   See N. Feldman, Does Sharia Mean the Rule of Law?, in: International Herald Tribune of 16 March 2008.

source of political legitimacy. The realisation of this idea of self-government in the circumstances of a complex society, however, represents a formidable challenge. In the following, I will adopt one of the most promising proposals on how this challenge could be met, namely the conception of legitimacy developed in *Habermas'* discourse theory of law and democracy.

In "Between Facts and Norms", *Habermas* argues that in a complex and pluralist modern society self-determination can only be realised as a discursive process in the course of which deliberation in parliament is linked to deliberation in the wider public sphere. This conception finds its expression in the "democratic principle", according to which

> "only those statutes may claim legitimacy that can meet with the assent (Zustimmung) of all citizens in a discursive process of legislation that in turn has been legally constituted".[25]

Discourse is central to *Habermas'* conception of democracy because he conceives of the practice of self-determination as a collective search for reasoned answers to a set of different questions:[26] Moral questions, that is questions of justice, are the most fundamental questions which citizens have to answer, because they delimit the range of options for the organisation of the community. *Habermas* characterises moral questions as those questions in which we consider what we ought to do in light of what would be equally fair to everyone[27] and the answers to which we consider to be universal and not particular to our community.[28] The point of reference in answering moral questions is thus the whole of mankind, the "generalised other" in the sense of *George Herbert Mead*. However, as *Habermas* points out, moral principles are often very abstract and therefore not sufficiently selective to tell us how we should organise our coexistence.[29] In the lawmaking process, moral discourse is therefore supplemented by ethical-political discourse, in which we answer the more specific question: How do we, as a community, want to live? What are our aims and aspirations? While the validity claims of moral norms, at least in *Habermas'* conception, are purely cognitive in nature – "we ought to obey moral precepts because we know they are right"[30] – with ethical-political questions,

---

25   J. Habermas, Between Facts and Norms. Contributions to a Discourse Theory of Law and Democracy (1998), p. 110.

26   See Habermas, Between Facts and Norms (1998), pp. 158 ff.; cf. J. Habermas, On the Pragmatic, the Ethical, and the Moral Employments of Practical Reason, in: J. Habermas, Justification and Application. Remarks on Discourse Ethics (1993).

27   See Habermas, Between Facts and Norms (1998), pp. 161 f.; cf. J. Habermas, Discourse Ethics: Notes on a Program of Philosophical Justification, in: J. Habermas, Moral Consciousness and Communicative Action (1990).

28   Examples include the permissibility of the death penalty, of abortion etc.

29   See Habermas, Between Facts and Norms (1998), p. 155.

30   Ibid. p. 153; cf. ibid. p. 155: "According to discourse theory, moral norms can appear

which refer to collective aims and identities, a "volitional moment" enters the political discourse and thus the "validity dimension (...) of legal norms".[31]

Since the question of how a particular community wants to live cannot be answered in the abstract, the legitimacy of legal norms is always relative to this particular community and can only be established with reference to the *de facto* will of the community's members.[32] The same is true for the pragmatic dimension of the lawmaking discourse, which comprises questions as to the strategies which the community should choose, given its political aims and moral convictions, as well as for situations in which a compromise between irreconcilable interests has to be found. These questions too can only be answered in relation to, respectively, the actual aims of and the actual constellations of interests in the legal community. In practice, the boundaries between the different dimensions of discourse are of course fluid and often contested.[33] It is certainly debatable whether there is a moral obligation to maintain certain social welfare policies or whether a commitment to the welfare state merely expresses the self-understanding of a particular community. And the discussion of economic policies, such as state-ownership of enterprises, often oscillates between ethical-political and pragmatic considerations. What matters in the present context is that, due to these different dimensions of the lawmaking discourse, the basis of the legitimacy of legal norms is a mixture of validity claims referring to moral norms, collective goals and identities, and pragmatic considerations. As *Habermas* sums it up,

> "valid legal norms indeed harmonize with moral norms, but they are "legitimate" in
> the sense that they additionally express an authentic self-understanding of the legal
> community, the fair consideration of the values and interests distributed in it, and the
> purposive-rational choice of strategies and means in the pursuit of policies".[34]

Habermas is of course not the first to recognise the mixed basis of political legitimacy. As Shane Mulligan puts it in his genealogical analysis of the uses of legitimacy in International Relations,

> "we find legitimacy emerging from a kind of communitarian basis, an agreement or
> even consensus among those whose opinion matters, as to a particular good [expression

---

with a purely cognitive validity claim because the principle of universalization provides a rule of argumentation that makes it possible to decide moral-practical questions rationally"; on the principle of universalisation, cf. Habermas, Discourse Ethics (1990).

31   Habermas, Between Facts and Norms (1998), p. 156.
32   See ibid.
33   Habermas acknowledges that the different forms of discourses can only be separated analytically and that, in practice, most political questions will touch upon all dimensions of discourse, see ibid. p. 565, fn. 3 (of the postscript).
34   Ibid. p. 156.

of self-understanding/collective goals, N.L.] (...). Yet there is also a sense in which the legitimacy that arises is suggestive of something more than a particular good, perhaps a universal or even moral good [compatibility with moral norms, N.L.]."[35]

Habermas' contribution lies in having conceptually come to grips with this mixed basis of legitimacy by tracing it, at least in the context of democratically enacted law, to the multiple dimensions of discursive self-government.

2.   The Active Dimension of Self-Determination[36]

In the domestic context, the implications of the active aspect of self-government are relatively straightforward: a people can only govern itself if its procedures for collective decision-making are effective. While there is certainly a trade-off between ensuring that all citizens can assent to a decision – the passive aspect of self-determination – on the one hand and the effectiveness of the decision-making procedure on the other hand, both are indispensable for democratic legitimacy: crudely put, without consent, there is no *self*-government, and without effectiveness, there is no self-*government*. Any system of democratic government thus presupposes a balance between consent and effectiveness. In almost all national jurisdictions this balance is struck differently depending on considerations such as the seriousness and urgency of a matter: constitutional amendments usually require a larger quorum than ordinary laws which in turn require the consent of more people and are thus more difficult to pass than government decrees or other administrative decisions.

The need for a balance between consent and effectiveness is all too familiar to students of international organisations, and there are some parallels in the way

---

35   Mulligan, The Uses of Legitimacy (2005), p. 364; cf. I. Claude, Collective Legitimization as a Political Function of the United Nations, in: International Organization 20 (1966), p. 369: "In the final analysis, the problem of legitimacy has a political dimension that goes beyond its legal and moral aspects. (...)[T]he process of legitimization is ultimately a political phenomenon, a crystallization of judgement that may be influenced but is unlikely to be wholly determined by legal norms and moral principles."

36   It should be noted that there are a number of problems associated with transferring Habermas' conception of discursive self-government to the international level. These cannot be addressed in this paper. Chief among them is the caveat that it is only meaningful to speak of democratic legitimacy at the international level when the states which take part in collective self-government in international forums are *self-determination units*, i.e. when their *individual* autonomy can be understood as an expression of the *collective* autonomy of the individuals under their respective jurisdictions. To what extent this is true in any particular situation has to be investigated on a case-by-case basis. All statements about the possibility of legitimate lawmaking in the WTO in this paper are thus subject to the condition that the states participating in lawmaking are self-determination units.

this balance is struck for different types of votes on the international and the national level: for example, votes on procedural matters are usually easier than votes on substantive issues.[37] However, for reasons of both legal formality and factual power realities, the element of consent is usually privileged in the design of international institutions: unlike citizens in democratic constitutional states, states are formally sovereign and cannot be legally bound against their will. Moreover, since there is no monopoly on the use of force at the international level, legal obligations which are not based on consent would also be extremely hard to enforce, at least against powerful states.[38] The resulting need to secure states' voluntary cooperation can create significant obstacles to the realisation of active self-determination on the international level.

Before I can discuss these obstacles in more detail, I need to clarify how the requirement of consensus can conceivably prevent the adoption of democratically legitimate decisions if, according to the democratic principle, the condition that a decision can meet with the assent of all affected actors makes this decision democratically legitimate in the first place. The key issue here is that *de facto* state consent is not the same as "assent in a discursive process of legislation". In the context of passive self-determination, the fact that a decision has been adopted by consensus does not guarantee that it could have met with the assent of all actors in a discursive process of legislation, since the consent might have been brought about by pressure or deception. Similarly, in the context of active self-determination, the fact that a state has vetoed a decision does not necessarily imply that the decision could not have met with universal assent in a discursive process of legislation. To take an obvious example: It would be inconceivable to claim that the fact that a state has vetoed a decision to abolish colonialism, slavery or apartheid implies that such a decision could not meet with universal consent in a discursive process; quite to the contrary, it is the decision not to abolish these practices that would be indefensible in a discursive process of legislation, since these practices violate the basic premises of the very discourse in which they would have to be justified. In this context, *Robert Alexy* has introduced the notions of "discursive necessity" and "discursive impossibility", respectively.[39]

---

37   See e.g. Article 27 of the UN Charter for the voting rules of the Security Council.
38   See C. Reus-Smit, The Constitutional Structure of International Society and the Nature of Fundamental Institutions, in: International Organization 51 (1997); according to Steinberg, this is one of the reasons why consensus decision-making has been maintained in organisations such as the GATT: R. Steinberg, In the Shadow of Law or Power? Consensus-Based Bargaining and Outcomes in the GATT/WTO, in: International Organization 56 (2002), p. 345.
39   R. Alexy, A Theory of Legal Argumentation. The Theory of Rational Discourse as Theory of Legal Justification (1989), p. 207: "To be sure, several judgments of value and of obligation as well as several rules are stringently required and flatly excluded by the rules of discourse. This holds true, for example, of rules which completely

The problem is that through its veto, a state can preserve a state of affairs which cannot, by definition, be discursively justified, since those who would need to assent to it are excluded from the discourse in the first place. It should also be recalled that, in *Habermas'* conception, it is a necessary (though not sufficient) condition for the legitimacy of a norm that it is in accordance with moral principles.[40] The veto allows states to perpetuate a status quo which is not justifiable according to any conceivable moral principle.[41] The refusal of the United States to agree to effective curbs on carbon dioxide emissions in order to slow global warming may be a case in point.[42] It is the ability of states to block a consensus on discursively indefensible grounds and thus to preserve a status quo which cannot be discursively legitimated that can make the requirement of consensus an obstacle to collective self-government, although consent is in principle a precondition for democratic government. The active dimension of self-determination therefore demands that there must be a possibility to overrule dissent that the dissenting state either cannot justify at all or on grounds which are "discursively impossible" or incompatible with moral principles.

The requirement of consent can also become an obstacle to active self-determination when a community faces a choice between two or more discursively possible options and needs to come to a decision because of time constraints. This is a further scenario – which is probably much more common than the choice between a discursively necessary and a discursively impossible decision – in which both *Habermas* and *Alexy* see majority decisions as justified.[43] Majority voting is not incompatible with discursive self-government, as long as decisions taken by majority vote are revisable at a later stage in the discourse.[44] The majority decisions then represent, as it were, snapshots

---

exclude some human beings from participation in discourses by imposing the legal status of a slave on them. In this sense it is possible to speak respectively of '*discursive impossibility*' and '*discursive necessity*'."

40   Habermas, Between Facts and Norms (1998), p. 155f.
41   See H. Müller, Internationale Verhandlungen, Argumente und Verständigungshandeln. Verteidigung, Befunde, Warnung, in: P. Niesen/B. Herborth (eds.), Anarchie der kommunikativen Freiheit. Jürgen Habermas und die Theorie der internationalen Politik (2007), pp. 206 ff., for an example of such a situation: "Konfrontiert mit einer überwältigenden Mehrheit, die sich auf die offensichtlich besseren Gründe stützte, wäre der mächtigen Delegation nur der Rückzug auf den begründungslosen politischen Willen geblieben nach dem Motto: Ihr habt recht, aber wir wollen das trotzdem nicht. Dieser Situation wollte man sich trotz überlegener Machtressourcen nicht aussetzen.", ibid. p. 208.
42   For an excellent discussion of conceivable moral principles on the basis of which carbon dioxide emissions could be regulated, see P. Singer, One World. The Ethics of Globalization (2004), chapter 2.
43   See Alexy, Theory of Legal Argumentation (1989), pp. 207 f; Habermas, Between Facts and Norms (1998), pp. 179 f.
44   See Alexy, Theory of Legal Argumentation (1989), pp. 207 f; Habermas, Between

of an ongoing self-determination discourse. When they meet these criteria – reversibility and embeddedness in an ongoing discourse – majority decisions present probably the most practicable answer to the need of balancing consent and effectiveness and thereby doing justice to both the passive and the active dimension of self-determination.

In light of the need to balance the imperatives of consent and effectiveness, the WTO's pride in the fact that virtually all decisions are taken by consensus appears unjustified already on the conceptual level. Even leaving aside the fact that in practice the consensus procedure "does not provide for equality (in terms of decision and influence) because not every Member has the same ability to maintain vetoes"[45], the WTO's contention that the consensus procedure is "in principle (…) even more democratic than majority rule because no decision is taken until everyone agrees"[46], is misleading in that it totally disregards the active dimension of self-determination: while the consensus procedure may in theory ensure that "every country has to be convinced before it joins a consensus"[47], the need for consensus makes it much more difficult for members to react to changes in economic or political conditions or to judicial law-making by changing the law. As *Singer* points out, "rule by consensus can also be called rule by the veto".[48] A single member can, through its *de facto* veto, preserve the status quo, even when an overwhelming majority favours changes to the law. This is not a mere theoretical possibility: for example, the decision by the United States to block the consensus on a waiver that would have allowed developing countries to import generic versions of patented medicines when faced with a public health crisis delayed the adoption of the waiver for eight months.[49] This one-against-all constellation seems to repeat itself in the context of the discussion on the relationship between TRIPS and the UN Convention on Biological Diversity, with the US blocking the consensus on a decision to grant the Convention's Executive Secretary observer status in the TRIPS Council.[50]

Facts and Norms (1998), pp. 179 f.

45   C.-D. Ehlermann/L. Ehring, Decision-Making in the World Trade Organization. Is the Consensus Practice of the World Trade Organization Adequate for Making, Revising and Implementing Rules on International Trade?, in: Journal of International Economic Law 8 (2005), p. 51.
46   WTO, Ten Common Misunderstandings (2007), p. 10.
47   Ibid.
48   Singer, One World (2004), p. 75.
49   See Ehlermann/Ehring, Decision-Making (2005), p. 64 for other examples; cf. L. Elliott/C. Denny, US Wrecks Cheap Drugs Deal, in: The Guardian of 21 December 2002: "Faced with furious opposition from all the other 140 members of the World Trade Organization, the US refused to relax global patent laws which keep the price of drugs beyond reach of most developing countries.".
50   See Intellectual Property Watch, TRIPS Council: Big Boost for Biodiversity Amendment; Enforcement Debated, www.ip-watch.org/weblog/index.php?p=643 (This and the following internet sources: 15 September 2009).

These examples show that the balance between consensus and the effectiveness of collective self-government in the WTO is highly skewed in favour of the former.[51]

3. Communicative Power

Given that power has at least in international relations always been primarily associated with coercion, it is not surprising that critical theorists as well as activist critics of globalisation tend either to reject power *per se* or at least to be very suspicious of it. As *David Chandler* observes, the newly emergent "global civil society" movement deems itself

"morally progressive in so far as its demands do not 'seek to replace one form of power with another' but instead have the 'objective of "whittling down" the capacity of concentrated centres of power'".[52]

Mary Kaldor, for example, finds the "ethos of civil society" in "anti-politics" which "was a new type of politics because it was not about the capture of state power; it was the politics of those who don't want to be politicians and don't want to share power".[53] As *Anthony Giddens* notes, this negative attitude towards power has also been a shared trait of Marxism and liberalism: both "participate (…) in a 'flight from power'", because they associate it with class or state oppression, respectively.[54]

In his report from the 2004 World Social Forum in Mumbai, Rahul Rao alludes to what is problematic about this view:

"Talk of 'power' made some people at the WSF very uncomfortable indeed. One panelist's [sic] reference to creating a 'non-power opposition to power' struck me as decidedly odd. Non-violent resistance is an effective tactic precisely because *its legitimacy gives one power* – power of a different kind from that which one opposes perhaps, but power nonetheless."[55]

---

51   See Ehlermann/Ehring, Decision-Making (2005), p. 68: "Consensus therefore creates a trade-off between the ability of easily objecting and the difficulty of achieving desired decisions.".

52   D. Chandler, Building Global Civil Society 'From Below'?, in: Millennium 33 (2004), p. 314, quoting N. Stammers, Social Movements and the Social Construction of Human Rights, in: Human Rights Quarterly 21 (1999), p. 1006.

53   M. Kaldor, Global Civil Society. An Answer to War (2003), pp. 56 f, quoted in Chandler, Building Global Civil Society (2004), p. 317.

54   A. Giddens, The Constitution of Society. Outline of the Theory of Structuration (1984), pp. 256 f.

55   R. Rao, Included Out?, www.metamute.org/en/Included-Out, emphasis added.

To embrace the idea that legitimacy can be a source of power, one first has to accept the premise that

"power is not necessarily linked with conflict in the sense of either division of interest or active struggle, and power is not inherently oppressive".[56]

And indeed: There is no reason why an actor should only be capable "to 'make a difference' to a pre-existing state of affairs or course of events" by overriding the will of others; "transformative capacity" can also result from the formation of a common will.[57]

Various authors have translated this basic idea into very different conceptions of power.[58] The concept which I will adopt in the following – *Habermas'* concept of communicative power – stands out in that it is directly linked to a particular mode of action, namely communicative action.[59] For *Habermas*, the distinction between communicative and coercive power is congruent with the distinction between action coordination through communicative and strategic action. Since the concept of communicative power is by definition inextricably linked to the coordination of action based on a common understanding and thus to the creation and maintenance of a social order based on legitimate law,[60] it is particularly well suited for an analysis that is concerned with the legitimacy of international law.

In *Habermas'* conception, communicative action can give rise to communicative power because discourses not only serve the cognitive purpose

---

56   Giddens, The Constitution of Society (1984), p. 257.
57   Giddens conceptualises power as the "the *capability* of [an actor] to 'make a difference' to a pre-existing state of affairs or course of events", or as "transformative capacity", ibid. pp. 14 f.
58   See e.g. H. Arendt, On Violence (1970), p. 44; J. Nye, Soft Power. The Means to Success in World Politics (2004), p. 2; T. Franck, The Power of Legitimacy Among Nations (1990); I. Hurd, Legitimacy and Authority in International Politics, in: International Organization 53 (1999); for discussions of Arendt's conception of power, see J. Habermas, Hannah Arendts Begriff der Macht, in: J. Habermas, Philosophisch-politische Profile (1987), and J. Schell, The Unconquerable World. Power, Nonviolence, and the Will of the People (2003), chapter 8.
59   On communicative action in international relations, cf. T. Risse, "Let's Argue": Communicative Action in World Politics, in: International Organization 54 (2000); and H. Müller, Arguing, Bargaining and All That: Communicative Action, Rationalist Theory and the Logic of Appropriateness in International Relations, in: European Journal of International Relations 10 (2004).
60   See J. Habermas, Faktizität und Geltung. Beiträge zur Diskurstheorie des Rechts und des demokratischen Rechtsstaats (1998), p. 185: "Verschwisterung der kommunikativen Macht mit der Erzeugung legitimen Rechts"; the intimate connection between communicative power, i.e. "arguing and persuasion", and legitimacy is also noted by T. Risse, Global Governance and Communicative Action, in: Government and Opposition 39 (2004), p. 310.

of producing rules and policies which can be presumed to be legitimate, but also have practical significance in that "discursively produced and intersubjectively shared beliefs have (...) a motivating force".[61] This "weakly motivating force of good reasons" transforms the common convictions reached in discourse into a common will and thus generates a power potential that can find expression in collective action and, as an "authorising force", in the creation of legitimate law.[62] Communicative power cannot be exercised "despite resistance", since it is based on the voluntary assent of the actors involved. It refers solely to the transformative capacity that is generated through the voluntary assent of individuals, and that "springs up between men when they act together".[63] This form of capacity does not exist between people with respect to any matter on which they do not agree.

4. The Paradigmatic Case: Amendment of the TRIPS Provisions on Compulsory Licensing

The paradigmatic case for a perspective on the legitimacy of WTO law that focuses on the active dimension of self-determination and the reconfiguration of power relations as a precondition for legitimate lawmaking is not the Seattle protesters hurling stones at the representatives of an unaccountable power, but rather a situation in which some of the poorest countries in the world managed to address a vital concern (admittedly created in large part by the WTO itself) by amending the TRIPS provisions on compulsory licensing. This case is instructive not only because it can tell us about what is positively required to make legitimate WTO law; in fact, it is perhaps most striking for all the elements that usually characterise WTO lawmaking but were not present in this case.

The amendment of the TRIPS provisions on compulsory licensing occurred in response to concerns by Least-Developed Countries (LDCs) that they would not be able to access generic drugs in public health crises, such as the one caused by HIV/AIDS, because the original TRIPS allowed the manufacturing of generic drugs under compulsory licences only for the domestic market. Poor countries without pharmaceutical manufacturing capacity were thus not in a position to take advantage of these provisions. Supported by considerable civil society activism and other international institutions such as the World Health Organization (WHO), the developing countries ultimately succeeded both in re-framing intellectual property protection of pharmaceuticals as a public health issue and in reconfiguring the power relations in the WTO in support of amending the TRIPS to allow the importation of drugs manufactured under

---

61   Habermas, Between Facts and Norms (1998), p. 147.
62   Ibid., pp. 147 f.
63   Arendt, On Violence (1970), p. 44.

compulsory licences into countries without sufficient manufacturing capacity in the case of a public health crisis. It is telling in how many respects the process by which this result came about differs from the usual lawmaking process in the WTO.

First, the amendment process started with the "Doha Declaration on TRIPS and Public Health" adopted at the Doha Ministerial in 2001, which put the negotiations outside the single undertaking. Second, since it was framed as an "implementation issue" of prior negotiating results, it was not treated as part of a reciprocal bargain. These two factors – that the negotiations were not part of the single undertaking and were not framed as a reciprocal bargain – ensured or made it at least much more likely that the issue would be decided on its merits. This was arguably a precondition for the advocates of the amendment to succeed in eroding the argumentative position of the US and ultimately change the law. One crucial factor in this regard was the US's own experience with a public health crisis in form of the Anthrax attacks, which prompted the US government to threaten Bayer, the producer of the drug Cipro, with compulsory licensing and rendered the US position on the compulsory licensing provisions in the TRIPS untenable in the negotiations.[64]

Third, while the negotiations where conducted under the consensus procedure, the normative implications of this procedure became clear in unusually stark terms when a single state, the US, blocked agreement for eight months: the consensus procedure allows a state to maintain a veto even in situations in which it is vital for other states to move forward with a decision and in which that state has for all intents and purposes lost the argument. What the episode showed, then, was that the consensus procedure can constitute a formidable (even if, in this case, temporary) obstacle to active self-determination and lawmaking governed by communicative power.

Two factors that positively contributed to the resolution of the TRIPS-Public Health controversy need to be noted: First, the formation of communicative power was certainly facilitated by the fact that the case was relatively clear from a moral point of view: The commercial interests of some of the world's most powerful corporations stood against the survival of millions of the poorest people on the planet. And second, the involvement of civil society was crucial.

---

64   S. Sell, Private Power, Public Law. The Globalization of Intellectual Property Rights (2003), pp. 160, 149; M. Wolf, Why Globalization Works (2004), p. 217; Singer, One World (2004), p. 73; on the rules of practical discourse at work here, see Alexy, Theory of Legal Argumentation (1989), p. 190 ("Every speaker may assert only those value judgments or judgments of obligation in a given case which he or she is willing to assert in the same terms for every case which resembles the given case in all relevant respects") and p. 203 ("Everyone who makes a normative statement that presupposes a rule with certain consequences for the satisfaction of the interests of other persons must be able to accept these consequences, even in the hypothetical situation where he or she is in the position of those persons").

The success of US activists and civil society campaigns promoting access to essential medicines in awakening the US public to the issue undoubtedly contributed to the reversal of US policy on compulsory licensing, facilitating the adoption of the Declaration on TRIPS and Public Health at the Doha Ministerial and the eventual resolution of the issue in a way that addressed developing countries' concerns.[65]

In sum, the amendment of the TRIPS provisions on compulsory licensing could be seen as an example for a power-to-legitimacy paradigm: Instead of focusing on how the law could be legitimised, this paradigm would direct attention to the obstacles to, and the potential for, the formation of communicative power in the lawmaking process, and hence the opening up of space for legitimate lawmaking in the first place.

IV.   Obstacles to the Formation of Communicative Power in the Lawmaking Culture of the WTO

The power-to-legitimacy paradigm directs our attention to institutional practices and discursive structures which currently inhibit active self-determination and the formation of communicative power in the WTO. Given that the three conceptual pillars of current WTO lawmaking – reciprocity, the single undertaking, and the consensus procedure – were conspicuous for their absence (reciprocity, single undertaking) or special role (consensus procedure) in the negotiations of the TRIPS amendment, I will in the following investigate their potential to hinder the formation of communicative power in the WTO, focusing on the concept of reciprocity. My central hypothesis is that the prominence of these three concepts in the WTO lawmaking discourse inhibits the discussion of issues on their merits. My purpose is not to argue that these institutions should necessarily be dispensed with. However, by problematising them, I hope to draw them into the legitimacy debate and highlight their role in inhibiting the formation of communicative power.

1.   Reciprocity

The idea that international trade negotiations are basically an exchange of reciprocal concessions is often portrayed as an unproblematic truism. As *Rorden Wilkinson* puts it, "bargaining is at the root of the international trade regime. Trade negotiations are based on reciprocal exchange."[66] And indeed, the WTO Agreement commits its members to

---

65   Sell, Private Power, Public Law (2003), pp. 146-162.
66   R. Wilkinson, Crisis in Cancún, in: Global Governance 10 (2004), p. 151.

"entering into reciprocal and mutually advantageous arrangements directed to the substantial reduction of tariffs and other barriers to trade and to the elimination of discriminatory treatment in international trade relations".[67]

At the same time, reciprocity does not represent a generally accepted standard that would allow one to determine a priori on which issues an agreement is viable. It is largely a matter of perception. As *Finger* has remarked, "operationally speaking, in the GATT/WTO system agreement defines reciprocity, not the other way around".[68] In a major study of the results of the Uruguay Round, *Finger* and his colleagues have found "little evidence of either equal sacrifice or of mercantilist balance".[69] The imbalance between concessions given and concessions received was on average more than half as large as the overall concessions that a member had received.[70] The researchers did not encounter a single delegation that had "attempted to calculate the depth of cut by each country, or even of major trading partners".[71] In sum, it appears that in purely numerical terms reciprocity does not shape WTO lawmaking as significantly as it is frequently assumed. That makes it no less important to examine its political role in the lawmaking discourse.

The picture of WTO lawmaking discourse that emerges when one reads the position papers and contributions of WTO members in the agricultural negotiations, for example, is quite different from what the conventional wisdom of the WTO as a bargaining forum would lead one to expect. The overwhelming majority of contributions make substantive historical, moral and theoretical arguments. Of course the countries present their own positions, but in almost all cases these are justified with and embedded within wider arguments about the historical context, common goals and considerations of fairness. Explicit demands of reciprocity are, first of all, extremely rare. And when they are introduced, they quite transparently serve the function of avoiding an engagement with the arguments offered by the other members on their merits.

Interestingly, a similar pattern can be observed in the agricultural negotiations leading up to the Punta del Este Declaration of 1985, which launched the Uruguay Round, and in the agricultural negotiations preceding the Doha

---

67   Preambles of the WTO Agreement and the GATT; cf. GATT, Article XXVIII bis ("negotiations on a reciprocal and mutually advantageous basis").
68   J. Finger, A Diplomat's Economics: Reciprocity in the Uruguay Round Negotiations, in: World Trade Review 4 (2005), p. 29; cf. the following statement by former GATT Director-General Arthur Dunkel: "Reciprocity cannot be determined exactly; it can only be agreed upon.", quoted in J. Finger/L. Winters, Reciprocity in the WTO, in: B. Hoekman/A. Mattoo/P. English (eds.), Development, Trade, and the WTO. A Handbook (2002), p. 51.
69   Finger, A Diplomat's Economics (2005), p. 35.
70   See ibid., pp. 35 f.
71   Ibid.

Declaration in 2000/2001: Among dozens of contributions, the only member that brings up reciprocity is in both cases – the European Community (EC). In the work of the Preparatory Commission for the Punta del Este Ministerial Meeting, the EC representative complained that it was

"disappointing that the previous comments on this subject [agriculture] had essentially been a list of claims and familiar complaints, with no indication of contributions or concessions that countries might be prepared to make. The community was being pressed to make concession, but no-one had indicated what it would receive in exchange."[72]

He went on to threaten that the negotiations would not be successful "if it were always the same countries that would be asked to make sacrifices" and if countries continued to insist "on a catalogue of demands without the accompanying obligations".[73] In a similar vein, the European representative in the pre-Doha agricultural negotiations criticised the US proposal for "demand[ing] more from some than from others" and for not being "faithful to the existing agreement [sic] on Agriculture" by giving up the principle that "all should move in a similar fashion".[74]

It is of course unsurprising that the EC would avoid engaging with the arguments of other members on their merits, since its own arguments for maintaining agricultural protection and in particular export subsidies would not have much purchase. But the fact that members can hide behind demands for "reciprocity" in order to avoid the discussion of issues on their merits suggests that, if one is interested in enhancing opportunities for the formation of communicative power, one should attempt to destabilise, rather than reinforce, the notion that reciprocity is an unproblematic pillar of WTO lawmaking.

There are a number of points one could make to that end. First, historically speaking, trade liberalisation based on reciprocity has by no means been the norm. In 19th century Britain, for example, "any departure from unilateralism – for example, towards a notion of reciprocity in trading relations – was criticised as disguised protectionism".[75] It was not until the adoption of the Reciprocal Trade Agreements Act of 1934 by the US Congress that reciprocity became a central principle in US trade policy, for example.[76] Second, as *Paul Krugman*

---

72   Preparatory Committee, Records of Discussions. Discussions of 4-5 February, PREP. COM (86) SR/2 of 18 March 1986, para. 30.
73   Ibid.
74   Second Special Session of the Committee on Agriculture, Statement by the European Community, G/AG/NG/W/24 of 11 July 2000, p. 2; cf. First Special Session of the Committee on Agriculture, Statement by the European Communities, Doc. G/AG/NG/W/3 of 4 April 2000, p. 1: "it [the EC, N.L.] will expect to obtain improved market opportunities for its exporters in balance with increased access to our market".
75   Lang, Reflecting on 'Linkage' (2007), p. 528.
76   See K. Dam, Cordell Hull, The Reciprocal Trade Agreements Act, and the WTO, in:

has famously put it, the economic theory underlying the reciprocal exchange of "concessions" in the form of tariff reductions "does not make sense on any level".[77] While this is widely acknowledged, it is often argued that from a political economy perspective, reciprocity in international trade negotiations has facilitated liberalisation by mobilising export interest to offset the domestic political influence of protectionist forces.[78] This political-economy justification, however, becomes problematic when the subject of the negotiations is no longer tariff reductions, but substantive public policies concerning e.g. the intellectual property regime or food safety standards: in these cases, reciprocity no longer facilitates what would be economically rational anyway, but represents the application of a decision-making procedure ultimately modelled on commercial transactions ("you get what you pay for"[79]) to substantive public policy choices with not only political, but also substantial economic costs.[80]

Beyond these general points, there are a number of specific ways in which the concept of reciprocity hinders the formation of communicative power. First, the insistence on reciprocity often represents an attempt to narrow down the deliberations to the "here and now". Demands for reciprocity not only deflect questions of historical responsibility, for example, whether the former colonial powers have a special responsibility to counteract trade patterns that are residues of the colonial era and are still upheld through mechanisms such as tariff escalation. They also ignore the more recent historical context of previous trade negotiations.[81] Many developing countries have perceived the outcomes of the Uruguay Round as grossly unbalanced and have hence seen a primary purpose of the implementation phase and the Doha Round in "rebalancing" the international trading system.[82] In such a situation, the demand for reciprocity is a convenient device for winners in previous negotiations to exclude from

---

E.-U. Petersmann (ed.), Reforming the World Trading System. Legitimacy, Efficiency, and Democratic Governance (2005).

77   P. Krugman, What Should Trade Negotiators Negotiate About?, in: Journal of Economic Literature 35 (1997), p. 114.

78   See e.g. Wolf, Why Globalization Works (2004), p. 208.

79   This is how an official of the United States Trade Representative characterised law-making in the WTO, see K. Abbott/D. Snidal, International Action on Bribery and Corruption: Why the Dog Didn't Bark in the WTO, in: D. Kennedy/J. Southwick (eds.), The Political Economy of International Trade Law. Essays in Honor of Robert E. Hudec (2002), p. 193.

80   See Krugman, What Should Trade Negotiators Negotiate About? (1997); Finger/ Winters, Reciprocity in the WTO (2002); D. Steger, The Culture of the WTO: Why It Needs to Change, in: Journal of International Economic Law 10 (2007), pp. 491 f.

81   Stiglitz/Carlton, Fair Trade for All (2005), p. 107.

82   Finger, A Diplomat's Economics (2005), p. 37: "In real economics (...) the developed countries gained, the developing countries lost from each of the three components [TRIPS, clothing and textiles, agriculture, N.L.].".

consideration the fairness of the outcomes of previous rounds and thus, as it were, reset the baseline for the negotiations to zero.

Apart from excluding historical considerations, reciprocity is also inimical to moral argumentation and hence, more broadly, to the formation of communicative power on the basis of shared normative understandings. As stated above, reciprocity reduces global public policymaking to the model of a commercial transaction in which "you get what you pay for". This is problematic not only because "many significant current issues (...) have a strong normative component that cannot readily be reduced to technical trade-offs".[83] It also leads to a discursive set-up whose counterintuitive features become particularly evident in comparison to the national sphere. As *Joseph Stiglitz* and *Andrew Carlton* remark,

"in national economic debates, we do not demand that the poor give up an amount commensurate with what they get. Rather, we talk about social justice and equity."[84]

Finally, negotiations based on reciprocity lead the parties to define issues "as a bargaining problem with divided interests rather than as an issue of common concern".[85] Given that communicative power depends on the formation of a common will, this tendency is obviously detrimental to legitimate lawmaking.

In sum, the idea that trade negotiations should be governed by reciprocity has the potential to systematically impede the formation of communicative power, which is premised on reaching a definition of a common interest and on reaching agreement on what would be fair and equitable.

2. The Single Undertaking

A second, and rather unique, feature of lawmaking in the WTO is the "single undertaking". The concept has two aspects: as a negotiating principle, it means that lawmaking should take place in comprehensive negotiating rounds and that "nothing is agreed until everything is agreed"; as a legal principle, it mandates that, with the exception of plurilateral agreements, all WTO members have to subscribe to all WTO agreements. While the latter principle is enshrined in the WTO Agreement as an explicit legal rule,[86] the former is an element par excellence of the WTO's lawmaking culture that persists although it is in no

---

83   Abbott/Snidal, International Action on Bribery and Corruption (2002), p. 202.
84   Stiglitz/Carlton, Fair Trade for All (2005), p. 107.
85   Abbott/Snidal, International Action on Bribery and Corruption (2002), p. 193.
86   WTO Agreement, Article II.2: "The agreements and associated legal instruments included in Annexes 1, 2 and 3 (hereinafter referred to as "Multilateral Trade Agreements") are integral parts of this Agreement, *binding on all Members.*" (emphasis added).

way mandated by the WTO Agreement;[87] in fact, the WTO was in part designed to obviate the need for comprehensive negotiating rounds,[88] as is evident in the built-in agendas contained in various WTO agreements.[89]

The "single undertaking" grows out of and compounds the logic of reciprocity in WTO negotiations. As a legal principle, it is usually justified as necessary to prevent the kind of "free-riding" that was possible in the fragmented legal order of the pre-Uruguay Round GATT.[90] Before the founding of the WTO, the contracting parties to the GATT could pick and choose which additional agreements (referred to as "codes") they wanted to join. As a result, non-members could benefit from adjustment made by the members to a particular code, e.g. a reduction in subsidies, without making any concessions of their own. While the term "free-riding" could be seen as implying an understanding of the international trade regime as a public good from which all states benefit and to which they therefore have to make a contribution,[91] historically the "single undertaking" has been used to extract concessions from developing countries in areas such as intellectual property rights and trade in services and thus to "make them pay" for concessions by developed countries in the areas of trade in agricultural products and textiles.[92]

---

87   See Steger, The Culture of the WTO (2007), p. 493: "The preference of WTO members for negotiating rounds is a long standing practice, but it is not required by the rules.".

88   See Moore, Democratic Roots (2005), p. 42: "One rationale for the creation of the WTO was to put an end to rounds by creating a permanent forum for negotiations, but so far this promise has not been realized.".

89   See e.g. Agreement on Agriculture, Article 20; it was on the basis of this article that free-standing negotiations on trade in agricultural products began prior to the start of the Doha Round; these were later integrated into the Doha Round single undertaking.

90   See Steger, The Culture of the WTO (2007), pp. 489 f.

91   For such a reading, see Wolf, Why Globalization Works (2004), p. 207.

92   At the start of the Uruguay Round, only negotiations on trade in goods were part of the single undertaking, while negotiations on trade in services were to be conducted separately; see Ministerial Declaration on the Uruguay Round, 20 September 1986, Part I, Section B (ii) (formulating the single undertaking for negotiations on trade in goods). However, towards the end of the Uruguay Round the US and EC managed to force the major developing countries into accepting trade in services as part of the single undertaking enshrined in Article II.2 of the WTO Agreement with a sophisticated legal manoeuvre, referred to internally among US negotiators as "the power play" (Steinberg, In the Shadow of Law or Power? (2002), p. 360): The WTO Agreement, which created a new institutional framework for the multilateral trading system, did not include the original "GATT 1947", but instead the basically identical, but legally distinct "GATT 1994" (see WTO Agreement, Article II.4). This would have allowed the US and the EC to *withdraw* from the original "GATT 1947" after they joined the WTO (including the "GATT 1994") and thereby to *terminate* the market access obligations which they had accumulated over the decades of the operation of the GATT *to any country which refused to join the WTO*. At the same time, signing

In a similar vein, the choice for the "single undertaking" as a negotiating principle is usually justified with reference to the increased opportunities for cross-linkages that present themselves when negotiations on a number of issue areas are held at the same time. Apart from compounding the capacity constraints of developing countries which are in themselves an obstacle to the formation of communicative power,[93] the package approach to trade negotiations arguably implies and reinforces a conception of WTO lawmaking in which members can demand that concessions in areas in which they have lost an argument be paid for by other members with concessions in entirely unrelated areas.

The single undertaking as a negotiating principle can also represent a formidable obstacle to active self-determination, because disagreement in one issue area can paralyse the entire negotiations. It is particularly telling to compare the amendment process of the TRIPS provisions on compulsory licensing discussed above with the fate of an initiative through which four West-African LDCs sought to put an end to the subsidisation of the production and export of cotton.[94] The subsidies, paid in particular by the US, and the ensuing low world market prices for cotton were endangering the livelihoods of millions of poor cotton farmers and their dependants in West Africa – a situation of arguably comparable urgency to the impact of TRIPS on public health. Similarly to the TRIPS amendment process, the sponsors of the initiative had a compelling moral case and were strongly supported by civil society. In 2005, they won a partial victory when a commitment to eliminate all forms of export subsidies for cotton in 2006 was enshrined in the Hong Kong Ministerial Declaration.[95] However, the practical impact of this partial solution has so far been *nil*, since it will not be implemented until the Doha Round is concluded in its entirety, which does not look likely to happen any time soon. The fact that the cotton initiative was integrated into the Doha Round single undertaking, whereas the TRIPS and

---

up to *all* of the covered agreements was made a condition for WTO membership (see Article II.2 WTO Agreement). This meant that any country that refused to sign any of the agreements negotiated in the Uruguay Round would not only lose the benefits of all other agreements negotiated during the Round, but would potentially be "giving up the cumulated market access rights as guaranteed by multilateral trading rules and as negotiated in all GATT rounds"; K. Stegemann, The Integration of Intellectual Property Rights into the WTO System, in: The World Economy 23 (2000), p. 1243.

93   The formation of communicative power necessarily presupposes that all members can participate in deliberations and have enough time and capacity to analyse the subject matter at hand and formulate a position on it.

94   See WTO Negotiations on Agriculture. Poverty Reduction: Sectoral Initiative in Favour of Cotton, Joint Proposal by Benin, Burkina Faso, Chad and Mali, Doc. TN/AG/GEN/4 of 16 May 2003.

95   See Ministerial Declaration, Hong Kong Ministerial Conference, Doc. WT/MIN(05)/DEC of 22 December 2005, para. 11; overall, the Declaration accorded priority to cotton in the context of the agricultural negotiations.

public health negotiations were not, thus made a big difference in terms of the capacity for active self-determination of least-developed WTO members.

It should be noted that the single undertaking in both its manifestations has been subject to sustained criticism, *inter alia* by the so-called Sutherland report on "The Future of the WTO".[96] The desirability of "early harvests" in negotiations (instead of the principle that nothing is agreed until everything is agreed) and "variable geometry" when it comes to membership in WTO agreements (instead of the principle that all members must join all WTO agreements) is now more widely considered. As a result, the single undertaking is probably the least stable of the three elements of the WTO's lawmaking culture discussed in this paper.

3.   The Consensus Procedure

I have already argued above[97] that, while consent is in principle a precondition for legitimate lawmaking, the consensus procedure can also represent an obstacle to active self-determination and lawmaking governed by communicative power. Whether the procedure represents such an obstacle depends largely on whether potentially obstructionist states face the prospect of being outvoted.[98] In the WTO, this possibility exists in principle: Article IX of the WTO Agreement provides for voting in cases where consensus cannot be reached. In practice, however, voting is not a realistic prospect.[99] As *Debra Steger* puts it, "the culture of the WTO forbids even thinking about voting".[100] The WTO's lawmaking culture thus does not contain any safeguards to ensure

---

96   Consultative Board to the Director-General Supachai Panitchpakdi, The Future of the WTO. Addressing Institutional Challenges in the New Millennium (2004), chapter 7; for criticism of the single undertaking, cf. Wolf, Why Globalization Works (2004), p. 211; Moore, Democratic Roots (2005), p. 42.

97   In section III.2.

98   Boyle and Chinkin emphasise the importance of voting as a "threat, an inducement to achieve consensus"; A. Boyle/C. Chinkin, The Making of International Law (2007), p. 158, quoting D. Vignes, Will the Third Conference on the Law of the Sea Work According to the Consensus Rule?, in: American Journal of International Law 69 (1975), p. 119; similarly, Ehlermann and Ehring argue that, if the WTO is to avoid "paralysis", "the possibility of a vote" has to be "a *shadow* under which the quest for consensus takes place"; Ehlermann/Ehring, Decision-Making (2005), p. 72.

99   See P. Kuijper, WTO Institutional Aspects, in: D. Bethlehem/D. McRae/R. Neufeld *et al.* (eds.): The Oxford Handbook of International Trade Law (2009), p. 96: "there is no example so far of a successful application of majority voting by any chair in the WTO's history. In reality, therefore, the WTO is governed entirely by consensus.".

100   Steger, The Culture of the WTO (2007), p. 488; for similar expressions of amazement about the fact that member states never even seem to consider a vote, see Ehlermann/ Ehring, Decision-Making (2005), e.g. pp. 65 f.

that "no one state or group of states can block final agreement *unreasonably*."[101] To the contrary, other elements of this culture, in particular the idea that trade negotiations are about the reciprocal exchange of concessions, tend to make it more likely that states make use of their *de facto* veto, since the idea makes it appear legitimate "for a state to tie its acceptance to narrow individual gains".[102] In the WTO context, the consensus procedure allows at least the more powerful states to adopt negotiating positions which are not formulated on generally acceptable premises. The procedure thus contributes to a lawmaking culture in which mercantilist calculus, rather than reasoned argument, is the primary currency.

V. Conclusion

In the present paper, I have argued that the current debate about the legitimacy of WTO law takes place within a legitimacy-to-power paradigm, as a result of which the debate appears as an attempt to legitimise the law as it stands within the parameters of the current power relations. This discursive structure furthers a limited view of what would be required to make WTO law legitimate. I have therefore proposed to supplement the current paradigm with a perspective that brings the importance of the active dimension of self-determination, i.e. states' capacity to effectively tackle issues of vital concern through international lawmaking, into sharper relief. At the same time, I have argued that in many cases legitimate lawmaking will not be possible without a major reconfiguration of power relations in the WTO. Drawing on *Habermas'* theory of law and democracy, I have suggested that the objective of such a reconfiguration should not be seen in terms of a redistribution of coercive power from some states to others, but of enhancing the role of communicative power in the lawmaking process. Such an approach would seek to destabilise, rather than reify, those elements of the WTO's lawmaking culture which currently inhibit the formation of communicative power in the lawmaking process.

---

101   Boyle/Chinkin, The Making of International Law (2007), p. 160 (emphasis added).
102   Abbott/Snidal, International Action on Bribery and Corruption (2002), p. 201.

Bibliography

Abbott, K.W./D. Snidal, International Action on Bribery and Corruption: Why the Dog Didn't Bark in the WTO, in: D. Kennedy/J. Southwick (eds.), The Political Economy of International Trade Law. Essays in Honor of Robert E. Hudec (2002).

Alexy, R., A Theory of Legal Argumentation. The Theory of Rational Discourse as Theory of Legal Justification (1989).

Arendt, H., On Violence (1970).

Bacchus, J., A Few Thoughts on Legitimacy, Democracy, and the WTO, in: E.-U. Petersmann (ed.), Reforming the World Trading System. Legitimacy, Efficiency, and Democratic Governance (2005).

Boyle, A./C. Chinkin, The Making of International Law (2007).

Chandler, D., Building Global Civil Society 'From Below'?, in: Millennium 33 (2004), pp. 313-339.

Cho, S., A Quest for WTO's Legitimacy, in: World Trade Review 4 (2005), pp. 391-399.

Claude, I., Collective Legitimization as a Political Function of the United Nations, in: International Organization 20 (1966), pp. 367-380.

Collony, W., Introduction: Legitimacy and Modernity, in: W. Collony (ed.): Legitimacy and the State (1984).

Consultative Board to the Director-General Supachai Panitchpakdi, The Future of the WTO. Addressing Institutional Challenges in the New Millennium (2004).

Dam, K., Cordell Hull, The Reciprocal Trade Agreements Act, and the WTO, in: E.-U. Petersmann (ed.), Reforming the World Trading System. Legitimacy, Efficiency, and Democratic Governance (2005).

Ehlermann, C-D./L. Ehring, Decision-Making in the World Trade Organization. Is the Consensus Practice of the World Trade Organization Adequate for Making, Revising and Implementing Rules on International Trade?, in: Journal of International Economic Law 8 (2005), pp. 51-75.

Elliott, L./C. Denny, US Wrecks Cheap Drugs Deal, in: Guardian of 21 December 2002.

Elsig, M., The World Trade Organization's Legitimacy Crisis: What Does the Beast Look Like?, in: Journal of World Trade 41 (2007), pp. 75-98.

Esty, D., The World Trade Organization's Legitimacy Crisis, in: World Trade Review 1 (2002), pp. 7-22.

Feldman, N., Does Sharia Mean the Rule of Law?, in: International Herald Tribune of 16 March 2008.

Finger, J., A Diplomat's Economics: Reciprocity in the Uruguay Round Negotiations, in: World Trade Review 4 (2005), pp. 27-40.

Finger, J./L. Winters, Reciprocity in the WTO, in: B. Hoekman/A. Mattoo/P. English (eds.), Development, Trade, and the WTO. A Handbook (2002).

Franck, T., The Power of Legitimacy Among Nations (1990).

GATT, Preparatory Committee, Records of Discussions. Discussions of 4-5 February, PREP. COM (86) SR/2 of 18 March 1986.

Giddens, A., The Constitution of Society. Outline of the Theory of Structuration (1984).

Habermas, J., Theorie des Kommunikativen Handelns. Vol. 1: Handlungsrationalität und gesellschaftliche Rationalisierung (1981).

— Hannah Arendts Begriff der Macht, in: J. Habermas (ed.), Philosophisch-politische Profile (1987).

— Discourse Ethics: Notes on a Program of Philosophical Justification, in: J. Habermas (ed.), Moral Consciousness and Communicative Action (1990).

— On the Pragmatic, the Ethical, and the Moral Employments of Practical Reason, in: J. Habermas (ed.), Justification and Application. Remarks on Discourse Ethics (1993).

— Between Facts and Norms. Contributions to a Discourse Theory of Law and Democracy (1998).

— Faktizität und Geltung. Beiträge zur Diskurstheorie des Rechts und des demokratischen Rechtsstaats (1998).

Howse, R., The Legitimacy of the World Trade Organization, in: J.-M. Coicaud/V. Heiskanen (eds.), The Legitimacy of International Organizations (2001).

Hurd, I., Legitimacy and Authority in International Politics, in: International Organization 53 (1999), pp. 379-408.

Intellectual Property Watch, TRIPS Council: Big Boost for Biodiversity Amendment; Enforcement Debated, www.ip-watch.org/weblog/index.php?p=643.

Kaldor, M., Global Civil Society. An Answer to War (2003).

Krugman, P., What Should Trade Negotiators Negotiate About?, in: Journal of Economic Literature 35 (1997), pp. 113-120.

Kuijper, P., WTO Institutional Aspects, in: D. Bethlehem/D. McRae/R. Neufeld et al (eds.): The Oxford Handbook of International Trade Law (2009).

Lang, A., Reflecting on 'Linkage': Cognitive and Institutional Change in the International Trading System, in: Modern Law Review 70 (2007), pp. 523-547.

Marks, S., Democracy and International Governance, in: J.-M. Coicaud/V. Heiskanen (eds.), The Legitimacy of International Organizations (2001).

Moore, M., The Democratic Roots of the World Trade Organization, in: P. Macrory/A. Appleton/M. Plummer (eds.), The World Trade Organization. Legal, Economic and Political Analysis, Vol. 1 (2005).

Moravcsik, A., In Defence of the 'Democratic Deficit': Reassessing Legitimacy in the European Union, in: Journal of Common Market Studies 40 (2002), pp. 603-624.

Müller, H., Arguing, Bargaining and All That: Communicative Action, Rationalist Theory and the Logic of Appropriateness in International Relations, in: European Journal of International Relations 10 (2004), pp. 395-435.

— Internationale Verhandlungen, Argumente und Verständigungshandeln. Verteidigung, Befunde, Warnung, in: P. Niesen/B. Herborth (eds.), Anarchie der kommunikativen Freiheit. Jürgen Habermas und die Theorie der internationalen Politik (2007).

Mulligan, S., The Uses of Legitimacy in International Relations, in: Millennium 34 (2005), pp. 349-375.

Nanz, P./J. Steffek, Global Governance, Participation and the Public Sphere, in: Government and Opposition 39 (2004), pp. 314-385.

Nye, J., Soft Power. The Means to Success in World Politics (2004).

Offe C./U. Preuss, The Problem of Legitimacy in the European Polity. Is Democratization the Answer?, in: Constitutionalism Webpapers 6 (2006), www.qub.ac.uk/schools/SchoolofPoliticsInternationalStudiesandPhilosophy/FileStore/ConWEBFiles/Filetoupload,52216,en.pdf.

Rao, R., Included Out?, www.metamute.org/en/Included-Out.

Reus-Smit, C., The Constitutional Structure of International Society and the Nature of Fundamental Institutions, in: International Organization 51 (1997), pp. 555-589.

Risse, T., "Let's Argue": Communicative Action in World Politics, in: International Organization 54 (2000), p. 39.

— Global Governance and Communicative Action, in: Government and Opposition 39 (2004), pp. 288-313.

Scharpf, F., Governing in Europe: Effective and Democratic? (1999).

Schell, J., The Unconquerable World. Power, Nonviolence, and the Will of the People (2003).

Sell, S., Private Power, Public Law. The Globalization of Intellectual Property Rights (2003).

Singer, P., One World. The Ethics of Globalization (2004).

Stammers, N., Social Movements and the Social Construction of Human Rights, in: Human Rights Quarterly 21 (1999), pp. 980-1008.

Stegemann, K., The Integration of Intellectual Property Rights into the WTO System, in: The World Economy 23 (2000), pp. 1237-1268.

Steger, D., The Culture of the WTO: Why It Needs to Change, in: Journal of International Economic Law 10 (2007), pp. 483-495.

Steinberg, R., In the Shadow of Law or Power? Consensus-Based Bargaining and Outcomes in the GATT/WTO, in: International Organization 56 (2002), pp. 339-374.

Stiglitz, J./A. Carlton, Fair Trade for All. How Trade Can Promote Development (2005).

Trebilcock, M./R. Howse, The Regulation of International Trade (2005).

Vignes, D., Will the Third Conference on the Law of the Sea Work According to the Consensus Rule?, in: American Journal of International Law 69 (1975), pp. 119-129.

Wilkinson, R., Crisis in Cancún, in: Global Governance 10 (2004), pp. 149-155.

Wolf, M., Why Globalization Works (2004).

World Trade Organization, First Special Session of the Committee on Agriculture, Statement by the European Communities, G/AG/NG/W/3 of 4 April 2000.

World Trade Organization, Ministerial Declaration, Hong Kong Ministerial Conference, Doc. WT/MIN(05)/DEC of 22 December 2005, para. 11.

World Trade Organization, Second Special Session of the Committee on Agriculture, Statement by the European Community, G/AG/NG/W/24 of 11 July 2000.

World Trade Organization, Ten Common Misunderstandings About the WTO (2007).

World Trade Organization, WTO Negotiations on Agriculture. Poverty Reduction: Sectoral Initiative in Favour of Cotton, Joint Proposal by Benin, Burkina Faso, Chad and Mali, Doc. TN/AG/GEN/4 of 16 May 2003.

Normative Reflections to Enhance Existing Modes of Governance – Comment

Alexander Brand and Tina Roeder

The question that guides the encounter with the three papers in this section is, not surprisingly, directed at the specific value of normative reflections to enhance existing modes of governance. However, two different (albeit interwoven) readings of this question are possible. First, what is the value of normative reflections to enhance existing modes of government/governance, or, in other words, how can legal structures be utilised to improve the handling of global risks? Each of the three articles suggests its own answer to this question. After examining those, the second reading of the question becomes relevant: Apart from the particular methods employed, what constitutes the specific value of normative reflections to enhance existing modes of governance? Both readings are equally important, and all three contributions to this section provide us with answers to them.

The first article in this group, *Vanessa Holzer's* reflections on the relevance of the 1951 Refugee Convention in times of armed conflict, examines existing normative structures and their adaptability to certain global problems, i.e. the flight of people from specific situations of violence. The Refugee Convention bases the special status and protection it gives to the individuals who fall within its scope on the existence of certain forms of persecution; understood and interpreted traditionally, it does not cover people fleeing purely from the intrinsic fears and terrors of armed conflicts *per se*. By, *inter alia*, interrelating the Convention's definition of a refugee to the rules of humanitarian and human rights law, *Holzer* shows how these situations of violence can be, if at least partly, included in the scope of the Convention, offering a heightened level of protection to those most desperately in need of it, while keeping the structure and *telos* of the Convention intact.

This approach, broadening the range of an existing legal instrument without changing the instrument itself or creating new sets of rules, can be seen as the gentlest, most frictionless way to enhance international governance – a subtle method, but perhaps, precisely because of its softness, rather more effective. After all, as *Holzer* rightly points out, the interpretation of international treaties can be – and has been – influenced by consecutive, amicable practice of the respective state parties. On the other hand, legal guarantees that exist purely behind the written words will by their very nature always be of a more elusive character; more easily agreed and accepted than the written legal text, but also, in reverse, much more easily discarded. State practice in other areas of refugee law shows that legal certainty is hard, if not impossible, to achieve this way:

Concerning the question of gender-related persecution under the Refugee Convention, state practice varies even within Europe considerably. The would-be refugee is left to wonder whether or not he or she will be accepted at the doors of the host country basically until he is standing on the very door step, more often than not with no sensible way to return.

Joris Larik's thoughts on the international criminal responsibility of corporations take us one step further along the road to matching existing international legal structures to the changing global reality. In his, the second, article, he takes another set of rules – those on the international criminal responsibility of the individual – and examines its applicability, not just to situations previously not covered, but nevertheless closely related to the theme of the original legal structure, but to a whole new group of addressees, namely international respectively multinational corporations (MNCs).

While the obstacles, accurately presented and scrutinised by *Larik*, are obvious – how to identify a legal person's *dolus*, and how to punish it effectively once it has been convicted –, the necessity to legally deal with the ever-growing influence of so-called "multis" on the international plane is just as evident. *Larik's* approach to the problem is quite manifest, especially in this respect that the risks presented by multinational corporations cannot be solved nationally. Even in the course of its normal, routine business, a multinational corporation presents numerous legal difficulties, perhaps even more so on the international than on the national plane. With all the legal problems related, for instance, to the acceptance or non-acceptance of foreign acts of state, it is impossible to see how a set of rules concerning certain forms of behaviour by international corporations, adopted nationally, could make any lasting impact on such a corporation. *Larik's* proposal offers a way to shift from national helplessness to a new level of international co-operation in this respect, with almost all the legal rules necessary for this transfer already in existence.

Legally sound, his approach nevertheless holds certain problems in relation to the implementation of such a set of rules for MNCs. *Larik* follows a trend which has been present in Public International Law for quite some time, the terminological criminalisation of certain acts committed on the international plane. Before setting up the rules laid down in the ICC's statute concerning criminal acts of individuals, it had already been tried to introduce a similar terminology in relation to states. In the Draft Articles on State Responsibility, the International Law Commission (ILC) originally included an article on so-called "international crimes" committed by states, mostly gross breaches of core human rights rules; a concept closely related to and in parts intertwined with the notion of obligations *erga omnes*. But while the existence of obligations *erga omnes* seems to have gained a firm footing in Public International Law over the years, the idea of "state crimes" has not. The relevant article 19 was finally deleted from the draft rules, since most states proved strictly unwilling to accept being criminalised for certain acts.

While international corporations are not states, and therefore not on a par with those main generators of Public International Law, they are not individuals either. Despite all human rights treaties, the individual's position on the international plane is not a particularly firm one (although it has been stabilised to some extent by the ICJ's *LaGrand* judgement); individuals still rely, in many areas and especially in relation to the enforcement of their international rights, on states. To put it more bluntly: From a purely legal point of view, individuals exist on the international level because states accorded them the possibility to do so. If the states agree on criminalising certain acts of individuals on this level, then there is, in simple terms, not too much the individual can do to overthrow this decision.

For international corporations, on the other hand, the international plane represents a natural habitat; if not legally, then certainly in practical terms. They exist, they act on this plane, and often, their actions entail grave repercussions. Whether Public International Law chooses to accept it or not, the processes of globalisation have put those corporations as players on the international board; and, other than individuals, they are power players. In their strongest form, as *Larik* also mentions, they are able to outweigh states both on the economic and the political level.

With this in mind, it is not easy to see how international corporations could be brought to accept the proposed criminalisation of certain forms of corporate behaviour. There are other attempts being made to legally bind them to the core framework of Public International Law, especially in relation to human rights guarantees; but, so far, to no avail. International corporations, as any entity created for the purpose of achieving purely economic goals, are not made to operate with moral or ethical principles in mind. Plainly speaking, they are made to do business, and business is what they will do and will, by all means, at all times, strive to keep on doing. Thus, it seems highly doubtful that they would not use all their considerable strength to avert a set of rules like the proposed, especially if it is accompanied by such a grave stigmatisation.

One also wonders if the true, unique risk really lies in the "multis'" own involvement in acts of genocide and other massive violations of human rights, with which *Larik* is mostly dealing. Lurking behind the obvious, there is another danger, subtler and, in terms of legal structures, probably almost impossible to grasp. Throughout the world, governments and economic entities have become increasingly intertwined; and it is not just the poor, unstable, violence-ridden countries that are prone to accept more influence from potent corporations than should wisely be done. Over the years, and especially in the current times of global economic insecurity, we are witnessing more and more rather disquieting scenarios in which corporations – international and national – are bargaining with worried states, successfully using catch phrases like "tightening job market" or "economic stagnation" to gain freedom from many essentially sound legal impediments.

With a view to this ever-increasing global influence of corporations, it must furthermore be doubted whether the contempt of public opinion that *Larik* envisages as a feasible punishment for certain corporate acts would truly be as effective as he imagines it to be. With these rather practical problems in mind, it seems quite manifest that the third contribution to this section, *Nicolas Lamp's* considerations on the WTO legitimacy debate, should go even one step further. To him, the real task is not to examine the existing rules in order to enhance their efficiency, but to delve deeper and look at the power relations at play below the legal surface. In doing so, his is by far the most radical approach. Looking at the recent wave of the "WTO legitimacy debate", *Lamp* proposes to shift the very perspective on what constitutes legitimacy with regard to the WTO. He argues, first, that the degree of active self-determination allowed to its members within the organisation's rule-making procedures has not received enough attention. Secondly, as one might have guessed given the recent deadlock situation, the WTO's legitimacy hinges on a reconfiguration of established power relations among its members and their respective constituencies. This in itself is not revolutionary, since both criticisms are directed, as *Lamp* notes, at a legitimacy "debate" that has at least partially adopted an agnostic attitude to power relations (obviously with fatal consequences) and thus become somewhat anaemic. What sets his treatment apart is his thoughtful and carefully constructed argument concerning the obstacles as well as the potential "remedies" for enhancing the legitimacy of the WTO and, by that, bringing about a more inclusive mode of governance.

Lamp, in his discussion of *Jürgen Habermas*, is quite aware of the rather sobering effect some of the more recent attempts at incorporating *Habermas'* thinking into international relations (IR) theory arguably have had. That is why he never aspires to treat the normative approach embodied in the concept of communicative action merely as an analytical toolbox, and he does wisely so. Thus, he illuminates that the consensus procedure of the WTO, widely hailed as an embodiment of democracy, does not qualify as the same as "assent" in a discursive process of legislation in the Habermasian sense. In other words, the opening-up of communicative space, the establishment of the very opportunity to debate the validity of the respective claims is qualitatively different from the bargaining procedures of states' representatives wielding veto powers. This might seem trivial at first glance but gains tremendous persuasive power in his analysis of the dynamics that led to the amendment of the TRIPS provisions on compulsory licensing. In this instance, some sort of discursive process took place, which not only re-asserted a certain measure of self-determination on behalf of seemingly less powerful states, but also (temporarily) led to a reconfiguration of power relations.

In the remainder of the article, *Lamp* returns to the obstacle-side of the legitimacy debate, again reconstructing (almost: de-constructing) a well-known pillar of WTO decision-making procedure, i.e. the principle of reciprocity. While on a general level one could interpret such "reciprocity" in its alleged *do ut des*-quality as a fairly just concept, *Lamp* convincingly shows that claims for reciprocity are strategically deployed precisely to hinder the formation of communicative power.

While this is all astutely argued and, on an abstract level, sounds promising, one nevertheless has to ask whether there is hope that the role of communicative power can systematically (more or less) be enhanced in the WTO lawmaking process. Is the paradigmatic case cited above the only case? What might contribute to or bolster the chances for further communicative processes? Do powerful (in the traditional sense) actors understand these dynamics and re-orient their behaviour according to such new, discursive dynamics beyond the simple recourse to reciprocity? These are question worth asking, and they might have been answered by the author, if only he had been given more space. For all its elaboration, however, there seems to be a minor shortcoming in the last paper: A more thorough assessment of the very idea of "risk" that has informed the contribution would have made it easier to compare all three papers in this section on the same level. It is in this sense (and only in this one) that the paper itself "risks" being slightly misunderstood, as if it was directed mostly at correcting the obvious shortcomings of the scholarly legitimacy debate, while in fact, as *Lamp* undoubtedly is quite aware of, there are major issues concerning life, survival and well-being of people at stake.

As has been shown, all three contributions employ normative reasoning far beyond the mere description of a certain ensemble of norms in a given field of action and the proposition of "technical" solutions to problems of risk. Thus, the articles compiled seem to suggest that (turning towards the second reading of the initial question) there is indeed a specific value to normative reflection on existing modes of governance, although each paper frames this issue in a different way.

Vanessa Holzer's paper makes the core claim that a lot (especially from the perspective of the refugees) depends on how the situation of "persecution" is assessed by specific institutions. Given the deliberately interpretative character of the Convention's text, it is left to states' practices and further juridico-legal refinement based upon political will and political acts to adapt the protection clause to several instances of endangerment. As *Holzer* is quite clear about it, the "floodgates concern" is a political and not a legal argument; but precisely because it is not merely a technical question of applying established rules (which in turn also involves politics), but in the end a politico-normative question, the reluctance to broaden the scope of protection needs to be explained. For it is, as the reflection on refugee issues makes painfully clear, the political question, which risk is deemed to be more dangerous – the risk of a refugee being persecuted or the risk of other societies giving potentially huge numbers of refugees a safe haven – that decides upon the fate of refugees. Nevertheless, in such a situation, where practices seem to be malleable through argumentative reasoning, it might be a wise and more effective way to show how an expanded reading of the Refugee Convention actually covers more phenomena than traditionally thought, if one is to help securing the status of refugees who fled the perils of armed conflict.

Larik's normative reasoning takes a different form. In making transparent that the enormous and still growing scope and power of MNCs entails global risks at least with regard to massively increased abilities to inflict (willingly or permissively) large-scale damage and that these abilities are hardly matched by regulatory measures and/or penalty structures, he presents an eminently normative problem. However, the clever move of *Larik's* approach is that, instead of lamenting such a (indeed lamentable!) "regime deficit" or trying to analyse what explains this gap as it is usually done in the large literature critical on MNCs, he actually engages this gap in a constructive way. Through attempting to show that there are not any insurmountable juridical grounds that justify this gap, he frames a normative problem (evolving risks that should be countered, but are regrettably left to some degree in the balance) in a legalistic argument. In other words, he anchors a normative claim (MNCs should be treated as if...) within existing legal frameworks undermining on a general level the claim that it is basically a problem of non-existing regulation or laws that simply cannot be constructed. This, on the other hand, arguably strengthens the argumentative power of the underlying normative claim.

In *Lamp's* Habermasian treatment of the WTO legitimacy debate, normativity abounds. He basically applies a normative approach to a host of normative questions, while at the same time illustrating his ideas with an interesting empirical case of normative change. In doing so he – rather than just confronting us with a normatively inspired plea for necessary change (of power relations etc.) – directs our attention to normative dynamics that might already have begun to alter existing structures of governance.

The articles show in manifold ways that, in answer to the question initially posed, normative reflections can indeed be of great value to enhancing governance in the face of global risks. But, and this is just as clear, such value is not without limits. Where underlying structures and dynamics are faulty, malfunctioning or simply out-dated, they may either render legal changes useless, or altogether block them. In the end, it all boils down to that seemingly simple task: To find the precious point of equilibrium between that which must be done, and that which can be done. Beyond that, there is no denying that altering legal structures, the content as well as application of rules etc. hardly functions as a panacea with regard to (global) risks. If at all, it might contribute to proper and just management of such risks, while their roots for a good part lie elsewhere.

C. Alternative Modes of Governance –
Examples from Different Policy Fields

The Exit Option in the Treaty of Lisbon: More Harm than Good?

Susanne Lechner

I. Introduction

It took over 50 years since the founding of the European Union (EU) for the idea of a Constitution for Europe to be tackled. The efforts to push the political integration were, however, put to an end when France and the Netherlands voted against the Draft Constitutional Treaty in 2005. Despite that backlash, government officials kept at the idea of forming a new institutional framework for Europe which finally resulted in the Treaty of Lisbon signed in December 2007. The ratification process, slowed down by the Irish veto in 2008, is finished. The outcome of the 2nd Irish referendum in October 2009 gave way to the final implementation of the treaty in December 2009.

What was first designed as a Constitution for Europe resulted in the diluted Treaty of Lisbon: the final product of intergovernmental negotiations on the way to a new legal fundament for the functioning of the European Union. As it aims at strengthening the European Union institutionally, in order to cope with the challenges of the 21st century, it pursues measurements that make the EU "more democratic, transparent and efficient".[1]

Whether the treaty can fulfil that promise continues to be the subject of ongoing discussions. It could be confirmed that the treaty leads to more democracy as, on the one hand, the power of the European Parliament will be strengthened and, on the other hand, the influence of national parliaments on European affairs will increase. In addition to that, direct democracy can be exerted by European citizens as they may bring in own initiatives.[2] In terms of transparency, however, the treaty has been blamed for raising new questions without clear answers and for granting too many exemptions in the form of declarations and protocols.[3] Instead of being more transparent, its complexity has increased, making the treaty less understandable.

It seems doubtful that a coherent framework for the functioning of the EU has been established with the Treaty of Lisbon. Revisions of the treaty will be unavoidable in the near future if the set goals are to be reached.[4] Keeping that

---

1   For detailed information on the Treaty of Lisbon and its expected changes see http://europa.eu (This and the following internet sources: 15 July 2009).
2   See S. Kurpas, The Treaty of Lisbon – How Much "Constitution" is Left? An Overview of the Main Changes, in: CEPS Policy Brief 147 (2007), p. 9.
3   Ibid.
4   See M. Höreth/J. Sonnicksen, Making and Breaking Promises. The European Union

in mind, it is hard to estimate how efficient the new treaty will be: having, in the future set-up, two new representatives (a European Council President and a High Representative for Foreign Affairs) will certainly make the EU more tangible, but it needs to be discussed whether these positions are indeed necessary.[5] Furthermore, voting procedures are supposed to be simplified in order to speed up decision-making processes in an increasingly heterogeneous EU. Prospectively, more decisions will be made by qualified majority voting: 137 policy areas have been decided upon by qualified majority so far; after the ratification process, qualified majority will be applied in 181 policy areas.[6] This will certainly facilitate the decision-making and reduce its costs, but it can be expected that the design of the qualified majority, i.e. a complicated double-majority, will narrow the potential efficiency of the voting procedure.

Valued at the key issues of democracy, transparency and efficiency, the Treaty of Lisbon will remain under intense scrutiny. It will not do, however, to rate the success of the treaty by means of only these three criteria. Another criterion has to be applied: flexibility (in terms of flexible integration). The treaty not only grants opt-outs, it also improves the conditions for enhanced cooperation, leading to different integration patterns for the member states.[7] In this context, it is not astonishing that the Treaty of Lisbon also includes a right to withdraw from the EU. Apart from supposedly being a democratic element stabilizing the Union, it also adds to the concept of flexible integration. The question that now needs to be discussed is whether this norm may indeed increase the stability of the Union, thus fostering the integration process, or whether it is the beginning of the end of the Union as member states can now legally and voluntarily exit from it.

This article is organized as follows. In Section two it is debated why or why not the right of withdrawal should be embedded in a constitutional framework. Section three analyses the wording and content of the right of withdrawal mentioned under Article 50 in the Treaty of Lisbon. Part four focuses on the impact of that right as a new voting rule in decision-making processes. In a game-theoretic setting it can be shown that member states might gain bargaining power in negotiations by threatening to exit. Section five introduces possible amendments to Article 50 as a means of restricting the misuse of the exit option. Section six concludes the article by answering the question posed in the title of this article: Does the right of withdrawal indeed cause more harm than good?

     Under the Treaty of Lisbon, in: ZEI Discussion paper 181 (2008), pp. 25 f.

5   See Höreth/Sonnicksen, Making and Breaking Promises (2008), p. 26.

6   See Centrum für Europäische Politik (CEP), EU-Reformvertrag: Beschlussfassung im Rat, www.cep.eu/445.html.

7   See Kurpas, The Treaty of Lisbon (2007), p. 9.

II.   The Right of Withdrawal: A "Must-have" in a Treaty?

The right to withdraw can be understood as the right of a member state to abandon an association of states such as the EU, thus regaining full sovereignty. For the first time since the creation of the European Union an explicit option to exit has found its way into a legal framework and the question arises as to whether such a right truly needs to be imbedded within a treaty, especially as no state has ever left the Union so far.[8]

First of all, there is the fear that the days of the EU in its present design are numbered if member states can unilaterally withdraw from the Union.[9] The principle of an ever closer Union that will last forever is being scrutinized and may lead to uncertainty on behalf of the member states as to how the future development of the EU may look like. It is also feared that member states may be less willing to cooperate in order to reach compromises on certain issues.[10] Instead of simply raising their voice in order to achieve better compromises or bargaining results, member states can consider an immediate exit, even more so if exiting entails almost no costs.[11]

Secondly, it can be argued that member states could lose their incentive to invest in collective goods provided by the EU as they fear that other member states behave as free riders enjoying the advantages of the EU but choosing to exit if they are unhappy with their membership, i.e. when they have to make payments to the community. The principle of unity is being challenged to such an extent that potential accession countries are less eager to join the Union as they are afraid of decreasing solidarity.[12]

Thirdly, there is the risk that the right of withdrawal can be misused to erode democratic rules and decisions as a "majority of a group could use this right for

---

8   It could be argued that the withdrawal of Greenland from the European Communities in 1982 may be considered as an example that an exit has already taken place under the current legal setting. However, Greenland is a former colony of Denmark which transformed itself into an overseas non-European country. If Greenland's withdrawal were to be considered as a precedent, then it would only be valid for those territories that are in the same position. See F. Harhoff, Greenland's Withdrawal from the European Communities, in: Common Market Law Review 20 (1983), p. 31.

9   See F. Harbo, Secession Right – An Anti-Federal Principle? Comparative Study of Federal States and the EU, in: Journal of Politics and Law 1 (2008), p. 143.

10 See C. Sunstein, Constitutionalism and Secession, in: University of Chicago Law Review 58 (1991), p. 650.

11 See A. Hirschman, Abwanderung und Widerspruch: Reaktionen auf Leistungsabfall bei Unternehmungen, Organisationen und Staaten (1974), p. 71. In this context no opportunity costs and one-time costs, for example through the reestablishment of border controls etc., are considered.

12 Although the right of withdrawal poses that risk to countries interested in EU membership, it guarantees them at the same time the option to withdraw.

the sole purpose of overruling federal laws which prevent them from oppressing the minority of the group".[13]

However, a minority could also enforce its opposition to a decision agreed on by majority voting by threatening with secession. In other words, an overruled minority could adopt blackmail as a strategy to impose its will on the majority.[14] The danger that the EU could be blackmailed by a single member state with the right of withdrawal had already been anticipated by the European Commission and the European Convention when discussing the Draft of the European Constitution. Whether or not the right of withdrawal bears the potential of being used as a threatening device will be discussed later.

Despite the counter-arguments brought forward, the right to withdraw has been written down explicitly in the Treaty of Lisbon. There must be advantages of having such an option in the treaty. First of all, member states can then unilaterally exit the Union without stating any reasons. Since no clear exit option was provided in the legal framework,[15] the Treaty of Lisbon now closes that gap and provides additional stability for the Union:

"History teaches us that there is no such thing as institutions which last forever. Integrated areas arise, change or decay – peacefully or violently. If in addition to the conditions for joining a club at the same time those for withdrawing from the club are regulated, then integration policy is given the necessary degree of symmetry, which – even if this appears paradoxical – contains an element of stabilization."[16]

---

13   T. Apolte, Secession Clauses: A Tool for the Taming of an Arising Leviathan in Brussels?, in: Constitutional Political Economy 8 (1997), p. 57.

14   See J. Buchanan, Democracy and Secession, in: M. Moore (ed.), National Self-determination and Secession (1998), p. 21.

15   Up to the Treaty of Lisbon, there was no explicit right permitting a unilateral withdrawal from the Union. Turning to International Law Art. 62 of the Vienna Convention, the doctrine of *clausula rebus sic stantibus* may be considered. According to that article, "(...) a party may withdraw from a treaty in case of a fundamental change of circumstances, when these circumstances constitute an essential basis of the consent of the other parties, and if the change of these circumstances may radically transform the extent of the withdrawing party's obligations under the treaty". Harhoff, Greenland's Withdrawal (1983), p. 30. A fundamental change of circumstances as such is currently unlikely and if indeed such a situation occurs, all conditions going along with Art. 62 must be fulfilled for that a member state may withdraw from any treaties. See A. Waltemathe, Austritt aus der EU. Sind die Mitgliedstaaten noch souverän? (2000), p. 96. In addition to that, it is also not clearly stated whether a member state may withdraw after the consent of the remaining countries. Here, Article 48 of the Treaty on European Union may be considered. In the article it is stated that treaties might be amended if certain conditions are fulfilled, thus also enabling the dissolution of the community. See J. Zeh, Recht auf Austritt, in: Zeitschrift für Europarechtliche Studien 2 (2004), p. 189.

16   W. Schäfer, Withdrawal Legitimised? On the Proposal by the Constitutional Convention for the Right of Secession from the EU, in: Intereconomics (2003), p. 183.

Secondly, it can be argued that an exit option may lead to economic growth: in the historic context it can be seen that decentralised medieval Europe, for example, spurred competition and growth among its countries. If a state has the opportunity to leave a union, it might receive an impetus to focus on its economic development and to pursue new strategies. This means in economic terms that the right to exit is the other side of the coin of economic integration. To put it another way, trade openness and political separatism, which are enabled by the right of withdrawal, go hand in hand.[17]

Economic integration is determined by free trade among countries that actually do not have to be part of a regional integration area such as the EU because they can profit from free trade anyway, without bearing the costs of membership.[18] Nevertheless, they prefer being part of a union because "external threats increase the incentives to form larger political unions for protection, and hence tend to reduce the probability of separatism."[19]

As long as the advantages prevail, member states will remain within the union, but if decisions are made that create higher costs, member states can choose to leave, which provides them with bargaining power – the right of withdrawal serves therefore as guarantee against collective decisions which are sub-optimal.[20] A governing majority, for example, is then restricted from imposing high taxes on a minority.[21] A right of withdrawal is therefore able to limit excessive redistribution flows as member states can raise their voice more effectively. This aspect is of special relevance especially as there is a never-ending conflict between the net payers and net receivers in the EU. By negotiating strategically, member states try to get the maximum out of available EU funds at the expense of other member states. The countries with a high average income contributing most to the EU budget may now demand a more efficient allocation of resources by threatening to leave the union if their voice is not heard.

Fourthly, the right to exit gives emphasis to the principle of subsidiarity. By transferring more state tasks vertically, institutional competition within the EU, which has been less intensive in the past due to increasing tendencies of centralisation, will be increased.[22]

---

17   See A. Alesina/E. Spolaore/R. Wacziarg, Economic Integration and Political Disintegration, in: American Economic Review 90 (2000), p. 1277.

18   See P. Bolton/G. Roland/E. Spolaore, Economic Theories of the Break-up and Integration of Nations, in: European Economic Review 40 (1996), pp. 701 f.

19   E. Spolaore, Civil Conflict and Secessions, in: Economics of Governance 9 (2008), p. 57.

20   See P. Kurrild-Klitgaard, Opting-Out: The Constitutional Economics of Exit, in: American Journal of Economics and Sociology 61 (2002), p. 124.

21   See J. Buchanan/R. Faith, Secession and the Limits of Taxation: Toward a Theory of Internal Exit, in: American Economic Review 77 (1987), p. 1031.

22   See Schäfer, Withdrawal Legitimised? (2003), p. 183.

When arguing whether or not the Treaty of Lisbon should include the right of withdrawal, advantages and disadvantages have to be taken into consideration and weighed up: The right of withdrawal clearly works against the idea of Europe being an everlasting construction. As soon as one member state decides to leave, others may follow suit and the whole integration project is challenged as the gains of integration through the Single Market and the Monetary Union threaten to disappear.

From an ex-ante point of view, a right of withdrawal should therefore not be included in a legal framework because the overall utility of the Union depends on its credible duration. From an ex-post point of view, however, a right of withdrawal should be mentioned in a constitutional set-up in order to keep exit costs low and not to risk a costly secession war.[23]

Keeping that in mind, it can be understood as a stabilizing factor of the integration process: member states do not lose their sovereignty altogether because they can leave the Union if they are not content with their membership.[24] By enhancing the principle of , the right of withdrawal may therefore be able to contribute to the cohesion of the Union. Last but not least: the right of withdrawal is a democratic element, thus adding to the stability of the EU.

III.   The Exit Option in the Treaty of Lisbon

According to Article 50 of the Treaty of Lisbon,[25] a member state may voluntarily exit the Union according to the following guidelines:

"1. Any Member State may decide to withdraw from the Union in accordance with its own constitutional requirements."

A country interested in withdrawing from the European Union has to deal first with the issue of whether its constitution allows it to exit.[26] The European Court of Justice (ECJ) would need to decide whether that decision has been made in accordance with national constitutional law. Whether the country may still legally withdraw in the case that the European Court of Justice questions the

---

23   See M. Bordignon/S. Brusco, Optimal Secession Rules, in: European Economic
       Review 40 (2001), p. 1812.
24   See D. Doering, Friedlicher Austritt. Braucht die Europäische Union ein
       Sezessionsrecht?, Discussion Paper, in: The Centre for the New Europe (2002),
       pp. 55 f.
25   See Treaty of Lisbon, Official Journal of the European Union 51 (2008).
26   A. Waltemathe (2000) provides a good overview of the different constitutional
       conditions for an exit from the European Union.

validity of the decision to withdraw has not been discussed so far.[27] Besides that if a country really wants to withdraw, it will not care at all about the decision of the court.

"2. A Member State which decides to withdraw shall notify the European Council of its intention. In the light of the guidelines provided by the European Council, the Union shall negotiate and conclude an agreement with that State, setting out the arrangements for its withdrawal, taking account of the framework for its future relationship with the Union. That agreement shall be negotiated in accordance with Article 218(3) of the Treaty on the Functioning of the European Union. It shall be concluded on behalf of the Union by the Council, acting by a qualified majority, after obtaining the consent of the European Parliament."

"3. The Treaties shall cease to apply to the State in question from the date of entry into force of the withdrawal agreement or, failing that, two years after the notification referred to in paragraph 2, unless the European Council, in agreement with the Member State concerned, unanimously decides to extend this period."

The state will notify the EU of its intention to withdraw and negotiate an exit agreement by considering the future relationships between both parties. The withdrawing member state may refuse to sign such agreement by anticipating that it can leave the union after a waiting period of two years anyway. In doing so, it may basically enforce its withdrawal.[28] Taking that into consideration, a member state may use the right as a "threat of withdrawal to force concessions from the other member states knowing that any putative withdrawal could itself be withdrawn before the two years have expired".[29]

"4. For the purposes of paragraphs 2 and 3, the member of the European Council or of the Council representing the withdrawing Member State shall not participate in the discussions of the European Council or Council or in decisions concerning it. A qualified majority shall be defined in accordance with Article 238(3)(b) of the Treaty on the Functioning of the European Union."

It is clearly stated that the withdrawing member state is excluded from any voting or discussion concerning its withdrawal, but it has not been mentioned

---

27   See R. Friel, Providing a Constitutional Framework for Withdrawal from the EU: Article 59 of the Draft European Constitution, in: International and Comparative Law Quarterly 53 (2004), p. 425.

28   See T. Bruha/C. Nowak, Recht auf Austritt aus der Europäischen Union? Anmerkungen zu Artikel I-59 des Entwurfs eines Vertrages über eine Verfassung für Europa, in: Archiv des Völkerrechts 42 (2004), p. 7.

29   Friel, Providing a Constitutional Framework (2004), p. 426. Even though such an agreement is not a precondition for an exit, it could be a worthwhile step: if a beneficial agreement can be reached, the costs of withdrawal will be lessened. See S. Berglund, Prison or Voluntary Cooperation? The Possibility of Withdrawal from the European Union, in: Scandinavian Political Science 26 (2006), p. 163.

whether the member state can still participate in discussions being of relevance for the future relationship between the EU and the member state in question. Should the withdrawing member state have the right to participate in those meetings? The article remains silent on that.[30]

> "5. If a State which has withdrawn from the Union asks to rejoin, its request shall be subject to the procedure referred to in Article 49."

After having withdrawn from the Union, the member state may (re)join it, but it cannot claim direct membership; rather, it has to run through the same entry proceedings as any other applicant country.[31]

Even though the article drafts the procedure, it does not provide any information on how to cope with the institutional changes that go along with the withdrawal of a country from the EU. How will the composition of the European Parliament and Commission change and how will the votes in the Council of Ministers and in the European Council be newly weighted?[32]

Indeed, the withdrawal clause has not been formulated in enough detail and leaves certain issues unclear, such as the design of the agreement or how to deal with the institutional challenges. It raises many questions and does not provide detailed solutions. It could be argued that a clear procedure has not been stated on purpose because the EU expects that an actual withdrawal will not happen; therefore, there is no need to worry about fuzzy details because the probability of an immediate withdrawal is supposed to be low.

Even though this might currently reflect a true perception, the future might tell a different story. Due to numerous enlargements, the composition of the EU has changed in a way that member states have more and more diverting preferences which hinder decision-making processes. As a reaction to that, voting procedures have changed: more decisions are made by majority instead of unanimity. For this reason, it is possible that individual member states might be overruled. If that happens often enough, the option of being either a sovereign state outside the Union or the member of another regional integration area could become an increasingly attractive alternative to EU membership.

By referring to the right of withdrawal, any member state could demand less centralisation so that it can remain within the community. In that case the right serves as a democratic device of federalism in the EU; at the same time, however, it bears the risk of being misused as a means of extracting concessions from other member states. Whether member states are indeed able to increase their bargaining power through the right of withdrawal and exploit it will be discussed in the next section.

---

30   See Friel, Providing a constitutional framework (2004), p. 426.
31   See Bruha/Nowak, Recht auf Austritt aus der Europäischen Union? (2004), pp. 7 f.
32   See Harbo, Secession Right – An Anti-Federal Principle? (2008), p. 143.

IV. The Impact of the Exit Option as a Third Voting Rule in the Treaty of Lisbon

With the help of a game-theoretic approach, *Lechner* and *Ohr*[33] analyse how the right of withdrawal increases a member state's bargaining power. The initial point is a decision that has to be made in the Council of Ministers, which will increase the benefits for the majority of EU member states except for the country, M1, whose benefits of EU membership will be reduced. In case the decision is made, M1 will demand a financial transfer compensating it for the loss. Its request is enhanced by the threat to leave the European Union if a transfer is not offered. *Lechner* and *Ohr* analyse how much compensation is offered to M1 by the EU in different decision-making scenarios: unanimity voting, majority voting without exit option under the current legal setting in the Treaty of Nice, and majority voting with the exit option as enabled in the Treaty of Lisbon. The amount offered to M1 reflects its bargaining power. How much is the EU willing to pay M1 for its agreement to the decision and for it to remain in the Union?

The theoretical framework of that analysis is the so-called Ultimatum Game: two players, a proposer and a responder, meet only once and bargain on how to split a certain amount. Both players have complete information on the amount to be redistributed. The proposer makes an offer to the responder that he can accept or deny. If he accepts, both players receive the respective amounts and the game ends. If he, however, rejects, both players receive nothing. According to the standard theory, the proposer would give the lowest amount necessary for the responder to accept. The responder should accept any offer higher than zero. If both agree, the respective pay-offs are provided with the proposer receiving a higher one than the responder.

Experimental tests were conducted to survey these theoretical implications. *Güth, Schmittberger*, and *Schwarze* show that players do not act according to the standard theory: In a one shot game, the responder rejects offers which were below 20-30 percent of the amount to be redistributed. The proposer, on the contrary, offers between 30-50 percent of the amount to be redistributed which is more than theory suggests.[34] Since the experiment by *Güth, Schmittberger*, and *Schwarze*, the Ultimatum Game has been intensively tested by modifying its underlining assumptions, such as assuming information asymmetries, auctioning the roles of the proposer or providing outside-options in order to find out how the test subjects decide. As an explanation for the contrary behaviour

---

33   See S. Lechner/R. Ohr, The Right of Withdrawal in the Treaty of Lisbon: A Game Theoretic Reflection on Different Decision Processes in the EU, in: Cege-discussion Paper 77 (2008), pp. 9 ff.

34   See W. Güth/R. Schmittberger/B. Schwarze, An Experimental Analysis of Ultimatum Bargaining, in: Journal of Economic Behaviour and Organization 3 (1982), pp. 384 f.

of the players, so-called social motives are brought forward. The behaviour of the proposer to offer more than predicted can be explained, on the one hand, by the notion of fairness: the proposer offers around half of the amount so that both are better off.[35] Fairness is an important factor in his utility function: He maximizes his utility by preferring a fair split of the amount even though he could have kept more for himself. On the other hand, he might be afraid that the responder could punish him for a too low offer and therefore prefers an equal split, thus giving the responder no reason to reject the offer.[36] Why the responder rejects low offers might be explained by the notion of envy: when both players compare their pay-off, the responder does not grant the proposer his amount – assuming that he kept more than the equal split for himself – and will therefore reject his offer.[37] These experimental results need to be taken into consideration when applying the Ultimatum Game in order to assess bargaining results. In the present treatment, the EU is the proposer and M1 the responder. The EU reacts to the demand of M1 by offering a certain amount that depends on the underlying voting procedure the decision requires. *Lechner* and *Ohr* identify which compensating transfers the EU will offer member state M1 against the background of the theoretical implications of the Ultimatum Game and its experimental results.

In the case of unanimity, the original Ultimatum Game as presented above comes into effect. Every member state has to agree to the decision, otherwise it cannot be realized. M1 signals its benefit loss resulting from the decision and demands compensation. According to theory, the EU would offer an amount compensating M1 for its loss. If M1 accepts, its net benefit of the decision and the provided transfer is marginally higher than zero, while the net benefit gain for the EU is at its maximum, as the decision benefits the majority of the member states. If M1, however, rejects the offer, it will not receive any payment and the decision will not be realized.

If a decision requires the majority of votes and member states do not have an exit option, the "dictator game" as a special version of the Ultimatum Game comes into play. In a majority voting scenario not everyone has to agree to the decision. If M1 gets overruled, it demands compensation, but no offer is necessary as the decision can be realized despite the opposition of one or more member states. The EU acts as a dictator, who can realize the decision no matter what M1 claims. Assuming that the majority of the remaining member states have already voted for the decision, it does not have to offer any compensating

---

35   See W. Güth/R. Tietz, Ultimatum Bargaining Behavior. A Survey and Comparison of Experimental Results, in: Journal of Economic Psychology 11 (1990), p. 446.
36   See D. Kravitz/S. Gunto, Decisions and Perceptions of Recipients in Ultimatum Bargaining Games, in: The Journal of Socio-economics 21(1992), p. 66.
37   See G. Kirchsteiger, The Role of Envy in Ultimatum Games, in: Journal of Economic Behavior and Organization 25 (1994), p. 388.

transfer. In the case of a majority vote and the explicit right of withdrawal, another special variant of the game is applied: the Ultimatum Game with a "one-sided outside option". Member state M1 will again ask for compensation and may enhance its demand by threatening to withdraw if no compensation is offered. The EU will offer a transfer which does not fully compensate M1 for its loss, it incurred due to the decision, but which makes M1 better off in staying within the Union and realising the decision instead of withdrawing. In this setting, the offered compensation will be lower than under unanimity.

Based on these theoretical implications, M1 has the highest bargaining power in the unanimity requiring voting procedure as it will be fully compensated for its loss. The 2nd highest bargaining power can be expected under majority voting with the right of withdrawal: M1 will not entirely be compensated for the loss of the decision, but be made better off to its situation outside the Union. M1 has the lowest bargaining power under the current setting of a decision requiring a majority vote and no withdrawal option because the EU is not dependent on M1's approval of the decision and will therefore not have to offer any compensation. Taking into consideration experiments conducted for testing the Ultimatum Game, different results can be expected. In practice, to make sure M1 consents to the decision and does not withdraw from the Union, the EU will make M1 higher offers in all three scenarios, compared to the theoretical implications. Again, M1 has the highest bargaining power under the unanimity rule, as the EU will offer the maximum amount needed to make sure M1 agrees.

Under certain conditions M1 may, in the case of a majority vote, have the same bargaining power as under unanimity, namely when it threatens to withdraw. If the loss in utility caused by M1's exit is higher than the expected utility gain of the decision, the EU will be willing to overcompensate M1 for the loss by offering an amount equivalent to the decision's utility gain in order to make sure that M1 does not leave the Union. If M1 rejects such an offer, the EU will drop the decision as it prefers M1 staying in the Union. In that scenario M1's bargaining power can be as high as under unanimity. If the loss in utility in case M1 exits is, however, lower than the expected utility gain of the decision, the EU will be prepared to offer what M1's membership is worth (to the European Union), keeping in mind that it wants to implement the decision by all means, even at the risk of M1's withdrawal. In that scenario, the bargaining power is lower compared to unanimity.

Even in a majority voting without the option to exit, M1 can count on some offers, based on the notion of fairness. In this case, the member state should accept any offer since a rejection will not punish the EU for a too low offer.

To sum up the analysis, *Lechner* and *Ohr* yield following results: when considering game-theoretic implications, the EU offers higher compensations in case of unanimity rule than in case of a decision by majority with the right to exit. In a majority system without the exit option, the provided transfers will be the lowest. When considering experimental results, the maximum amount M1 can receive in case of a withdrawal option can be as high as under unanimity voting. M1 may expect some payments in case of a decision by majority voting without the right to exit.

Member states do gain bargaining power – a fact which is reflected in the amount of transfers they can get. Here, the amount of the offered transfers is determined by the loss M1 would suffer due to the decision, the loss M1 would suffer in case of withdrawal, the loss the EU would suffer in case M1 withdraws and the gain of the decision for the EU. The most the EU can offer is what the decision is worth to the community. If M1 denies such transfer, the decision will be dropped.[38] Based on these implications, the stability aspect of the right of withdrawal needs to be questioned: in a majority vote with exit option, the EU is willing to toss the decision when compensation payments do not suffice, which is the case when M1's loss of withdrawal is very small. This is especially true for bigger states within the EU that can remain outside the Union without too big loss. It is apparent that the right of withdrawal increases the bargaining power of the bigger states that can credibly threaten to leave the Union. The smaller states, however, are less able to induce enough compensation transfers since their withdrawal is unlikely.

The right of withdrawal that is supposed to stabilize the Union cannot fulfil its promises as it benefits those member states that have a bigger size and/or economic power. It might turn out as a credible instrument for net payers and less for net receivers that cannot credibly threaten to leave the Union if no compensation is offered. As the EU is interested in keeping all member states within the Union, there remains the incentive for a member state to blackmail the EU. Hereby, the amount of offered transfers increases, the more utility the member state generates for the EU, thus putting bigger states at an advantage.

V.   Restrictions on the Right of Withdrawal?

After having discussed the impact of the right of withdrawal on member states' bargaining power, it needs to be discussed whether the article should be modified in order to contain or better avoid any misuse of the right of withdrawal. The first option is to raise exit costs per se, which would make the exit less likely and therefore reduce the potential of the exit option being used as a threatening instrument. One way of doing so is to include a referendum requiring that the majority of the citizens vote in favour of withdrawal. This would keep especially Euro-sceptic politicians from posing threats to the EU as their bargaining power shrinks because they have to conduct a referendum before the country can actually withdraw from the Union. If, as *Erola*,

---

38   See Lechner/Ohr, The Right of Withdrawal in the Treaty of Lisbon (2008), pp. 9-19.

Määttänen, and *Poutvaara* expect, the majority of those citizens opposing further integration prefer to keep up the *status quo* rather than to leave the EU, the threat of withdrawal loses credibility.[39] Another way to raise the costs is to introduce an exit fee. This seems plausible since a withdrawal would cause a certain amount of costs anyway, such as the necessity to undertake institutional changes in order to adapt to the new situation.[40] In this context it has been suggested by Convention Member *Badinter* that the withdrawing member state should pay for the loss it causes when leaving the European Union. Any initiative of withdrawal would be scotched as the remaining member states might have the incentive to overdraw the costs the country causes when leaving the Union, thus further diminishing the probability of an exit.

The second option that needs to be discussed is to enhance the power of the EU by allowing it to punish the country when the right of withdrawal is used to blackmail other member states. By disposing of such a right, the EU may increase its bargaining power and thus avoid being subdued by a single member state. The punishment could have different options: the member state may be excluded from further negotiations or it could even be expelled from the Union if it oppresses the EU severely enough.

The decision on how to deal with the member state could be taken by the European Court of Justice, otherwise member states may have an incentive to punish a threatening member state inappropriately. The difficulty in having such a punishment option is that it needs to be proven that a member state intentionally blackmailed the Union. In practice, this intent would be very hard to determine. The primal idea of having the right of withdrawal as a means of strengthening federalism and of opposing tendencies towards centralisation is not given anymore because blackmail could immediately be imputed to the member state demanding any changes by referring to the right of withdrawal. The country would therefore have no opportunity of standing up against any reproaches.

The third option is to use the right of withdrawal as an opt-out clause: "An opt-out is an exemption from a treaty provision or a directive granted to a Member State that does not wish to join the other Member States in a particular area of community co-operation."[41] Member states would have the legal option, in the form of the right of withdrawal, to opt out of certain policy areas if they are no longer interested in participating in this policy.[42] This would be

---

39   See E. Eerola/N. Määttänen/P. Poutvaara, Citizens Should Vote on Secession, in: Topics in Economic Analysis and Policy 4 (2004), pp. 5 f.

40   See Kurrild-Klitgaard, Opting-Out (2002), p. 149.

41   R. Adler-Nissen, The Diplomacy of Opting Out: A Bourdieudian Approach to National Integration Strategies, in: Journal of Common Market Studies 46 (2008), p. 665.

42   This might be due to, for example, increased tendencies of integration in that policy realm.

considered as a partial secession, however, retaining EU membership. When allowing an opt-out, it needs to be considered that EU membership cannot be combined with every opt-out type in the sense that a country might choose to withdraw, for example, from the Single Market while still keeping its EU membership. Therefore, it needs to be determined to which policy areas in the sense of a "core acquis communautaire"[43] member states must belong to in order to guarantee the proper functioning of the EU.[44] In other areas, opting out would be allowed, which is especially relevant for areas with a high degree of harmonisation, redistribution and market regulations. According to this concept, the European Union would act as an arbitrator between clubs[45], which member states can enter or exit, while full membership as such remains intact. If a member threatens to leave in case it does not receive any compensation, the EU might decide whether or not the demand of the member state is justified, and if not, it can suggest the member state to leave that particular club and be part of another club that better suits its interests. Member states would participate in different clubs according to their integration level.[46]

This idea could be implemented with the so-called enhanced cooperation that was already introduced in the Treaty of Amsterdam. Enhanced cooperation enables the most ambitious member states to deepen cooperation between them while keeping the door open to other countries to join them at a later stage. In doing so, different integration levels in form of various "enhanced cooperation clubs" may be reached, where flexible entry and exit are possible[47] with the help of the right of withdrawal, thus strengthening the future European integration process through flexibility.[48]

---

43   This "core acquis communautaire" would regulate principles of the Internal Market such as the freedom of goods and services, the full convertibility of currencies, competition rules, environmental standards or cooperation with respect to the Security and Defence Policy, where withdrawal is not possible in order to guarantee the stability of the European Union.

44   See Schäfer, Withdrawal Legitimised? (2003), p. 185.

45   In this setting, the European Union can be interpreted as a club providing a variety of integration goods to its members that cannot be enjoyed by states outside the club such as the participation at the Single Market or the European Monetary Union.

46   See J. Ahrens/H. Hoen/R. Ohr, Deepening Integration in an Enlarged EU: A Club-theoretical Perspective, in: European Integration 27 (2005), pp. 417 ff.

47   See M. Wohlgemuth/C. Brandis, Europe à la Carte? A club-theoretical vindication, in: J. Varwick/K. Lang (eds.), European Neighbourhood Policy. Challenges for the EU-Policy Towards the New Neighbours (2007), p. 167.

48   Which concrete role enhanced cooperation will play in the future is not clear yet. It would enhance the integration process if it became an appropriate instrument to deal with the growing heterogeneity as well as with the trade-off between deepening and widening of the EU. There is however the risk that member states engaging in enhanced cooperation use their "first-mover advantage" in forming a club and exclude other interested member states from joining in at a later stage. Therefore, states should

The arguments presented here support the idea of making it difficult to misuse the right of withdrawal. At the same time any tendencies of withdrawal will be hindered, thus making it difficult to withdraw. As already mentioned, it is hard to detect an intentional abuse of the right. By attaching too many conditions to Article 50, however, the risk of a violent break-away from the European Union will increase. Therefore, it was politically decided not to condition the exit, as member states should decide for themselves whether to stay or to leave.

VI.   Conclusion: More Harm than Good?

The Treaty of Lisbon is seen as another step to deepen the level of political integration within the EU. At the same time it enables its member states to legally exit the Union. Taking that into consideration, the question arises as to whether such a right will cause more harm than good. There are indeed risks involved in constitutionally guaranteeing an explicit right of withdrawal. Moreover, the potential of this right being used as a threatening instrument against the EU persists as member states gain bargaining power.

Whether they make use of such potential can only be speculated about. The integration process has already seen some threats of withdrawal: The French president *de Gaulle* threatened to leave the Union in 1965 if no unanimity rule was applied in the Council's proceedings. His request was granted in the form of the Luxembourg Compromise of 1966. Former Prime Minister *Thatcher* demanded payment facilities for the UK in 1973 and threatened to hold a referendum if no such concession were to be given: the citizens should decide whether to stay in the Union or to leave. As a result, the UK was given the so-called British rebate that relieved its household.[49]

In this article it was also discussed whether such a risk should be reduced by attaching conditions to the withdrawal clause which would eventually raise exit costs and thus reduce the utility of an exit. In order to avoid costly secession wars and to warrant member states their own will to decide for themselves whether to stay or to go, no (costly) conditions have been attached. Even the mentioned agreement outlining the details of the withdrawal is not binding.

The EU places considerable trust into the member states that they will not abuse the right by blackmailing the Union and rather consider that option as ultima ratio, when staying in the Union is no longer preferred. Whether they appreciate the right is left to be seen. In the current situation, however, an

---

commit themselves not to change the rules (of entry) but if they do, then they should be forced to provide compensation for excluded countries. See M. Bordignon/S. Brusco, On Enhanced Cooperation, in: Journal of Public Economics 90 (2006), p. 2085.

49   See Lechner/Ohr, The Right of Withdrawal (2008), p. 8.

immediate withdrawal of a member state as a sign of dissatisfaction with its membership is unlikely as the costs of withdrawal are higher than the expected gains of returning to full sovereignty. Keeping in mind that the European Union has become more heterogeneous in the course of its enlargement, the right of withdrawal could become an important instrument. It might have the potential to stabilize it by allowing flexible integration: member states may form clubs according to the concept of enhanced cooperation or a group of them could even exit from the Union and form a new compound of states characterised by their preferences.[50] Ultimately, that right could indeed cause more good than harm.

Bibliography

Adler-Nissen, R. The Diplomacy of Opting Out: A Bourdieudian Approach to National Integration Strategies, in: Journal of Common Market Studies 46 (2008), pp. 663-684.

Ahrens, J./H. Hoen/R. Ohr, Deepening Integration in an Enlarged EU: A Club-theoretical Perspective, in: European Integration 27 (2005), pp. 417-439.

Alesina, A./E. Spolaore/R. Wacziarg, Economic Integration and Political Disintegration, in: American Economic Review 90 (2000), pp. 1276-1296.

Apolte, I., Secession Clauses: A Tool for the Taming of an Arising Leviathan in Brussels?, in: Constitutional Political Economy 8 (1997), pp. 57-70.

Berglund, S., Prison or Voluntary Cooperation? The Possibility of Withdrawal from the European Union, in: Scandinavian Political Science 26 (2006), pp. 147-167.

Bolton, P./G. Roland/E. Spolaore, Economic Theories of the Break-up and Integration of Nations, in: European Economic Review 40 (1996), pp. 697-705.

Bordignon, M./S. Brusco, Optimal Secession Rules, in: European Economic Review 40 (2001), pp. 1811-1834.

—   On Enhanced Cooperation, in: Journal of Public Economics 90 (2006), pp. 2063-2090.

Bruha, T./C. Nowak, Recht auf Austritt aus der Europäischen Union? Anmerkungen zu Artikel I-59 des Entwurfs eines Vertrages über eine Verfassung für Europa, in: Archiv des Völkerrechts 42 (2004), pp. 1-25.

Buchanan, J./R. Faith, Secession and the Limits of Taxation: Toward a Theory of Internal Exit, in: American Economic Review 77 (1987), pp. 1023-1031.

Buchanan, J., Democracy and Secession, in: M. Moore (ed.), National Self-determination and Secession (1998).

Calliess, C./M. Ruffert, Verfassung der Europäischen Union. Kommentar der Grundlagenbestimmungen (2006).

Centrum für Europäische Politik (CEP), EU-Reformvertrag: Beschlussfassung im Rat, www. cep.eu/445.html.

Doering, D., Friedlicher Austritt. Braucht die Europäische Union ein Sezessionsrecht?, Discussion Paper, The Centre for the New Europe (2002).

---

50   See Callies/Ruffert, Verfassung der Europäischen Union (2006), p. 639.

Eerola, E./N. Määttänen/P. Poutvaara, Citizens Should Vote on Secession, in: Topics in Economic Analysis and Policy 4 (2004).

Friel, R., Providing a Constitutional Framework for Withdrawal from the EU: Article 59 of the Draft European Constitution, in: International and Comparative Law Quarterly 53 (2004), pp. 407-428.

Güth, W./R. Schmittberger/B. Schwarze, An Experimental Analysis of Ultimatum Bargaining, in: Journal of Economic Behavior and Organization 3 (1982), pp. 367-388.

Güth, W./R. Tietz, Ultimatum Bargaining Behavior. A Survey and Comparison of Experimental Results, in: Journal of Economic Psychology 11 (1990), pp. 417-449.

Harbo, F., Secession Right – An Anti-Federal Principle? Comparative Study of Federal States and the EU, in: Journal of Politics and Law 1 (2008), pp. 132-148.

Harhoff, F., Greenland's Withdrawal from the European Communities, in: Common Market Law Review 20 (1983), pp. 13-33.

Hirschman, A., Abwanderung und Widerspruch: Reaktionen auf Leistungsabfall bei Unternehmungen, Organisationen und Staaten (1974).

Höreth, M./J. Sonnicksen, Making and Breaking Promises. The European Union Under the Treaty of Lisbon, ZEI Discussion Paper 181 (2008).

Kirchsteiger, G., The Role of Envy in Ultimatum Games, in: Journal of Economic Behavior and Organization 25 (1994), pp. 373-389.

Kravitz, D./S. Gunto, Decisions and Perceptions of Recipients in Ultimatum Bargaining Games, in: The Journal of Socio-economics 21(1992), pp. 65-84.

Kurpas, S., The Treaty of Lisbon – How Much "Constitution" is Left? An Overview of the Main Changes, in: CEPS Policy Brief 147 (2007).

Kurrild-Klitgaard, P., Opting-Out: The Constitutional Economics of Exit, in: American Journal of Economics and Sociology 61 (2002), pp. 123-158.

Lechner, S./R. Ohr, The Right of Withdrawal in the Treaty of Lisbon: A Game Theoretic Reflection on Different Decision Processes in the EU, Cege-discussion Paper 77 (2008).

Schäfer, W., Withdrawal Legitimised? On the Proposal by the Constitutional Convention for the Right of Secession from the EU, in: Intereconomics (2003), pp. 182-185.

Spolaore, E., Civil Conflict and Secessions, in: Economics of Governance 9 (2008), pp. 45-63.

Sunstein, C., Constitutionalism and Secession, in: University of Chicago Law Review 58 (1991), pp. 633-670.

Treaty of Lisbon, Official Journal of the European Union 51 (2008).

Waltemathe, A., Austritt aus der EU. Sind die Mitgliedstaaten noch souverän? (2000).

Wohlgemuth, M./C. Brandi, Europe à la Carte? A Club-theoretical Vindication, in: J. Varwick/K. Lang (eds.), European Neighbourhood Policy. Challenges for the EU-Policy Towards the New Neighbours (2007), pp. 159-180.

Zeh, J., Recht auf Austritt, in: Zeitschrift für Europarechtliche Studien 2 (2004), pp. 173-210.

Challenging the Conventional Banking System: Does Islamic Banking Provide More Financial Stability?

Ewa Karwowski

I.   Introduction

Islamic and increasingly Western scholars identify Islamic banking to be a stable alternative and dignified challenge to the crisis-ridden conventional banking system. Critique and alternative are perceived to be fundamental and fundamentally different since they target debt financing and interest rates in conventional banking. The claim that Islamic banking has a stabilising effect on the economy is based on (1) the morality of the *homo islamicus* surmounting moral hazard and adverse selection problems; (2) the developmental character of Islamic banking promoting growth and wealth redistribution; and most importantly, (3) its inherent stability in reducing economic fluctuations and reoccurring crises.

This chapter will explore the theoretical vindication of this challenge with some reference to empirical findings. Generally, Islamic and Western economic thought appear to differ only on one aspect significantly: the *homo islamicus* who maximes profit in a moral way compliant with Islamic law. The methodology applied by Islamic economics does not differ fundamentally from Western economics.[1] A reduction to individual choice and the focus on trust and its betrayal cannot generate a comprehensive theory of the workings of the economy. Nonetheless, such a theory is essential in identifying factors, which destabilise the system. Therefore, Islamic economics contribute little original ideas towards the concern of economic stability mainly borrowing from Western economic theory. The borrowed concepts are often absorbed superficially, resulting in the intuitive claim of a superior Islamic alternative. In fact, whether a banking system exercises a stabilising or a destablising effect on the overall economy depends on the direction and purpose of lending. Hence, the claim of Islamic banking towards inherent stability is doubtful. For a while already, Islamic banking has been perceived to be at its 'tipping point' turning into a

---

[1]   This claim can be reinforced by pointing towards the vast literature produced by economist, sociologists and politcal economists on bounded rationality and collective action, which allow for individual motivations other than the exclusively selfish, materialistic ones of the homo econocus. See M. Weber, Die protestantische Ethik, Eine Aufsatzsammlung (1969); J. Elster, The Cement of Society: A Study of Social Order (1989). Hence, the assumption of a morally guided individual can be hardly claimed as unique to Islamic economics.

mainstream product[2] despite still marginal assets as share of total international banking assets. What could not be achieved by phenomenal growth rates, particularly in the Middle East and Southeast Asia, was established by the current economic crisis. The international visibility of Islamic banking has been raised dramatically as it is increasingly advocated as stable alternative to our crisis-ridden financial system.

The prohibition of interest and collateral constitutes the difference between conventional and Islamic banking that most attention focuses on. Simultaneously, the prohibition constitutes the basis for the claim of many Islamic scholars, but also of an increasing number of Western economists, that Islamic banking is superior to conventional banking. This superiority manifests itself in three aspects:

(1) The absence of interest represents the moral dimension of Islamic economics.[3] Morality in turn is inherent to the *homo islamicus* whose values do not tolerate the injustice of charging interest. Consumption credit is injust because it exploits the needy while production credit is injust because of the uncertainty inherent to every investment project is not shared between borrower and lender.

(2) The developmental character of the Islamic economic system. Apart from optimum growth rates, social welfare including need fulfilment and full employment are explicit goals of Islamic economics.[4] This social welfare dimension also refers to justice because the aim is to strive for a (more) equitable wealth distribution. *Zakat*, a compulsory Islamic contribution towards charity, and Muslim inheritance law are the main instruments of redistribution.[5]

(3) Increased stability. Financial and economic stability are understood as original features of the Islamic economic system, conceptually ensured by morality, development and a relatively equitable wealth distribution and practically by the abolition of interest and promotion of wealth redistribution.

These three aspects constitute the objectives of the Islamic financial system as well as its main differences to the conventional one. In the following, this study focuses on the claim of Islamic financiers and politicians that Islamic banking is more stable than conventional banking and the thesis of Islamic scholars

---

2   See BBC News, Islamic Banking 'Goes Mainstream', http://news.bbc.co.uk/1/hi/
     business/4264939.stm (July 2008); BBC News, Banks Move into Islamic Finance,
     http://news.bbc.co.uk/1/hi/world/middle_east/5064058.stm (July 2008); Credit Suisse,
     Islamic Banking, Der Profit des Propheten, http://emagazine.credit-suisse.com/app/
     article/index.cfm?aoid=153319&fuseaction=OpenArticle&lang=de (July 2008); The
     Economist, Is Islamic Finance at Tipping Point?, http://www.economist.com/sponsor/
     qfc/index.cfm?pageid=article104 (June 2008).
3   See M. U. Chapra, Why Has Islam Prohibited Interest? Rationale Behind the
     Prohibition of Interest, in: A. Thomas (ed.), Interest in Islamic Economics (2006).
4   See M. U. Chapra, Why Has Islam Prohibited Interest? (2006); M. K. Lewis/L. M.
     Algaoud, Islamic Banking (2001).
5   See M. A. Khan, The Theory of Employment in Islam, in: Islamic Literature (1968).

that Islamic banking is inherently stable as opposed to conventional banking. However, Islamic economics provides little theory on which these claims can be convincingly based. Effectively, it distinguishes itself from conventional theory mainly through the concept of the *homo islamicus* as opposed to the *homo economicus*. Concentrating on moral values and consequently trust, Islamic economic theory lacks a systemic understanding of the economy and the banking system's role in it. This short-fall it shares with conventional economics. In fact, the question whether banking structures have a (de-) stabilising effect on the economy as a whole can only be answered by examining lending patterns and purposes.

II.   Increased Stability of Islamic Banking

Western and Islamic understanding of banks and their role within the economy do not differ significantly. In economic theory, banks are typically understood in a generic sense as financial intermediaries. Their main task is to channel funds from the surplus sector to the deficit sector. In principle, households, firms, the government and foreigners can possess a surplus or a deficit in funds and consequently supply or demand credit. However, conventional economic theory identifies households as most important "lender-savers" while businesses and the government are the major "borrower-spenders".[6] Hence, banks are understood to transform household savings into corporate credit, which is used for production. In this setting, banks stabilise the economic system, providing a source of finance to businesses when internal or financial market financing is impossible. As far as Islamic scholars are concerned, Islamic banks should engage in exactly the same activity. In other words, they should create corporate credit using household savings. However, the credit mode should be a different one. Islamic banks should primarily lend through profit-and-loss-sharing (PLS) activities.[7] Three partners can be identified in an Islamic finance contract: the depositor, the bank and the borrower. Depositors supply funds to the bank. They can choose to put their savings into demand deposits, which are non-remunerated accounts, or into remunerated *mudharabah* (partnership) deposits.[8] While the bank is not obliged to share profits with holders of demand (i.e. current or savings) deposits, it is obliged to encash these deposits on demand. Holders of investment and special investment accounts under the partnership agreement are entitled to a share in the bank's profit. These accounts typically

6   See F. S. Mishkin/S. G. Eakins, Financial Markets and Institutions (2006), p. 18.
7   See M. U. Chapra, The Future of Economics, An Islamic Perspective (2000); M. N. Siddiqi, Muslim Economic Thinking, A Survey of Contemporary Literature (1981); M. N. Siddiqi, Banking Without Interest (1983).
8   See H. van Greuning/Z. Iqbal, Risk Analysis for Islamic Banks (2008).

entail a long-term commitment just like time deposits and sometimes also a share in losses.

Concerning the demand for finance, the borrower who is assumed to be an entrepreneur is only liable as to his time and effort invested. The bank and him share the profit (or loss) at a predetermined ratio. In the case of *mudharabah* (partnership) projects the bank cannot exercise any direct influence on the investment, whereas in the case of a *musyarakah* (equity participation) arrangement it possesses rights similar to those of a joint venture partner.[9] These are primary financing modes or so-called PLS agreements. Secondary financing modes are meant to take a subordinate role since they are effectively mark-up pricing or leasing arrangements, and because a true emphasis on productive investment is lacking, they are not "truly Islamic".[10] Interestingly, in the context of borrowing and lending the Islamic economy in its ideal state does not differ from the neoclassical economy in its ideal state. In a perfectly functioning market setting, as *Kenneth Arrow* and *Gerard Debreu* assumed, there would be as little need for financial intermediaries as for firms.[11] Here information is complete and universally held, thus, all market participants possess perfect foresight. Contracts are enforced costlessly, competition is perfect and all markets clear instantly. This state is a general equilibrium (GE) where frictions or exogenous shocks are absent. The existence of banks is unnecessary since individuals possess perfect foresight and can easily decide by themselves whose investment project will be successful and whose a failure. The price of credit is determined similarly to all other prices: the sum of individually demanded funds is equated to the sum of individually supplied funds. The intersection of an upward sloping supply curve and a downward sloping demand curve provides the interest rate on loanable funds – the price for credit.

This is the loanable funds theory of interest, which however ignores that in a developed fractional-reserves system commercial banks create credit at their discretion and not according to the supply of saving.[12] This is visible during periods of crisis when banks are very reluctant to lend money and signal this reluctance through elevated interest rates on credit. Modern conventional economics – most prominently New Keynesian ideas – inherited the confusion

---

9   See M. U. Chapra, The Future of Economics (2000); R. Dhumale and A. Sapcanin, An Application of Islamic Banking Principles to Microfinance, Technical Note (2004); Greuning/Iqbal, Risk Analysis for Islamic Banks (2008).

10   See V. Sundararajan/L. Errico, Islamic Financial Institutions and Products in the Global Financial System: Key Issues in Risk Management and Challenges Ahead (2002), p. 18; M. U. Chapra, The Future of Economics (2000).

11   See K. Arrow/G. Debreu, The Existence of an Equilibrium for a Competitive Economy, in: Econometrica 22 (1954).

12   See V. Chick, The Evolution of the Banking System and the Theory of Saving, Investment and Interest in: P. Arestis/S. C. Dow (eds.), On Money, Method and Keynes (1992).

between savings and credit. Without revisiting credit, New Keynesians drop two of the assumptions of the frictionless GE: (1) Information is assumed to be imperfect and asymmetric and therefore, (2) contracts are not costlessly enforceable.[13] In contrast to the *Arrow-Debreu* setting, where individuals could easily lend and borrow amongst themselves, informational imperfection prevents individuals with surplus funds and those with deficit funds finding each other. Banks take on the role of connecting potential borrowers with potential lenders. More importantly, financial intermediaries possess a comparative advantage in setting the premium for external finance, i.e. the interest rate. Since they specialise in the provision of credit, they are assumed to possess more information about systemic and idiosyncratic risk than individual lenders. Systemic risk refers to instability risk originating from the setup and structures of the financial system itself. Idiosyncratic risk results from the fact that the lender does not know the borrower, holds less information about the investment project, and that their interests increasingly diverge the higher the share of external finance in the envisaged investment. If information was perfect and contract enforcement costless, lending and borrowing would reach point (E') in graph 1. All investment projects, yielding at least as much return as to cover the principle and the interest rate (r) equal to the riskless rate plus a premium for systemic risk, would be financed. There are no differences between external and internal financing of investment and consequently, the *Modigliani-Miller* theorem holds. Introducing imperfect and asymmetric information creates a need for the so-called external finance premium (P_e). The premium constitutes the difference between funding investment externally as opposed to internally. This discrepancy is explained in New Keynesian models through idiosyncratic risk, promoting the idea of asymmetric information as the economic philosopher's stone. If we accept that information is imperfect, the asymmetric information paradigm portrays the impossibility of trusting economically rational agents as the main source of frictions in the economic system. Instability arises from the fact that information is lacking and individual incentives might be socially detrimental. Thus, to prevent frictions the availability of information has to be increased and individual incentives have to be aligned with social ones, eliminating moral hazard and adverse selection.[14]

---

13   See for example B. S. Bernanke/M. Gertler, Agency Costs, Net Worth, and Business Fluctuations in: The American Economic Review 79/1 (1989).

14   Moral hazard refers to situations in which individuals can incur a (share of the) profit from their decision, it is, however, not liable for a potential loss. In the context of credit, a bank's attempt to account for this risk through raising the cost of credit results in an adverse selection situation exacerbating the risk of default. Higher credit cost will squeeze those borrowers out of the market who undertake relatively safe but low-yielding projects and potentially leave the lender with those borrowers who can meet the increased cost through excessively risky investment.

Consequently, the riskless interest rate (r) can only be granted to borrowers up to the point where the quantity of credit equals the borrowers' perfectly collaterisable net worth (point (W) in graph 1) up to where incentives are understood to be aligned. Thereafter, the existence of the external premium (P$_e$) makes the credit supply curve (S) slope upwards and diverge from the perfectly elastic supply curve (S') in the *Arrow-Debreu* setting. Equally, the credit demand curve (D') shifts inwards for the imperfect information case because attempting to align lender's and borrower's interests the lender transfers risk towards the borrower who in turn is supposedly risk averse and demands less external finance.[15] Financial repression takes place – less investment undertakings are realised than in the *Arrow-Debreu* world – to prevent instability.

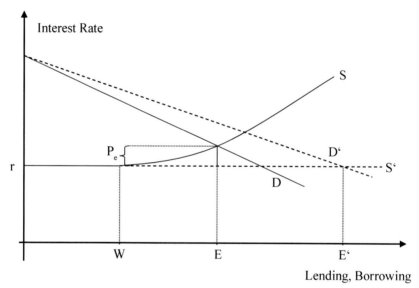

Graph 1: The Premium for External Finance[16]

The information and incentive alignment problems that New Keynesians stress are addressed referring to behavioural norms. Leading Islamic economists mainly criticise the concept of the exclusively profit-orientated *homo economicus* in (Western) neoclassical economics contrasting him with the morally aware *homo islamicus*. The focus on morality within Islamic

---

15   See M. Gertler/A. Rose, Finance, Public Policy and Growth, in: G. Caprio/I. Atiyas/
      J.A. Hanson (eds.), Financial Reform: Theory and Experience (1994).
16   See ibid., p. 22.

economics is understood as the discipline's *raison d'être*.[17] In the ideal Muslim community, collateral would not be needed since religious norms prevent moral hazard problems from arising. In other words, in this ideal community, borrowers would not abuse money credited to them but would strive to employ it productively. Equally, asymmetric information – referring to the fact that borrower and lender do not have access to the same amount and kind of information – would not be relevant. Trust among borrowers and lenders aligns their interests in the PLS dividing profits or losses fairly between them. Consequently, the economy of perfect competition, information and market clearing is a parallel world to the perfect Muslim community.[18] In both worlds, neither a premium for external finance nor collateral is necessary to reach the socially optimal level of lending and borrowing – point (E') in graph 1. The riskless interest rate r could be easily transformed into a fixed charge the bank receives for its services turning the model *Shari'a*-compliant.

The outcome is Pareto optimal – profits of some agents in society increase without an adverse effect on anyone else's pay-off – in contrast to the financial repression case. Here, all investment undertakings that have been realised under credit rationing are still financed. Furthermore, those investments that can cover principle and the riskless interest rate or fee (r), but that could not amortise (r) plus the external financing premium, will also be realised (E' – E).

The prohibition of interest combined with the common belief that banks channel funds towards productive investment makes Islamic banking and Western economic theory inconsistent with each other. Curve (S), indicating the supply price of credit, disappears in a PLS framework because the absolute profit is not known to the bank until the investment is realised. A predetermined return to the lender, dependent on the borrowing period and independent of the borrower's uncertainty, is not permissible under Islamic banking. Hence, primary modes of Islamic banking are incomprehensible for Western economists. This might explain why there is little Western theory applied and developed. Alternatively, many attempts exist to make Islamic banking resemble conventional banking schemes. This includes the claim that the majority of Islamic lending has a debt-like character.[19] Obviously, the theoretical conception of banking given above and the phenomenon of Islamic banking are very much reconcilable for secondary modes of Islamic finance, resulting in predetermined debt servicing, which in fact constitute the majority of Islamic banking transactions and in Malaysia almost their totality.[20]

---

17   M. N. Siddiqi, Islamic Finance and Beyond (2000); M. U. Chapra, Why Has Islam Prohibited Interest? (2000).

18   See H. A. Dar/J. R. Presley, Islamic Finance: A Western Perspective, in: International Journal of Islamic Financial Services, 1 (1999).

19   See R. K. Aggarwal/T. Yousef, Islamic Banks and Investment Finance (1996).

20   See Bank Negara Malaysia, Annual Reports (2001-2005).

III. Inherent Stability of Islamic Banking

Economic stability is one of the main – if not the single main – preoccupations of Islamic economics forming the foundation of the challenge toward conventional banking. In the following, the most salient Islamic arguments will be reviewed in the light of their Western counterparts, beginning with microeconomic issues and moving towards increasingly comprehensive macroeconomic theory of economic instability.

Facing the dominance of interest-based banking, some Islamic economists ask whether a financial system based on PLS would be stable and could perform as well as an interest-based one. As Islamic financial systems on a national level did not emerge until the late 1970s[21] answering this question was somewhat obstructed. Using a GE framework, *M. Ali Khan* and *M. Nejatullah Siddiqi* assert that a financial system based on PLS is stable. However, even among Islamic economists the work refuting the destabilising effect of *ex ante* undetermined credit price characteristic for primary modes of Islamic finance was perceived as merely intuitively convincing while lacking the formal rigour of GE analysis.[22]

Considering the supply side of financial funds, *Waqar Massod Khan*, in a microeconomic partial equilibrium model, claims to show formally the superiority of Islamic lending schemes. The expected utility from an Islamic variable rate of return is higher than the expected utility from a conventional fixed rate and will be preferred by the lender. Yet, an interest/debt-based banking system prevails despite *Khan's* results. Reasons for this paradox are arguably tax deducibility – governmental distortions of the price mechanism – and incentive and information based explanations.[23] With respect to the demand side of financial funds, Islamic banks are arguably more run-proof than their conventional counterparts. If the bank's profits decline, the incentive to withdraw funds invested in a PLS contract should also decrease.[24] Yet, it could be equally argued that Islamic banks are in fact even more prone to bank runs. In order to avoid potential losses, already an expected fall in profitability could result in withdrawal of funds given the favourable conditions granted to *mudharabah* clients enabling them to withdraw funds on short notice.[25]

---

21   Since 1979 in Iran and Pakistan and in 1984 in Sudan. See Khan *et al.*, Islamic Banking (1989). Central Bank of Sudan, http://www.bankofsudan.org (4 June 2008).

22   See Z. Iqbal/M. F. Khan, A survey of Issues and a Programme for Research in Monetray and Fiscal Economics of Islam (1981).

23   See W. M. Khan, Towards an Interest-Free Islamic Economic System, A Theoretical Analysis of Prohibiting Debt Finance (1985).

24   See Lewis/Algaoud, Islamic Banking, (2001).

25   Generally, a notice of one month suffices. See M. Cihak/H. Hesse, Islamic Banks and Financial Stability: An Empirical Analysis (2008).

Research by the IMF supports the claim that Islamic banks are more stable, but only if their assets do not exceed one billion US Dollars.[26] Considering larger banks, conventional ones seem stronger. This study implies that smaller banks operate based on "character-lending" with a manageable number of borrowers who can be assessed, monitored and controlled effectively rendering collateral unnecessary. As the number of borrowers rises, this business model dependent on intense generation of information becomes excessively costly and non-lucrative. The IMF measures bank stability using a score summing up equity capital, reserves as percentage of assets and the bank's average return as percentage of assets and dividing this sum by the standard deviation of return on assets. This ratio constitutes the "number of standard deviations a return realisation has to fall in order to deplete equity".[27] The higher the score the higher is a bank's stability according to this measure. The study is based on observations from 20 countries including 77 Islamic and 397 commercial banks. The period covered is 1993 to 2004. Using panel regressions, data across time and countries are treated equally. This methodology is problematic since the term "bank" is understood generically while in fact it differs from economy to economy being differently defined by domestic statistics agencies across countries. Significant differences already exist within the Organisation for Economic Cooperation and Development (OECD). While the English definition refers to merchant banks excluding activities in the capital market, German banks also operate in the capital market due to their universal tradition.[28] Countries with such different regional and developmental backgrounds as those making up the sample are very likely to have different definitions for banks. In the case of Islamic banking the problem of fungibility occurs. Islamic banks in mixed financial systems are in some cases subsidiaries of conventional banks. Therefore, their profitability is hard to measure independently from the conventional bank's profit since funds are likely to be transferred between the holding company and the subsidiary one. Usually such a practice is illegal according to Islamic law, but the problem is undeniable when Islamic banks do not even possess separate balance sheets from their mother companies. Consequently, the regression undertaken by *Martin Cihak* and *Heiko Hesse* is questionable, which is reflected in the results. The calculated scores are statistically significant in a sample of large Islamic banks only.[29] Moving towards the macroeconomic perspective, *W. M. Khan* considers the work of a

---

26   See ibid.
27   See ibid., p. 7.
28   See J. Toporowski, European Destiny and Macroeconomic Responsibility in the Financial Systems of Germany and the U.K.: A Balance Sheet Approach, in: S. F. Frowen/F. P. McHugh (eds.), Financial Competition, Risk and Accountability, British and German Experiences (2001).
29   See Cihak/Hesse, Islamic Banking (2008).

wide range of Western economists, most prominently *Friedrich A. von Hayek* and *Milton Friedman*, to support his argument against interest.[30] *Friedman*[31] was convinced that exogenous shocks rather than interest rate changes determine the quantity of money in the economy contributing substantially towards economic disturbances. *Hayek* presented a more elaborated theory. For the latter the idea advocated by *Friedman* that the disturbing influence of money only emerges with changes in the price level – based on *Knut Wicksell's* ideas – was extremely naive.[32]

For *Hayek*, the short-comings in *Wicksell's* work lie in the marginalist methodology applied, where the interest rate is regarded as the price equilibrating supply of savings and demand for credit – i.e. the loanable funds theory.[33] Arguably, growing economies have interest rates below those equilibrating demand and supply of funds because the former exceeds the latter. Hence, credit exceeds the level of savings supplied. Economic up- and downswings originate from misalignments between the equilibrium rate of interest and the money rate of interest, caused by changes in the volume of effective money present in the economy. However, *Hayek* understands credit expansion and subsequent contraction as endogenous to the financial system meaning these swings cannot be avoided.[34] In contrast to some Islamic scholars such as *Khan*, *Hayek* did not advocate the elimination of credit. Without credit, businesses are completely exposed to the destabilising effects of household savings, which goes together with under-consumption. Most Islamic scholars, just like conventional economists, advocate models of fractional reserve banking, like the one put forward by *Siddiqi*, *Uzair* and *Ahmed* for the Islamic economy.[35]

The latter, *Shaikh Mahmud Ahmad*, took up *Keynes's* concept of the marginal efficiency of capital to explain why interest rates destabilise the economy and cause cycles of booms and busts.[36] *Keynes* argued that the money rate of interest

---

30   See W. M. Khan, Towards an Interest-Free Islamic Economic System (1985).

31   Friedman can be regarded to write in a Wicksellian tradition starting from an equilibrium position and statically considering changes in the quantity of money. But contrary to Wicksell, Friedman did not attribute any importance to the rate of interest.

32   See F. A. von Hayek, Geld- und Konjunkturtheorie (1929).

33   See ibid.

34   See ibid.

35   See W. M. Khan, Towards an Interest-Free Islamic Economic System (1985); M. N. Siddiqi, Banking Without Interest (1983). Based on Monzer Kahf and some other Islamic economists, such as Masudul Alam Choudhury and Mohammad Ziaul, Hoque advocates 100 percent reserve banking until today. See M. A. Choudhury/M. Z. Hoque, An Advanced Exposition of Islamic Economics and Finance (2004).

36   See S. M. Ahamd, Economics of Islam (1952).

hinders investment, production and full employment.[37] Yet according to *Ahmad*, *Keynes* failed to spell out the crucial conclusion and solution to economic crisis: the prohibition of interest. Yet, *Keynes* understood interest as an inherent part of every traded good not only money. Interest consists of the output an asset produces minus its carrying cost and plus its liquidity premium. The liquidity premium is the amount of money individuals are willing to spend on the convenience to possess the good. Money is the only commodity for which by definition the liquidity premium exceeds the carrying cost. Thus, the money rate of interest is the determinant rate of interest.[38] Replacing interest entirely by PLS would mean that return to money did not contain the premium. This might – e.g. in a liquidity trap – deter agents to place funds into Islamic investment accounts because they would lose liquidity or it might transfer the liquidity premium from demand deposit holders to the Islamic bank.

Muhammad Akram Khan's and *Sayyid Abdul A'la Mawdudi's* support *Ahmad's* proposition. Arguably, depression and stagnation are caused by interest rate payments introducing imbalances between production and consumption. Through interest-payments, wealth and purchasing power are transferred from the borrower to the lender. By definition, the borrower has a higher propensity, i.e. a stronger inclination, to consume. While demand for consumption goods decreases, as the debtor has to pay interest on the debt, supply increases because the creditor presumably invests the received funds into further production. In the context of entrepreneurial credit, interest causes prices for consumption goods to rise transferring funds from individuals with a relatively high propensity to consume to those with a relatively low one.[39] This analysis introduces consideration about the income distribution, arguing that large income inequalities are economically destabilising. *Ahmad's* work refers to Western economists such as *John A. Hobson* and *Thorstein Veblen*.[40] Yet, *Hobson* identified excessive income inequality levels as condusive to speculation and the emergence of a rentier class that lives of unearned profit,[41] both being destabilising. For *Ahmad*, however, the mere existence of interest destabilises the economy, because it encourages unproductive or speculative activity rendering capital for productive undertakings consequently scarce. Interest is seen to play a role in bringing about economic crisis. During an economic boom, credit expands and interest payments raise the marginal cost

---

37   See J. M. Keynes, The General Theory of Employment, Interest and Money (1936), p. 235.
38   "There is no remedy but to persuade the public that green cheese is practically the same thing and to have a green cheese factory (i.e. central bank) under public control", J. M. Keynes, General Theory (1936), p. 235.
39   See M. A. Khan, The Theory of Employment in Islam (1968); M. N. Siddiqi, Muslim Economic Thinking (1981).
40   See S. M. Ahamd, Economics of Islam (1952).
41   See J. A. Hobson, Imperialism: A Study (1938).

of production. Profit increases and, while wages stagnate, unproductive and speculative investment rises. Increased demand for capital pushes interest rates up, while squeezing profit margins. Over-confidence emerges arguably causing over-production. Recognising that more production is financed than would be efficient and can be covered by expected returns, the central bank puts up interest rates. Commercial banks follow suite raising interest rates and are also forced to recover loans. Business confidence drops and households postpone consumption exacerbating the started economic downturn.[42] Yet, it is unclear what the systemic causalities behind booms and busts are in Islamic economic theory. *Mohamed Ariff* points out that none of the Islamic scholars "really succeeded in establishing a causal link between interest, on the one hand, and employment and trade cycles, on the other".[43]

Looking for Western economic theory supporting interest prohibition, *Ben Bernanke* and *Mark Gertler's* accelerator is an economic model of instability claiming to possess rigorous micro-economic foundation. Moreover, *Bernanke*'s approach has allegedly more credence than *Hyman Minsky's* Financial Instability Hypothesis (FIH) – whose tradition it follows by self-confession[44] – as informational asymmetries are incorporated and can explain credit cycles without relying on individuals' irrationality unlike the FIH.[45]

Based on *Irving Fisher's* Debt Deflation Theory, the FIH assumes companies to speculate in production equipment during economic booms. The majority of their investment is presumably financed through credit. In the course of a boom the volume of credit demanded will rise until the interest rate is affected. As firms' balance sheets deteriorate due to an increasing debt ratio and once decided investment is interest-inelastic, a relative rise in production costs or a relative drop in prices will set off a debt deflation scenario as described by *Fisher*.[46] Interest rates determine the debt servicing cost for a project. As consequence, the mere existence of debt and also interest are understood to be destabilising.[47] Therefore, Islamic banking eliminates one possible source of economic fluctuations since Islamic financial commitments should be undertaken on an interest-free and long-term basis that aligns financial obligations and actual profit.

It can be doubted whether an Islamic (PLS-based) credit system will be more stable than the conventional (debt-based) one, particularly because debt

42   See S. M. Ahamd, Economics of Islam (1952).
43   M. Ariff, Islamic Banking, in: Asian-Pacific Economic Literature 2 (1988).
44   See B. S. Bernanke/M. Gertler, Inside the Black Box: The Credit Channel of Monetary Policy Transmission, in: Journal of Economic Perspectives 9 (1995).
45   See P. S. Mills/J. R. Presley, Islamic Finance: Theory and Practice (1999).
46   See H. P. Minsky, Stabilizing an Unstable Economy (1986).
47   See M. U. Chapra, The Future of Economics (2000).

has stabilising influences on the financial system.[48] A steady inflow of funds into stock and real estate markets – like experienced during the run-up to the subprime mortgage crisis in the US – can inflate markets, increasing the fragility of the economic system as a whole. Debt obligations can only inflate to a limited extent since they are characterised by a maturity span and an underlying fixed value.

Generally, Islamic and Western economic thought appear to differ only on one aspect significantly: the *homo islamicus* who maximises profit in a moral way compliant with Islamic law. The methodology applied by Islamic economics does not differ fundamentally from Western economics.[49] A reduction to individual choice and the focus on trust and its betrayal cannot generate a comprehensive theory of the workings of the economy. Nonetheless, such a theory is essential in identifying factors destabilising to the system. Therefore, Islamic economics contribute little original ideas towards the concern of economic stability mainly borrowing from Western economic theory. The borrowed concepts are often absorbed superficially, resulting in the intuitive claim of a superior Islamic alternative.

Economists tend to overlook that typically Islamic banking cannot exist in isolation from conventional finance. Therefore, Islamic finance has to be analysed in the context of domestic and global economic and financial flows, which are dominated by non-Islamic finance. Such an analysis shows that it is impossible for Islamic banks to isolate themselves from conventional banks – at least in a developed financial system. This forces Islamic banks to copy patterns from Western financial systems.[50]

IV. Banking from an Systemic Point of View

Although conventional theory assumes that banks act as financial intermediaries, channelling funds from the household to the business sector, it hardly explains the underlying reasons and mechanisms. In actual fact this assumption is only valid for a specific set of institutions and by no means universal. Today's

---

48 See J. Toporowski, The End of Finance, The Theory of Capital MarketInflation, Financial Derivatives and Pension Capitalism (2000).

49 This claim can be reinforced by pointing towards the vast literature produced by economists, sociologists and political economists on bounded rationality and collective action, which allow for individual motivations other than the exclusively selfish, materialistic ones of the homo economicus. See M. Weber, Die protestantische Ethik, Eine Aufsatzsammlung (1969); J. Elster, The Cement of Society: A Study of Social Order (1989). Hence, the assumption of a morally guided individual can hardly be claimed as unique to Islamic economics.

50 See E. Karwowski, The Significance and Distinctiveness of Islamic Banking for Financial Stability in Malaysia (2008).

generation of economists inherited the assumption and neglect a revision in light of today's institutional setting. In an economic system where industrial small and medium enterprises (SMEs) contribute a major share to gross domestic product (GDP) bank credit to businesses is crucial. SMEs are typically forced to demand bank loans once internal financing is exhausted since their access to financial markets is limited. Equally, large enterprises[51] need bank credit once they fully absorb internal funds and the possibility to issue new shares.[52] In a pre-financialised world,[53] bank lending, regardless whether interest-based or not, stabilises the economy acting against households' hoarding of funds. If households hoard funds excessively in the form of saving, companies have to take out credit to meet production costs. Firms are forced into indebtedness and further investment is discouraged since funds are primarily needed to cover costs and serve increasing debt. Imagining the level of economic activity as the water level in a system of pipes, saving is a destabilising leakage. Due to saving, less funds are channelled back to the firms than spent on capital investment and labour, resulting in a fall of economic activity in the system. Hence, bank credit is stabilising in this context since it compensates the lack of finance that firms experience pouring in new "water".

The traditional view that household saving funds firms' investment tends to perceive households as passive economic units whose consumption and saving adapt to current income. Here, saving is a procyclical variable, rising during booms and falling during busts. Yet, according to *Joseph Steindl*, saving tends to be stable over the business cycle or even increases (decreases) during periods of economic downswings (upswings) and, therefore, moves counter-cyclically.[54]

---

51 Keynes distinguishes "speculation" meaning the investment for capital gains and "enterprise" referring to investment for future income. Enterprise in this context follows Keynes's definition and merely includes non-speculative firms. See J. M. Keynes, General Theory (1936). However, as will be discussed below, the number of large, non-speculative firms is decreasing rapidly at least since the 1970s in US and U.K. because big business tends to be over-capitalised using internal funds increasingly to generate gains in the financial markets and not by capitalist production. See J.Toporowski, The End of Finance (2000).

52 Although financial markets offer them additional ways to raise funds this does not equate to an infinitely elastic supply of finance since the emission of new shares – to take just one example – will impact on the prevailing share price. Especially in times of crisis, when additional funds are most needed, this price might be very sensitive.

53 Although an increase in remuneration and influence of shareholders as opposed to stakeholders is present – and therefore the claim arises that capital gains at the expense of labour – this is regarded as side effect. The more significant institutional change is that the line between financial and non-financial large enterprises is blurred and therefore the (industrial) profit-led business cycle is replaced by a (financial) demand-led one.

54 See J. Steindl, Saving and Debt, in: A. Barrere (ed.), Money, Credit and Prices in Keynesian Perspective (1989).

The assumption of passive households might have been adequate for pre-War Europe where significant saving across society was absent and investment in durable goods or housing was not strongly exercised by households. In the post-War era, however, households accumulated significant savings, undertaking major investment in durable consumer goods and real estate. There is statistical evidence that the saving ratio increased over the post-War period (1960-1979) in the developed world.[55] This development can be explained by the rising income inequalities in developed societies and by the increasing presence of institutional savers such as life insurance companies and pension funds. Major structural changes in the institutions of post-War economies take place: (1) capital market inflation[56] and (2) the breakdown of the industrial business cycle.

(1) An increasing saving leakage discourages businesses from undertaking productive investment. Firms' expenditure on labour (wages) returns to a smaller and smaller extent to them, meaning that profit from manufacturing falls. Simultaneously, the financial liberalisation of the post-Bretton Woods era encourages financial innovation. Consequently, lack of household demand forces big businesses to look for alternative profit opportunities in the financial markets. This alternative source of profit becomes increasingly attractive as it constitutes the very pool into which the saving leakage is channelled. The entry of institutional investors into the stock markets caused share prices to inflate. Conventional theory assumes that share prices reflect a company's marginal profitability being determined by supply and demand. This claim becomes groundless once the workings of the stock market are examined. The crucial fact is that businesses are not obliged to buy back shares they issue due to the existence of a secondary market. Since the bulk of the investment return on shares – except for dividends – will be provided by other investors, who are willing to buy the purchased shares at a higher price, the liquidity of the market rather than supply and demand decides over price. Hence, the conventional claim that prices determine financial flows is a myth.

In fact, the reverse is true. Due to the excessive accumulation of saving pouring into these markets and the nature of market dynamics, increases in share prices tend to be inflationary. Rising share prices typically attract even larger inflows of liquidity, resulting in further price increases, which further exacerbate the price rise. Substitution effects which would suggest that investors shift from relatively more expensive to now relatively less expensive shares are weak because it is not gross substitutability which dominates the investment decision but expectations about the future price developments.[57] Here, econometric data manipulation and especially linear extrapolation support the belief that past trends will also continue in the future, favouring capital market inflation.

---

55   See ibid.
56   See J. Toporowski, *The End of Finance* (2000).
57   See ibid.

Price inflation in financial markets mainly affects liabilities with an open or no maturity span. Debt liabilities with fixed repayment dates tend to not inflate significantly or fall in price when repayment approaches since the underlying value determines the price. Debt then, despite its destabilising effect on the individual firm, can affect the whole system in a stabilising way preventing price inflation.[58]

(2) Despite their inability to finance productive investment, capital markets provide, especially during times of boom, a valuable source of and destination for excess capital for firms. Excess capital can be

"the excess of a company's liabilities over its productive capital, i.e., the plant, equipment, materials, and stocks of unsold products and semi-fabricates that a firm holds".[59]

In such a case, the capital market is used as source of funds that are not needed for the firm's production process but for investment into financial assets issued by other companies, banks and financial institutions. The firm is over-capitalised. Evidently, excess capital undermines the importance of the industrial business cycle in favour of a financial one. Nonetheless, the financial business cycle is not completely outstripped of industrial production. Productive activity is induced by households and their demand, not by businesses and their profits. The business cycle transforms from a profit-led one into a demand-led one because the private sector holds big amounts of funds that are used for investment into durable goods and real estate. However, firms and households do not merely swap positions. The structural shift is brought about by the emergence of institutional savers and consequently financial market inflation is more fundamental. This new business cycle is increasingly fragile since there are various leakages operating and financial markets constitute an alternative circular flow for funds. Households' saving flows on the one hand into the housing market, which offers individuals a way to invest for capital gain. On the other hand, saving flows into financial markets such as the capital market through the intermediation of institutional investors.

Equally, firms invest their excess capital into financial markets. Both flows constitute a leakage away from the industrial business cycle and into an alternative circular flow of finance. Due to financial innovation, these pools absorbing the flow of leakages are not strictly separate from each other as the

---

58　See J. Toporowski, Theories of Financial Disturbance, 2005.
59　J. Toporowski, Notes on Excess Capital and Liquidity Management (mimeo), p. 1.

US subprime mortgage crisis shows.[60] The role banks, and more specifically Islamic banks, play in the modern setting highly depends on the purpose of their activity. It can no longer be assumed that funds simply flow from households to firms since households engage in investment activities and firms hoard funds in the form of excess capital. Therefore, it is necessary to analyse the origin and direction of bank lending to assess its overall impact on economic stability. For the case of Malaysia – which is generally perceived to be a role model for other countries aiming at establishing a comprehensive Islamic financial system and which represents due to its general openness a paradigm of the effects that Islamic banking and international finance exert on each other – Islamic banks actually channel funds from the corporate to the household sector favouring housing price inflation.[61]

V. Conclusion

The claim of Islamic financiers, politicians and scholars that Islamic banking is inherently stable or at least more stable than conventional banking increased while the US financial crisis was unfolding. This chapter reviewed the theoretical foundations of this claim. Generally, Islamic economic theory contributes little to understanding financial instability and its impact on the overall economy. Its main challenge towards conventional economics, i.e. *the homo islamicus*, is a concept, which focuses on trust and its betrayal. A systemic understanding of the financial system and its interaction with the overall economy is lacking. This feature Islamic economics shares with dominant conventional theory such as the New Keynsian approach. In fact, a banking system's stability does not depend on the presence or absence of interest and collateral, but on the direction and purpose of lending. Islamic banking can be equally destabilising as conventional banking if bank lending channels surplus funds from the corporate to the household sector, favouring asset price (mainly housing price) inflation.

---

60   Financial innovation tends to take on increasingly risky shapes. This is a side effect of companies' over-capitalisation. The existence of excess capital means that bank loans are no longer of essential importance to companies as in the Kalecki-Steindl model. Although this development reduces firms' indebtedness it destabilises banks' operations, which lose (except for governments) their most reliable clients. As consequence, banks are forced to lend to more risky customers – SMEs and households – and additionally look for alternative income sources in financial market operations. See J. Toporowski, The End of Finance (2000).

61   See E. Karwowski, The Significance and Distinctiveness of Islamic Banking (2008).

Bibliography

Aggarwal, R. K. /T. Yousef, Islamic Banks and Investment Finance, Social Science Research Network (1996).

Ahamd, S. M., Economics of Islam (1952).

Ariff, M., Islamic Banking, in: Asian-Pacific Economic Literature 2 (1988), pp.48-64.

Arrow, K./G. Debreu, The Existence of an Equilibrium for a Competitive economy, in: Econometrica 22 (1954), pp. 265-290.

Bank Negara Malaysia, Kuala Lumpur, http://www.bnm.gov.my of July 2008.

BBC News, Islamic Banking 'Goes Mainstream', http://news.bbc.co.uk/1/hi/buness/4264939. stm of February 2005.

— Banks Move into Islamic Finance, http://news.bbc.co.uk/1/hi/world/middle_ east/5064058.stm of June 2006.

Bernanke, B. S./M. Gertler, Agency Costs, Net Worth, and Business Fluctuations, in: The American Economic Review 79 (1989), pp. 14-31.

— Inside the Black Box: The Credit Channel of Monetary Policy Transmission, in: Journal of Economic Perspectives 9 (1995), pp. 27-48.

Central Bank of Sudan, Khartoum, http://www.bankofsudan.org of August 2008.

Cihak, M./H. Hesse, Islamic Banks and Financial Stability: An Empirical Analysis, IMF Working Paper, International Monetary Fund (2008).

Chapra, M. U., The Future of Economics, An Islamic Perspective (2000).

— Development Economics: Lessons that Remain to be Learned, in: Islamic Studies 42 (2000), pp. 639-650.

— Why Has Islam Prohibited Interest? Rationale Behind the Prohibition of Interest, in: A. Thomas (ed.), Interest in Islamic Economics (2006).

Chick, V., The Evolution of the Banking System and the Theory of Saving, Investment and Interest Arestis, in: P. and S. C. Dow (eds.), On Money, Method and Keynes (1992).

Choudhury, M. A./M. Z. Hoque, An Adavnced Exposition of Islamic Economics and Finance (2004).

Dar, H. A./J. R. Presley, Islamic Finance: A Western Perspective, in: International Journal of Islamic Financial Services 1 (1999).

Credit Suisse, Islamic Banking, Der Profit des Propheten, http://emagazine.credit- suisse.com/ app/article/index.cfm?aoid=153319&fuseaction=OpenArticle&lang=de of June 2006.

Dhumale, R./A. Sapcanin, An Application of Islamic Banking Principles to Microfinance, Technical Note, Washington: Study by the Regional Bureau for Arab States, United Nations Development Programme in Cooperation with the World Bank (2004).

El-Gamal, M., An Attempt to Understand the Economic Wisdom (Hikma) in the Prohibition of Riba, in: T. Abdulkader (ed.), Interest in Islamic Economics (2006).

Elster, J., The Cement of Society: A Study of Social Order (1989/90).

Friedman, M., A Program for Monetary Stability (1959).

Gertler, M./A. Rose, Finance, Public Policy and Growth, in: G. Caprio Jr./I. Atiyas/J. A. Hanson (eds.), Financial Reform: Theory and Experience (1994).

Greuning, H. van/Z. Iqbal, Risk Analysis for Islamic Banks (2008).

Hassan, V./B. Shanmugan/V. Perumal, Corporate Governance: An Islamic Paradigm (2005).

Hayek, F. A. von, Geldtheorie und Konjunkturtheorie (1929).

Hobson, J. A., Imperialism: A Study (1938).

Iqbal, M./M. F. Khan, A Survey of Issues and a Programme for Research in Monetray and Fiscal Economics of Islam (1981).

Karwowski, E., Financial Stability: The Significance and Distinctiveness of Islamic Banking in Malaysia, Levy Economics Institute Working Paper No. 555 (2009).

Keynes, J. M., The General Theory of Employment, Interest and Money (1936).

Khan, M. A., The Theory of Employment in Islam, in: Islamic Literature 14 (1968), pp. 5-16.

Khan, W. M., Towards an Interest-Free Islamic Economic System, A Theoretical Analysis of Prohibiting Debt Finance (1985).

Lewis, M. K./L. M. Algaoud, Islamic Banking (2001).

Mills, P. S./J. R. Presley, Islamic Finance: Theory and Practice (1999).

Minsky, H. P., Stabilizing an Unstable Economy (1986).

Mishkin, F. S./S. G. Eakins, Financial Markets and Institutions (2006).

Robertson, D. H., Money (1928).

Siddiqi, M. N., Muslim Economic Thinking, A Survey of Contemporary Literature (1981).

— Banking Without Interest (1983).

— Islamic Finance and Beyond, Proceedings of the Third Harvard University Forum on Islamic Finance (2000).

Steindl, J., Saving and Debt, in: A. Barrere (ed.), Money, Credit and Prices in Keynesian Perspective (1989).

Sundararajan, V./L. Errico, Islamic Financial Institutions and Products in the Global Financial System: Key Issues in Risk Management and Challenges Ahead, IMF Working Paper (2002).

The Economist, Is Islamic Finance at Tipping Point?, http://www.economist.com/sponsor/qfc/index.cfm?pageid=article104 of June 2008.

Toporowski, J., Notes on Excess Capital and Liquidity Management, mimeo.

— The End of Finance, The Theory of Capital Market Inflation, Financial Derivatives and Pension Capitalism (2000).

— European Destiny and Macroeconomic Responsibility in the Financial Systems of Germany and the U.K.: A Balance Sheet Approach, in: S. F. Frowen/F. P. McHugh (eds.), Financial Competition, Risk and Accountability, British and German Experiences (2001).

— Theories of Financial Disturbance (2005).

— The Economics and Culture of Financialisation, Paper presented to the Workshop on Credit and Debt in Present Day Capitalism, University of Manchester (2008).

Veblen, T., The Theory of Business Enterprise (1904).

Weber, M., Die protestantische Ethik, Eine Aufsatzsammlung (1969).

Wicksell, K., The Influence of the Rate of Interest on Prices, in: The Economic Journal 17 (1907), pp. 213-220.

Risking War to Take a Chance on Peace?
The Risk Paradox of Self-Perpetual Violence

Carolin Görzig

I. Introduction

In a provocative manner *Edward Luttwak* claims in his article "Give War a Chance" that minor wars should be let burn out by themselves because war leads to peace.[1] Although symmetric warfare between equal conflict parties constitutes a form of cooperation[2] and is, especially against the background of the rising costs of warfare ultimately aimed at leading to a fast outcome, the today prevailing security risks such as asymmetric warfare and terrorist challenges follow a different logic and assume different functions.[3]

The often termed "new wars" between sometimes unequal warring parties as state and sub-state actors and more often between sub-state actors themselves do not burn out easily and after a short time, but usually continue for decades. Instead of resolving political conflicts and bringing peace after passing a culminating phase of violence, the new wars fall into a self-perpetuating dynamic which decisively prolongs the fighting and makes war its own cause.

Similarly, the notion of the "new" terrorist holding apocalyptic aspirations undermines the deterrent function of force. The backlash of pre-emptive strikes and the vicious terror/counter-terror conundrum evidence the inroad of adapting old concepts to new challenges and only serve to confirm the blurring of lines between non-state and state terror.

While *Luttwak* claims that war serves to exhaust the belligerents and suggests that the United Nations (UN) would do more good if it "helped the strong to defeat the weak faster", this paper argues that violence itself can become a cause of violence. This self-reinforcing feature turns violence into a risk paradox.

What is a paradox? A paradox is "the situation in which the condition of possibility is also the condition of impossibility".[4] A prototype is the famous liar paradox wherein the claim that everybody is a liar becomes a contradiction *en se*. This contradiction results from negating a self-referential statement, e.g. employing violence to reach peace – an example that clearly fulfills the

---

1   See E. N. Luttwak, Give War a Chance, in: Foreign Affairs 78 (1999), p. 36.
2   See C. Daase, Strategische Assymetrie als Herausforderung für die Friedens- und Konfliktforschung, http://www.evangelische-akademie.de/Daase.pdf.
3   See ibid.
4   C. Daase/O. Kessler, From Insecurity to Uncertainty: Risk and the Paradox of Security Politics, in: Alternatives 33 (2008), p. 212.

paradoxical meaning of sacrificing values in the present in order to realize them in the future. It takes "the end justifies the means" literally. The self-referential nature of paradoxes highlights the stake of an actor in bringing himself into a paradoxical situation in the first place. Accordingly, *Christopher Daase* states that risk policy itself is risky. Political action can become paradoxical and produce more problems than it actually solves.[5] Violence, for example, constitutes such a risk paradox. In order to strengthen this argument and qualify *Luttwak's* provocative claim, this chapter will elaborate on three different mechanisms underlying the self-perpetuation of violence: the commercialisation of warfare, terrorism as provocation, and spirals of radicalisation.

The first mechanism concerns the privatisation and commercialisation of violence and war. While states formed the sole holders of the monopoly of violence in classical interstate war,[6] different actors are appearing on the scene of inner-state conflict, mainly of private character. For these "new" units, above all consisting of paramilitary groups, warlords, criminal gangs, foreign mercenaries and soldiers,[7] war has become a form of pure self-preservation or personal enrichment. The increased presence of foreign mercenaries or the "whores of war"[8] and numerous warlord groups signals the progressing commercialisation and privatisation of warfare.[9]

The use of violence as a source of income leads to the apoliticisation of war and turns conventional patterns of warfare around.

The renunciation of the Clausewitzian understanding of war is described by *David Keen* as war being the "continuation of economics by other means".[10] Fighting war profiteers with war therefore becomes futile. If it is greed that drives conflict, then making war is just like giving the greedy exactly what they want. If crime lives from illegality, rewarding illegality will not fight it. The second mechanism underlying the self-perpetuation of war concerns terrorism as a strategy of provocation. Warring groups often instrumentalise attacks in order to gain publicity by playing the theatre of terrorism choreographed for the media.[11] The principle of provoking through

---

5   See C. Daase, Einleitung, in: C. Daase/S. Feske/I. Peters (eds.), Internationale Risikopolitik (2002), p. 21. An illustrious case of point can be found in driving behaviour: drivers whose security in traffic is increased through technical advances such as airbags lean towards more risky driving behaviour, see Daase, Einleitung (2002), p. 22.

6   See H. Münkler, Die neuen Kriege (2002), p. 7.

7   See M. Kaldor, New & Old Wars (1999), p. 8.

8   W. Burchett/D. Roebuck, The Whores of War. Mercenaries Today (1977).

9   See Münkler, Die neuen Kriege (2002), p. 40.

10   D. Keen, Incentives and Disincentives for Violence, in: M. Berdal/D. Malone (eds.), Greed and Grievance: Economic Agendas and Civil Wars (2000), p. 27.

11   See B. M. Jenkins, International Terrorism: A New Mode of Conflict, in: D. Carlton/C.

violence and terror is thereby nothing new: from being formulated in Russia in the late nineteenth century to being adopted by leftist extremists in South America in the 20th century to guiding Western European leftists, terrorism as provocation continues to be used throughout the world. The goal of winning the masses will thereby be more successful when the state is more repressive. The imperative not to let a small minority impose a major change is, ironically, foiled by the very change violent non-state actors such as terrorists impose if the state does not concede. Following *Luttwak's* suggestion to employ brute force may fail to deter terrorists simply because concessions might not be their primary goal: "terrorists get benefits from their violent acts even if their targets do not immediately yield to their demands."[12] That *Zawahiri* thanks God for "appeasing us with the dilemmas in Iraq and Afghanistan"[13] can be understood in this context. A third mechanism underlying the self-reinforcing dynamic of violence concerns the radicalisation of the warring actors. The concept of "new", irrational or absolute terrorists and its implications shed light on the inherent contradiction in the discourse on combating those who are assumingly beyond negotiation. "New"[14] terrorists are namely (by definition) too irrational to be deterred. As a consequence, military counter-terrorism strategies are futile. Effective deterrence is precisely conditioned by the rationality of the potentially deterred. *John Mearsheimer* brings the essence of deterrence to the following point:

"Deterrence, in its broadest sense, means persuading an opponent not to initiate a specific action because the perceived benefits do not justify the estimated costs and risks."[15]

As such, terrorists capable of being deterred would become aware of their terrorist action's immense costs which outweigh possible benefits. However, absolute terrorists cannot be deterred, simply because there is nothing tangible

---

Schaerf (eds.), International Terrorism and World Security (1975), p. 16.

12   D. Tucker, Skirmishes at the Edge of Empire (1997), p. 75.

13   Cited by B. Hoffman, The Changing Face of Al Qaeda and the War on Terrorism, in: Studies in Conflict and Terrorism, 2 (2004), pp. 549-560.

14   The term of the new terrorists became infamous since the bombing of New York's World Trade Centre and the attack of Tokyo's underground in the mid 90's. From Walter Laqueur, who suggests that "there has been a radical transformation, if not a revolution, in the character of terrorism", to Bruce Hoffman to whom new terrorism seems "a (...) far more lethal threat than the more familiar 'traditional' terrorist groups", most terrorism experts agree that "all of this renders much previous analysis of terrorism based on established groups obsolete". See W. Laqueur, The New Terrorism: Fanaticism and the Arms of Mass Destruction (1999), p. 4; B. Hoffman, Inside Terrorism (1998), p. 200; I. Lesser/B. Hoffman/J. Arquilla *et al.*, Countering the New Terrorism (1999), p. 2.

15   J. Mearsheimer, Conventional Deterrence (1985), p. 14.

one could threaten to take away from them. Rather than serving to deter violence, repression ushers in radicalisation.

The three described mechanisms – the commercialisation of warfare, terrorism as provocation, and radicalisation spirales resulting from violence can turn violence into it's own cause. In order to present the argument, this chapter is structured into two major parts. The first part will elaborate on the three mechanisms more closely. The following second part will give three examples for these mechanisms[16] before the conclusion will underline the argument brought forward.

II.   Three Mechanisms and the Self-Perpetuation of Violence

1.   The Commercialisation of Violence and the Futility of Fighting War Profiteers with War

Fighting war profiteers with war is futile. Nonetheless, a common approach still attempts to tackle the supply side by denying insurgents access to resources, for example by waging a war on drugs. In order to influence the economic incentives of the combatants, sanctions are imposed or punishment for informal trade is raised to increase deterrence effects.[17]

Yet, these policies encounter enormous obstacles and can even be counterproductive.[18] Embargos on conflict goods and international narcotics prohibition regimes are easily circumvented, since lootable natural resources are difficult to regulate.

---

16   The three chosen examples are based on field research in Egypt, Colombia and Turkey. The inclusion of interview material gathered in these countries are not used to depict objective truth, but rather to contrast Luttwak's assumption with a different perspective.

17   Examples for such supply-orientated policies are the UN sanctions against the National Union for the Total Independence of Angola (UNITA) and the Revolutionary Unity Front (RUF) of Sierra Leone which worked as an embargo on conflict diamonds and the Plan Colombia initiated by the United States to fight Colombian drug trafficking. See K. Ballentine, Beyond Greed and Grievance: Reconsidering the Economic Dynamics of Armed Conflict, in: K. Ballentine/J. Sherman (eds.), The Political Economy of Armed Conflict - Beyond Greed and Grievance (2003), p. 275.

18   Vanda Felbab-Brown writes accordingly: "Eradication will frequently have a dubious effect on the financial resources of the terrorist group (...). Effective suppression of the production of the illicit commodity may actually increase the international market prices for the commodity to such an extent that the total revenues may be even greater.", V. Felbab-Brown, The Intersection of Terrorism and the Drug Trade, in: J. Forest (ed.), The Making of a Terrorist. Recruitment, Training, and Root Causes (2006), p. 172.

Additionally, sanctions have the effect of raising the value of the targeted good thereby further increasing economic incentives.[19] Thus, it has been argued that narcotics law enforcement has above all served to create considerable profits for drug dealers.[20] Furthermore, deterrence measures motivate persons actively in the underground to dive even deeper into illegality in order to complicate detection. Consequently, shadow activities become more criminalised and hence harder to influence. Lastly, one trading good can be replaced by another one or worse, the possibility of plundering civilian assets opens up. These measures of supply-side policies will hence exacerbate criminality and conflict.[21] Instead of addressing deep-rooted grievances, resources are channeled into prohibition measures. Such an approach ignores the important task of identifying structural and social causes and can only establish a negative peace at best.

A direct link between excluding criminal actors and their flourishing on a global scale is given by *Mark Duffield*, who remarks that

"it is the (parallel) economy that has expanded and reintegrated the South within the liberal world system following its exclusion from the formal networks of the informational economy".[22]

Through clandestine business such as drug trafficking, frauds etc., people in poor countries reintegrate themselves into the world economy on new terms.[23] Civil war thus does not necessarily equal "development in reverse"[24], but rather the emergence of new wealth creation systems. Being the very product of illegality, these systems will not be prevented by a war on illegal goods. To the contrary, war profiteers will be encouraged to substitute or, even worse, ramp up predation.

2. Terrorism as Provocation and the Counterproductive Effects of Weakening the Weak

Warring groups often instrumentalise violence in order to provoke counter-violence. The formula is simple: the more repressive the state the more successful the non-state in reaching its goal of winning the masses. While non-state actors instrumentalise small wars to legitimise themselves, state actors

---

19 See Ballentine, Beyond Greed and Grievance (2003), p. 275.
20 See J. A. Inciardi, American Drug Policy: The Continuing Debate, in: J. A. Inciardi (ed.), The Drug Legalization Debate, (1999), p. 5.
21 See Ballentine, Beyond Greed and Grievance (2003), p. 275.
22 M. Duffield, Global Governance and the New Wars (2001), p. 142.
23 See W. Reno, The Meaning of Contemporary State Collapse for Self-Determination, in: The Somali Land Times of July 5 July 2003.
24 P. Collier/L Elliott/H. Hegre et. al., Breaking the Conflict Trap: Civil War and Development Policy (2003), p. ix.

lose legitimacy especially when engaging in dirty warfare.[25] Violence against an internal threat forces the state "to conduct an unconventional 'dirty' war and betray its own principles".[26] Yet, even maintaining public support against an external terrorist threat such as Al Qaeda is a complication. The legitimacy of a state only remains unthreatened if the state limits its war measures both in time and within the scope of the legal order.[27] Obviously, the lengthy Iraq war and terrorist suspect detention in Guantanamo Bay fall neither within legitimate time limits nor a legal order frame. Extreme Islamists, on the other hand, found an "easy" way

"to place their own issues on the international agenda by provocation aimed at intensifying the conflict between the Muslim world and leading Western or pro-Western governments".[28]

This attempt to provoke a response has been a clear success. *Luttwak* suggests that the UN should help the strong defeat the weak instead of prolonging war with disinterested interventions. The logic of minority resistance aimed at provocation defies this reasoning. If a small minority namely resorts to suicide missions as the strategy of the weak to provoke the strong, tactics aimed at further weakening the weak will lead to the very opposite of what they are trying to achieve.

For example sub-state terrorism, often the last in a number of choices,[29] is characterised precisely by the lack of mass support such that "small organizations resort to violence to compensate for what they lack in numbers".[30] And while guerrilla warfare is dependent upon a sympathetic population, moving within it like a "fish in the water"[31], terrorism aims at winning this support as a result of the psychological consequences of their violence.[32] Lacking such a sympathetic population, users of terrorism methods emphasise that they had no other choice. *Martha Crenshaw* remarks accordingly that "it is indeed true that terrorism often follows the failure of other methods".[33] This is

---

25   See C. Daase, Kleine Kriege - Große Wirkung. Wie unkonventionelle Kriegführung die internationale Politik verändert (1999), p. 223.
26   Ibid.
27   Ibid.
28   A. Kurz, New Terrorism: New Challenges, Old Dilemmas, in: Strategic Assessment, 6 (2003).
29   See M. Crenshaw, The Logic of Terrorism: Terrorist Behavior as a Product of Strategic Choice, in: W. Reich (ed.), Origins of Terrorism. Psychologies, Ideologies, Theologies, States of Mind (1990), p. 11.
30   Ibid.
31   H. Münkler, Gewalt und Ordnung (1992), p. 162. Münkler is referring to a statement by Mao Tse Tung.
32   See ibid.
33   Crenshaw, The Logic of Terrorism (1990), p. 10.

further elaborated by *Leonard Weinberg* who investigates the conditions under which political parties turn to terror. He summarises the body of writing on the causes of terrorism: "perhaps terrorism is most likely to occur precisely where mass passivity and elite dissatisfaction coincide."[34] But if terrorism is a result of a lack in numbers, decreasing numbers increases terrorism.

3. Radicalisation Spirals and the Illusion of Deterring Absolute Terrorists

Violence can serve to radicalise warring actors. When these warring actors radicalize such that they no longer hold rationale demands, the deterrence function of violence and repression is seriously questioned. For example, absolute terrorists are classified as not clinging to a specific goal such as territory, independence, or anything else tangible or political – in short, a goal which could be threatened. Manipulation via threat captures, as *Patrick Morgan* argues, the essence of deterrence.[35] It is this very notion of a visible threat which collides with the reality of terrorism.

Even before the advent of "new" terrorism, deterrence critics were eager to point out the weakness of conflict management tools. *Morgan* noted as early as 1977 that "arming to preserve us from clashes of arms"[36] lacks plausibility. But this is not the only futile attempt to square the circle which deserves criticism. Indeed, as *Morgan* notes – decades before Tokyo 1995 or September 11th – the theory of deterrence reduces humans' complex psychological reactions to the interplay among "rational" decision makers.[37]

If non-state warring actors are ultimately psychologically motivated, then the goal of violence often is violence itself as authors like *Jerold Post* postulate: "[The statement] 'it's not us – it's them' (...) provides a psychologically satisfying explanation for what has gone wrong in their lives."[38] The terrorists' logical conclusion is to destroy the establishment – another way of searching for identity. Striking out against this establishment is an attempt to strike out against the enemy within.[39] Why, asks *Post*, does "ETA not clap its collective hands in satisfaction, declare victory, dissolve the organization, and go back to work in the region's factories?"[40] Or why did members of the IRA act as to prolong the

---

34 L. Weinberg, Turning to Terror: The Conditions Under Which Political Parties Turn to Terrorist Activities, in: Comparative Politics 23 (1991).
35 See P. Morgan, Deterrence: A Conceptual Analysis. (1977), p. 9.
36 Ibid, p. 13.
37 See ibid. See also the literature on bounded rationality.
38 J. Post, Terrorist Psycho-Logic: Terrorist Behavior as a Product of Psychological Forces, in: W. Reich (ed.), Origins of Terrorism. Psychologies, Ideologies, Theologies, States of Mind (1990), p. 27.
39 See ibid., p. 26.
40 Ibid., p. 37.

cycle of violence when the moment for conciliation seemed ripe?[41] The group, Post argues, must be

"successful enough in its terrorist acts and rhetoric of legitimation to attract members and perpetuate itself, but it must not be so successful that it will succeed itself out of business".[42]

III.   Three Examples of the Self-Perpetuation of Violence

1.   The Futility of Fighting Colombian War Profiteers with War

After over four decades of persistent conflict in Colombia, left-wing guerrillas such as the FARC[43] and the ELN[44], rightwing paramilitary groups and the state continue to be locked in a violent competition. The struggle among these groups centers on determining who exercises political control, redressing socio-economic grievances, and contesting ideas on the appropriate political and economic Colombian system.[45]

Since many recent peace initiatives have failed in spite of seemingly favourable conditions, the attention of politicians and academics has increasingly shifted towards the economic dimensions of the Colombian conflict. Although the war cannot be explained by referring solely to economic sources of conflict, the ample financial resources of all three warring parties have complicated the dynamics of the conflict.[46] Whereas the FARC and ELN obtain revenues from extortion, kidnapping, and the international narcotics trade, paramilitaries were even closer involved in the trafficking of drugs;[47] meanwhile, the government's fight against the rebels and drug trade is financed in substantial part by the economic and military aid from the USA.[48] Colombian armed actors are clearly involved in plundering (illegal) resources. Like no other, the Colombian conflict therefore seems to vindicate *Clausewitz* and

---

41   See ibid., p. 38.
42   Ibid.
43   Fuerzas Armadas Revolucionarias de Colombia (The Revolutionary Armed Forces of Colombia).
44   Ejercito de Liberación Nacional (National Liberation Army).
45   See A. Guáqueta, The Colombian Conflict: Political and Economic Dimensions, in: K. Ballentine/J. Sherman (eds.), The Political Economy of Armed Conflict. Beyond Greed and Grievance (2003), p. 73.
46   See ibid., p. 74.
47   In fact, it was through a demobilisation agreement between the Colombian government and the Colombian paramilitary that the paramilitary laid down their arms. However, this demobilisation agreement remains contested.
48   Guáqueta, The Colombian Conflict (2003), p. 73.

confirm *Keen*: "war is the continuation of economy by other means".[49] Fighting Colombian war actors with war has been and continues to be futile. The war on drugs in particular contributed to war-benefiting by non-state actors. Some would surely disagree with this argument. According to one interviewee, the Plan Colombia is successful, because "violence is going down, the fear of the people is shrinking, prices in the US for heroine and cocaine are rising".[50] This perception clashes clearly with the facts brought forward by another interviewee, who tells how the illegal combatants constantly adapt and find easy ways to circumvent such war measures as coca plant fumigation, as well as how the whole Plan Colombia is merely a business to protect the interests of a few companies.[51]

From this person's perspective, waging war against war profiteers defeats the purpose: "the more they try a military solution – the more the state destabilizes – the more society falls into chaos."[52]

Several factors help to explain this vicious circle. Returning to the first interviewee above – this time in search of possible negative effects of the Plan Colombia – the answer highlights a clear favouring of security over development: "there are debates about the balance between the focus on security and military and alternative development programs. And yes, there should always be more development programs. But firstly you need more security."[53]

Yet, giving priority to security over development ignores the mutuality of both. This mutuality is key to understanding the nature of the Colombian conflict. The paramilitary is able to create a stronger social base of support than the guerrilla precisely because it provides means derived from cocaine cultivation. According to *Alexandra Guáqueta*, they are therefore legitimate on a local basis.[54] It is the lack of development, along with a lack of alternatives, which plays into the hands of those warring actors who privatise the state's monopoly of violence. What emerges are alternative systems of wealth creation.

The involvement of guerrilla groups and paramilitaries in narcotics trade and extortion emerged predominantly in the last two decades and expanded significantly in the late 1990s. Concurrently, conflict-related violence has increased such that there seems to be a direct correlation between growth of guerrillas and paramilitaries and the escalation of the conflict on the one hand and an increase in drug production and trade on the other. The increasing commercialisation of violence has decisively weakened the government, eroding state institutions through corruption and the diverting resources which

---

49   Keen, Incentives and Disincentives for Violence (2000), p. 27.
50   Author Interview in Bogota, Spring 2006.
51   See Author Interview, Bogota, Spring 2006.
52   Ibid.
53   Author Interview in Bogota, Spring 2006.
54   See Guáqueta, The Colombian Conflict (2003).

could be used for economic development.[55] The inability of the government to provide security and the weakening of police and judicial institutions in turn enable the privatisation of security, fostering a climate conducive to the use of commercialised violence.[56] A vicious circle ensues.

The rise in narcotics trade is related to economic decline and inequality. Thus, the ability of guerrillas and paramilitaries to benefit from the production and trafficking of drugs is facilitated by a needy agrarian work force, which, after the Colombian agricultural crisis in the 1990s, is eager to engage in drug production.[57] Furthermore, the economic deterioration in the late 1990s has augmented inequalities and unemployment,[58] providing the armed groups with favourable recruitment possibilities.[59] The increased violence and escalating drug trade, in turn, has contributed to the economic slowdown by destabilising the Colombian economy.

The drug trade has, moreover, evolved into a political force. The part drug trafficking organisations took over in the counterinsurgency enabled them to control vast territories upon which they imposed their control. "Through drug cultivation", a former commander of the smaller guerrilla force ELN states, "the armed groups derive their social base"[60], because "if you control drug cultivation you control the people".[61] This form of "colonisation" gives them control over territories the state has lost its grip on. "La coca" – its cultivation, production and trade – allows a form of social mobility which people in "a divided class society with a very strong sense of exclusion of the have-nots"[62] cannot obtain otherwise:

"In a country where every attempt of social reform failed, with high indexes of rural and urban poverty (...) where the mechanisms of social mobility are scarce, the narco-traffic found all the possibilities to grow – in the middle of an ethical collapse induced by the peak of the social pyramid."[63]

---

55   See ibid., p. 91.
56   See E. Garfield/J. Arboleda, Violence, Sustainable Peace, and Development, in: M. M. Giugale/O. Lafourcade/C. Luff (eds.), Colombia. The Economic Foundation of Peace (2003), p. 49.
57   See Guáqueta, The Colombian Conflict (2003), p. 90.
58   See ibid., p. 95.
59   In both legal and illegal armed groups young men from poor families are on the front-line. See Garfield/Arboleda, Violence, Sustainable Peace, and Development (2003), p. 41.
60   Author Interview in Bogota, Spring 2006.
61   Author Interview in Bogota, Spring 2006.
62   Author Interview in Bogota, Spring 2006.
63   J. Guerrero Barón, La sobre-politización del narcotráfico en Colombia en los años ochenta y sus interferencias en los procesos de paz, in: R. Peñaranda/J. Guerrero Barón (eds.), De las armas a la politica (1999), p. 226.

The Colombian war has escalated especially against the background of increasingly globalised flows of funds and weapons.[64] The access to global markets and criminal networks has helped the armed groups to translate drug production into money and military strength.[65] The direct link between excluding criminal actors and these actors' flourishing on a global scale, as argued by *Duffield*[66], can be evidenced in Colombia. Through clandestine business such as drug trafficking, people in Colombia reintegrate themselves into the world economy on new terms. New wealth creation systems emerge which are fueled, ironically, by a war on drugs. Fighting Columbian war profeteers with war becomes futile.

2.   The Counterproductive Effects of Turkey's Attempts to Isolate the PKK

Turkey aims at isolating the PKK from the population. However, Kurds perceive Turkey's current divide-and-rule policies as just another attempt to colonise the Kurds. Thus, since the early 20th century the territory and the people which constitute Kurdistan seem at the mercy of history. According to *Ismail Besikci*, Kurdistan is thereby "not even a colony, a nation that is not even colonized".[67] Arguably, Kurdistan's status ranks lower. It lacks political status and identity, because "the goal is to eradicate Kurdish identity".[68] Kurds experienced and continue to experience modernisation as traumatic. Turkey's inability to solve the problem by democratic means has produced a vicious circle of violence. Not only has its unitary approach of "one state, one nation and one and one and one"[69] brought those Kurds who speak Kurdish behind closed doors but are officially Turks[70] into a precarious situation. Further still, Turkey never "welcomed the Kurds with open mouth and heart"[71], and thereby forgot that its actions directly contribute to what it fears the most – the splitting of the country. According to an interview with a commander of the ARGK[72] in the July 1992 edition of the Kurdistan Report,"it is the Turkish government which is losing the masses."[73] The PKK, in turn, has achieved the mobilisation of its people. This coincides with the perception of a Turkish terrorism expert who concludes

---

64   See Garfield/Arboleda, Violence, Sustainable Peace, and Development (2003), p. 73.
65   See ibid., p. 82.
66   See M. Duffield, Global Governance and the New Wars (2001), p. 142.
67   I. Besikci, Kurdistan. Internationale Kolonie (1991), p. 16.
68   Ibid., p. 17.
69   Author Interview in Diyarbakir, Summer 2006.
70   Ibid.
71   Ibid.
72   ARGK is a unit within the PKK army.
73   Kurdistan Report Nr. 48, July 1992, "Es ist die türkische Regierung, die die Massen verliert" (Interview mit dem ARGK-Kommandanten, Cemil Bayik).

that the presence of the PKK demands that the state be more oppressive. And if the Turkish state becomes more oppressive as a consequence, then the PKK is conclusively strengthened as it thus achieves its goal.

Feeding into the awakening of Kurdish nationalism, divide-and-rule policies and the suppression of Kurdish identity do indeed lead to the very opposite of what such policies are meant to achieve. The resulting radicalisation can be traced from the very beginning of the PKK. Thus, the Kurdistan Workers Party was founded when the state suppressed earlier civil actions and incarcerated the demonstrators. As one former prisoner recounts, isolation practices within prison took on gruesome forms: "People are also isolated from each other in prison, they are made strangers. If you stay alone for ages, you cannot get social relations anymore."[74] Even more tellingly, when asked whether he would regret anything, the former prisoner did not hesitate before replying: "I was wondering in prison: Am I lucky or not. And yes, I am lucky, I am the person who is not oppressing others, but who is oppressed, I am not torturing anyone, I am being tortured."[75]

That Turkey neglects the PKK boosts the PKK's identity.[76] Young Kurds are not only conscious of their own Kurdish identity. Their reinforced identification also goes along with identifying against the Turks: "young people are now getting more conscious about their own identity and that increases the hate from inside."[77] Many interviewees were apparently preoccupied about where things are going, worrying that if the problems would not be solved "they may start coming back again and in a harder way".[78] The "hate from inside" comes to the fore quickly during the interviews. Divide-and-rule tactics radicalise the youth. When the village guard system was established, many village guards were forced into it. The resulting maxim "if you are not with us, you are against us"[79] is a dangerous simplification. "If they namely manage to increase the hate between Turks and Kurds, a real civil war could emerge."[80]

Divide-and-rule tactics in Turkey materialise moreover on a very rudimentary, worrisome level. A February 2008 article in the magazine *Der Spiegel* titled "Is your father a Terrorist?" describes the recent use of questionnaires in Turkish schools, asking for example "Is your father a terrorist?", or: "Does your sister

---

74   Author Interview with Former Prisoner and Former PKK Member.
75   Ibid. These statements are reinforced by claims of human rights institutions. For example, the European Court of Human Rights has issued 210 judgements against Turkey in 2008 for torture, extrajudicial execution, unfair trial and other violations. See Human Rights Watch: World Report, Chapter: Turkey, www.hrw.org.
76   See Author Interview in Ankara, Summer 2006.
77   Author Interview in Turkey, Summer 2006.
78   Ibid.
79   Author Interview in Diyarbakir, Summer 2006.
80   Author Interview with a Kurd in Bavaria, 2007.

go to the mountains?"⁸¹ This questionnaire is a good example for the negative consequences of policies aimed at further weakening a minority. The article quotes *Ihsan Babaoglu*, head of the leftist teacher syndicate, as saying that the cleavage between Turks and Kurds is only further deepened:

"About 90% of the respondents are of Kurdish origin. A part of them reacts with anger and defiance to the questioning and the mistrust. The stronger the Turkish side talks upon them, the stronger they identify with their Kurdishness."⁸²

The fact that diminishing the number of terrorist groups increases terrorism is evidenced in the Kurdish case by the temporary use of suicide bombings. Interviewees argued that

"there was a losing of hopes within the organization in the late '90s, they lost a lot of militants, so they had limited options; the suicide mission is a kind of a last mission".⁸³

Similarly, a former PKK member describes that the situation was somehow stuck: "there was a deadlock, nothing was done by the state, so these were some individual decisions to do this".⁸⁴ *Crenshaw's* note that "it is indeed true that terrorism often follows the failure of other methods"⁸⁵ is given evidence here. Also on an individual level, the seemingly irrational can make sense.⁸⁶ Accordingly, an interviewee states that one has to know the motivation of these people:

"if a married man is captured by the state and is being tortured, then the woman is next and then the relatives – at some point you say: life is over".⁸⁷

---

81   Spiegel Online, Schul-Fragebogen in der Türkei "Ist dein Vater Terrorist?" (School Questionnaire „Is your Father a Terrorist?"), http://www.spiegel.de/schulspiegel/ausland/0,1518,536404,00.html of 29 February 2008.
82   Ibid.
83   Author Interview in Ankara, Summer 2006.
84   Author Interview with Former Prisoner and Former PKK Member.
85   Crenshaw, The Logic of Terrorism (1990), p. 10.
86   Mohammed Hafez, in turn, doubts "rationalist explanations of individualist motivations for carrying out suicide attacks. Strategic calculus helps explain why organizations choose to dispatch human bombers, but it cannot explain why ordinary men and women accept the role of the 'martyr'. To explain why individuals do it, we must go beyond instrumental rationality and we must first seek to understand the social meaning bombers give to their actions.", see M. Hafez, Dying to be Martyrs: the Symbolic Dimension of Suicide Terrorism, in: A. Pedahzur (ed.), Root Causes of Suicide Terrorism. The Globalization of Martyrdom (2006), p. 75.
87   Author Interview with a Kurd in Bavaria, 2007.

3.   The Illusion of Deterring the Egyptian Gama'a Islamiya with Violence

All the available evidence clearly indicated a classification of the Gama'a Islamiya[88] as an absolute terrorist organisation without a rational mindset and thus without hope for change of its ideology and goals. When *Omar Abdel Rahman*[89] tried to justify the violence asking "How can we cry for a tourist and not cry for the hundreds of thousands of the oppressed?"[90], it became clear that the group had turned to indiscriminate violence. As they admit now themselves: "they were very young and immature".[91] As their ambitions were far from being realised, they also never considered exactly what it was they were striving for or how their goals could be implemented. With jihad turning into an end in itself, a rationale based on applying their views to reality has become infeasible.

Deterrence strategies face a dilemma when confronting such absolute terrorists: effective deterrence is conditioned by the rationality of the potentially deterred.[92] Characterised as lacking tangible goals,[93] absolutes can not be deterred, simply because there is nothing tangible one could threaten to take away from them.

A case in point, Egypt's military counterterrorist strategy from the 1970s through the 1990s bore no fruit. Over two decades of persecution resulted in the detention of the majority of the Gama'a Islamiya's members – the biggest terrorist threat in Egypt during this period. But despite of thousands of arrests, dozens of executions, and long term prison sentences, the campaign of violence did not cease; rather, it intensified even further. Gama'a's members continued attacking Egypt's security and government officials as well as the tourism industry. They were involved in the assassination of President *Anwar al-Sadat* in 1981 and the Speaker of the Egyptian Parliament in 1990. In 1992, a leading secularist figure and Egyptian author was killed by a splinter of the group for his views which were contrary to their ideology as he promoted the idea of a secular Egyptian state. The peak of the group's violent campaign was reached in 1997, when more than sixty foreign tourists and local tour guides were

---

88   However, it was through dialogue with the government and in-group debate, that the Gama'a Islamiya came to transform and renounce violence.

89   Omar Abdel Rahman led a coalition of jihadi groups including the Gama'a Islamiya, a coalition which led to the assassination of Sadat on October 6, 1981. Rahman is currently sentenced to life imprisonment in an American prison for planning the WTC attack in 1993. For more see M. Al-Zayyat, The Road to Al-Qaeda (2002).

90   Cited by M. Hafez, Why Muslims Rebel (2003), p. 183.

91   Author Interview in Cairo, Summer 2006.

92   The terrorists, so the ambition of deterrence policies, are to become aware of the immense costs of their terrorist action which outweigh possible benefits.

93   See W. Zartman, Negotiating with Terrorists, in: International Negotiation 8 (2003), pp. 443-450.

massacred in Luxor. Although this attack was not authorised nor commissioned by Gama'a's leadership, but was rather conducted by a few rogue members from the organisation, the international community for the first time felt directly threatened by an organisation already labeled as terrorist in Europe and the USA.[94] The Egyptian government pushed international agreements in order to capture and extradite suspected Islamists to Egypt. Through these agreements, militants from Afghanistan, Albania, Bulgaria, Bosnia, Sudan, Yemen etc. could be captured and extradited.[95]

Overall, 95 percent of violence in Egypt in the 1980s and 1990s was blamed on the Islamic Group.[96] The Egyptian government resorted to military means and arrested thousands of Gama'a's members. Torture was now applied indiscriminately.[97] Those who were not executed or arrested were either killed in shootouts with security forces, left for Afghanistan to fight the Soviets, or sought refuge all over the world, including the United States and Western Europe.

Especially after the murder of Sadat in 1981, the Egyptian government initiated a major offensive against the Gama'a Islamiya:

"It was really very nasty what happened here. Nothing like Algeria, I mean Islamic Algeria. A nightmare, this was done very nasty. How many people were killed here."[98]

Emergency laws imposed once again after the assassination of President *Sadat* allowed the security forces to detain thousands of Islamists without court order or judicial supervision. The police and military were free in devising security strategies in the manner which they deemed most suitable to the circumstances. And when the government adopted a shoot-to-kill policy in the 1990s, the number of injured Islamists declined while the number of Islamists killed increased.[99]

Despite the government's efforts, however, the jailed Gama'a Islamiya leadership still found ways to communicate with their members outside prisons. The attempted assassination of President *Muhammad Husni Mubarak* in Addis Abeba in June 1995 was coordinated by the Gama'a Islamiya, most of whose

---

94   The Gama'a Islamiya is considered a terrorist organisation by the US, the EU and Egypt.
95   See Hafez, Why Muslims Rebel (2003), p. 86.
96   See D. Rashwan, The Obstacle Course of Revisions: Gamaah versus Jihad, in: Al-Ahram Commentary 80 of 30 May 2007.
97   See Hafez, Why Muslims Rebel (2003), p. 86.
98   Author Interview in Cairo, Summer 2006. According to Amnesty International, the Egyptian Authorities are committing systematic abuses of human rights in the name of national security. For more information see "Egypt: Planned anit-terror law could intensify abuses," www.amnesty.org (11 April 2007).
99   Hafez, Why Muslims Rebel (2003), p. 86.

members were already jailed.[100] While the Egyptian government refused to listen to and negotiate with terrorists, the campaign of violence and terrorist attacks continued unabated. The government, strongly supported by security forces, used all possible means at its disposal to fight Islamists. Extra judicial arrests, military tribunals, arrests without warrants, prison stays without trials, torture, and finally executions all failed to deter Islamists from their use of violence.[101]

Why is this the case? Because repression originally intended to deter violence nurtures what it tries to prevent: radicalisation. Thus, according to *Montasser Al-Zayyat* the Gama'a was initially very close to the more moderate Muslim Brotherhood. To him this fact only changed once the government pushed the group towards violence:

> "First the Gama'a Islamiya used peaceful means (…) but it was the result of the government's treatment and behavior towards the Gama'a Islamiya, so the group responded with violence."[102]

This view is confirmed by *Mohammed M. Hafez*, according to whom indiscriminate repression by the Egyptian government contributed to the group's radicalisation. When the government killed the official spokesman of the Gama'a Islamiya in 1990, the group formed an armed wing and retaliated by assassinating the former Speaker of Parliament. The state's massive counter-reaction not only targeted militants but also their families, friends, "virtually anyone who had a beard with a trimmed moustache".[103] Through witnessing the state's hostage-taking of Islamists' relatives to pressure militants into turning themselves in, mistreatment and torture of those captured, and further restrictions such as the imposition of curfews, violence became a justified response in the eyes of the Gama'a. As evidenced in the group's statements, the Gama'a Islamiya began its fight against the state in order to stop mass arrests and the takeover of private mosques.[104] Moreover, the government's brute response served to augment the oversimplified theological reasoning of the extremists. According to the theological reasoning for violent jihad, a strong desire to seek "justice, revenge, and defend honor" plays a crucial part.[105]

---

100   Furthermore, in June 1992 the secular intellectual Faraj Fuda was assassinated and in October 1994 the Nobel Prize winner Najib Mahfouz was wounded.

101   See K. Al-Hashimi/C. Görzig, Change through Debate. Egypt's Counter-terrorism Strategy towards the Gama'a Islamiya, paper delivered at Sixth Pan-European Conference on International Relations, Turin, 2007.

102   Author Interview with Montasser Al-Zayyat, Cairo, Summer 2006.

103   Hafez, Why Muslims Rebel (2003), p. 85.

104   See ibid., p. 86.

105   C. Görzig/K. Al-Hashimi, Baseless Jihad, in: W. Heitmeyer *et al.* (eds.), Control of Violence (Forthcoming).

In their published revisions, former fundamentalists point to torture and long unjustified prison sentences that contributed to the rise of Islamic extremism.[106]

While in prisons throughout the 1960s, many Islamic activists began to question the reasons for such harsh treatment: If they were true Muslims who had to be punished so severely, than can the police be Muslim as well?

True Muslims do not cause harm to others; thus the regime, the police, and all individuals who follow orders from authorities must be infidels, or "jahiliyin"[107]. Under these conditions and reasoning, the notion of the enemies of Islam took hold and evolved into an ideology of which we still see consequences today. *Mawil Izzi Dien* also argues that Egypt's crackdown on Islamists in the 1960s created a backlash against Arab and Muslim regimes who were supported by foreign powers:

"The crushing of the Muslim Brotherhood by Egyptian authorities created a ripple effect of 'Islamic resurgence', 'government opposition', and 'Islamic hero movement' which was duplicated in most of the Muslim world that was formerly part of the Ottoman empire, such as Iraq, Syria, Saudi Arabia, Palestine, and Jordan."[108]

It was in prisons where most people turned to extremism and terrorism, where members of various groups began labeling everyone other than their "brothers" an infidel.[109] According to Gama'a Islamiya accounts, those who began labeling others as infidels became like cluster bombs – spreading fanaticism dangerously and accusing everyone of being an infidel.[110] Instead of deterring absolute terrorism, repression ushers in radicalisation turning terrorism and counter-terrorism into a self-perpetuating vicious circle.

IV. Conclusion

This chapter demonstrated how violence becomes self-perpetuating, reinforcing its own reason. What might appear as a minor risk can turn global – for example when old concepts such as the notion of a purposeful, peace-bringing war is applied to today's challenges such as catastrophic terrorism or the new wars. Surely it is not new that risk policy itself is risky. Paradoxical effects – consequences which are more costly than the risk itself – are not seldom.

---

106   See O. I. Hafez *et al.*, Mubadara Waq'f Al Anf - Ru'uia Waqiiya wa Nazra Shariia (2002).
107   A. M. Al-Sharif *et al.*, Tasslit al-Addwaa ala ma Waqaa fi al-Jihad min al-Akhtaa (2002).
108   M. I. Dien, Islamic Law - From Historical Foundations to Contemporary Practice, (2004), p. 130.
109   See N. I. Abdellah *et al.*, Harma Al Ghouloun Fi Al Din Wua Takfir Al Muslimin (2002), p. 6.
110   Ibid.

But even when the Club of Rome states that the change towards modern civilisation implies consequences from which some have the opposite effect of what was intended, we are not halted to justify inconsistent policies. On the very contrary, the disclosure of paradoxes can sometimes be traced back to an actual instrumentalisation of arguments which scrutinised more closely lose explanatory power.

According to *Luttwak*, "peace takes hold only when war is truly over." However, peace itself is already a highly contested concept. What is violence and what not is also in the eye of the beholder.

Interviewees from different backgrounds often described their situation with poignant metaphors. Especially in dialogues with Islamists, the metaphor of knocking on a door was popular. Interestingly, Colombians liked to talk of windows of opportunity. Kurds, for their part, stressed that they had no mouth, no eyes or no nose and Hamas eventually emphasised that it has no space and that its house is occupied. Clearly, offering rooms, opening doors and windows of opportunity is a language expressive of hopes and desires to talk and to be heard. War and violence, as this chapter argued, closes doors and windows of opportunity turning violence into a self-perpetuating conundrum.

Considering this excursion on new security challenges and the self-perpetuation of violence, alternative modes of governance and the inclusion of violent non-state actors – for example through dialogue – become relevant.

Bibliography

Abdellah, N. I. *et al.*, Harma Al Ghouloun Fi Al Din Wua Takfir Al Muslimin (2002).
Al-Hashimi, K./C. Görzig, Change through Debate. Egypt's Counter-terrorism Strategy towards the Gama'a Islamiya, paper delivered at Sixth Pan-European Conference on International Relations, Turin, 12-15 September 2007.
Al-Sharif, A. M. *et al.*, Tasslit al-Addwaa ala ma Waqaa fi al-Jihad min al-Akhtaa (2002).
Al-Zayyat, M., The Road to Al-Qaeda (2002).
Ballentine, K., Beyond Greed and Grievance: Reconsidering the Economic Dynamics of Armed Conflict, in: K. Ballentine/J. Sherman (eds.), The Political Economy of Armed Conflict - Beyond Greed and Grievance (2003), pp. 259-284.
Besikci, I., Kurdistan. Internationale Kolonie (1991).
Burchett, W./D. Roebuck, The Whores of War. Mercenaries Today (1977).
Collier, Paul/L. Elliott/H. Hegre et. al., Breaking the Conflict Trap: Civil War and Development Policy (2003).
Crenshaw, M., The Logic of Terrorism: Terrorist Behavior as a Product of Strategic Choice, in: W. Reich (ed.), Origins of Terrorism. Psychologies, Ideologies, Theologies, States of Mind (1990), pp. 7-24.
Daase, C./O. Kessler, From Insecurity to Uncertainty: Risk and the Paradox of Security Politics, in: Alternatives 33 (2008), pp. 211-232.
Daase, C., Kleine Kriege - Große Wirkung. Wie unkonventionelle Kriegführung die internationale Politik verändert (1999).

— Einleitung, in: C. Daase/S. Feske/I. Peters (eds.), Internationale Risikopolitik (2002), pp. 9-35.

— Strategische Assymetrie als Herausforderung für die Friedens-und Konfliktforschung, http://www.evangelische-akademie.de/Daase.pdf.

Dien, M. I., Islamic Law - From Historical Foundations to Contemporary Practice (2004).

Duffield, M., Global Governance and the New Wars (2001).

Felbab-Brown, V., The Intersection of Terrorism and the Drug Trade, in: J. Forest (ed.), The Making of a Terrorist. Recruitment, Training, and Root Causes (2005), pp. 172-188.

Garfield, E./J. Arboleda, Violence, Sustainable Peace, and Development, in: M. M. Giugale/O. Lafourcade/C. Luff *et al.* (eds.), Colombia: The Economic Foundation of Peace (2003), pp. 35-58.

Goerzig, G./K. Al-Hashimi, Baseless Jihad, in: W. Heitmeyer *et al.* (eds.), Control of Violence (Forthcoming)

Guáqueta, A., The Colombian Conflict: Political and Economic Dimensions, in: K. Ballentine/J. Sherman (eds.), The Political Economy of Armed Conflict. Beyond Greed and Grievance (2003), pp. 73-106.

Guerrero Barón, J., La sobre-politización del narcotráfico en Colombia en los años ochenta y sus interferencias en los procesos de paz, in: R. Peñaranda/J. Guerrero Barón (eds.), De las armas a la politica (1999), pp. 219-295.

Hafez, M., Why Muslims Rebel (2003).

— Dying to Be Martyrs: the Symbolic Dimension of Suicide Terrorism, in: A. Pedahzur (ed.), Root Causes of Suicide Terrorism. The Globalization of Martyrdom, (2006), pp. 54-80.

Hafez O. I. *et al.*, Mubadara Waq'f Al Anf - Ru'uia Waqiiya wa Nazra Shariia (2002).

Hoffman, B., Inside Terrorism (1998).

— The Changing Face of Al Qaeda and the War on Terrorism, in: Studies in Conflict and Terrorism, 27 (2004), pp. 549-560.

Inciardi, J. A., American Drug Policy: The Continuing Debate, in: J.A. Inciardi (ed.), The Drug Legalization Debate (1999), pp. 1-8.

Jenkins, B., International Terrorism: A New Mode of Conflict, in: D. Carlton/C. Schaerf (eds.), International Terrorism and World Security (1975), pp. 13-49.

Kaldor, M., New & Old Wars (1999).

Keen, D., Incentives and Disincentives for Violence, in: M. Berdal/D. Malone (eds.), Greed and Grievance: Economic Agendas and Civil Wars (2000), pp. 19-42.

Kurdistan Report Nr. 48, July 1992, „Es ist die türkische Regierung, die die Massen verliert" (Interview mit dem ARGK-Kommandanten, Cemil Bayik).

Kurz, A., New Terrorism: New Challenges, Old Dilemmas, in: Strategic Assessment, 6 (2003).

Laqueur, W., The New Terrorism: Fanaticism and the Arms of Mass Destruction (1999).

Lesser, Ian/B. Hoffman/J. Arquilla *et al.*, Countering the New Terrorism (1999).

Luttwak, E. N., Give War a Chance, in: Foreign Affairs 78 (1999), pp. 36-44.

Mearsheimer, J., Conventional Deterrence (1985).

Morgan, P., Deterrence: A Conceptual Analysis (1977).

Münkler, H., Gewalt und Ordnung (1992).

— Die neuen Kriege (2002).

Post, J., Terrorist Psycho-Logic: Terrorist Behavior as a Product of Psychological Forces, in: W. Reich (ed.), Origins of Terrorism. Psychologies, Ideologies, Theologies, States of Mind (1990), pp. 25-42.

Rashwan, D., The Obstacle Course of Revisions: Gamaah versus Jihad, in: Al-Ahram Commentary 80 of 30 May 2007.

Reno, W., The Meaning of Contemporary State Collapse for Self-Determination, in: The Somali Land Times of 5 July 2003.

Spiegel Online, Schul-Fragebogen in der Türkei "Ist dein Vater Terrorist?" (School Questionnaire „Is your Father a Terrorist?"), http://www.spiegel.de/schulspiegel/ausland/0,1518,536404,00.html of 29 February 2008.

Tucker, D., Skirmishes at the Edge of Empire (1997).

Weinberg, L., Turning to Terror: The Conditions Under Which Political Parties Turn to Terrorist Activities, in: Comparative Politics 23 (1991), pp. 423-438.

Zartman, W., Negotiating with Terrorists, in: International Negotiation 8 (2003), pp. 443-450.

Alternative Modes of Governance – A Critical Appraisal

Regina Heller and Cornelia Manger-Nestler

Managing global risks is a difficult endeavor: Risks are intricate to predict, most often there is no clarity about the causer and the causal responsibility. Global risks transcend borders, i.e. they can affect everyone, everywhere. In short: Uncertainty is a distinctive feature of global risks. Moreover, sources of global risks are wide-ranging: They can be political, legal (caused by uncertain rules), economical, ecological or technological in nature. Clearly, such diffuse but complex challenges require specific international governance approaches and joint efforts to fight them effectively.

The preceding chapters have taught us how global risks are addressed through conventional, existing modes of governance. But in some instances, such conventional mechanisms proof inadequate. Then, alternative modes of governance come to the fore. The three contributions of this chapter deal with alternative modes of governing global risks – although with quite different empirical foci and from the angle of various scientific disciplines. But they all have in common that they make us familiar with and urge us to think about more "unconventional" ways to collective problem-solving in the international realm. In that sense, they are truly interdisciplinary.

But how do alternative modes of governance look like and what can they contribute to a better and more effective problem-solving with regard to global risks? When do such alternatives become relevant? What issues do the authors look at empirically, what ideas do they propose and how do they generate their results theoretically? What are the problems or consequences from the findings proposed in the three studies? And finally: What can we learn from the authors' considerations?

Firstly, *Susanne Lechner* shows that alternative modes of governance can become relevant when a central authority among a multiplicity of state actors with heterogeneous interests is missing. In such cases, other forms of interaction than hierarchical steering need to be considered in order to overcome decision deadlocks and to maintain the capability to act. From a macroeconomic perspective, *Lechner's* article amply shows how the European Union (EU) is trying to overcome the increasing problem of actor-multiplicity and heterogeneity within the enlarged Union by introducing a withdrawal procedure in the Lisbon Treaty (EU-L). The exit-option fixed in Article 50 EU-L gives each Member State the constitutional right to withdraw from the EU when it encounters a loss in its benefits that is caused by a majority vote decision. Via a game-theoretical modeling, *Lechner* reveals that the introduction of the exit-option is not, as it might seem in the first place, destabilizing the internal coherence of the EU, but rather strengthens the effectiveness and legitimacy of political rule within the EU. The exit-option encourages more open methods of coordination, particularly bargaining processes and, thus, allows for more flexibility and a speed-up of decision-making processes among the Union of the 27.

However, looking at the issue from a legal point of view, the positive assessment derived from game theory becomes highly questionable. A legal evaluation would rather assume that the exit-option is more a political threatening posture than a serious juristic opportunity. Based to the *sui generis*, supranational legal system of the EU, the exit-option establishes an – up to now not existing – constitutional right for any Member State to quit the membership of the Union in case of the decision "to withdraw from the Union in accordance with its own constitutional requirements" (Article 50 para. 1 EU-L). The phase of legal disentanglement will be started by the notification of the intention of the exit-willing member states to the European Council.

"In the light of the guidelines provided by the European Council, the Union shall negotiate and conclude an agreement with that State, setting out the arrangements for its withdrawal, taking account of the framework for its future relationship with the Union." (Article 50 para. 2 EU-L)

Upon a closer view, Article 50 EU-L includes two legal modes of an exit: on the one hand, by a mutual agreement of the residual members (Article 50 para. 2, 3 – 1st alt., 4 EU-L "Sunset-Clause"), and on the other hand, in case of a "quarrel separation" without a mutual consent (Article 50 para. 2, 3 – 2nd alt. EU-L). In the case of a successful agreement between the European Council and the exit-willing state, "the Treaties shall cease to apply to the State in question from the date of entry into force of the withdrawal agreement" (1st alt.); if the agreement is failing, the membership ends by timing "two years after the notification" (2nd alt.). Concerning the concrete procedures of the withdrawal, the Lisbon Treaty contains very vague provisions seeming like an "all-or-nothing-solution" without e.g. time limits or periods for reflection and settlement. Furthermore there is no provision concerning the re-delegation of state powers and sovereign rights transferred to the EU within the scope of admission back to the former Member State; this would be a very long process with considerable practical problems.

Nevertheless, the European Union is still characterised as a voluntary community of sovereign states not being a "prison of nations"; that is why the interaction between the Member States (and the EU) should be dominated by rational decisions being the result of interest adequate compensation and reciprocal acceptance. Based on these principles, the EU shall aspire a flexible integration process – according to a "Europe of different speeds" in the Economic and Monetary Union (Article 99 et seq. EU) – with the effect that the practical relevance of the exit-option will be very small. Thus, the game-theoretic analysis simply ignores the existence and potential impact of other than interest-based mechanisms to sustainable cooperation and interaction. Moreover, the power of Europe as a guiding "idea" and source of identity for its Member States should not be underestimated. From such a normative perspective, the EU represents not an "everlasting alliance for better or worse", but a "common chance" for all.

Secondly, we learn from *Ewa Karwowski* that alternative modes of governance may need to be considered when conventional governance mechanisms themselves fail or create instability. *Karwowski* discusses the potential of Islamic banking as an alternative to the crisis-ridden conventional (Western or occidental) banking system. As *Lechner*, she takes on a macroeconomic perspective, but looks at the issue through a systemic lens. The systemic view differs from the game theoretic approach in that it shifts away the focus of analysis from the individual (economic and interest-driven) actor to the influence of political, social and cultural factors on a system's stability. *Karwowski* argues that the stability of any banking system – including the stability of Islamic banking – depends rather on the direction and purpose of lending than on the presence or absence of (whatsoever) interests and collaterals/securities.

While some studies indeed found out that Islamic banks are more stable, the author argues that, from a systemic point of view, this only holds for smaller contexts. When acting globally, conventional banks seem significantly stronger. Given the narrowness of Islamic banking operability, there is reason to believe that this system would hardly be able to manage financial flows globally. On the other hand, *Karwowski's* contribution also makes an interesting stance in favour of Islamic banking: In our globalized world, she argues, Islamic banks cannot operate in isolation from and have to interact with other, particularly Western, financial systems. This means they are – willingly or unwillingly – exposed to a multitude of diffusion effects and influenced by the Western banking system. As both systems come closer this way, the question arises whether it is only Islamic banks that learn from and are being influenced by the West, or whether Western banks can and actually should learn from its Islamic counterparts? Yet, after the 2008 financial crisis, Western banks would be well advised to adopt, respectively come back to a "culture" of morality. All the same, Islamic banking is a niche market – and it will be in the future wherefore an approximation to or integration in the conventional (occidental) banking system would be very difficult. *Ipso facto,* the Islamic prohibition of interests (rîba) and the Sharia rules which are no secular law induce to a completely different banking system as well as array and design of banking products. Added to these and due to the wide social differences between single Islamic states, a uniform and binding regulatory framework does not exist and even in developed states (like

Malaysia and Indonesia) only rudiments are increasing. Particularly Malaysia is a very special case because the Malaysian banking system is one of the highly developed banking systems in the Islamic world; anyway the south-east-Asian states altogether pursue a more liberal approach in Islamic finance. In Malaysia, we can find a dual banking system consisting of conventional banks offering products from conventional banking as well as – in a special division – Islamic finance products ("Islamic window"); besides Islamic banks exist only offering Koran-conformable products. The Islamic Banking Act from 1993 – as one of the first acts in the Asian Islamic area – defines the conditions for an Islamic banking business; especially, the act negotiates establishing a Sharia advisory board

"to advise the bank on the operation of its banking business in order to ensure that they do not involve any element which is not approved by the religion of the Islam." (Article 2 Islamic Banking Act)

Apart from that, Malaysia has another particular feature: a "National Sharia Advisory Council on Islamic Banks and Takaful" founded in 1997 by the Central Bank of Malaysia. The Council established common advisory strategies for Islamic finance products, the principle of equal treatment and mutual recognition for Islamic and conventional banking products as well as the Islamic Finance Arbitration Rules and the "Kuala Lumpur Regional Centre for Arbitration". In spite of the pictured development, the existence of a Sharia board must be an Islamic phenomenon not applicable in the Western legal system. Even the financial crisis has shown that we need strict and reliable supervisory rules in the banking business made by national, better supranational authorities who are legitimized by the voting of the commons – and not by a religious law with unpredictable awards.

Finally, *Carolin Goerzig's* article teaches us that alternative modes of governance need to be considered when we face new sorts of risk actors, particularly non-state actors, who are not part of and whose strategies and interests cannot be captured through traditional institutionalized orders. Her contribution addresses the problem of risk actors and the relevance of understanding their multiple interests and motives as a precondition for ending self-perpetual violence. While her subject matter – non-state actor violence as a security risk – is clearly positioned within the discipline of International Relations (IR), *Goerzig's* argumentation is theoretically highly inspired by microeconomic thinking and supplemented by theories of rational choice. The way in which the author embeds traditional IR theory into the "economics of (un-)security" enables her to show that "new forms of violence" follow a completely different logic than conventional warfare. Most importantly, these "new forms of violence" are far from being a uniform challenge. Instead, they are driven by very different motives and are underpinned by very different interest structures. The three mechanisms underlying the self-perpetuation of terrorist violence – privatisation and commercialisation, provocation, radicalisation – also exhibit different levels and shapes of "rationality": Privatisation and commercialisation are driven by material well-being and profit-making, not or not primarily by political or ideological goals. Provocation, the second mechanism, echoes the attempt to attract attention to a group's problems within a society and might hint at a general willingness to bargaining and dialogue on the part of these actors. Radicalisation reflects a state of mind, where individuals are ideologically deadlocked and – regardless of any, even personal consequences – willing to use (mass) violence in order to pursue their political goals.

However, the disclosure of different "rationalities", interest structures and motivations on the part of the various non-state actor groups, which *Goerzig* examines in her article, reveals something else and probably something most important: that is the fact that sometimes it seems politically opportune for state actors to label resistance and violence "terrorism", although, when taking a closer look, political interests are missing or only play a subordinate role, or when the re-integration of marginalized political and ethnic groups or separatists into the political process is not welcomed by a government. Thus, the delineation between a "terrorist" and a "freedom fighter" can sometimes be drawn arbitrarily and is subject to the interpretations and interests of governmental actors. *Vice versa*, the categorisation suggested by *Goerzig* helps to draw a useful and more objective line. The international community should, therefore, be highly critical and most careful when adopting and "legitimizing" views and interpretations from national governments about who a "terrorist" is and who is not. It is most obvious that when policy-makers need to react to such different forms of violence without understanding the underlying mechanisms and the actors' motives, countermeasures will gain little or no traction, trigger paradoxical effects and more resistance, and will in the end spur the spiral of violence even further. *Goerzig's* article suggests a way out: Instead of categorically denying concessions to violent groups, policy-makers should use "windows of opportunity" which correspond to the specific rationales of the violent non-state actors. Response-strategies would then need to include, *inter alia*, bargaining and the offering of different forms of incentives as well as dialogue. Building on inclusion instead of exclusion might be a bitter pill to swallow for national governments and societies, who are exposed to violence from non-state actors. But in some instances, this may be the only way to successfully and lastingly transform such violence into peace.

All in all, dealing with global risks beyond traditional forms of governance has both its chances and limits. Alternative governance modes clearly provide for more flexibility and adequate, sometimes even unusual responses to complex problems. At the same time though, it should not be forgotten that any interaction in the international realm and problem-solving efforts beyond hierarchy remain to a great extent subject to the interests of the actors involved. At the end of the day, it remains to them and their choices whether or not they want to constructively make use of new forms and approaches to the governance of global risk. It is no surprise that despite the empirical and disciplinary variety of the three articles presented here, the three authors all use, make recourse to or complement their research approaches with economic thinking and rational choice theory in one or the other way. At the same time, the contributions discussed also point to other factors that determine whether alternative modes of governance become a "success" or a "failure". In this sense, an interdisciplinary approach to the analysis of new modes of governing global risks, as presented here, can both practically and theoretically be very illuminating.

Notes on Contributors

Alexander Brand, M.A., is lecturer and doctoral researcher at the Chair of International Politics and the School of International Studies (ZIS), both Technische Universität Dresden. He has just finished his PhD manuscript on mass media and the discursive construction of international relations. Further research areas include: US foreign policy, politics of global development and the sport/politics nexus. Among his recent publications is: ‚Lagos is not Lehman' - The Differentiated Impact of the Global Financial Crisis on Emerging Markets and Developing Countries, in: Adam Fireš/Igor Varga (eds.): Crucial Problems of International Relations, Prague: University of Economics Press, 2009, pp. 73-103.

Christian Burckhardt, M.Sc., is currently an Associate Expert at the United Nations Secretariat in New York. He will submit his PhD thesis "Civilian Power Europe? The nature of European Union foreign policy" at the University of Oxford in mid-2010. During his PhD studies, Christian was a visiting researcher at the European University Institute in Florence and at IEP (Sciences Po) Paris. He holds a B.A. in International Relations from Technische Universität Dresden and an M.Sc. in European Studies from the London School of Economics and Political Science (LSE). His research interests include discourse analysis, realism, EU trade policy, EU military operations, UN-EU cooperation and the EU as a model in international relations.

Anke Dahrendorf, LL.M., is a PhD fellow at the Institute for Globalisation and International Regulation at Maastricht University. She also works as a junior researcher for the department of International and European Law of the Faculty of Law at Maastricht University. This article incorporates some of the ideas that Anke is working on in her PhD dissertation which will be published in 2012 or 2013. Anke holds a B.A. in International Relations from Technische Universität Dresden and a cum laude LL.M. degree of the Master programme Magister Iuris Communis from Maastricht University.

Kinka Gerke-Unger, Dr., is economic specialist at the U.S. Consulate General Frankfurt. She received her B.A. in History-Political Science from Jamestown-College, Jamestown, North Dakota, USA, before obtaining a Masters degree in Economics from the Johann Wolfgang Goethe-Universität, Frankfurt. Prior to obtaining her PhD in Political-Science from the Goethe-Universität, Frankfurt, for a dissertation on the US policy towards dispute settlement reform of the GATT in 2008, she was research fellow at the Peace Research Institute Frankfurt (PRIF), and legislative assistant to U.S. Senator Bob Packwood. From

1999 to 2005 she worked as economic specialist and project manager for the German Agency for Technical Cooperation (GTZ), designing and implementing technical assistance projects related to WTO accession and economic and legal reform. In 2006 she taught an undergraduate course at the School of International Studies, Technische Universität Dresden, on the multilateral trade regime of the WTO. She has published numerous articles on US foreign and US foreign trade policy.

Carolin Goerzig, Dr., M.A., is currently post-doctoral fellow at the European Union Institute for Security Studies in Paris, working on the transformation of non-state armed groups. She holds a doctorate from the University of Munich and a Masters degree from Kent University/Brussels School of International Studies. Her doctoral research on the topic "Negotiating with Terrorists" has led her to complete field research in Colombia, Egypt, Syria and Turkey. She has been a visiting researcher at the London School of Economics, a participant in the Young Scientist Summer Program of the International Institute of Applied Systems Analysis and a Marie Curie Fellow at the Department for Peace and Conflict Research at Uppsala University.

Regina Heller, Dr., is a senior researcher at the Institute for Peace Research and Security Policy at the University of Hamburg (IFSH). She studied Political Science and East Slavic Studies at the University of Mainz, at the Middlebury College, VT/USA and at the University of Hamburg. In 2006, Regina Heller completed her PhD on norm socialisation in Russia and the role of the EU in the transfer of international human rights norms to the Russian Federation. She used to work at the Conflict Prevention Network (CPN) at the Stiftung Wissenschaft und Politik in Ebenhausen and Berlin and as coordinator of the research project „International Risk Policy" at the Center for Transatlantic Foreign und Security Policy at the Freie Universität Berlin.

Jana Hertwig, Dr., LL.M., serves as research associate at the Institute for International Law of Peace and Armed Conflict (IFHV), Ruhr-Universität Bochum. Prior to joining IFHV, she worked as consultant to the United Nations Association of Germany and as research assistant at the Chair of International Law, European Union Law and International Relations, Faculty of Law of Technische Universität Dresden. She graduated and obtained her PhD from the Technische Universität Dresden. Her areas of expertise include European (CFSP) and International Non-proliferation Policies of Weapons of Mass Destruction (WMD) and Terrorism, Methods and Means of Warfare (e.g. Ban on Cluster Munitions), and Protecting Women and Children in Armed Conflict.

Vanessa Holzer, LL.M., is a visiting fellow at the Refugees Studies Centre, Oxford University, and a doctoral candidate at Frankfurt University focusing on "war refugees" in international law. She was previously a research fellow at the Max Planck Institute of Comparative Public Law and International Law, Heidelberg. She holds an LL.M. in International Law from the London School of Economics and Political Science (LSE) and a B.A. in International Relations from Technische Universität Dresden. Her LL.M. thesis, which analysed the human rights-based approach to the protection of refugee children, was awarded the Blackstone Chambers Prize of the LSE Law Department. Vanessa holds a scholarship from the German National Academic Foundation.

Ewa Karwowski, M.A., is currently an ODI fellow and works as senior economist in South Africa. She studied International Relations at the Technische Universität Dresden as well as the Panthéon-Assas/Paris II, and Economics at the School of Oriental and African Studies, London. She has experience working in (inter-)governmental institutions in Germany, Poland, France, and Malaysia. Her research work was published by the Levy Institute of Bard College, New York, the School of Oriental and African Studies in London as well as the Technische Universität Dresden.

Nicolas Lamp, M.A., LL.M., is a PhD candidate in Public International Law at the London School of Economics and Political Science (LSE). He holds a B.A. and M.A. in International Relations from Technische Universität Dresden and Jacobs University, Bremen, respectively, and an LL.M. in Public International Law from the LSE. His PhD research focuses on international lawmaking processes, in particular the lawmaking process in the WTO. He is currently also a Visiting Fellow at the Institute of International Economic Law at Georgetown University in Washington, D.C., and works as Editorial Assistant to Professor John H. Jackson at the Journal of International Economic Law.

Joris Larik, LL.M., M.A., is PhD candidate in law at the European University Institute and visiting lecturer at the School of International Studies, Technische Universität Dresden. Previously, he studied at the School of International Studies, Technische Universität Dresden (B.A.), Leiden University (LL.M.), and the College of Europe (M.A.). His research interests centre on the relationship between international and EU law, new actors in international relations, EU external relations, international economic law, and security and defence policy. The present contribution stems from a chapter of the author's LL.M. thesis at Leiden University under the supervision of Dr. Larissa van den Herik.

Susanne Lechner, Dr., studied International Relations at the Technische Universität Dresden and at the IEP Strasbourg from 1999 to 2002. She continued with a Master program in International Economics at Goettingen University and at the Athens University of Economics and Business. From 2004-2009 she worked as a research associate at the Center for European, Governance and Economic Development Research and at the Chair of Economic Policy. After having finished her thesis in 2009, she has become Director of European Economic Policy and Industrial Policy at the Association of German Chambers of Industry and Commerce (DIHK e.V.) in Brussels.

Cornelia Manger-Nestler, Dr., is a full professor of German and International Economic Law at Leipzig University of Applied Sciences. Following a degree in law and a Master of European Law, she worked as a research assistant for Prof. Dr. Ulrich Fastenrath, Faculty of Law, TU Dresden, and Prof. Dr. Ludwig Gramlich, Faculty of Economics and Business Administration, TU Chemnitz. Her doctoral dissertation dealt with the changing role of the Deutsche Bundesbank in the European System of Central Banks. Her research focuses on European and International Monetary Law, legal problems of prudential supervision and regulatory control of public sectors.

Sylvia Maus, LL.M., is a lecturer and doctoral researcher at the Chair of International Law, European Union Law and International Relations at the Faculty of Law, Technische Universität Dresden. She holds a B.A. in International Relations from the Technische Universität Dresden and an LL.M. in Public International Law from the University of Nottingham. She is currently working on her PhD project on the United Nations and human rights in post-conflict situations as a contribution to *ius post bellum*. Her research interests include international human rights law, international humanitarian law and United Nations law and politics.

Almut Meyer zu Schwabedissen, M.A., is a researcher and lecturer at the School of International Studies (ZIS), Technische Universität Dresden. She has studied at the University of Manchester, Great Britain, and at Technische Universität Dresden, where she has earned her degree in Political Science and German as a Foreign Language. Currently, she is conducting research and joint classes with lecturers from Great Britain, Poland and the Czech Republic in a multinational project on New Dimensions of Security in Europe (NewSecEU), funded by the European Commission. She is also the project coordinator of NewSecEU.

Jörn Richert, M.A., is currently writing his PhD thesis at the German Institute for International and Security Affairs (Stiftung Wissenschaft und Politik, SWP), Berlin and the University of Bielefeld. At SWP he is associated with the research project „Competing for Scarce Resources", after having worked for the SWP-project "Climate Change and Security". He received his M.A. in Political Science, Economics and Psychology from the University of Kiel (2008). He studied in Madrid (2005/06) and worked at the Kiel Institute for the World Economy (2006/07).

Solveig Richter, Dr., is working as Senior Research Associate in the Research Division EU External Relations at the German Institute for International and Security Affairs (Stiftung Wissenschaft und Politik), Berlin. Her main emphasis is on EU Enlargement, the Western Balkan and the European Security Architecture. She received her PhD from the Technische Universität Dresden and the Centre for OSCE Research at the Institute for Peace Research and Security Policy (IFSH) in Hamburg. Her dissertation focused on the role of the OSCE in the democratisation process in South Eastern Europe. After studies in political science, history and communication science in Dresden and Strasbourg, she worked as research fellow, lecturer and consultant in Dresden and Hamburg.

Tina Roeder, Dr. iur., is currently working for her postdoctoral lecture qualification at the Chair of Public Law, European and Public International Law, Technische Universität Dresden. In her doctoral thesis, she studied the question of return of Palestinian refugees to Israel; her teaching thesis deals with national and international aspects of human dignity.

Matthias Schuler, M.A., is a lecturer and research assistant at the School of International Studies (ZIS), Technische Universität Dresden. He holds a B.A. in International Relations from the Technische Universität Dresden and an M.A. in International Political Economy from the University of Warwick. In 2009 he acted as Administrative Director and Programme Coordinator at the School of International Studies. His research interests focus on Global Political Economy, especially financial markets, global financial governance and monetary policies.

Index

Dresdner Schriften zu Recht und Politik der Vereinten Nationen
Papers on Law and Policy of the United Nations

Herausgegeben von Sabine von Schorlemer

www.peterlang.de

Alpago Alpago

Power and Poverty
Is the EU a New Planet?

Frankfurt am Main, Berlin, Bern, Bruxelles, New York, Oxford, Wien, 2010.
163 pp.,1 fig., num.tab.
ISBN 978-3-631-60382-6 · hardback € 29,80*

This book focuses on the economic and political relations between the EU, Turkey, Morocco and Mediterranean Countries. It examines these relations from a global and pluralistic perspective and investigates them through a comparative analysis. The study reveals the untold issues and that's why it leads the readers to go beyond the borders. It is a professional and important source, particularly for economic and political decision makers. Furthermore this book addresses everyone, who wants to know about the background of international economic and political happenings.

Content: The theoretical background of the EU-Integration policy towards Turkey in comparison to the Mediterranean cooperation agreement · Customs Union with Turkey · EU-Mediterranean Cooperation · Comparative Analysis in Research · Country Facts: Turkey and Morocco · MEDA- Projects with Maghreb-countries

Peter Lang · Internationaler Verlag der Wissenschaften

Frankfurt am Main · Berlin · Bern · Bruxelles · New York · Oxford · Wien
Distribution: Verlag Peter Lang AG
Moosstr. 1, CH-2542 Pieterlen
Telefax 00 41 (0) 32 / 376 17 27

*The €-price includes German tax rate
Prices are subject to change without notice
Homepage http://www.peterlang.de